Knowledge-Infused Learning

Knowledge-infused learning directly confronts the opacity of current "black-box" AI models by combining data-driven machine learning techniques with the structured insights of symbolic AI. This guidebook introduces the pioneering techniques of neurosymbolic AI, which blends statistical models with symbolic knowledge to make AI safer and user-explainable. This is critical in high-stakes AI applications in healthcare, law, finance, and crisis management.

The book brings readers up to speed on advancements in statistical AI, including transformer models such as BERT and GPT, and provides a comprehensive overview of weakly supervised, distantly supervised, and unsupervised learning methods alongside their knowledge-enhanced variants. Other topics include active learning, zero-shot learning, and model fusion.

Beyond theory, the book presents practical considerations and applications of neurosymbolic AI in conversational systems, mental health, crisis management systems, and social and behavioral sciences, making it a pragmatic reference for AI system designers in academia and industry.

MANAS GAUR is an assistant professor in the Department of Computer Science and Electrical Engineering at the University of Maryland, Baltimore County (UMBC). A pioneer in knowledge-infused learning (2016–2022), Gaur's research has earned multiple best paper awards and recognition through USC Eminent Profiles and AAAI New Faculty Highlights. His cutting-edge work continues to attract major funding, including grants from NSF and EPSRC-UKRI in partnership with the Alan Turing Institute.

AMIT P. SHETH is the NCR Chair and Professor of Computer Science and Engineering at the University of South Carolina, where he founded the university-wide AI Institute in 2019 and grew it to nearly 50 AI researchers in four years. He is a fellow of IEEE, AAAI, AAAS, ACM, and AIAA. His awards include the IEEE CS Wallace McDowell Award and the IEEE TCSVC Research Innovation Award. He has co-founded four companies, run two of them, and advised or mentored over 45 PhD candidates and postdocs to exceptional careers in academia, in industry, and as entrepreneurs.

Knowledge-Infused Learning
Neurosymbolic AI for Explainability, Interpretability, and Safety

MANAS GAUR
University of Maryland Baltimore County

AMIT P. SHETH
University of South Carolina

Shaftesbury Road, Cambridge CB2 8EA, United Kingdom

One Liberty Plaza, 20th Floor, New York, NY 10006, USA

477 Williamstown Road, Port Melbourne, VIC 3207, Australia

314–321, 3rd Floor, Plot 3, Splendor Forum, Jasola District Centre, New Delhi – 110025, India

Cambridge University Press is part of Cambridge University Press & Assessment, a department of the University of Cambridge.

We share the University's mission to contribute to society through the pursuit of education, learning and research at the highest international levels of excellence.

www.cambridge.org
Information on this title: www.cambridge.org/9781009513746
DOI: 10.1017/9781009513722

© Manas Gaur and Amit P. Sheth 2026

This publication is in copyright. Subject to statutory exception and to the provisions of relevant collective licensing agreements, no reproduction of any part may take place without the written permission of Cambridge University Press & Assessment.

When citing this work, please include a reference to the DOI 10.1017/9781009513722

First published 2026

Cover image: Pobytov/DigitalVision Vectors via Getty Images

A catalogue record for this publication is available from the British Library

A Cataloging-in-Publication data record for this book is available from the Library of Congress

ISBN 978-1-009-51374-6 Hardback

Cambridge University Press & Assessment has no responsibility for the persistence or accuracy of URLs for external or third-party internet websites referred to in this publication and does not guarantee that any content on such websites is, or will remain, accurate or appropriate.

For EU product safety concerns, contact us at Calle de José Abascal, 56, 1°, 28003 Madrid, Spain, or email eugpsr@cambridge.org

Contents

	Preface	*page* ix
1	**Introduction**	1
2	**Knowledge Graphs for Explainability and Interpretability**	11
	2.1 Knowledge Graphs	11
	2.2 Construction of the Empathi Ontology	13
	2.3 Integration of External Vocabularies	14
	2.4 Evaluating Quality of *empathi*	21
	2.5 Personalized Health Knowledge Graph	36
	2.6 Knowledge Graph for Explainability	40
	2.7 Knowledge Graph for Interpretability	44
3	**Knowledge-Infused Learning: The Subsumer to NeuroSymbolic AI**	47
	3.1 Why Neurosymbolic AI?	48
	3.2 What Is Neurosymbolic AI and How Do We Achieve It?	49
	3.3 Knowledge-Infused Learning	55
	3.4 KiL for Language Modeling	57
	3.5 Process Knowledge in KiL	58
	3.6 KiL for Knowledge-Intensive Language Understanding	60
	3.7 Recommender Systems	67
	3.8 Computer Vision	67
4	**Shallow Infusion of Knowledge**	69
	4.1 What Is Shallow Infusion?	71
	4.2 Methods of Shallow Infusion	72

v

4.3	Shallow Infusion for Mental Health	76
4.4	Explainable Data Creation and Use in Suicide Context	78
4.5	Description of Explainable Data	88
4.6	Explainability as a Metric: Perceived Risk Measure (PRM)	91
4.7	Summary	92

5 Semi-deep Infusion Learning — 94
- 5.1 Benefits of Semi-deep Infusion — 94
- 5.2 Methods to Achieve Semi-deep Infusion — 98
- 5.3 Semantic Encoding and Decoding Optimization (SEDO) — 104
- 5.4 TDLR: Top (Semantic)-Down (Syntactic) Language Representation — 108
- 5.5 Ensemble Learning — 112
- 5.6 Summary — 120

6 Deep Knowledge-Infused Learning — 121
- 6.1 Deep Infusion Module — 123
- 6.2 Differential Knowledge Engine — 127
- 6.3 Summary — 130

7 Process Knowledge-Infused Learning — 131
- 7.1 PKiL for Safety Constrained and Explainable Question Generation in Mental Health — 139
- 7.2 PKiL for Suicidality Assessment — 144

8 Knowledge-Infused Conversational NLP — 155
- 8.1 ISEEQ Architecture and Evaluation — 160
- 8.2 Personalized Conversation Agent — 172
- 8.3 Mental Health Conversational Agent — 181
- 8.4 KiL for Mental Health Conversations — 189
- 8.5 Safe and Explainable Language Models in Mental Health — 191

9 Neurosymbolic Large Language Models — 203
- 9.1 Introduction — 203
- 9.2 Consistency and Safety Issues in LLMs — 207
- 9.3 Defining Consistency, Reliability, User-Level Explainability, and Safety — 210
- 9.4 The CREST Framework — 221

9.5	Consistency as a Metric for LLMs	226
9.6	Ethical Considerations	240
9.7	Contextual Bias Assessment	243

References	258
Index	300

Preface

As I pen this preface, I reflect on my exploration into artificial intelligence (AI) – a journey ignited by a profound curiosity and the urgent need to unravel the complexities of AI for broader, socially impactful applications. My motivation is deeply rooted in the significant effects AI has shown across various fields, such as healthcare informatics, crisis management, and mental health services. This exploration has underscored a major issue: the opacity of current AI systems, which often leaves potential users confused and reluctant to integrate these technologies into critical human-centered applications. This book began to take shape following a series of insightful discussions at the AAAI conference in early 2020, just before the global spread of COVID-19. A particularly memorable fireside chat with Turing laureates Yann LeCun, Geoffrey Hinton, Yoshua Bengio, and Nobel Prize-winner Daniel Kahneman highlighted both the transformative potential of AI and the critical issues related to its explainability, interpretability, and adherence to standards in high-stakes decision-making. This contrast inspired my deep dive into knowledge-infused learning (KiL), an innovative approach within neurosymbolic AI that combines data-driven techniques with the structured insights of symbolic AI. I was particularly inspired by the advancements in models like AlphaFold, which underscored the potential of AI when augmented with human-understandable knowledge. This book aims to bridge the gap between advanced AI functionalities and the transparent, accessible technologies we aspire to achieve. Building on my PhD dissertation under IEEE W. Wallace McDowell Award-winner Professor Amit P. Sheth, this edition incorporates recent AI developments, including large language models, new case studies on mental health and well-being, and updated methodologies. It introduces a novel conceptual framework, CREST – consistency, reliability, explainability, safety, and trust – to enhance our understanding of KiL. Writing this book posed challenges in making complex technical content accessible. It required constant updates to keep pace with the rapidly evolving AI landscape (e.g., conversational agents to chatbots to co-pilots) and ensure its relevance and accuracy. My hope is that this book not only enlightens but also inspires our collective journey toward creating more transparent, interpretable, and safe AI systems. By sharing this knowledge, I aim to empower the next generation of researchers and practitioners to develop AI technologies that are powerful, trustworthy, and beneficial for society at large.

Audience

This book is ideal for readers with a background in computer science, especially in AI, data mining, natural language processing (NLP), and information retrieval. A basic understanding of linear algebra, probability, and statistics will enhance comprehension. It serves as a primer on KiL, a form of neurosymbolic AI in which knowledge enhances neural networks. This book targets computer science students and faculty, as well as interdisciplinary centers on data science.

The content can also be valuable for those in psychology, social science, linguistics, information systems, mathematics, and computing. The book offers insights into theories, experiment design, and evaluation strategies, emphasizing the use of knowledge graphs (KGs) from non-computer science research.

It can independently serve as a seminar course on KiL, Trusted AI, Data Science for Social Good, or AI for Social Good. Industry researchers and practitioners will benefit from the tangible use cases, theories, and evaluation strategies to address field-specific issues. The book provides a detailed guide on KGs and their role in developing knowledge-infusion techniques for interpretable learning from text, video, images, and graphical data on the Web.

Computation and cognitive theories are used to introduce KiL, detailing different forms of knowledge, automatic KG construction, modeling, and infusion in machine- and deep learning techniques. The book also covers application-specific evaluation methods for explainability and reasoning using benchmark and real-world datasets. It concludes with future directions, grounding readers in KG and robust learning for the Web and society.

1
Introduction

To create genuinely effective artificial intelligence (AI), we need to build systems that think, explain, and reason like humans. This perspective from Gary Marcus aligns with Andrew Ng's view that the hype around big data is overblown and that AI must advance in intelligence. Early on in the heyday of machine learning (ML), Pedro Domingos (2012) observed that "Data alone is not enough." These experts agree that merely scaling up AI models to billions of parameters has led to fundamental challenges such as "hallucinations" (Thoppilan et al., 2022a).

Large language models (LLMs), such as BlenderBot 1 and BlenderBot 2, have demonstrated these problems by generating incorrect and sometimes unsafe responses (Lee et al., 2022). Policymakers and practitioners are particularly concerned about using AI in critical areas like healthcare, crisis response, and scientific discovery due to serious usability and privacy issues (Cornelio et al., 2021). To address these concerns, most companies (91%) insist that AI models be understandable and explainable to earn the trust of users and stakeholders (IBM, 2021; Longo et al., 2020a).

As recognized by DARPA (2019), the future of AI lies in hybrid models that combine human knowledge and expertise with AI's computational power for better, more explainable decision making. Human expertise during the first wave of AI involved creating handcrafted rules to identify patterns in data. AI's strength lies in its ability to process large datasets with immense computational power. For instance, models like GPT-4 excel in narrowly defined tasks that do not necessarily require additional context. An example of this is language translation, where GPT-4 can translate text from one language to another with high accuracy without needing to understand the broader context of a conversation. Another example is sentiment analysis, where the AI can accurately determine whether a given text expresses positive, negative, or neutral sentiments based solely on the text provided without needing further context about the situation or the individuals involved. However, data-driven models alone are insufficient for tasks like mental health and well-being (Gyrard et al., 2024), crisis informatics (Ara et al., 2024), and estimation of autism (Tilwani et al., 2023), as these tasks are driven by experts, and various experts can interpret their results differently. Integrating human expertise with AI's computational strengths is crucial for developing effective AI systems. This hybrid approach, whether combining the capabilities of symbolic AI (i.e., the first wave of AI) and statistical AI (i.e., the second wave of AI) loosely or tightly, will help balance the benefits of both methods. Just as the brain uses system 1 and system 2 processes, as characterized by Kahneman (2011), or what may be characterized by AI based on perceptual and cognitive capabilities (Sheth et al., 2016), the future AI will also need capabilities developed in both waves of AI.

To understand the importance of combining human knowledge with AI, consider the ongoing quest of ML researchers to achieve high accuracy and confidence in their models. To reach these goals, researchers must curate high-quality datasets, establish clear guidelines for annotators with the requisite knowledge, and even review annotators' backgrounds to ensure consistent annotation.

Despite these processes, annotators often consult external knowledge sources or rely on their experience to ensure the correctness of their work. This additional information, which we refer to as knowledge, is the crucial missing piece that AI lacks for achieving trustworthy outcomes. Integrating human knowledge with AI is essential for providing context and enhancing the reliability of AI systems, which are crucial components in building trustworthy AI.

Consider the example shown in Figure 1.1, which illustrates how annotators perceive sentences to be annotated and how their backgrounds influence their work. Annotators who lack expertise on the topic often seek additional sources to gain the necessary knowledge, ensuring they complete the annotation task accurately and with high quality. These external pieces of information are unavailable to data-driven AI models during training or fine-tuning, causing them to approximate their learning behavior and sacrifice consistency and robustness (Figure 1.2 provides an additional example).

Hybrid AI has been a topic of interest for achieving consistent and robust AI for over 50 years. The journey started in 1968 with McCarthy and Hayes (1981), who identified several philosophical challenges in AI. Among these, the following two are central to this book:

- How can AI facilitate reasoning, particularly in estimation, models (e.g., self-consistency, knowledge conflicts), and knowledge representation?

Introduction

Data Point: The ___ bartender is an alcoholic.

	Our representation of the kind of contexts annotators considered	Our interpretation of annotators' *rule* to classify into the Yes class
Annotator 1	The young/underpaid/single bartender is an alcoholic.	Possible context must be representative of real-world scenarios.
Annotator 2	The Irish/arrogant/local bartender is an alcoholic.	Possible context must maintain lexical correctness.
Annotator 3	The short/tall/boring bartender is an alcoholic.	Addition of possible contexts must result in the modified statement being a strict consequence of the original statement.

Figure 1.1 Qualitative analysis of annotators' thought processes after the annotation task. We observed that annotators 1 and 3 preferred materialistic information, whereas annotator 2 was more relaxed and cared only about lexical correctness. *Note: These examples are for representation purposes only and are not the real annotations.* Credit: Govil et al. (2024)

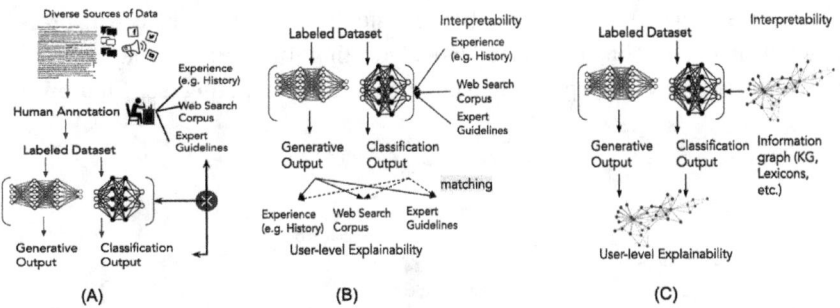

Figure 1.2 This illustration explains how human annotators create high-quality datasets. (A) Annotators use extra information not available to ML/DL models. (B) Incorporating this knowledge into ML/DL models improves interpretability and user-level explainability. (C) Integrating diverse knowledge sources is resource-intensive. However, using machine-readable information graphs can replace these sources, reducing computational costs without compromising data quality.

- How can AI capture causality in various situations?

McCarthy and Hayes emphasized that practical AI systems need epistemological frameworks to store facts about the world and use them for informed decision making.

In 1979, Hofstadter (1979) questioned "Why is AI far from being intelligent?" by pointing out the artistic and beautiful nature of human thinking in his book *Gödel, Escher, Bach*.

During the "AI winter," various methods were developed, including teacher forcing (a part of student–teacher modeling), sequential models based on humans' ability to learn using local knowledge, and convolutional models based on humans' ability to process global knowledge. In 2001, Sheth et al. (2001) introduced the concept of a world model to enhance search, personalization, and user profiling, demonstrating the effectiveness of human-curated knowledge bases in achieving state-of-the-art results with small-scale and interpretable AI models like hidden Markov models. They also developed a semantic search engine using knowledge graphs (referred to as a world model or ontologies), combining knowledge-based and statistical classifiers to enrich content similarly to Infobox, later known as the rich content model (Sheth et al., 2002; Sheth, 2003; Sheth et al., 2004).

In 2006, Turing Award winner Leslie Valiant posed the question, "How can machines acquire and manipulate commonsense knowledge?" Kahneman's (2011) book *Thinking, Fast and Slow* addresses this by proposing the integration of System 1 (Statistical AI) and System 2 (Symbolic AI) (see Figure 1.3). Sheth et al. (2017) reinforced this idea, stating that knowledge will propel machine understanding of content and advocating for hybrid AI that integrates semantic, cognitive, and perceptual components in computing (see Figure 1.4).

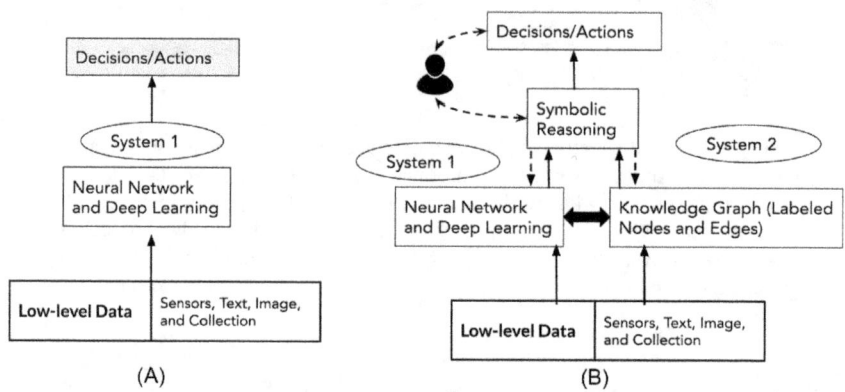

Figure 1.3 (A) Neural networks and deep learning models, including classification/discriminative models and generative models, are often viewed as "black boxes" because their decisions and actions lack user-level explainability. The internal workings of these models are not easily interpretable, requiring analysis of low-level data to understand them. This black box is called System 1 (LeCun et al., 2015). (B) System 2 represents symbolic knowledge, which can be structured as an knowledge graph (KG), semantic lexicons (dictionaries), or rules (sets of constraints). These symbolic forms of knowledge are machine understandable and can be integrated into System 1 to enhance model interpretations. By combining System 1 with System 2, user-level explainability is achieved, allowing for a clearer understanding of the model's outcomes.

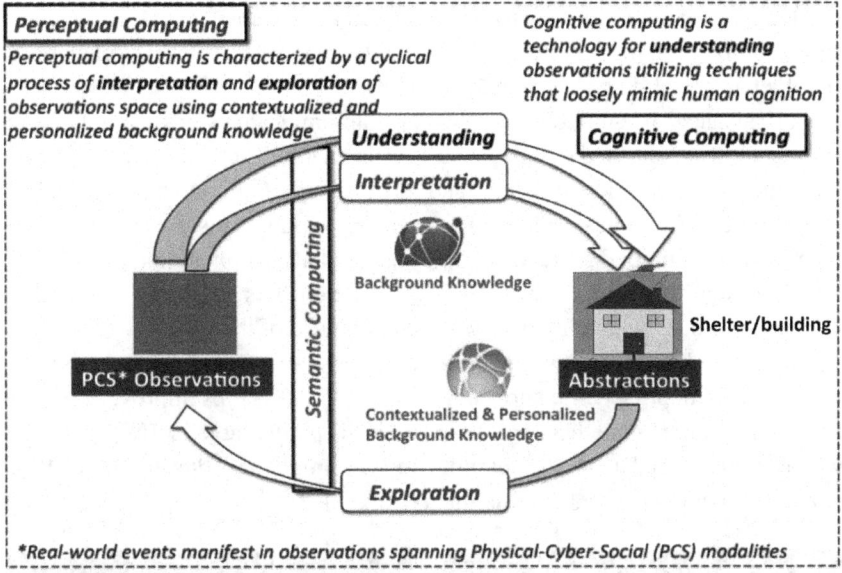

Figure 1.4 Semantic computing (SC) adds context to unstructured data, enabling comprehensive analysis across physical, cyber, and social realms. Cognitive computing (CC) utilizes these SC annotations to interpret and understand the data, while perceptual computing (PC) continuously gathers and refines environmental data to tailor knowledge to specific contexts and needs. This cyclical process enhances the system's ability to adapt and respond dynamically (Sheth et al., 2016).

Unlike data-driven AI, the human brain does not follow a rigid script but instead combines perception (highly statistical) and cognition (based on explicit, structured knowledge) for complex decision making and communication (Garcez and Lamb, 2023). There has been significant progress in incorporating knowledge into deep learning (DL) (Dash et al., 2022).

Humans can process information at various abstraction levels, akin to how we navigate different learning stages. A knowledge-driven AI should tap into diverse human-curated sources, like general or domain-specific knowledge bases, whether in lexical formats or graph-based structures (Sheth and Thirunarayan, 2021). This approach helps AI to draw connections between facts and observations, making the outcomes more relatable and understandable to humans.

Neurosymbolic AI and **Knowledge-Infused Learning** (KiL) exemplify techniques within this broader framework. KiL, in particular, emphasizes the integration of various forms of knowledge – lexical, domain-specific, commonsense, or constraint-based – into AI. This integration helps overcome challenges commonly associated with symbolic or statistical AI approaches, such as improving model interpretability and providing user-level explanations (Dash et al., 2022; Hitzler et al., 2022).

For instance, in autonomous driving, combining knowledge graphs with machine learning has led to significant advancements. These knowledge graphs facilitate a better understanding and processing of autonomous vehicles' diverse and voluminous data, such as sensor outputs. This process not only helps achieve a unified representation of data but also supports the completion of knowledge graphs by predicting new relationships or filling in missing information, thus enhancing the overall intelligence of the system.

Moreover, KiL has shown its utility in diverse areas like healthcare, where integrating domain-specific knowledge into AI models helps improve accuracy and reduce biases in medical predictions. This is particularly useful in contexts where conventional machine learning models might fail due to the lack of nuanced domain knowledge (Kursuncu et al., 2018).

> **Definition of Knowledge-Infused Learning**
>
> `Knowledge-Infused Learning` is a class of neurosymbolic AI techniques that incorporate broader forms of knowledge (lexical, domain-specific, common-sense, and constraint-based) into addressing limitations of either symbolic or statistical AI approaches, such as model interpretations and user-level explanations. Compared to powerful statistical AI that exploits data, KiL benefits from data and knowledge.

> **Words from the pioneers in neurosymbolic AI**
>
> **Leslie Valiant**'s vision: "The aim here is to identify a way of looking at and manipulating broader and other richer forms of knowledge that are consistent with and can support what we consider to be the two most fundamental aspects of intelligent cognitive behavior: *the ability to learn from experience, and the ability to reason from what has been learned*. Therefore, we seek a semantics of knowledge that can computationally support the basic phenomena of intelligent behavior." Further, Knowledge-Infused Learning aims to incorporate broader forms of knowledge: linguistic, lexical, domain-specific, rule-based, and word sense-based (Sheth and Thirunarayan, 2021).

> **Douglas Hoftstader** mentioned the reasons for the question "Why is AI far from being intelligent?" by pressing on human thinking being artistic and beautiful. Later, you will see that knowledge-infused learning introduces the concepts of entity normalization, semantic query expansion, zero-shot learning, and contextual bandits using knowledge graphs to generate probable outcomes that intuitively lie in human understanding of the problem.

> **Gary Marcus** reflected on the lack of common-sense reasoning in deep language models, much like Leslie Valiant. Considering Marcus's example: "What happens when you stack kindling and logs in a fireplace and then drop some matches is that you typically start a ___," a KiL approach will look for a connection between "kindling," "log," "fireplace," "matches," giving "fire" as the concept with most closely related representations.

KiL has seen a continuum of strategies for infusing knowledge that has been broadly categorized as a shallow, semi-deep, and deep infusion. *Shallow knowledge infusion* contextualizes the training examples with expert knowledge to capture meaningful patterns. Some of the shallow infusion examples include contextual modeling (Bhatt et al., 2019), entity normalization (Gaur et al., 2021a), and others (Gaur et al., 2021d). *Semi-deep infusion* attempts to embed expert knowledge in the parametric space of the model or guides the model's learning process using constraints (Faldu et al., 2021a; Gunaratna et al., 2021; Gaur et al., 2021b). Though this infusion method has yielded significant gains, it fails to assist deep learning models in learning high-level abstractions through its multiple layers. *Deep knowledge infusion* combines the stratified representation of knowledge at varying abstraction levels to be transferred in different layers of deep learning models (Sheth et al., 2019c). A KiL model can provide user-level explanations by mapping tokens in the input data to concepts in the knowledge graph (Roy et al., 2023a). Further, a KiL model is an interpretable procedure whose learning curve can be monitored by either (a) a weighting function that demonstrates the correlation between the tokens in the input and concepts in the knowledge source (Gaur et al., 2018) or (b) logical constraints that monitor the amount of knowledge infusion (Sheth et al., 2022).

In This Book

The black box statistical/generative AI has gained substantial notoriety but needs more explainability and safety for critical applications in domains such as healthcare and finance. This book showcases techniques, systems, and measures for neurosymbolic AI driven by knowledge in graphs and guidelines, enabling machines to achieve cognitive abilities in domains that support the required capabilities. The book will guide you through distinct stages of incorporating knowledge into AI, highlighting the disparities between inferences drawn from statistical AI and symbolic AI methodologies. While it remains focused on various enhancements introduced to statistical AI, including the popular and extensively used attention mechanisms, the book will also deliver an exhaustive and well-informed account of topics such as machine learning and knowledge-guided machine learning; data transformation, and knowledge-guided data transformation; posthoc explainability and safety with knowledge; ante-hoc explainability and safety with knowledge, explainability, and safety integrating various forms of knowledge; and more profound levels of integration. Technically, the book's explorations of advancements will encompass domains such as reinforcement learning and policy gradients, zero-shot learning, active learning, and model ensembles. On a pragmatic level, the book will deeply examine innovations applied to applications such as conversational systems, mental health, crisis management systems, and social and behavioral sciences.

Chapter Summaries

Chapter 2 *Role of Knowledge Graphs in AI:* We introduce a primer on knowledge graphs (KGs), which are structured, machine-readable, and symbolic representations of information. They can enhance statistical AI methods by offering contextualization and abstraction. A range of KGs (WordNet, Wikidata, SNOMED-CT) is examined, serving as stores of general, commonsense, and specialized knowledge. Further, we provide a brief overview of the construction, enrichment, and learning representation of KGs. Such a stratum of knowledge would enable statistical AI to be consistent, reliable, interpretable, explainable, and safe when providing trustworthy decision support. We briefly explore the present state of statistical AI and discuss how integrating knowledge can achieve these attributes.

Chapters 3–6 *Knowledge-Infused Learning: The Subsumer to Neurosymbolic AI:*

We introduce the different categories of KiL and how they achieve the five attributes of trustworthiness in statistical AI. First, we will cover shallow infusion of knowledge, which concerns knowledge-guided data transforming, post-hoc explainability, knowledge retrieval, and augmentation, and knowledge-based vectorization techniques. Second, we will cover a semi-deep infusion of knowledge concerning the design of loss function, active function, and attention mechanisms concerning statistical AI's internal machinery. Third, we will have a deep infusion of knowledge to provide current AI architectures to blend with KGs or any other machine-readable knowledge to monitor latent representations, information fidelity, end-to-end intrinsic interpretability, and safety considerations. We will extensively delve into the technical intricacies of each KiL category, presenting general methodologies alongside specialized frameworks that highlight the practical value of KiL.

Building on these three methods of knowledge infusion, we introduce process knowledge-infused learning (PKiL) in the context of conversational systems. PKiL methods are particularly effective in applications with established guidelines, protocols, or processes, offering a deeper appreciation and understanding of their benefits in such structured environments.

Chapters 7–8 *Knowledge-Infused Learning for Conversational Systems in NLP*

Conversational systems amalgamate two distinct realms of research within the domain of natural language processing (NLP): the domains of question generation (QG) and response generation (RG), augmented by the intricacies of response shaping. These systems are colloquially referred to as chatbots or conversational agents. Recently, they have captured the focus and interest of researchers spanning diverse fields, largely due to the emergence of large language models (LLMs). These models, often likened to the nucleus of conversational systems, have ignited a renewed enthusiasm for and exploration of the capabilities and potential of such systems. However, the concerns inherent in statistical AI are equally evident in LLMs employed within conversational systems. In this chapter, we delve into the intersection of KiL and conversational systems, exploring how integrating external and varied knowledge sources can counterbalance the limitations of LLMs and elevate the functionality of these systems. By enhancing conversational systems' contextual understanding, coherence, and domain-specific expertise, KiL offers a promising pathway to overcoming the challenges of relying solely on statistical AI approaches. This integration enables these systems to provide more accurate, informed, and nuanced responses, elevating their overall performance and utility. In this chapter, we will delve into specific applications of KiL in conversational systems, focusing on its implementation in healthcare contexts and its role in improving general-purpose information-seeking interactions. Some of the key topics in these chapters include: (a) safety and explainability of conversational systems: Where are we and what is required to achieve AI safety and human-level explainability?; (b) process knowledge-infused learning; (c) the designing of explainable conversational agent; (d) the designing of knowledge-driven and adaptive personalization conversational agent; (e) contextualized question generation using knowledge graph-guided RAG: The why, what, and how of agents' information seeking, clarification, and factoid question generation in general purpose and critical applications.

Chapter 9 *Neurosymbolic Large Language Models:*

Modern AI methodologies, particularly sophisticated large language models (LLMs), often operate as black boxes in decision-making processes, raising concerns about their outcomes' reliability, consistency, and validity. In critical fields such as healthcare, emergency response, and nutrition, users demand transparency to maintain trust in AI-driven decisions. Furthermore, AI systems must evaluate whether the outcomes they generate are safe and suitable for users or if it's better to withhold a response. These factors are crucial in building AI credibility.

This chapter expands the KiL framework to detail five essential attributes for creating trustworthy AI: consistency, reliability, explainability, safety, and bias. While the first four attributes are discussed in other chapters, this section focuses on the crucial role of context elicitation and its role as an intrinsic property of LLMs for handling bias. KiL can mitigate bias by incorporating diverse viewpoints and historical contexts, promoting a more balanced and equitable language representation. It also helps identify and correct biased patterns in language generation.

2
Knowledge Graphs for Explainability and Interpretability

2.1 Knowledge Graphs

A knowledge graph (KG) is a machine-readable structured representation of knowledge consisting of entities (entity and entity type) and relationships in various forms (e.g., labeled property graphs and resource description frameworks (RDFs)) (Sheth et al., 2019b). KiL based on Machine Learning/Deep Learning seamlessly integrates external knowledge to address challenging problems in low-resource and open-domain natural language processing tasks and domain-specific problems. Domain-specific problems require the application of task-specific knowledge (implicit or explicit) to generic AI models. For example, to detect emerging events in a stream of crisis-related posts (e.g., Hurricane, COVID-19 Pandemic), a generic language model (e.g., Word2Vec Mikolov et al., 2013, BERT) can be fine tuned using the concepts and relationships found in disaster ontology (e.g., empathi from Gaur et al., 2019a). Low-resource problems are characterized by having few labeled samples, making further labeling difficult in terms of effort, quality, and time. For instance, annotating millions of posts from users in various mental health communities on Reddit would require (a) establishing guidelines for annotation, (b) training annotators, (c) resolving annotation conflicts, and (d) enriching quality over multiple iterations to achieve high annotator agreement. A study by Gaur et al. (2021b) proposed a KiL pipeline to annotate such extensive social data at scale, shifting the human role from annotators to evaluators.

There are various forms of KG, which are constructed either through manual effort, automatically, or semi-automatically, as illustrated in Figure 2.1. KG constructed with manual effort and following expert-defined guidelines are called Ontologies. For instance, in Figure 2.1E, the empathi ontology by Gaur et al. (2019a) is constructed from archives of the Federal Emergency Management Agency (FEMA), disaster ontology (Bhatt et al., 2014), geonames,

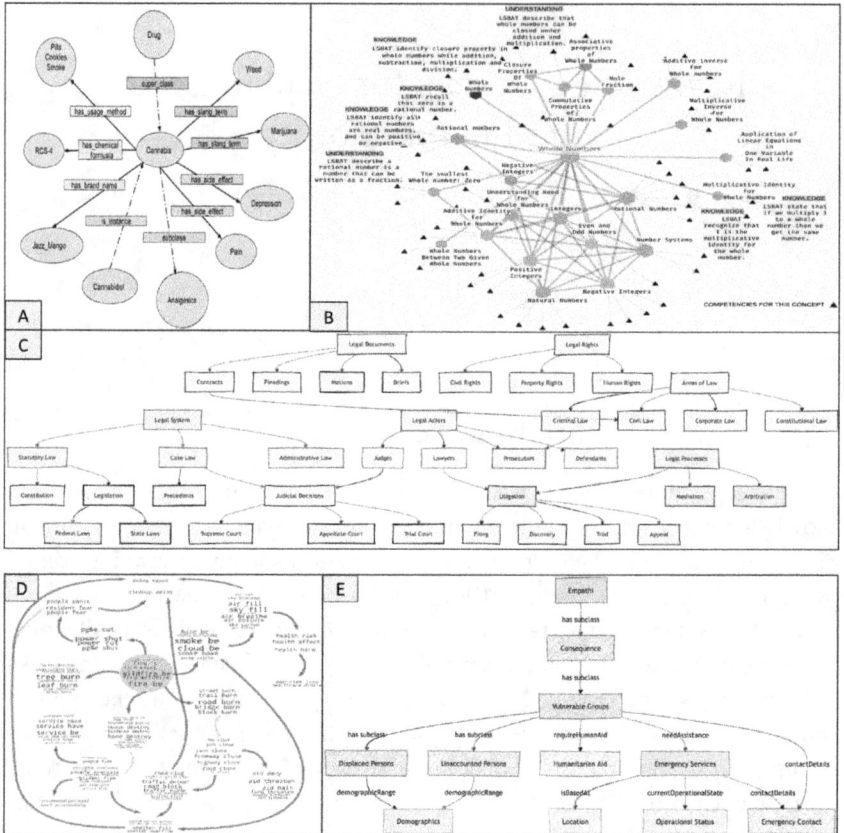

Figure 2.1 (A) Drug use ontology; (B) Education knowledge graph; (C) Legal knowledge graph; D Wildlife crisis event subgraph; E Empathi, a crisis ontology that models such a graph. Example KG constructed either from manual effort (A, C, E), automatically (D), or semi-automatically (B). Drug abuse ontology is created by Lokala et al. (2020). Empathi ontology is created by Gaur et al. (2019a). Wildfire crisis event subgraph is created by Jiang et al. (2019).

and others. The structure of the ontology is laid out based on the process in which an event is described in the FEMA archives. Figure 2.1B illustrates an educational knowledge graph (Dhavala et al., 2024) constructed from epubs of Amazon books and other course textbooks to assess a student's learning outcome and suggest ways to intervene. These domain-specific KGs are at the core of KiL to provide necessary information aid for ML/DL algorithms for domain adaptation and reasoning over the outcomes.

2.2 Construction of the Empathi Ontology

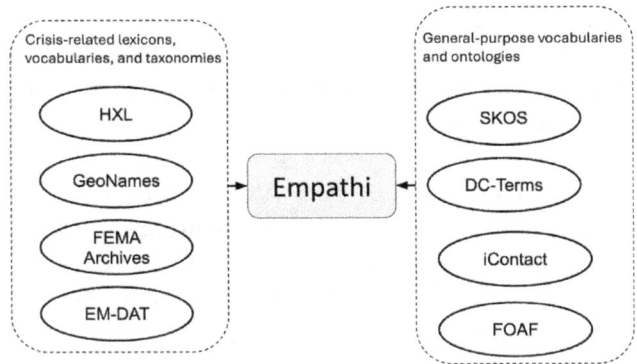

Figure 2.2 Importing existing ontologies in *empathi*.

2.2 Construction of the Empathi Ontology

Empathi represents a significant fusion of diverse ontologies related to crises and semantic information delivery (see Figure 2.2). The state-of-the-art vocabularies concerned with the hazard and crisis management domains are as follows:

HXL HXL stands for humanitarian exchange language. The HXL standard (2015) aims at information sharing during humanitarian calamities by overcoming the burden of interoperability. HXL ontology has a total of 50 classes and 66 relations. The main concepts contained in HXL are `Place`, `Survey and assessment`, `Operation`, `Cash and Finance`, and `Crisis`. Furthermore, the Keßler and Hendrix (2015) provides links to UN OCHA vocabularies such as global coordination groups and disaster types (ReliefWeb, 1996), organization types (United Nations Office for the Coordination of Humanitarian Affairs (OCHA), Centre for Humanitarian Data, 2023), vulnerable groups, and humanitarian themes under the United Nations Office for the Coordination of Humanitarian Affairs (UNOCHA) (2024). Furthermore, HXL provides a hashtag schema containing related social media tags such as #channel, #crisis, #impact, #event, etc. (Clark et al., 2015).

MOAC MOAC, which is concerned with the management of crises, is a vocabulary (Gaur et al., 2019a; Liu et al., 2013) providing concepts mainly related to crisis management. It was created by the Inter-Agency Standing Committee (2023), Emergency Shelter Cluster (2010) in Haiti, UN-OCHA 3W Who What Where Contact Database, and Ushahidi (2023) Platform.

DoRES DoRES stands for document-report-event-situation ontology. DoRES is an ontology sharing information between individuals and organizations using situational reports for describing the situation (Burel et al., 2017). It helps humanitarian organizations to structure their plans.

EDXL-RESCUER Ontology EDXL-RESCUER stands for emergency data exchange language reliable and smart crowdsourcing solution for emergency and crisis management (Fraunhofer IESE, 2023). It is an ontology based on EDXL developed for coordinating and interchanging information with legacy systems (Barros et al., 2015).

Emergency Fire (EF) EF is an ontology explicitly designed for fires in buildings. It comprises 131 terms along with definitions created after subjective research. It serves as a protocol for information sharing, analysis, evaluation, and comprehension by an organization in the situation of a disaster caused by fire (Bitencourt et al., 2015).

Social Media Emergency Management (SMEM) When faced with a sudden natural disaster, social media platforms become inundated with various types of information, including situational updates, expressions of concern, weather reports, and accounts of the crisis's effects. Amid this flood of data, it becomes crucial to identify the portions that are both contextually relevant and actionable for personnel responsible for coordinating relief efforts. The SMEM ontology offers a structured framework of concepts organized hierarchically. This framework enables the transformation of the large volume of unstructured content found on social media into a more manageable, action-oriented format, as discussed in Moi et al.'s (2016) work on ontology in emergency management.

Disaster Ontology This is one of the ontologies listed in the Finnish Ontology Library Service ONKI. Disaster Ontology (DO) by the Onki Finnish Ontology Library (2000) comprises 97 concepts (classes) concerning man-made and natural hazards. This ontology is useful for managing disaster situations but disregards concepts related to social media (e.g., news reports, modality of data, surveillance, prayer, and monitoring the status of the services provided by organizations).

2.3 Integration of External Vocabularies

In this section, we list the external vocabularies that have been partially integrated into *empathi*. Not all of them are necessarily related to hazard or

2.3 Integration of External Vocabularies

crisis management (we reuse generic concepts from well-known vocabularies, e.g., friend-of-a-friend (FOAF) ontology). Figure 2.2 concisely represents an integration that aims at reusing the existing vocabularies following ontology design methodologies (Methontology by Fernández-López et al. (1997) and NeOn by Suarez-Figueroa et al. (2012)) or interlinking *empathi* to other vocabularies that enhance its visibility. External vocabularies included in the *empathi* ontology are:

- **Federal Emergency Management Agency (2017) (FEMA)** provides a glossary of terms related to disaster preparation and management (Anderson, 2002).
- **Emergency Disasters Database (EM-DAT)** provides a precise definition of concepts and, furthermore, a categorization of disturbance-related events (Jonkman et al., 2005; Delforge et al., 2025).
- **MA-Ont** supports detailed properties describing media files and appropriate metadata mapping (Lee et al., 2012).
- **iContact** offers conceptual classes for defining international addresses. This is particularly useful when utilizing GeoNames (Nalchigar and Fox, 2010; Wick et al., 2015) as an ontology for describing locations (University of Toronto, 2010).
- **Friend Of A Friend (FOAF)** was created for describing people, relations, and associated events. Coupled with SIOC (Breslin et al., 2005) and the disaster domain model (Purohit et al., 2014; Bhatt et al., 2014), it can describe social media communities formed during disaster scenarios (Brickley and Miller, 2007; Miller and Brickley, 2007).
- **Geonames (2006)** is a part of the GeoNames Database, providing information about 11 million places (toponyms) covering all countries. Integrating the GeoNames ontology into our ontology adds geospatial semantic information that is critical for actionable hazard response. The ontology contains 150 classes and two relations forming 758 axioms on location dereferencing. The mapping syntax provided by this ontology is compatible with schema.org, the DBpedia ontology, the LinkedGeoData ontology, and the INSEE ontology (Wick et al., 2015).
- **Linked Open Descriptions of Events (LODE)** defines an event as an action that takes place at a certain time and has a specific location. It can be a historical action or a scheduled action. Thus, it provides the generic concept of Event along with locational (i.e., atPlace), temporal (i.e., atTime) aspects, and people who play a role (i.e., involvedAgent) (linkedevents.org, 2021).

16 *Knowledge Graphs for Explainability and Interpretability*

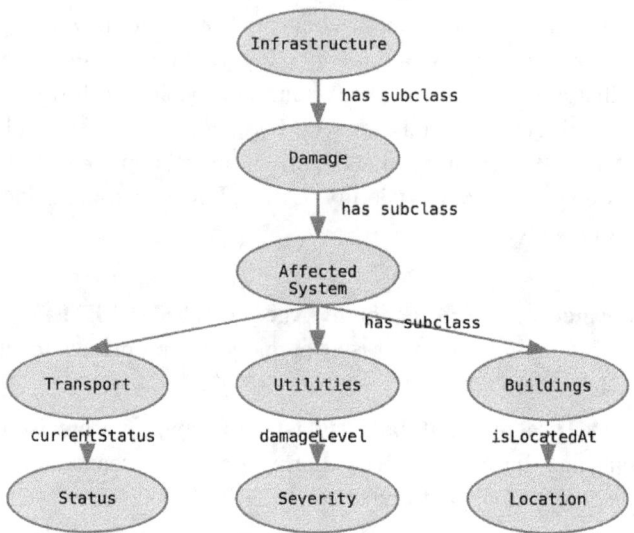

Figure 2.3 Partial representation of the Infrastructure Damage concept in *empathi*.

- **Simple Knowledge Organization System (SKOS)** is a data model we used to describe the concepts of our domain. It provides a better organization of domain knowledge (i.e., Hazard Crisis) (Miles et al., 2005; Miles and Bechhofer, 2009).
- **Semantically-Interlinked Online Communities (SIOC)** is a W3C ontological standard to describe information from online communities. It can support a volunteer or caregiver with actionable information in the realm of social media (Breslin et al., 2005; Passant et al., 2010).

Core Concepts of Empathi The *empathi* ontology contains 423 classes and 338 relations. In Figure 2.3, concepts linked to "Affected Population" via solid lines form structural concepts ("is-a"/"subclass"), while the concepts linked via colored dotted lines are semantically related concepts to "Affected Population." In the following, we present only the super-classes which imply generic coverage.

- **Age Group:** classifies people based on their age similarity by providing the following sub-classes: (i) Adolescent, (ii) Adult, (iii) Child, and (iv) Infant.
- **Event:** defines events along with spatial and temporal constraints happening in any phase of hazard. This concept embodies the following sub-classes: (i) Climate Change, (ii) Criminal Activity, (iii) Emergency Exercises, (iv) Evacuation Plan, (v) Humanitarian Event, (vi) Recovery Plan, (vii) Rescue

Operation, (viii) State Mitigation Plan, (ix) Volunteer Support, and (x) Early Warning.
- **Facility:** defines an amenity made accessible for a specific purpose. It is attributed to the following sub-classes: (i) Communication, (ii) Electricity, (iii) Gas Facility, (iv) Water Facility, and (v) Education Resources.
- **Hazard Type:** lists different types of hazards that can affect the human community. It is an entity type that embodies sub-classes (i) Airburst, (ii) Coastal erosion, (iii) Drought, (iv) Earthquake, (v) Explosion, (vi) Fire, (vii) Flood, (viii) Hurricane, (ix) Landslide, (x) Sandstorm, (xi) Storm, (xii) Tornado, (xiii) Toxic Radioactivity, (xiv) Tsunami, (xv) Volcano, and (xvi) Winterstorm.
- **Hazard Phase:** categorizes different activities carried out by various organizations before, during, and after a catastrophic event into three sub-classes: (i) During Hazard, (ii) Pre-Hazard, and (iii) Post-Hazard.
- **Impact:** affects someone or something in an unprecedented manner. This concept embodies sub-classes (i) Affected Population, (ii) Animal Loss, (iii) Health Issues, (iv) Food Shortage, (v) Financial Crisis, (vi) Contamination, (vii) Infrastructure Damage, and (viii) Severity.
- **Involved Actors:** associates people or organizations with any catastrophic event. Sub-classes of this concept are (i) Organization and (ii) People.
- **Modality of Data:** conveys or represents information (raw, structured, or semi-structured) using a text, audio, video, or photo sequences. Sub-classes of this concept are (i) Audio, (ii) Photo, (iii) Text, and (iv) Video.
- **Place:** defines a physical surrounding by longitude, latitude, and area, providing a relative position of someone or something during a hazardous situation. One sub-class of Place is Location, described by longitude, latitude, and the area of the affected place.
- **Report:** documents evidence of the destruction caused by the natural disaster. The report states all the activities carried out by various governmental and nongovernmental organizations (NGOs). The report is a way to keep people vigilant. Sub-classes encompassed under the concept are (i) Expert Report, (ii) Human Sensing Report, and (iii) Media Report.
- **Service:** is an act of providing support to someone in a situation of distressing incidents. Core sub-classes of this concept are (i) Financial Care, (ii) Healthcare Service, (iii) Helpline, (iv) Human Remains Management, (v) Resource and Information Centre, (vi) Supply, (vii) Transportation, and (viii) Prayer Location.
- **Status:** defines the state of services that are planned during the pre/in/post hazard phases. Associated sub-classes are (i) Available, (ii) Offered, (iii) Requested, and (iv) Unavailable.

- **Surveillance Information:** A systematic, ongoing collection, collation, and analysis of data and the timely dissemination of information to those who need to know so that action can be taken. The surveillance concept in the setting of natural disasters can help to identify the resulting health-related needs, which, in turn, will lead to the more rational and effective deployment of resources to affected populations.

Populating Empathi and Evaluation A substantial impact of the *empathi* ontology is empowering us to semantically annotate text (e.g., posts posted during the hazard). Figure 2.4 shows the mapping of segments within a given post to *empathi* concepts. Thus, at an abstract level, this post is related to the flood that occurred in Chennai and reports two associated impacts (*Airport Closed, 188 Killed*). In this respect, in the first experiment, we compiled 53 million posts from 30 significant hazards that have happened in the past, such as Hurricanes Sandy in 2012 and Irma in 2017, the Oklahoma Wildfires in 2017, the Chennai Flood in 2005, the Alaska Earthquake in 2018, the Florida Rains in 2000 and 2016, the Houston Floods in 2017, the New Zealand Earthquake in 2016, Typhoon Haima in 2016, Winter Storm Kayla in 2016, and many more. After that, we identified the posts related to the seven central concepts of *empathi*, i.e., (i) impact, (ii) modality of data, (iii) hazard type,

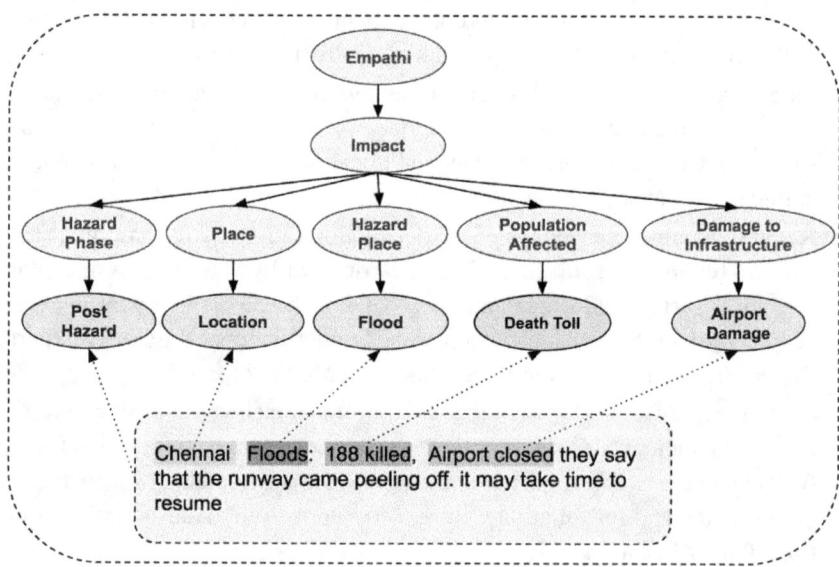

Figure 2.4 Mapping posts and their words to *empathi* concepts.

2.3 Integration of External Vocabularies

Table 2.1 *Mapping concepts of* empathi *to posts of hazards.*

Concepts of empathi	Posts
Hazard Type	3,034,257
Impact	618,446
Modality of Data	509,645
Facility	258,117
Place	16,397
Transportation	6,694
Surveillance	1,588
Water Facility (Sub-Concept of Facility)	218,968
Gas Facility (Sub-Concept of Facility)	33,047
Involved Organization (Sub-Concept of Involved)	4,249
Severity (Sub-Concept of Impact)	1,344

(iv) place, (v) transportation, (vi) surveillance, and (vii) facility. Table 2.1 shows the statistics of identified posts related to each of the chosen concepts and sub-concepts. The mapping was performed by training a word embedding model over 53 million posts and utilizing it in generating vectors of ontology classes and posts (Řehůřek, 2023). In the mapping process, first, we generate embedding of n-grams of a post and aggregate them using an averaging operation to create a representation of a post. We calculate cosine similarity scores to determine the relevant ontology classes to the post. After finding the relevant ontology classes to the post using a threshold of 70% similarity, we perform a similar process to find the similarity between n-grams of the posts and the sub-concepts within an ontology class. Moreover, considering the dynamic nature of the disaster domain, we assume our approach to be a feasible component of ontology evolution and population process. Table 2.2 represents samples of these posts (column two) along with the mapped *empathi* concepts (column three) from various hazard types (column one).

Extensive coverage by *empathi* provides the capability of extracting structured information from unstructured and sparse content (e.g., X) Derczynski et al. (2013). For identifying relevant information from unstructured social media text and classifying posts as relevant or irrelevant to the crisis, it is essential to map the words to ontology classes. For instance, in Figure 2.4, the post *Chennai Floods: 188 killed, Airport closed they say that the runway came peeling off. it may take time to resume* is identified as a post-hazard post. *Chennai* links to the concept *Place*, *Floods* links to the concept *Hazard type*, *188 killed* links to the concept *Affected population*, and *Airport closed* links to the concept *Infrastructure Damage*. Moreover, such a procedure is termed semantic annotation using expanded concepts (also known as hypernyms).

Table 2.2 *Sample of hazard-related posts from different hazard types. AP: Affected Population, ID: Infrastructure Damage, HP: Human Prayer, VS: Volunteer Support, H: Helpline, CA: Criminal Activity, S: Supply, L: Location, ER: Expert Report, SH: Shelter, Hazard Type (*): One hazard (Earthquake) causing another hazard (Landslide).*

Hazard type	Post	Hazard concept
Flood	1. 188 were killed; Airport closed. They say that the runway came peeling off. it may take time to resume.	Impact (AP, ID)
	2. @? Hope people get adequate relief and no one is left out.Nation stands with Chennai.	Event (HP)
	3. @? in who can offer places to stay, pls fill the form for volunteers collating info #chennairains	Event (VS)
	4. @? Chennai has been declared a disaster zone. Army has been deployed. Army Helpline - +XXX XXX XXXX #ChennaiRains	Service (H)
Hurricane	5. Surveillance video captures several people looting a Houston store #Harvey in the wake of Hurricane	Event (CA)
	6. The aftermath. 10,000 people are now homeless because of Hurricane Irma. #WednesdayWisdom #climatechange	Impact (AP), Event (CC)
	7. #HurricaneIrmaRecovery Drive for #Homestead & #FloridaKeys today! Drop off supplies at @? #DJLMS #dontgivebackjustgive.	Service (S)
	8. At least 56 of Florida's 639 nursing homes still have *no* electricity this morning, five days after #HurricaneIrma	Impact (ID)
Blizzard	9. @? "2-3 days, what could it take before airlines begin to clear the backlog? @? at on #blizzard2016.	Impact (ID)
	10. @?: I-75 in Kentucky closed due to a large number of accidents, state patrol says #blizzard2016	Impact (AP, ID)
	11. @?: The baton is passed. Buoy 50 miles south of Wilmington #Jonas #blizzard2016	Place (L)
	12. @?: Blizzard with "life and death implications" hits Washington, Mid-Atlantic #blizzard2016	Place (L), Impact (AP)
	13. @?: Be sure to follow @BGSLandslides for lots of up to date information on landslides across the UK #StormFrank	Report (ER)
Landslide	14. #StormFrank landslide at Glasscarraig Norman Motte & Bailey in Co Wexford	@? #archaeology #floods	Place (L)
	15. SRI LANKA: At least 73 dead after a week of flooding, landslides; 243,000 in temp shelters	TorStar #ExtremeWeather	Service (SH), Impact (AP)
	16. @?: #EcuadorEarthquake - landslides closing down roads & making it challenging for help to reach hardest-hit towns	Impact (ID), Hazard Type (*)

It can improve understanding of social media messages, which pose challenges like ill-formed sentences, ambiguous word senses, poor syntactic structure, and implicit referencing. Semantic features formed using *empathi* can enhance supervised and unsupervised learning in the crisis domain (Khare et al., 2018).

2.4 Evaluating Quality of *empathi*

To build up a quality ontology, we followed the principles of ontology methodologies such as NeON and Methontology, which encourage the reuse of existing ontologies. However, to quantitatively measure the quality of *empathi*, we designed a user evaluation survey. This survey contained 17 questions concerning hierarchical, relational, and lexical aspects of *empathi* inspired by Hlomani and Stacey (2014).

Precisely, the participants (e.g., researchers, PhD students) in the survey evaluated the following criteria: (1) the correctness of structure (hierarchy), (2) the correctness of relations between concepts, and (3) lexical evaluation, i.e., the quality of annotations associated with both concepts and relations. In the following, we elaborate on these criteria.

Structural Evaluation In this evaluation, the hierarchical structure is assessed concerning the correctness of the "is-a" relationship as to whether the given concept A is a particular type of the given concept B. For instance, "Animal Loss" is a subclass of "Impact" in *empathi*. Such evaluation is necessary to confirm the utility of the ontology for the classification task (Imran et al., 2015). We presented parts of hierarchy in the survey and asked the participants how far this hierarchy makes sense to them. They had to rate in the range 1 (fully disagree) to 5 (fully agree).

Semantic Relational Evaluation The ontology is evaluated for holding semantically correct relations between concepts. For instance, there is a relation between the concept "Affected Population" and the concept "Service" referring to "need for help." Thus, the Affected Population is the domain, and the Service is the range. Such an example of relations where entities are semantically tagged with their attributes enable high-quality summarization, subgraph extraction, and contextualized question answering. We presented a number of relations of *empathi* to the participants and asked them whether or not they confirm such relations exist.

Lexical Evaluation This part examines the *expressiveness*, *completeness*, and *clarity* of annotations of a given ontology. Expressiveness states the efficacy of the ontology in identifying relevant information using natural language processing techniques. Completeness (Cordì and Mascardi, 2004) evaluates whether an illustration of a concept using definitions and labels adequately defines various scenarios in the crisis domain. For instance, with respect to the concept "Human Prayer," the definition "prayer is a message to God from victim's relatives and family for protecting their lives and health" is provided along with the labels "send prayers," "heart prayers," "heart praying," "join praying," "love prayers," "prayers affected," "temple," "church," "prayers city," "prayers families," "prayers involved," etc. Clarity evaluates whether or not the concept name in the ontology is meaningful and easily understandable to humans and machines.

Results Our survey had 13 participants who understood the *crisis* domain and have published articles in relevant conferences (e.g., ISCRAM). The results recorded through survey are illustrated in Figure 2.5.

The structural evaluation section is comprised of seven questions: (SQ1) Concerning a hazard situation, are "Mental stress" and "Physical stress" two important concepts under "Health issues"? (SQ2) Do "No Effect," "Minor," "Major," "Hazardous," and "Catastrophic" represent sub-classes of "severity"? (SQ3) Are "Financial Crisis," "Food Shortage," and "Contamination" probable impacts of a Hazard? (SQ4) Are the following triples meaningful: "Animal Loss is Impact," "Communication Lines Failure is Infrastructure Damage," "Power Outage is Infrastructure Damage," and "Survived People is an Affected Population"? (SQ5) Do you consider a nongovernment organization's (NGO's) report to be an expert report? (SQ6) Do health reports, service feedback, and weather reports define human sensing? (SQ7) Can "News Agencies Report" and "Social Media Report" be categorized under "Media Report," a sub-class of "Report"? Questions SQ1–SQ6 were Yes/No questions, and SQ7 followed the Likert scale. The detailed results are represented in Figure 2.5. We observe the average agreement rate above 84.5%.

Regarding the evaluation of semantic relations, we designed seven questions as follows. SRQ1: Do you think the following triples make sense; "Event occurs in a Place," "Service is offered in a Place," "Each Hazard is associated to a couple of Events," and "Each Hazard leads to a couple of Services"? SRQ2: Can "Event" and "Service" concepts be linked to the concept "Place" using the "isLocationAt" relation? SRQ3: Do you think two different types of hazards can be related to an event, service, and place? SRQ4: Is the "current status" relation between Facility and Status semantically correct? SRQ5: Are available, offered, requested, and unavailable suitable categories for Status? SRQ6: Can the concepts "Service" and "Organization" apply to the concept

2.4 Evaluating Quality of empathi

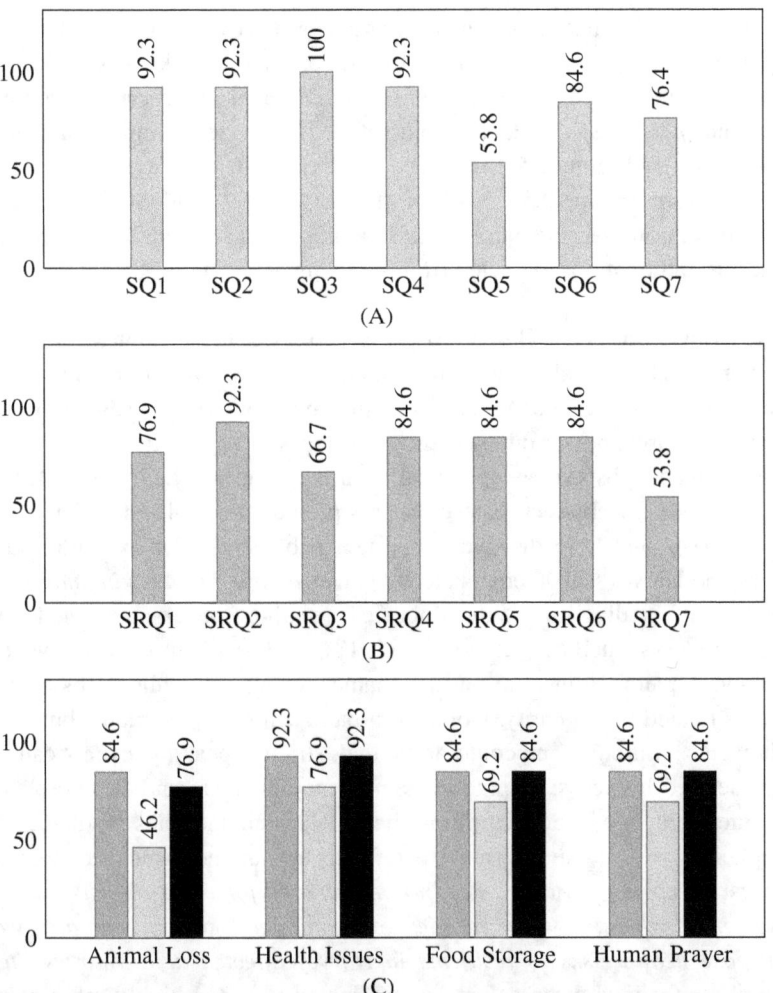

Figure 2.5 Agreement of 13 evaluators having some understanding of the domain. (A) Seven questions that evaluate Structure of *empathi*, (B) Seven questions that evaluate Semantic Relations of *empathi*, and (C) Three questions that evaluate lexical characteristics of *empathi* for four concepts: Animal Loss, Health Issues, Food Shortage, and Human Prayer. The agreement percentage is calculated as the percentage of evaluators who responded "agree" or "yes" in the ontology evaluation form. Each bar within each category represent LQ1, LQ2, and LQ3, respectively.

"Hazard Type"? SRQ7: Does the relation "needHelp" correctly link "Affected Population" with "Organization" and "Service"? Questions SRQ2–SRQ7 are Yes/No, and SRQ1 follows the Likert scale. From Figure 2.5, an average agreement of 75.4% was concluded in confirming the above facts.

The lexical evaluation of *empathi* was performed by representing definitions and synonyms (or labels) describing each concept and asking participants to respond to the following questions: (LQ1) Do labels appropriately represent the concept? (LQ2) Are labels complete? (LQ3) Are definitions and labels clear enough? Figure 2.5 shows the results with a total agreement rate of 78.8%. From Figure 2.5C, we see that LQ2, SR7, and SQ5 have a low agreement; however, the ontology will be improved with additional emerging concepts and relations extracted from social media content.

Case Study: Subevent Detection using Empathi In the context of a crisis, an **event** is a large-scale disaster that causes massive devastation (e.g., a hurricane). Such large-scale emergencies include many important **sub-events** (e.g., bridge collapses, power outages, drug shortages, etc.). We detect such events in social media posts (more specifically, on X) and group them into collections called **sub-event clusters**. These clusters provide a high-level understanding of the crisis and help discover important sub-events. For example, during Hurricane Harvey, an X post stated: *"power outage in west kingman due to flooding."* "Flooding" and "power outage" are sub-events of Hurricane Harvey.

Prior works, such as Rudra et al. (2018), *exclusively* model sub-events as noun–verb pairs. Nouns are entities, names, or places, while verbs describe actions related to the entity. Noun–verb pairs can represent many, but *not all* sub-events. Although one could argue that, strictly speaking, events can only be described by verbs, in practice, emergency planners and first responders are interested in a wider definition that could include topics or themes. For simplicity, we use "sub-events" to refer to events and topics or themes of interest. X posts such as *we need to be prepared for infectious diseases that may spread when the water recedes #chennaifloods* and *contaminated water still pose health risks to residents in Harvey affected area #harvey #texas* describe infectious diseases and contaminated water as highly relevant sub-events but do not conform to the noun–verb pair structure.

We use a two-word phrase detection model that captures frequent phrases to extract these kinds of sub-events. Our approach combines noun–verb pairs and phrases as a more comprehensive approach for sub-event detection. The number of automatically identified noun–verb pairs and phrases is large on large datasets and requires pruning. Our method identifies the most important sub-events by ranking candidate sub-events using the *empathi* ontology and discarding noun–verb pairs and phrases that do not occur more than once in the dataset. Subsequently, we cluster the top-ranked noun–verb pairs and phrases.

Datasets and Processing: We use Hurricane Harvey (2017) and the Nepal Earthquake (2015) as two case studies for our experiments. We use publicly

2.4 Evaluating Quality of empathi

Table 2.3 *Description of the two large-scale unlabeled and labeled post datasets used in the study.*

Event type	Hurricane Harvey	Nepal earthquake
Time period	Aug 27–Sept 2, 2017	April 25–30, 2015
Unlabeled posts	4.6 Million	635, 150
Labeled posts	4,000	4,639
Labels	Informative/Not-Informative	Informative/Not-Informative

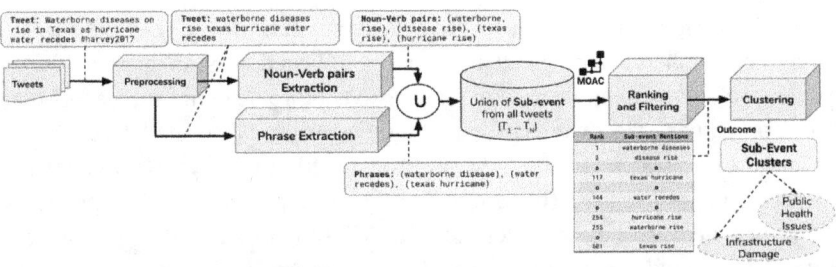

Figure 2.6 Our framework shows how candidate sub-events are extracted and clustered through an example posts.

available X posts related to both crises from CrisisNLP, a repository made public by Qatar Computing Research Institute (2023). The resource provides both unlabeled post IDs (concerning privacy constraints) and a small labeled post corpus for both Hurricane Harvey and the Nepal Earthquake. We used the Twitter Hydrator doc (2023) to extract posts associated with the post IDs. The labeled posts were marked as either relevant to the crisis events or not relevant to the crisis. A description of the datasets is provided in Table 2.3. We combined the unlabeled and labeled data to develop our model. The results of our approach were compared to the baseline, executed over the same labeled posts. We performed an initial preprocessing of the datasets comprising removal of (1) white spaces, (2) stop words and words with less than three characters, (3) strings with numeric characters, and (4) hashtags (e.g., #harvey, #hurricane, #hurricaneharvey).

Methodology: The method is divided into three components: (1) extraction of sub-events from text, (2) ranking of candidate sub-events, and (3) clustering (see Figure 2.6).

1. Extraction of Sub-events We form a single corpus of posts by appending processed labeled posts to unlabeled posts. We utilize the spaCy dependency parser to extract nouns and verbs present in the corpus of posts (Honnibal and Montani, 2020). The parser iteratively constructs a dependency tree for each post and removes all parent and child nodes that are either nouns or verbs. The number of noun–verb pairs identified from this method is numerous, and a large number of the candidates are not sub-events. To filter out the noisy pairs, we only consider noun–verb pairs that occur more than once in the dataset. This helps to substantially reduce the number of candidate sub-events without missing out on essential sub-events.

While noun–verb pairs can identify plenty of sub-events, they miss interesting and implicit sub-events that are not manifested as noun and verb pairs. Hence, we complement them with phrases to capture potential sub-events that occur as co-occurring words. We run a Gensim, a phrase model developed by Řehůřek (2023), over the X post corpus, setting the minimum count for co-occurring words as 2 (bigrams). The Gensim phrase model implements the phrase detection method described in Mikolov et al. (2013). Consider a sample processed post: *waterborne diseases hurricane water recedes*. The dependency parser identifies "waterborne recedes" and "water recedes" as noun–verb pairs. The phrase model recognizes "waterborne diseases" as a phrase. Their composition is considered as a candidate sub-event.

2. Ranking of Sub-events Using our method described above, we need to rank the candidate sub-events to identify the most important ones. For example, in the post *Waterborne diseases on the rise in Texas as hurricane water recedes #harvey2017*, "waterborne diseases" is a more important sub-event than "water recedes." Hence, our ranking method should be able to understand the semantic meaning of the pairs to rank them. To achieve this goal, we use a Empathi ontology containing 62 terms related to crisis scenarios. We compare our candidate sub-events with terms in the Empathi ontology and score the max of the cosine similarity between each candidate sub-event and the terms in the ontology. We need to generate embeddings of our candidate sub-events and terms in the ontology to make the comparisons. Embeddings provide a numerical vector representation that captures the context of a word in a corpus. Embedding algorithms, including Word2Vec (Mikolov et al., 2013), GLoVe (Pennington et al., 2014), and FastText (Joulin et al., 2016), have proven to be effective for creating rich representations tuned to a specific domain. We trained FastText on 53 million crisis-related posts covering the Florida Rains (2000 & 2016), the Chennai Floods (2005), Hurricane Sandy (2012), Typhoon Haima (2016), the New Zealand Earthquake (2016), Hurricane Irma (2017), Hurricane

Harvey (2017), the Houston Floods (2017), and the Alaska Earthquake (2018). We choose FastText since the method can generate embeddings for out-of-vocabulary words by leveraging character embeddings. This characteristic of FastText is important due to the noisy nature of social media text, in which there are many misspellings, neologisms, and hashtags. The trained model generated vector representations of tokens in unlabeled post datasets. The vector representation of a noun–verb pair or phrase was generated through the summation of individual word vectors. Further, we normalize the word vectors, as our downstream task of ranking and clustering requires the computation of cosine similarity between noun–verb pairs or phrases with concepts in the Empathi ontology. Our ranking approach gives a higher score to candidate sub-events that are semantically related to crisis terms in the *empathi* ontology.

3. Sub-event Clusters Aggregation of candidate sub-events is critical for rapid situational awareness. It will address the use cases of first responders (e.g., navy, firefighters, local emergency manager) and humanitarian organizations. We cluster our filtered list of candidate sub-events to enable us to label a cluster as belonging to a type/category (see Figure 2.6). Our clusters should be diverse and should group related sub-events such that each cluster will represent a cohesive category of sub-event. We investigated various clustering approaches (e.g., DBSCAN (Schubert et al., 2017), OPTICS (Ankerst et al., 1999), K-Means, and Gaussian mixture model) and found spectral clustering gave the most stable clusters for our task (Ng et al., 2002). The manifolds created in spectral clustering involve the creation of the similarity matrix using cosine similarity as a distance measure between the candidate sub-events. Our resulting clusters are topically diverse and evenly distributed, as we will show in the qualitative evaluation.

4. Experiments and Evaluation We analyze the performance of our approach on two disaster events: Hurricane Harvey and the Nepal Earthquake. The success of a sub-event and categorization scheme depends on (1) how accurately it can identify underlying sub-events in the data and (2) how practical the categories are in describing the event types in the dataset. In this regard, we provide quantitative and qualitative evaluations for our tasks where they apply.

5. Baseline Approaches We compare our method to a recent state-of-the-art approach for sub-event identification described by Rudra et al. (2018). The methodology, DEPSUB, outperforms several baseline methods in their evaluation. DEPSUB uses only noun–verb pairs for sub-event identification. Furthermore, it employs a different ranking scheme: a product of the

Szymkiewicz–Simpson overlap score of the sub-events and a discounting factor to reduce the count of infrequent sub-events.

We also compare our method to a variant of the baseline that uses only noun–verb pairs but employs our ranking methodology (*empathi*+NV). The difference between our method and this approach illustrates how phrases alone contribute to detecting comprehensive sub-events. For homogeneity, we followed similar pre-processing steps in the baseline study. However, we utilized the spaCy dependency parser as opposed to the X POS tagger for the extraction of noun–verb pairs. We considered the speed and accuracy of the spaCy parser to be preferable to the X POS tagger (Dutt et al., 2018).

2.4.1 Quantitative Evaluation

For our quantitative evaluation, we compare our approach with the baselines by measuring how good the top-ranked sub-events are at retrieving informative posts from the annotated datasets. In particular, given the ranked list of sub-events, we pick the top-k sub-events represented by NV-pairs and phrases and check their occurrence in labeled posts. A true positive is an annotated informative post that includes at least one of the top-k sub-events; otherwise, it is a false negative. We measure the precision and recall at different values of k. We define precision as the ratio of the number of informative posts identified to the total number of posts identified. Our recall is the ratio of the number of identified informative posts to the total number of informative posts in the dataset. We report F1-scores at the different values k and the ROC curve. Through these two metrics, we evaluate the effectiveness of our approach over the baseline methods in retrieving informative posts.

Hurricane Harvey: We used 795,461 distinct unlabeled posts from the hydrated 4.6 million posts together with 4,000 (3,027 informative and 973 un-informative) labeled posts to train the methods. The number of unique noun–verb pairs identified was 769,670, while the number of phrases totaled 27,122. Hence, the baseline method (DEPSUB) had 769,670 candidate sub-events, while our approach (without filtering) had 796,792. First, we show the performance of our approach compared to the baseline method without our filtering approach. Then, we show the performance of our approach with filtering applied compared to without filtering and to the baseline.

We observe in Figure 2.7 that our approach outperforms the baseline (DEPSUB) in F1-score over a various number of top-ranked sub-events. We also observe that we obtain marginal gains by adding phrases to noun–verb pairs for sub-event detection. Moreover, the curve illustrates that our ranking methodology identifies the most important sub-events compared to

2.4 Evaluating Quality of empathi

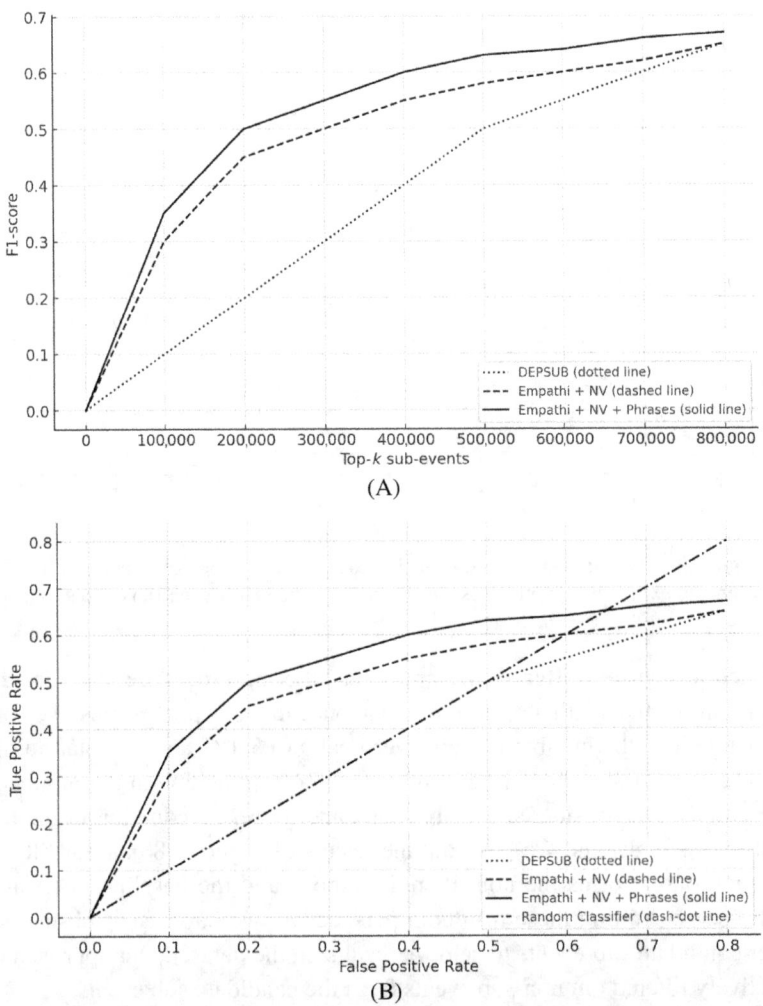

Figure 2.7 Assessing the relevance of candidate subevents in identifying informative posts in labeled Hurricane Harvey dataset. (A) F1-score over varying sub-events thresholds; (B) ROC curve. The sub-events were not filtered based on the noun–verb pairs.

the ranking used in DEPSUB. Considering Figure 2.7A, we observe that with the top 250,000 ranked sub-events, we achieve optimal results concerning precision and recall of retrieved informative posts. Additionally, we see in the Figure 2.7B plot that our method performs well compared to the baseline, which performs slightly better than random.

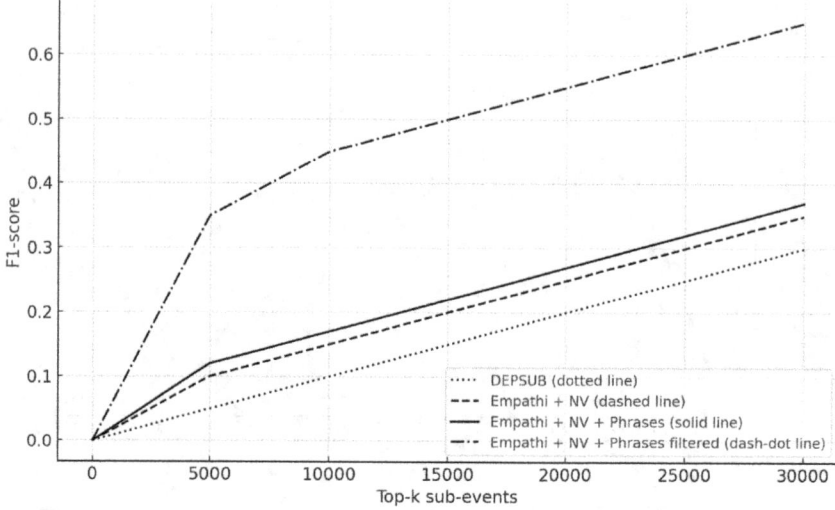

Figure 2.8 Variation in F1-score on increasing the number of candidate sub-events to extract informative posts from the annotated Hurricane Harvey dataset.

Hurricane Harvey Filtered: We apply our filtering procedure that considers only noun–verb pairs that occur more than once in the X post corpus. By doing this, we reduce the number of noun–verb pairs to 3,187 and the total number of sub-events to 30,309. This constitutes a 99.6% reduction in the number of noun–verb pairs considered as sub-events and a 96.2% reduction in the total number of sub-events. We see from the results of Figure 2.8 that our filtering approach outperforms the non filtered methods and the baseline in terms of the F1-score. Putting these results in perspective, we have used substantially fewer candidate sub-events to achieve results on the dataset. Our approach has effectively filtered out non-sub events from the candidate sub events.

Nepal Earthquake: To confirm the generalizability of our approach, we confirm our results on a different crisis event dataset. We used 635,150 distinct unlabeled posts from the hydrated posts together with 3,479 (1,636 informative and 1,843 un-informative) labeled posts to train the methods. The number of unique noun–verb pairs identified was 577,914, while the number of phrases totaled 36,980. In this regard, the DEPSUB method had 577,914 candidate sub-events, while our approach (without filtering) had 614,894 potential sub-events. As with the previous experiment, we first show the performance of our approach compared to the baseline method without our filtering approach. Then, we show the performance of our approach with filtering applied compared to without filtering and to the baseline.

2.4 Evaluating Quality of empathi

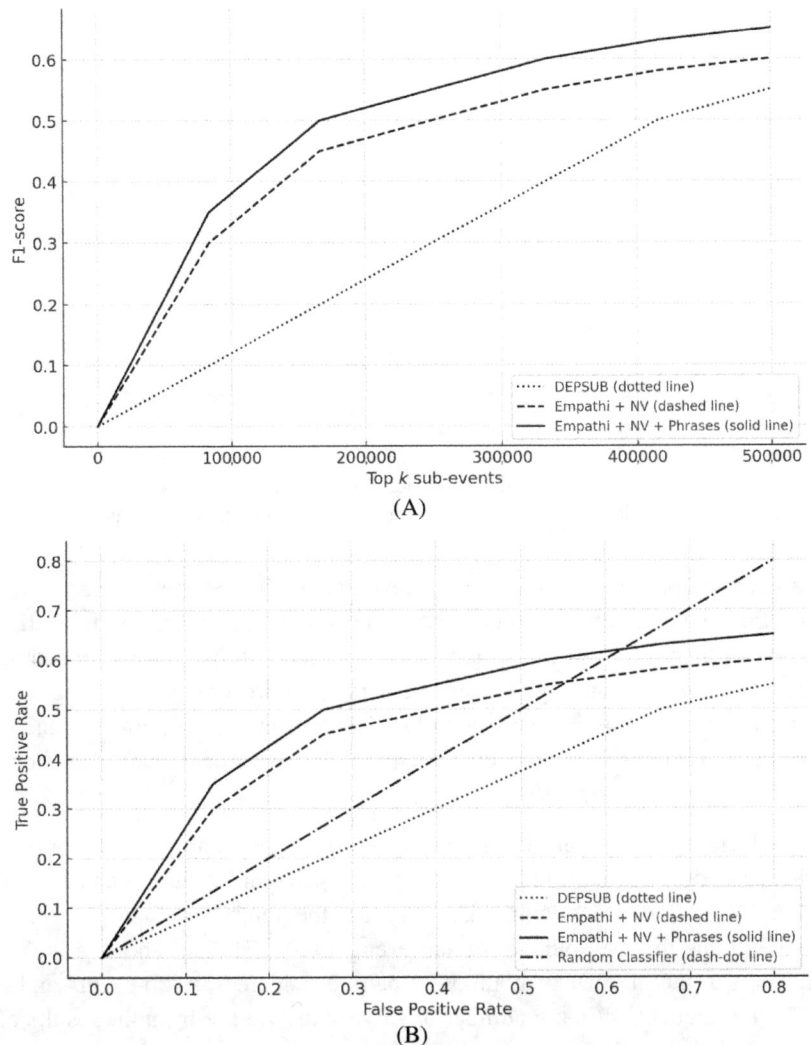

Figure 2.9 Assessing the relevance of candidate sub-events in identifying informative posts in the labeled Nepal Earthquake dataset. (A) F1-score over varying sub-events thresholds; (B) ROC curve. The sub-events were not filtered based on the noun–verb pairs

We observe in Figure 2.9 that our approach outperforms the baseline in F1-score with fewer sub-events than DEPSUB. Additionally, we see in the Figure 2.9B plot that our method performs better than the baseline method, which performed worse than random for most of the threshold values. This

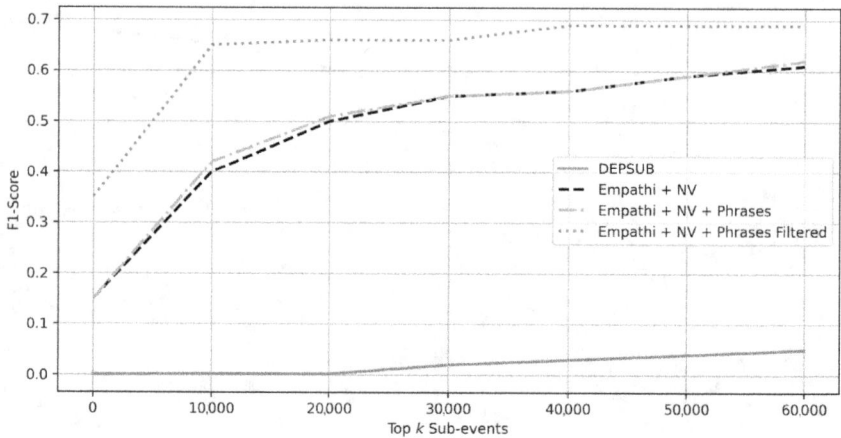

Figure 2.10 Variation in F1-score on increasing the number of candidate sub-events to extract informative posts from annotated Nepal Earthquake dataset.

was because the informative posts retrieved using DEPSUB were *negatively correlated* with the actual result (in other words, identified more uninformative posts). Furthermore, the utilization of the domain-specific crisis embedding model and *empathi* ontology enriched our ranking process by up-voting sub-events that are relevant in crisis scenarios. The contribution of phrases alone in this dataset is not as prominent as in the previous experiment, but it does help, as can be seen in Figure 2.9B.

Nepal Earthquake Filtered: Similar to the first experiment, we apply our filtering procedure that considers only noun–verb pairs that occur more than once in the X post corpus. By doing this, we reduce the number of noun–verb pairs to 19,229 and the total number of sub-events to 55,571. This shows a 96.7% reduction in the number of noun–verb pairs considered as sub-events and a 90.7% total reduction in the number of sub-events. We see from the results of Figure 2.10 that our filtering approach significantly outperforms the nonfiltered method and the baseline in terms of the F1-score. This result confirms that our approach generalizes over crisis events and substantially reduces noise from the candidate sub-events identified with all noun–verb pairs.

2.4.2 Qualitative Evaluation

Beyond our quantitative analysis, we also evaluate our methods in terms of quality. We conduct two qualitative evaluations: (1) for our sub-events and (2) for the categories in our clusters.

2.4 Evaluating Quality of empathi

Table 2.4 *List of top-ranked sub-events in the Hurricane Harvey dataset.*

Empathi-NV+phrase-filtered	DEPSUB baseline
feeding centers	foxnews flooding
road blocked	victims buzzfeed
shortage fuel	flotus donated
price gouging	redcross serving
hundreds trapped	spca need
shelter supplies	mullins flooding
drug shortage	coldwell impacted
infectious disease	sentedcruz impacted
medical equipment	peoples lost
water contamination	hurr impacted

Table 2.5 *List of top-ranked sub-events in the Nepal Earthquake dataset.*

Empathi-NV+phrase-filtered	DEPSUB Baseline
internet access	jeetpur tell
persons missing	people livez
public health	country redefined
power outage	waves clifton
shelter needs	machineries started
water hygiene	parliament subsidized
gtfc human remains	ayurveda words
riot cops	pepoles lost
thugs looting	tsunamy trying
reported deaths	chen missing

Ranked Sub-events

We posit that a good sub-event identification method should be able to identify important and diverse sub-events. Tables 2.4 and 2.5 show the top-ranked sub-events using our Empathi ranking and filtering approach compared to the top-ranked sub-events using DEPSUB. Our approach (Empathi-NV+Phrases-filtered) extracts important and diverse sub-events compared to DEPSUB. Though the baseline yielded some relevant sub-events ("machinery started," "parliament subsidized," "Flotus donated," "redcross serving") in its top ranks, the other sub-events do not accurately represent incidents that occurred during the crisis events. Thus, our top sub-events can inform first responders of the most pressing needs during a crisis scenario (see Figure 2.11).

Table 2.6 *A collection of crisis-related sub-event type labels derived from the MOAC crisis ontology for the MTurk assessment.*

Label 1	Emergency Response (e.g., search and rescue, volunteering, donation)
Label 2	Property Damage (e.g., damage, loss)
Label 3	Public Health (e.g., pollution, hospital)
Label 4	Affected Individuals (e.g., injured/missing/found)
Label 5	Security/Public Safety (e.g., violence, theft)
Label 6	Infrastructure and Utility (e.g., electricity, road infrastructure)
Label 7	Politics/Entertainment

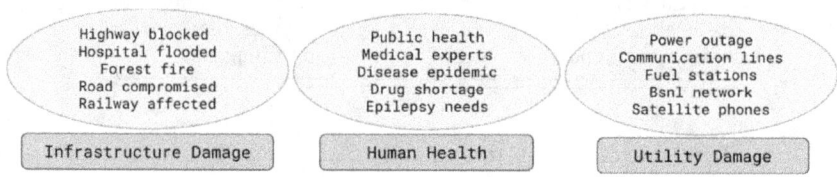

Figure 2.11 Sample sub-event (oval shape) and sub-event clusters (rectangle shape) in our experiments.

2.4.3 Human Evaluation of Cluster Quality

As illustrated in Figure 2.6, the terminal component of our approach involves clustering the ranked sub-events to identify categories that summarize the sub-events. Using spectral clustering, we cluster the sub-events generated using our filtering approach. We generated 40 and 50 clusters for Hurricane Harvey and the Nepal Earthquake, respectively. To get a sense of the quality of clusters, we point to an inherent property of spectral clustering: **Homogeneity** introduced by Xu and Ke (2016). Unfortunately, it is difficult to characterize the quality of the clusters with respect to this property. However, we describe a crowd-sourced qualitative evaluation using human annotators. We used the Amazon Mechanical Turk platform to determine that the sub-events within a sub-event cluster are more homogeneous than those within a random baseline. Each sub-event cluster is randomly sampled for a set of social media posts, and these posts are presented to a human evaluator as a cohesive collection. The evaluator is asked to provide up to three *sub-event type* labels (Table 2.6) that best describe the collection. Collections of random posts are provided as an alternative for collection construction to provide a baseline for comparison. The sampling methodology is summarized as follows:

2.4 Evaluating Quality of empathi

Table 2.7 *Student's T-test to show statistical significance of our approach over random baseline.*

Treatment A	Average number of labels in the collection: 2.00
Treatment B	Average number of labels in the collection: 2.11
Student's T-test p-value	0.0205
Statistical Significance	Yes with p-value < 0.05

Table 2.8 *Human annotators' label distribution by treatment (where $0.1 = 10\%$).*

Labels	Proposed method (Treatment A)	Random (Treatment B)
1	0.31	0.36
2	0.15	0.11
3	0.10	0.096
4	0.12	0.15
5	0.043	0.051
6	0.050	0.049
7	0.21	0.18

- **Treatment A:** 100 collections of posts (five posts in each collection) that all belong to the same sub-event cluster using the methodology proposed in this book.

- **Treatment B:** 100 collections of randomly sampled posts (five posts in each collection) from the entire set of posts in the Harvey dataset.

The annotations provided by the human evaluators show that the sub-event clustering methodology proposed in this book generates collections of posts that are significantly more cohesive than a random collection. The results in Table 2.7 show that human annotators provide *fewer* topic labels more often when labeling post collections from the sub-event cluster output than when labeling randomly sampled collections of posts.

Table 2.8 shows the distribution of labels selected by human annotators for the different methods. Our proposed method (treatment A) is different from the randomly sampled collection case (treatment B). The distributions are observed to have a statistically significant difference using the chi-square test with a p-value of 0.00176.

2.5 Personalized Health Knowledge Graph

A personalized healthcare knowledge graph (PHKG) is a representation of all relevant medical knowledge and personal data for a patient. The PHKG can support the development of innovative applications such as digitalized personalized coach applications that can keep patients informed, help manage their chronic condition, and empower physicians to make effective decisions on health-related issues or receive timely alerts as needed through continuous monitoring. Typically, the PHKG formalizes medical information in terms of relevant relationships between entities. For instance, a knowledge graph (KG) for asthma can describe causes, symptoms, and treatments for asthma, and a PHKG can be the subgraph containing just those causes, symptoms, and treatments that are applicable to a given patient.

State-of-the-Art of Health Knowledge Graphs: The Google Healthcare Knowledge Graph is a manually curated health knowledge graph by Rotmensch et al. (2017) that integrates ICD-9 and UMLS from the National Library of Medicine (2023) along with probabilistic machine learning and physician support to provide relevant information upon a user search. In Shi et al. (2017), a KG is applied to a pneumonia use case by performing a contextual pruning algorithm on knowledge graphs. DepressionKG is a disease-specific KG created by Huang et al. (2017) that can benefit representation and reasoning about major depressive disorder (MDD), requiring overcoming challenges in (1) heterogeneity of datasets, (2) highly contextual text processing, (3) incompleteness and inconsistency in datasets, and (4) expression, representation, and reasoning of medical knowledge.

PHKG is one solution to achieving the vision of the **Data – Information – Knowledge – Wisdom (DIKW)** pyramid. DIKW describes a hierarchical relationship between data, information, knowledge, and wisdom, an example of which has been applied to the healthcare domain in the context of managing blood pressure (Sheth et al., 2013). At each layer of the DIKW pyramid, the contextualization becomes finer and becomes finest at the wisdom stage. To create a PHKG, we integrate pertinent domain-specific medical knowledge bases to provide context for information related to health diseases.

Designing the Personalized Health Knowledge Graph (PHKG)
The architecture designed to build our PHKG is introduced in Figure 2.12. PHKG uses heterogeneous sources of knowledge: (1) IoT data provided by sensors, (2) medical datasets from Alchemy API that provide access to

2.5 Personalized Health Knowledge Graph

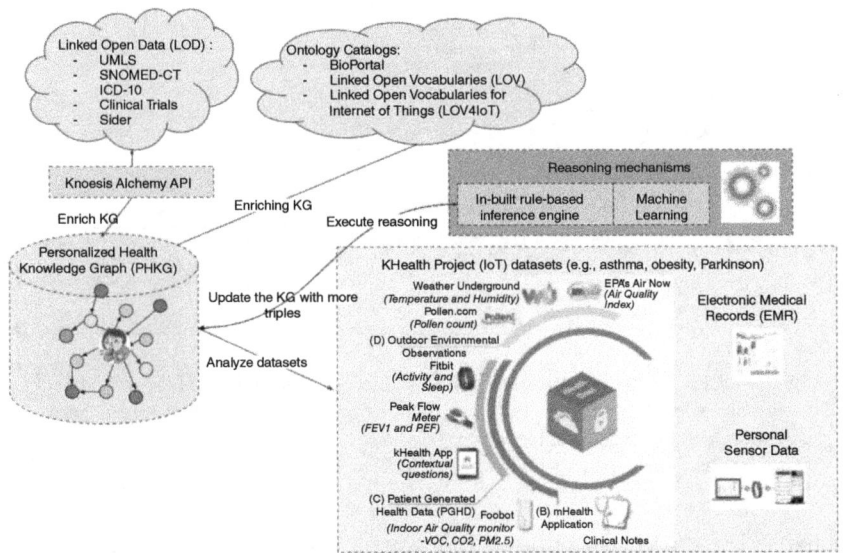

Figure 2.12 PHKG Architecture.

SNOMED-CT, UMLS, and ICD-10, (3) ontology catalogs to reuse models (e.g., asthma ontology), and (4) a set of unified rules to interpret data.

The **kHealth project** developed at the Kno.e.sis Research Center, is a framework for continuous monitoring of the patient's personal data and for generating notifications as needed to assist clinicians (Sheth et al., 2014). kHealth integrates data from three different sources: (1) *Electronic medical records*, (2) *Environment* using IoT devices (e.g., Foobot) and querying Web services (for weather data), and (3) *Personal health signals* using IoT devices (e.g., Fitbit) to provide data on sleep, activity, heart rate, etc. The kno.e.sis Asthma Ontology (kAO) from Gyrard et al. (2018) integrates : (1) W3C SOSA ontology to semantically annotate sensor observations (e.g., the peak flow meter is a subclass of the sosa:Sensor class), (2) the Asthma Ontology (AO) from BioPortal to reuse relevant concepts, (3) the FOAF ontology to describe people, and (4) the weather ontology to deduce meaningful information from weather datasets. The **asthma dataset** consists of data generated by IoT devices such as peak flow meters, Foobot, Fitbit, AirNow, and from Web services obtaining air quality parameters, pollen index and type, outside humidity, and temperature. The **obesity dataset** consists of data generated by IoT devices such as weighing scales, pill and water bottles, and Fitbit to obtain parameters such as weight, medication consumption, heart rate, and sleep

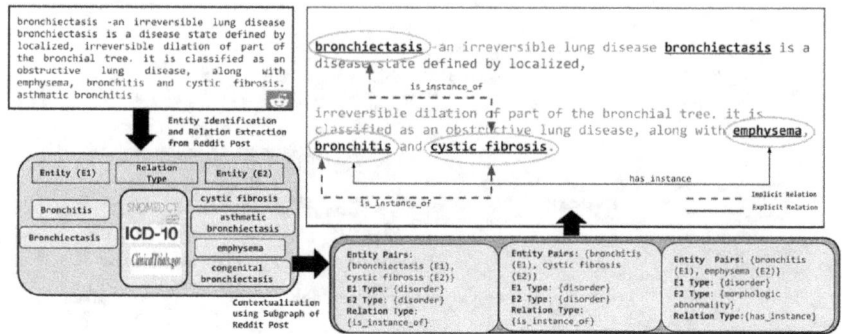

Figure 2.13 Sample annotation of entities and relations identified from a Reddit post on r/Health subreddit. Implicit relations are discovered after 1 hop, and explicit relations are present in 1 hop.

activity. The **Parkinson dataset** from Kaggle consists of mobile sensor data from the accelerometer, compass, microphone, and others on the smartphone to synthesize patient symptom information such as unsteady walking, lack of balance, a fall, and slurred speech. This information can be used to both diagnose and monitor the progression of Parkinson's disease.

Kno.e.sis Alchemy API by Gaur and Sheth (2017) identifies healthcare-related entities, entity types, and relations from social media text (e.g., Reddit) to define the context. Figure 2.13 demonstrates the utilization of medical datasets such as SNOMED-CT, ICD-10, and clinical trials to achieve entity extraction (e.g., the cough concept is a taxonomy itself within SNOMED-CT). Furthermore, SIDER (a drug and side-effect knowledge base) is utilized to identify treatment, disorder, side-effects, drugs, drug-dosage form, drug-dosage level, and adverse drug reactions using the entities and their type defined in the context.

Gyrard (2015) describes the **kHealth reasoner** as a rule-based reasoning engine that builds upon previous frameworks to derive meaningful insights from diverse data sources. This engine processes data collected from clinicians, patient questionnaires, and IoT devices to provide comprehensive health assessments (as depicted in Figure 2.14). The framework is designed to address specific reasoning challenges within the healthcare domain. By integrating heterogeneous data inputs, the kHealth reasoner enhances the ability to make informed healthcare decisions based on a wide range of patient information, ensuring a robust analysis of patient health status and needs.

A kHealth IoT dataset is semantically annotated using an appropriate ontology (e.g., the asthma dataset is annotated according to the kAO ontology)

2.5 Personalized Health Knowledge Graph

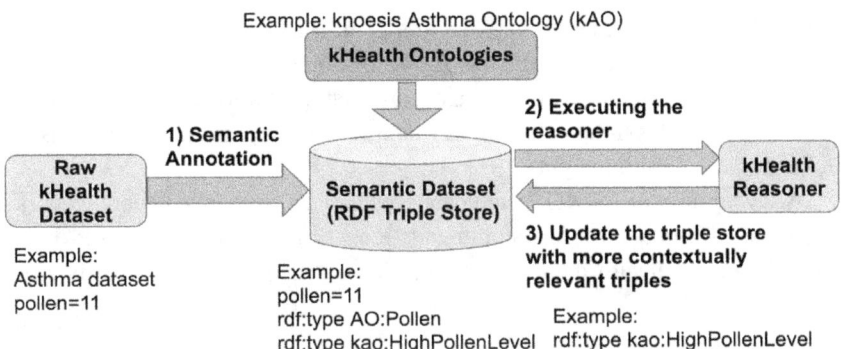

Figure 2.14 kHealth reasoner framework. For details on kAO, refer to this wiki page from the AI Institute at the University of South Carolina: https://wiki.aiisc.ai/index.php?title=KHealth:_Semantic_Multisensory_Mobile_Approach_to_Personalized_Asthma_Care (AIISC, 2024).

to make its meaning explicit and later deduce abstractions. The rules to support reasoning reflect domain knowledge and are mainly extracted from scientific publications, from web services explicitly describing the domain expertise, or manually curated as required to interpret the data. The formalism is inspired by the Jena inference grammar, which we enrich to be compliant with a dictionary of IoT devices (e.g., thermometer) and IoT observation types (e.g., outside temperature) classified within the kAO ontology. The execution of the rule provides meaningful abstractions from IoT observations (e.g., high temperature) and links the IoT data to specific domain ontologies (e.g., weather) from ontology catalogs or datasets from the linked open data (LOD) cloud.

Discussion: Designing the PHKG is essential for developing digital health coaches, such as chatbots, that aid doctors and patients. The PHKG tailors generic knowledge to individual patient needs, enhancing personalized healthcare delivery. This design is challenging because it necessitates the semantic integration of diverse data sources, including healthcare providers, IoT devices, and web data. It must account for context and personal history to derive high-level abstractions and actionable insights.

The PHKG integrates data from multiple heterogeneous sources, such as clinical notes, electronic medical records (EMRs), and IoT devices, to provide a comprehensive view of a patient's health. This integrated approach helps in understanding symptoms, hypothesizing and explaining disease progression, and inferring potential management and treatment plans. For instance, the PHKG can be used in managing chronic diseases such as asthma, obesity, and Parkinson's by integrating integrating information from environmental sensors and web data, and emphasizing the salient concepts. This approach exemplifies the principles of the data, information, knowledge, and wisdom (DIKW) pyramid, synthesizing various data sources to provide comprehensive and actionable health insights.

By leveraging the PHKG, healthcare applications can move beyond generic solutions, offering tailored recommendations and interventions based on a patient's unique health data, improving the overall quality and effectiveness of care.

2.6 Knowledge Graph for Explainability

A knowledge graph's primary impact lies in deciphering the opaque aspects of AI through detailed explanations. Take, for instance, Table 2.9, where we outline three vital domains. Through the clarity offered by a domain-specific knowledge graph, deep learning not only boosts its predictive confidence but also delivers well-founded explanations, serving as a tangible indicator of AI comprehension.

Understanding or explaining the behavior of a model depends on the perspective of the stakeholder. To interpret the model's results and understand its functionality, specific knowledge (like domain expertise or context-specific guidance) is necessary. We differentiate explainability into two types based on the integration of a knowledge graph (KG): system-level explainability and user-level explainability. Figures 2.15A and 2.15B in Gaur et al. (2021e) provide examples of these two forms of explainability.

- **System-Level Explainability (SysEx)** generates explanations after the analysis of word- and token-level feature importances through a suitable visualization mechanism, such as a saliency map. For instance, first-derivative saliency-based methods explain the decision of an algorithm by assigning values that reflect the importance of input features in their contribution to that decision in the form of a gradient map (heat map) (Ribeiro et al., 2016; Lundberg and Lee, 2017; Zafar and Khan, 2019). Another method for SysEx is layer-wise relevance propagation, which decomposes the prediction of a deep neural network for a specific example into individual contributions from sub-parts of the text (Samek et al., 2016; Yang et al., 2018a; Montavon et al., 2019). Input perturbations and attention models are other methods for SysEx developed by Bahdanau et al. (2014), Yang et al. (2016), and Vaswani et al. (2017a).

2.6 Knowledge Graph for Explainability

Table 2.9 *Benefits of context capture by KiL.*

Domain	Post	Outcome from DL	Outcome from KiL
Mental Health	Really struggling with my bisexuality which is causing chaos in my relationship with a girl. Being a fan of the LGBTQ community, I am equal to worthless to her. I'm now starting to get drunk because I can't cope with the obsessive, intrusive thoughts, and need to get it out of my head.	<struggling, worthless, drunk> **Prediction:** Depression (True: 0.71) (✗)	<struggling, bisexuality, chaos, relationship, worthless, drunk, intrusive thoughts> **Explanations (high-level concepts):** <health-related behavior, level of mood, drinking, obsessive-compulsive personality disorder, disturbance in thinking> **Prediction:** Obsessive Compulsive Disorder (True: 0.96) (✓)
Radicalization	Here is the fragrance of Paradise. Here is the field of Jihad. Here is the land of #Islam. Here is the land of the Paradise.	<Jihad, Islam> **Prediction:** Extremist (True: 0.90) (✗)	<Paradise, Jihad, Land, Islam> **Explanations:** <Paradise_Land, Jihad_Islam> **Prediction:** Non-Extremist (True: 0.87) (✓)
COVID-19	#Flu and #Pneumonia killed six times more people as #Covid19	<kill, more people, covid19> **Prediction:** Fact (True: 0.64) (✓)	<affected population, communicable diseases> **Prediction:** Fact (True: 0.865) (✓✓)

- **User-level Explainability (UseEx)** is the ability to generate explanations that are comprehensible to humans and support them in a well-informed decision-making process. Explanations would generally be in natural language or with a visual depiction traced over generic or domain-specific knowledge.

There is a growing trend of fine tuning the pre-trained models with limited labeled data. These have succeeded when (a) the distribution of the labeled dataset is similar to unlabeled data used for pretraining and (b) tasks are relatively straightforward, like natural language entailment and span extractive

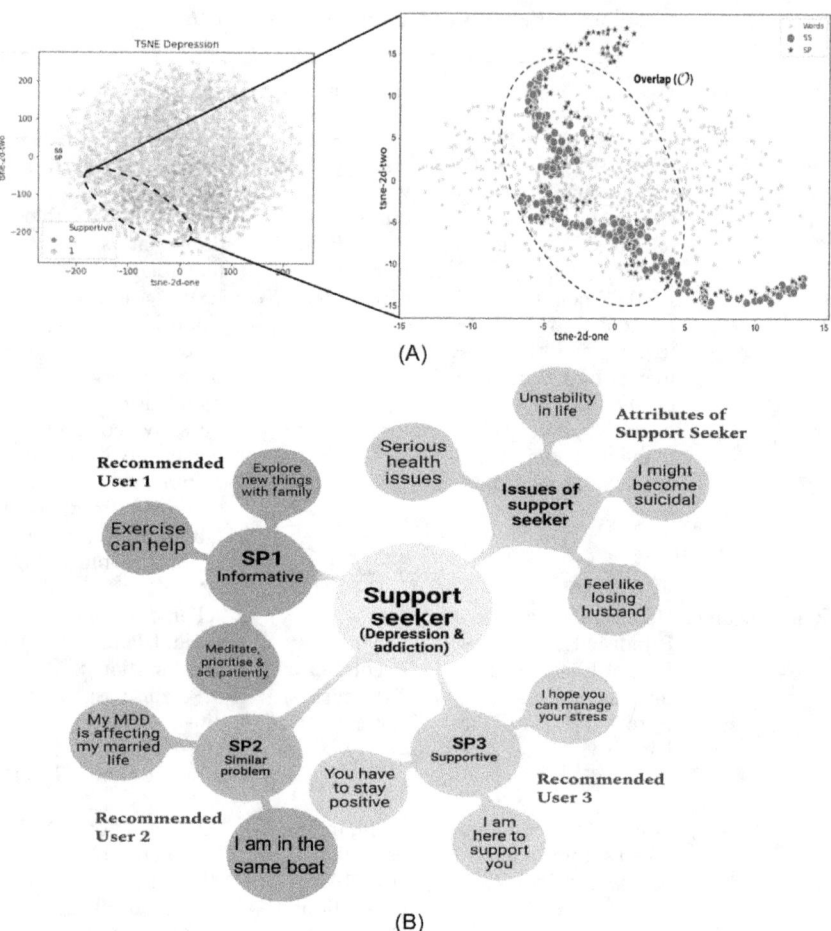

Figure 2.15 (A) System-level explainability showing the overlap (a proxy for matching a support seeker (SS) with its nearest support providers (SPs) using T-SNE visualization). (B) User-level explainability shows the reason behind mapping semantically-related SPs to an SS through the use of phrases that are semantically similar to concepts in the Patient Health Questionnaire Lexicon (PHQ-9).

question answering. However, real-world scenarios are often more complex, which poses the following challenges: (a) Fine-tuned models for domain-specific tasks with limited labeled data may not be sufficient to capture domain knowledge (Mosbach et al., 2020); (b) self-supervised training objectives over unlabeled data are not attempting to learn/acquire the domain knowledge required for the real world.

2.6 Knowledge Graph for Explainability

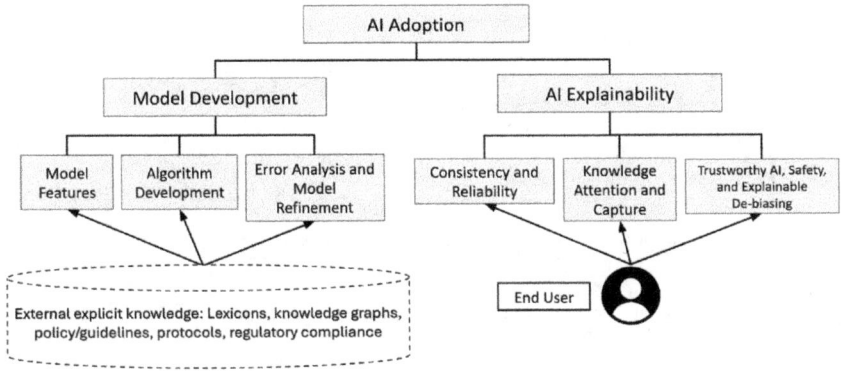

Figure 2.16 Adoption of AI systems occurs in two stages – the model building phase and the model explanation phase. Explicit knowledge as abstract concepts, processes, policy/guidelines, and regulations are essential to infuse into the AI system to yield sensible explanations comprehensible to humans.

Methods for Explainable AI: Recent research on explainability, such as from Goebel et al. (2018), has attempted to address several aspects of *opening this black box* to help humans, both system users and domain experts, understand such models' functioning and decision-making process. The adoption of AI systems occurs in two stages (see Figure 2.16):

- **Model-Building Phase:** This includes model features, algorithmic development, error analysis, and model refinement. Explicit knowledge as abstract concepts, processes, policies/guidelines, and regulations are essential to infuse into the AI system for sensible explanations comprehensible to humans.
- **Explaining Phase:** This includes decision making, knowledge capture, and trust and bias analysis. This phase includes user-in-the-loop (e.g., stakeholder) to assess consistency in the model and match user expectations (Riveiro and Thill, 2021).

Developing a high-quality explainable AI system necessitates the involvement of domain experts during the annotation, supervision, and evaluation stages (Roy et al., 2021; Gaur et al., 2021e). These experts require explanations that mimic the manner and terminology of a professional in their specific field. For instance, in the medical domain, model outcomes should be explained in alignment with the conceptual knowledge found in clinical guidelines, as analyses at the word or token level are typically unhelpful to domain experts (Lewis et al., 2020). Methods that utilize knowledge graphs (KGs) to provide

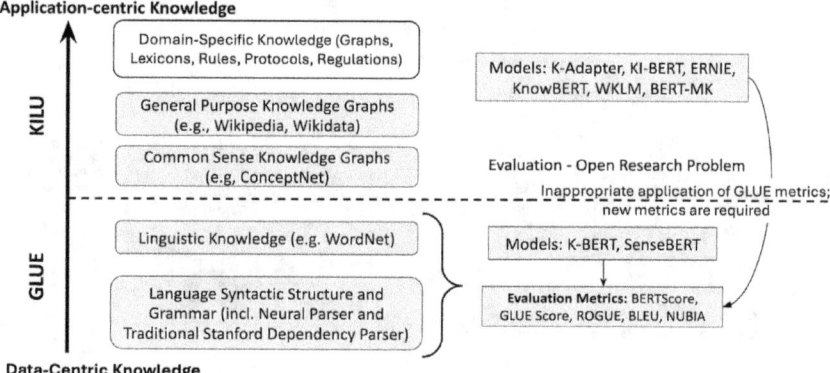

Figure 2.17 Different sources of knowledge. GLUE tasks are evaluated using BERT score, GLUE score, ROUGE-L, BLEU, BLEURT, and NUBIA metrics. However, for knowledge-intensive knowledge understanding, evaluations require domain knowledge-guided explanations.

conceptual-level explanations can enhance the clarity and evaluability of AI systems. To foster trust and facilitate real-world adoption, it is recommended that popular metrics for evaluating language understanding models, such as BLEU, ROUGE-L (Lin and Och, 2004), QBLEU4 (Nema and Khapra, 2018), BLEURT (Sellam et al., 2020), and MAUVE (Pillutla et al., 2021), incorporate a component to measure the alignment of predicted outcomes with KG concepts (Gaur et al., 2021b). This approach will help build end-user trust and promote faster integration of these systems into practical applications (see Figure 2.17).

2.7 Knowledge Graph for Interpretability

Interpretability is the ability to discern the internal mechanisms of an optimization module within an AI or data mining framework. For example, consider a transformer model whose key modules are (a) input embeddings, (b) type of encodings (positional (Vaswani et al., 2017a)/rotational (Su et al., 2024)), (c) attention layer, (d) loss function, and (e) batch normalization with or without dropout. We can call a transformer model interpretable if we can meaningfully interpret the functioning of each internal component ((a)–to–(e)) and can affirm that the model is functioning in our intended way. There are four methods to construct an interpretable model:

- **Probing:** Probes are shallow neural networks (e.g., 2-layer neural network, Restricted Boltzmann machine) placed over intermediate layers of a larger neural network, whose functioning needs to be interpreted. They help investigate what information is captured by different layers or attention heads. Probes are trained and validated using auxiliary tasks to discover if such auxiliary information is captured. Through probing, it is fairly interpretable to see how input tokens are contextualized in successive layers using attention mechanisms and how the model performs in sub-tasks that are decompositions of the major task. A KG can help in probing by computing the distance between the intermediate hidden representations of a DL model and concepts in a KG (Sheth et al., 2021).

- **Fine Tuning:** A pre-trained model that is not fine tuned comprises learned parameters supporting global parametric knowledge. Fine tuning allows the model to respond sensibly to a given task. It is a process of precisely adjusting the model's parameters to observations that are related to or similar to the observations on which the model was trained. Problems that require fine tuning would require a known mechanism to explain the model's behavior and support reasoning. This is seen in the form of human evaluation tasks, visual inspection of the model's output, or qualitative error analysis (Gritta et al., 2022). There are various fine-tuned transformer models on Wolf et al. (2019b), but for an interpretable fine tuning, a KG component is required (Liu et al., 2020). This has been shown in K-BERT, where a KG is augmented to a data representation. For example, in K-BERT, the representation of the term "cholesterol" is enhanced by augmenting the representation of the triple "<cholesterol> <causes> <heart attack>." For the downstream task, the relationships and entities captured in the KG can help in improved prediction.
- **Multi-task Learning:** This is a popular phenomenon to train the same model for multiple tasks. It enriches the semantic representations of models and avoids them overfitting. Auxiliary tasks could also be part of such a setup. For instance, sentiments associated with a medical text can be well studied automatically through DL if the algorithm can master the identification of medical conditions, treatment, and medication. This forms a multi-task learning problem solvable through a suitable DL algorithm (Yadav et al., 2018).
- **Autoencoders:** These are interpretable models as they are weighting functions and contextual representation learners because of their optimization function, which is a reconstruction loss. The encoder–decoder architecture is a container that can accept a DL model (e.g., sequence-to-sequence long short-term memory (LSTM), graph neural networks (GNN), convolutional neural networks (CNN)) and trains it to learn a representation by mapping input to output. The amazing utility of an autoencoder comes from replacing the decoder end with a knowledge source. This can be a KG if the internal

Table 2.10 *Comparison between different methods that make DL algorithms interpretable.*

Interpretability methods	Probes	Fine tuning	Multi-task learning	Autoencoder
Goal	Auxiliary task	Primary task	Primary task	Optimize input with knowledge for primary task
Update model parameters	No	Yes	Yes	Yes
Access model internals	Yes	No	No	Yes
Complexity	Shallow	Shallow or semi-deep	Shallow or semi-deep	Semi-deep

component is a GNN, a document if the internal component is an LSTM model, a lexicon if the internal component is the simple continuous bag of words embedding model, and many others (Gaur et al., 2018).

It is important to note that model interpretability achieved by probing and fine tuning provides system-level explainability and not user-level explainability. Autoencoders differ from fine tuning and probing by making the model interpretable and explainable through user-level knowledge, which is introduced by calculating conceptual information loss and proportionately propagating it in the neural network by modulating hidden representations (see Table 2.10 for comparison). A model's capability to be interpretable and user-level explainable also lies in the type of dataset it is trained on.

3

Knowledge-Infused Learning: The Subsumer to NeuroSymbolic AI

Humans interact with the environment using a combination of perception – transforming sensory inputs from their environment into symbols – and cognition – mapping symbols to knowledge about the environment for supporting abstraction, reasoning by analogy, and long-term planning. Human perception-inspired machine perception, in the context of AI, refers to large-scale pattern recognition from raw data using neural networks trained using self-supervised learning objectives such as next-word prediction or object recognition. In contrast, machine cognition encompasses more complex computations, such as using knowledge of the environment to guide reasoning, analogy, and long-term planning. Humans can also control and explain their cognitive functions. This seems to require the retention of symbolic mappings from perception outputs to knowledge about their environment. For example, humans can follow and explain the guidelines and safety constraints driving their decision making in safety-critical applications such as healthcare, criminal justice, and autonomous driving. While data-driven neural network-based AI algorithms effectively model machine perception, symbolic knowledge-based AI is better suited for modeling machine cognition. This is because symbolic knowledge structures support explicit representations of mappings from perception outputs to the knowledge, enabling traceability and auditing of the AI system's decisions. Such audit trails are useful for enforcing application aspects of safety, such as regulatory compliance and explainability, through tracking the AI system's inputs, outputs, and intermediate steps. This chapter introduces neurosymbolic AI, combining neural networks and knowledge-guided symbolic approaches to create more capable and flexible AI systems. These systems have immense potential to advance both algorithm-level (e.g., abstraction, analogy, reasoning) and application-level (e.g., explainable and safety-constrained decision-making) capabilities of AI systems.

3.1 Why Neurosymbolic AI?

Neurosymbolic AI refers to AI systems that seek to integrate neural network-based methods with symbolic knowledge-based approaches. We present two perspectives to understand the need for this combination better: (1) algorithmic-level considerations, for example, the ability to support abstraction, analogy, and long-term planning; (2) application-level considerations in AI systems, for example, enforcing explainability, interpretability, and safety.

Algorithm-Level Considerations: Research has identified distinct systems within the human brain specialized for processing perceptual and cognitive information. These systems collaborate to facilitate human intelligence, enabling individuals to understand and interact with their surroundings. Kahneman (2011) highlighted the distinction between System 1 and System 2. System 1 helps individuals process vast amounts of raw environmental data, transforming it into meaningful symbols (e.g., words, digits, colors) for cognitive processing. System 2, by contrast, engages in conscious and deliberate higher-level functions such as reasoning and planning, using background knowledge to accurately interpret the output of the perception module. Despite their different functions, Systems 1 and 2 are interconnected and work together to create the human experience, allowing individuals to perceive, comprehend, and act based on their environmental knowledge.

Over the past decade, neural network algorithms trained on large datasets have shown exceptional performance in machine perception tasks, such as predicting the next word and recognizing digits. Training on simple self-supervision tasks has led to solutions for complex problems like protein folding, efficient matrix multiplication, and solving intricate puzzles (Jumper et al., 2021; Fawzi et al., 2022). However, human cognition involves processes beyond the explicit data, such as making analogical connections between concepts through knowledge structures (Gentner, 1983).

Current generative AI systems, like GPT-4, might acquire knowledge structures to support cognitive functions from data alone (Bubeck et al., 2023). The hypothesis is that extensive text prediction can lead to an emergent "cognitive model" of the world within the neural network. However, the black-box nature of these systems raises concerns about their cognitive capabilities' evaluation. While symbolic models excel at supporting human-like cognition using knowledge structures (e.g., knowledge graphs), they are not suited to processing high-volume data. Therefore, integrating neural network-based System 1 tools, which excel at big-data processing, with symbolic knowledge-based Systems 2 tools, which excel at knowledge-dependent cognition, appears to be a more effective approach.

Application-Level Considerations: The combination of Systems 1 and 2 in neurosymbolic AI can enable important application-level features, such as explainability, interpretability, safety, and trust in AI. Recent research on explainable AI (XAI) methods that explain neural network decisions primarily involves post-hoc techniques like saliency maps (Goferman et al., 2011), feature attribution (Baehrens et al., 2010; Zhou et al., 2022b), and prototype-based explanations (Koh and Liang, 2017). Such explanations are useful for developers but not easily understood by end-users. Additionally, neural networks can fail due to uncontrollable training-time factors like data artifacts, adversarial attacks, distribution shifts, and system failures. To ensure rigorous safety standards, it is necessary to incorporate appropriate background knowledge to set guardrails during training rather than as a post-hoc measure. Symbolic knowledge structures can provide an effective mechanism for imposing domain constraints for safety and explicit reasoning traces for explainability. These structures can create transparent and interpretable systems for end-users, leading to more trustworthy and dependable AI systems, especially in safety-critical applications (Sheth et al., 2022).

> **Why Neurosymbolic AI?**
>
> *Embodying intelligent behavior in an AI system must involve both perception – processing raw data – and cognition – using background knowledge to support abstraction, analogy, reasoning, and planning. Symbolic structures represent this background knowledge explicitly. While neural networks are a powerful tool for processing and extracting patterns from data, they lack explicit representations of background knowledge, hindering the reliable evaluation of their cognition capabilities. Furthermore, applying appropriate safety standards while providing explainable outcomes guided by concepts from background knowledge is crucial for establishing trustworthy models of cognition for decision support.*

3.2 What Is Neurosymbolic AI and How Do We Achieve It?

Neurosymbolic AI is a term used to describe techniques that aim to merge the knowledge-based symbolic approach with neural network methods to improve the overall performance of AI systems. These systems have the ability to blend the powerful approximation abilities of neural networks with the symbolic reasoning capabilities that enable them to reason about abstract concepts, extrapolate from limited data, and generate explainable results (Garcez and Lamb, 2023). Together, these components support both the algorithm-level and application-level concerns introduced in the previous sections. Neurosymbolic AI methods can be classified under two main categories: (1) methods that compress structured symbolic knowledge to integrate with neural patterns and reason using the integrated neural patterns and (2) methods that extract information from neural patterns to allow for mapping to structured symbolic knowledge (lifting) and perform symbolic reasoning. Furthermore, we sub-categorize (1) into methods that utilize (a) compressed knowledge-graph representations for integration with neural patterns and (b) compressed formal logic-based representations for integration with neural patterns. We also sub-categorize (2) into methods that employ (a) decoupled integration between the neural and symbolic components and (b) intertwined integration between the neural and symbolic components. These methods enable both algorithm-level and application-level functions in varying degrees of effectiveness spanning low (**L**), medium (**M**), and high (**H**) scales. Figure 3.1 details our categorization of neurosymbolic AI methods.

Algorithm-Level Analysis of Methods in Category 1: For category 1(a), previous work has used two compression methods. One approach is to use knowledge graph embedding methods, which offers a promising approach by transforming knowledge graphs into high-dimensional vector representations using graph neural networks. This compression technique converts the discrete, symbolic structure of knowledge graphs – with their entities, relationships, and facts – into dense numerical vectors that capture semantic meaning. The resulting embeddings allow the structured knowledge to be seamlessly integrated with a neural network's internal representations, enabling the model to leverage both learned patterns from data and explicit domain knowledge simultaneously. The other approach is to use knowledge graph-masking methods, which encode the knowledge graphs in a way suitable for integration with the inductive biases of the neural network. Figure 3.2 illustrates the two approaches. The ability of neural networks to process large volumes of raw data also translates to neural networks used for knowledge graph compression when processing millions and billions of nodes and edges, that is, large-scale perception ((**H**) in Figure 3.1). Utilizing the compressed representations in neural reasoning pipelines improves the system's cognition aspects, that is, abstraction, analogy, and planning capabilities. However, the improvements are modest ((**M**) in Figure 3.1) due to the lossy compression of the full semantics in the knowledge graph (e.g., relationships aren't modeled effectively in

3.2 What Is Neurosymbolic AI and How Do We Achieve It?

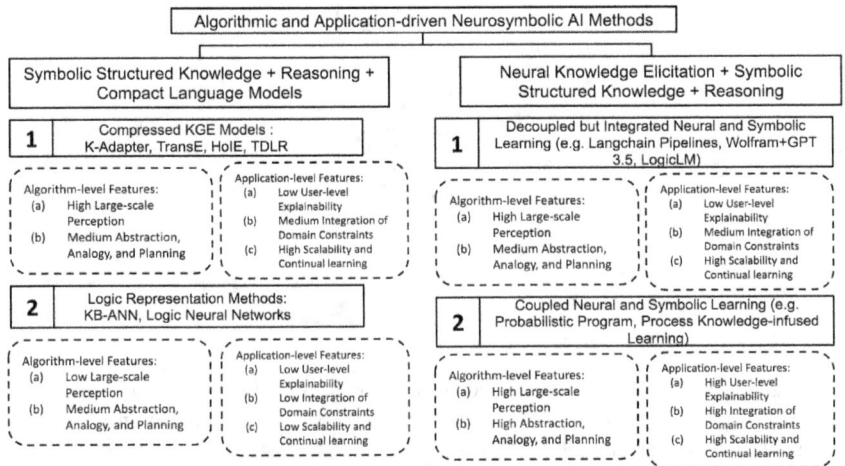

Figure 3.1 The two primary types of neurosymbolic techniques – lowering and lifting – can be further divided into four sub-categories. Across the low (**L**), medium (**M**), and high (**H**) scales, these methods can be used to provide a variety of functions at both algorithmic and application levels. Compressed KGE Models apply LoRA (Dettmers et al., 2024) over knowledge graph embedding (KGE) models (Wang et al., 2017). Logic-LM is a recent decoupled neurosymbolic AI approach to solve logical reasoning problems, wherein a large language model translates natural language problems into symbolic formulations, which are then passed to a deterministic symbolic solver for automated theorem proving (Pan et al., 2023b).

compressed representations). Category 1(b) methods use matrix and higher-order tensor factorization methods to obtain compressed representations of objects and formal logic statements that describe the relationships between them (such as propositional logic, first-order logic, and second-order situation calculus). Improvements in cognition aspects follow a similar trend as in 1(a). However, compression techniques for formal logic are computationally inefficient and do not facilitate large-scale perception ((**L**) in Figure 3.1).

Application-Level Analysis of Methods in Category 1: For category 1(a), its full semantics are no longer explicitly retained when compressing the knowledge graph for integration into neural processing pipelines. Post-hoc explanation techniques, such as saliency maps, feature attribution, and prototype-based explanations, can only explain the outputs of the neural network. These explanations are primarily meant to assist system developers in diagnosing and troubleshooting algorithmic changes in the neural network's decision-making process. Unfortunately, they are not framed in domain or application terms

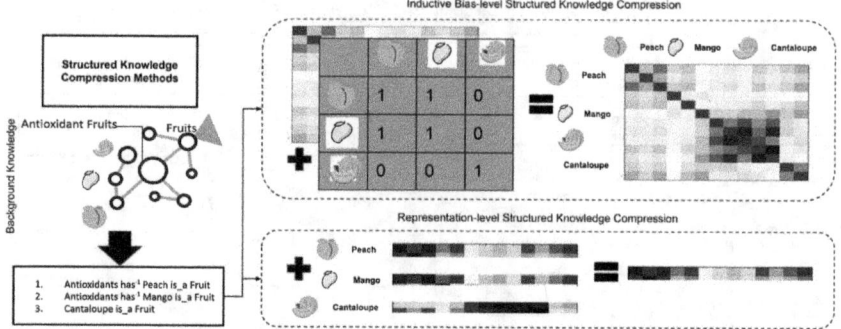

Figure 3.2 The figure illustrates two methods for compressing knowledge graphs to integrate them with neural processing pipelines. One approach involves embedding knowledge graph paths into vector spaces, enabling integration with the neural network's hidden representations. The other method involves encoding knowledge graphs as masks to modify the neural network's inductive biases. An example of an inductive bias is the correlation information stored in the self-attention matrices of a transformer neural network (Rawte et al., 2020; Wang et al., 2020). The △ on the Fruit node represents an extension of this graph to other fruits that may or may not have antioxidants.

and hence have limited value to end-users ((**L**) for low explainability in Figure 3.1). Knowledge graph-compression methods can still be utilized to apply domain constraints, such as specifying modifications to pattern correlations in the neural network, as depicted in Figure 3.2. However, this process has limited constraint specification capabilities because large neural networks have multiple processing layers and moving parts ((**M**) in Figure 3.1). It is challenging to determine whether modifications made to the network are retained throughout the various processing layers. Neural processing pipelines do offer a high degree of automation, making it easier for a system to scale across various use cases (such as plugging in use case-specific knowledge graphs) and to support continual adaptation throughout the system's life cycle (such as making continual modifications to the knowledge graphs). This capability is indicated by the letter (**H**) in Figure 3.1. For category 1(b), when compressed formal logic representations are integrated with neural processing pipelines, system scores tend to be low across all application-level aspects of user-explainability, domain constraints, scalability, and continual adaptation, as denoted by the letter (**L**) in Figure 3.1. This is primarily due to the significant user–technology barrier. End-users must familiarize themselves with the rigor and details of formal logic semantics to communicate with the system (e.g., to provide domain constraint specifications).

3.2 What Is Neurosymbolic AI and How Do We Achieve It?

Algorithm-Level Analysis of Methods in Category 2: For category 2(a), the proliferation of large language models and their corresponding plugins has spurred the development of federated pipeline methods. These methods utilize neural networks to identify symbolic functions based on task descriptions that are specified using appropriate modalities such as natural language and images. Once the symbolic function is identified, the method transfers the task to the appropriate symbolic reasoner, such as a math- or fact-based search tool. Figure 3.3 illustrates a federated pipeline method that utilizes the LangChain library. These methods are proficient in supporting large-scale perception through the large language model ((**H**) in Figure 3.1). However, their ability to facilitate algorithm-level functions related to cognition, such as abstraction, analogy, reasoning, and planning, is restricted by the language model's comprehension of the input query ((**M**) in Figure 3.1).

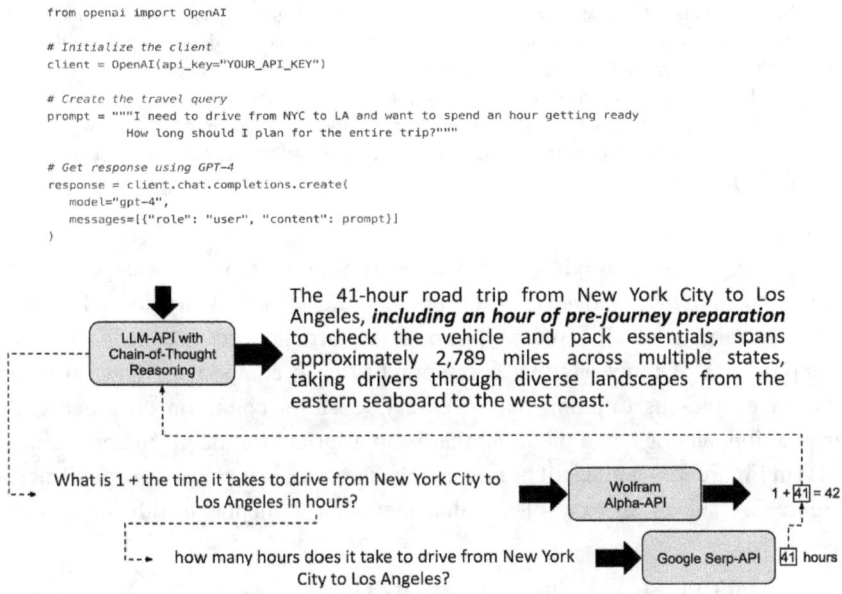

Figure 3.3 Illustrates a federated pipeline method using the LangChain library. The method employs a language model trained on chain-of-thought reasoning to segment the input query into tasks. The language model then utilizes task-specific symbolic solvers to derive solutions. Specifically, the language model recognizes that search and scientific computing (mathematics) symbolic solvers are necessary for the given query. The resulting solutions are subsequently combined and transformed into natural language for presentation to the user.

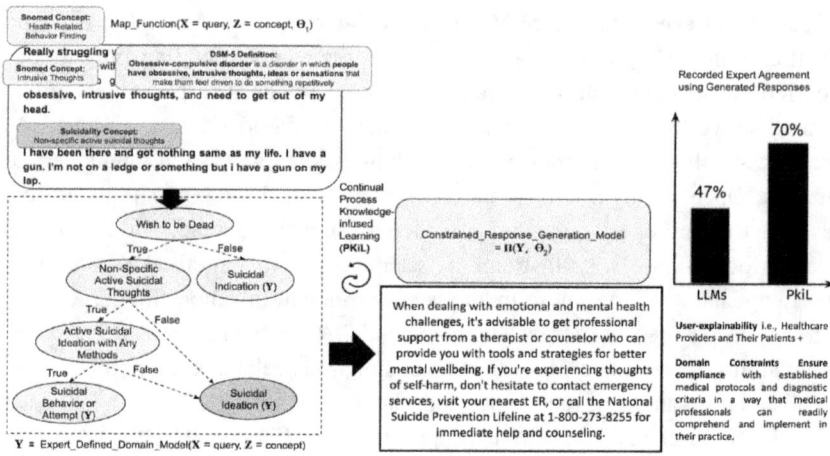

Figure 3.4 This illustration shows a fully integrated pipeline for AI systems that can be easily trained from start to finish. The process involves using trainable functions to convert raw data into relevant concepts for the specific application. In the example, the system is used for mental health diagnosis and conversational assistance. The trainable functions link pieces of raw data to decision points in the diagnosis model, which then apply rules to the patient's responses generated by the AI. Results from an existing implementation demonstrate that expert satisfaction levels reached 70% using such a pipeline, compared to 47% with LLMs in federated pipelines, such as OpenAI's text-Davinci-003 (Roy et al., 2022a).

Category 2(b) methods use pipelines similar to those in category 2(a) federated pipelines. However, they possess the added ability to fully govern the learning of all pipeline components through end-to-end differential compositions of functions that correspond to each component. This level of control enables us to attain the necessary levels of cognition on aspects of abstraction, analogy, and planning that is appropriate for the given application ((**H**) in Figure 3.1) while still preserving the large-scale perception capabilities. Figure 3.4 shows an example of this method for mental health diagnostic assistance.

Application-Level Analysis of Methods in Category 2: For the systems belonging to category 2(a), tracing their chain of thought during processing immensely enhances the application-level aspects of user explainability. However, the language model's ability to parse the input query and relate it to domain model concepts during response generation limits this ability ((**M**) in Figure 3.1). Furthermore, the specification of domain constraints in natural language using prompt templates also limits the constraint modeling capability, which depends on the language model's ability to comprehend application or domain-specific concepts ((**M**) in Figure 3.1). Federated pipelines excel in scalability since language models and application plugins that facilitate their use for domain-specific use cases are becoming more widely available and accessible ((**H**) in Figure 3.1). Unfortunately, language models require an enormous amount of time and space resources to train, and hence, continual domain adaptation using federated pipelines remains challenging ((**L**) in Figure 3.1). Nonetheless, advancements in language modeling architectures that support continual learning goals are fast gaining traction. Category 2(b) methods show significant promise as they score highly regarding all application-level aspects, including user-explainability, domain constraints, scalability across use cases, and support for continual adaptation to application-specific changes ((**H**) in Figure 3.1). This is due to the high modeling flexibility and closely intertwined coupling of system components. Thus, a change in any particular component leads to positive changes in all components within the system's pipeline. Notably, in an implemented system for the mental health diagnostic assistance use case, shown in Figure 3.4, we see drastic improvements in expert satisfaction with the system's responses, further demonstrating the immense potential for 2(b) category methods.

3.3 Knowledge-Infused Learning

KiL is a continuum that comprises three stages for the infusion of knowledge into the machine/deep learning architectures. As this continuum progresses across these three stages, it starts with a Shallow Infusion in the form of embeddings, and attention and knowledge-based constraints improve with a Semi-Deep Infusion. For deeper incorporation of knowledge, we articulate the value of incorporating knowledge at different levels of abstraction in the latent layers of neural networks. We consider it to be a Deep Infusion of Knowledge as a new paradigm that will significantly advance the capabilities and promises of deep learning. When we talk about knowledge infusion, we consider two forms of knowledge:

- **Unordered Knowledge:** This is defined as any structural information that **does not** enforce logical ordering in the outcome. Examples include all the existing KGs, such as DBPedia, which is non-sequential knowledge of Wikipedia, and UMLS (Unified Medical Language System), which is non-sequential knowledge of medical information (disease, symptoms, treatment, medication, etc.), and many others (refer to Figure 3.6). Figure 3.6 shows an illustration of SNOMED-CT KG used to explain why a

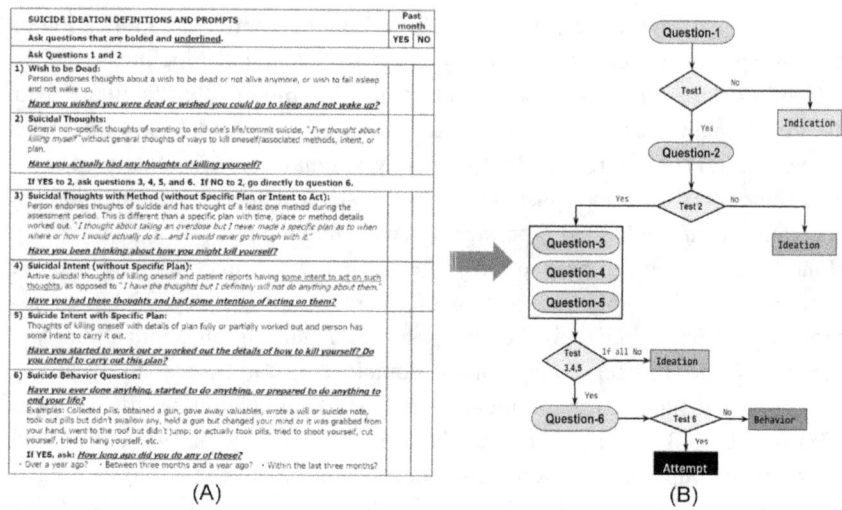

Figure 3.5 (A) Columbia Suicide Severity Rating Scale. (B) The induced process knowledge.

transformer's attention. Semantic lexicons are another form of non-sequential knowledge. Compared with KGs, lexicons are driven by a purpose and can be considered a subset of KGs. For instance, Linguistic Inquiry Word Count (LIWC) is a competitive lexicon to capture psycho-linguistic information (Pennebaker et al., 2001). ANEW and GoEmotions are example lexicons to capture emotions (Bradley and Lang, 1999; Demszky et al., 2020). The severity of suicide risk and depression are specialized use cases under mental healthcare that require dedicated lexicons. Recent studies have developed lexicons to capture entities that contribute to assessing suicide risk or depression from noisy social media communications (Yazdavar et al., 2017; Gaur et al., 2019b). Non-sequential knowledge infusion is helpful in classification and generative tasks as long as it does not mandate logical ordering.

- **Ordered Knowledge:** This is defined as any structural information that enforces logical ordering manifested in conceptual flow in the output of an AI model. This form of knowledge is required for generative tasks, such as question generation, response generation, or response shaping, wherein information is desired in a particular way. Figure 3.5 shows an example illustration of sequential knowledge. It sees wide application in current conversational AI research, wherein the task is to engage with the user meaningfully. For instance, the task of conversational information seeking requires the agent to either ask the user questions or respond to the user

3.4 KiL for Language Modeling

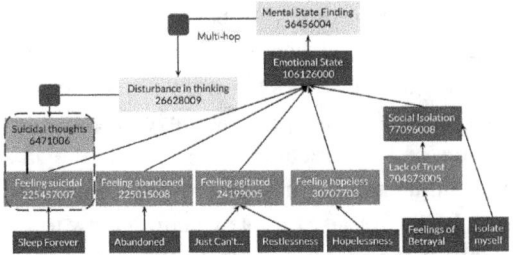

Figure 3.6 An illustration that associates system-level explainability with user-level explainability. The highlighted phrases on the left side of the figure are obtained from a DL model trained using the method in Gaur et al. (2018). This is a manifestation of system-level explanations. Highlighted phrases in the input text are queried in SNOMED-CT(Systematized Nomenclature of Medicine - Clinical Terms), thus forming a contextual tree (right side of the figure). This is a manifestation of user-level explanations. Formation of this tree is stopped when a node that has a high similarity to either leaf nodes or one-hop parent nodes is hit. The numbers in the boxes are SNOMED-CT IDs.

in a particular order. At a broad level, this order can be seen as categories: <Definition> is followed by <Method> is followed by <Application/Use Case>. Consider an example utterance from a user, "How to prepare Hibiscus tea?" A convincing response would have the following order: <Ingredients> is followed by <Method> is followed by <Use>. If an AI model is able to formulate the sequential nature of the knowledge, it can generalize over a set of similar tasks. So far, there has been one study that utilizes such sequential knowledge (also known as procedural knowledge or process knowledge) in generating sentences that describe the severity of suicide risk of an individual (Roy et al., 2022a).

3.4 KiL for Language Modeling

> **Research Question**
>
> Can the inclusion of explicit knowledge help Explainable AI provide human-understandable explanations and enable decision making?

Understanding language is essential for machines to communicate with humans and achieve trust effectively. Until recently, the focus on improving language models has been purely on improving statistical techniques (e.g., Word2Vec, Transformer models, etc.) based on word distribution and frequency. However, symbolic knowledge captured in KGs can help these language models capture entity-specific information better. Further, with knowledge, we achieve broader semantics, including named and taxonomic relationships, synonyms, acronyms, and others, which support contextualization and abstraction. As a result, the language-model encoding in the embedding space can be richer. Take an infusion of entity information together with BERT for an example where shallow to semi-deep infusion happens (e.g., ERNIE (Zhang et al., 2019d)). We consider deep infusion of knowledge to be a new paradigm that will significantly advance the capabilities and promises of deep neural networks.

One inherent advantage of using knowledge in language models is that they get the additional information through entities or KG triples that otherwise require a lot of data to learn. This knowledge may not be learned from statistical data as cleanly as by direct infusion techniques. Language models treat each word/subword (or token) without much differentiation. Hence, specific information that an entity or phrase represents in a sentence is difficult to capture without such special processes. For example, the entity "Donald Trump" may not be captured as two words collectively in a language model and hence miss the important knowledge that those two words collectively refer to the current US president.

Donald Trump will be a common sub-word in BERT, for example. It may get to the point that it represents a person when considering the complete sentence but will surely miss all structural information that the knowledge graph will bring in if the model can understand it is an entity. If such language models are used to facilitate a conversation with a user, they end up losing the context, resulting in the generation of factually incorrect responses (Ji et al., 2022). Furthermore, the conversations that are not context controlled result in random conversations and generate sentences that are incoherent and irrelevant to the user (Thoppilan et al., 2022a). In a complex domain, such as mental health, such models can end up generating unsafe questions or responses that can have severe consequences on the user's health (Roy et al., 2022a).

3.5 Process Knowledge in KiL

Information in KGs can guarantee context capture, but we need another type of knowledge called "process knowledge" to ensure that language models do not hallucinate. This form of knowledge extends the other forms of knowledge, comprising the following: (a) *Knowledge graphs:* These are structured but not ordered; they can support context capture but cannot enforce conceptual flow (Gaur et al., 2021b). (b) *Semantic lexicons:* These are a flattened form that makes deep language models context sensitive and adds constraints but cannot enforce conceptual flow (Manas et al., 2021). (c) *Ontologies:* These are curated schematic forms having classes, instances, and constraints. Thus, ontologies can provide stricter control over context and constraints (Lai et al., 2020a). Using process knowledge, an ontology can enforce order in question generation using deep language models and act as alternate process knowledge. For example, ADOS (Autism Diagnostic Observation Schedule) is a diagnostic tool used by a caregiver to improve clinical evaluation and guide therapy. In addition, it is often used in schools that have special care facilities for children with autism. Suppose a robotic system is situated in this setting to conduct the activities of a human caregiver. In that case, it needs a set of rules and classes, very much in the form of an ontology, to guide its interaction. Such an ontology is called a process knowledge-inspired ontology. Likewise, an ontology created using MoCA (Montreal Cognitive Assessment) can support the automation of aphasia detection methods.

Consider a scenario where a user asks the following question to a typical agent *without process knowledge*: "Can you recommend calorie-sensitive dishes?" If the agent is augmented with search and retrieve capabilities using the internet, it will accumulate responses to the following related questions listed under *people-also-ask questions*:

- Are restaurants required to put calories on menus?
- Are calorie recommendations accurate?
- Should I eat fewer than my recommended calories?
- What food can you recommend?

There are two fundamental problems here: (a) The AI system behind these recommendations is confused about whether "calorie sensitivity" is a positive or negative concept. (b) The AI system fails to bridge the gap between dishes and calorie sensitivity. Furthermore, a response to such a question is dependent on the time of day: breakfast, lunch, or dinner. A conversational agent with process knowledge can generate the following information-seeking-type questions:

(i) Do you have any preference for cuisine?
(ii) Do you want to know about low-calorie food in this cuisine for breakfast/lunch/dinner?
(iii) Do you want me to book reservations for restaurants that have this cuisine?
(iv) Do you want me to save your preferences?

If the answer to any question is no, then an alternate path in process knowledge is triggered. Here the process knowledge is the procedure for recommending

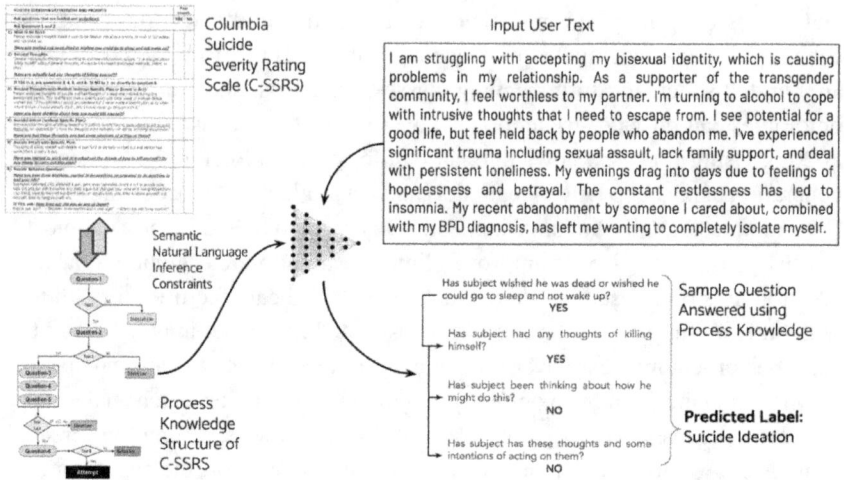

Figure 3.7 A two-stage pipeline comprises creating process knowledge and its infusion into a deep neural network to identify which questions can be answered from the user's input and which questions can be considered as follow-up questions for the complete assessment (Posner et al., 2010). The construction of process knowledge is manual for quality and safety purposes. Its infusion in the deep neural network is automated by an interplay of deep language models and an interpretable decision tree algorithm.
Note: Original text modified to ensure anonymity of the user.

and ordering food. Moreover, the agent can benefit from the 2015–2020 Dietary Guidelines for Americans (US Department of Health and Human Services, 2015) to emphasize overall healthy eating patterns supported by five food groups: fruits, vegetables, grains, protein foods and dairy.

Process knowledge can be used by KiL for additional capabilities, such as preventing conversational agents from generating sentences that have severe consequences, such as in mental healthcare (see Figure 3.7).

3.6 KiL for Knowledge-Intensive Language Understanding

Language models (LMs) inspired by deep learning exemplify a black-box nature, except for attention transformers (Mohammadi et al., 2024). These models have sparked debates, with conflicting opinions regarding their explainability and lack thereof (Bibal et al., 2022). Nevertheless, we take them as black box and examine ways to achieve transparency in these models. The reasons behind labeling them as blackbox are:

3.6 KiL for Knowledge-Intensive Language Understanding

- **Conceptual vs. Ambiguous Entities:** Consider an example from the Quora Question Pairs (QQP) dataset by Iyer et al. (2017), where we asked a DL model to classify whether two sentences, "What would have happened if Facebook was present in *World War I*?" and "What would have happened if Facebook was present in *World War II*?", were the same, and the model's classification was incorrect. It was because the DL model tokenized *conceptual entities*: World War I and World War II, giving attention to the phrase "World War" and ignoring "I" and "II." Then the question arises: "How to bracket conceptual entities so that DL model generates their representation together rather token-wise." One way is to leverage a ConceptNet KG to create a knowledge context surrounding these conceptual entities independently and generate better representation by concatenating representations of neighboring contexts.

    Ambiguous entities (e.g., polysemic words) are shown in the following two sentences: "What *eats* the phone battery quickly?" and "What would cause the battery on my phone to *drain* so quickly?" In these two sentences, "eat" and "drain" are polysemic words as they carry similar word senses in these two sentences. KGs like BabelNet or WordNet can provide senses for these words, along with definitions and relationships through synonyms, which can help DL create concatenated representations of these words independently, resulting in high similarity scores compared to representation without KG infusion (Navigli and Ponzetto, 2010; Goodman, 2023). Figure 3.8 provides examples of ambiguous and conceptual entities, showing cases where BERT needs external knowledge to capture the context for correct classification on the QQP dataset.

- **Long-Tail Entities:** DL models in NLP provide representations after learning a large volume of raw text. Essentially, they create and store an index of words and word–word co-occurrences, which considers distributional semantics to generate a numerical representation (Mikolov et al., 2013). Most of the time, the entity representing the document's theme is sparsely present. As a result, its representation is not as rich as other words that occur frequently. These sparsely distributed entities are called long-tail entities and affect any DL model by missing context. This is often the case in multi-hop question answering problems (Yang et al., 2018b). Consider an example (Gaur et al., 2020):

Question: **Sodium azide** is used in **air bags** to rapidly produce **gas** to inflate the bag. The products of the **decomposition** reaction are:
  (i) Na and water
  (ii) Ammonia and sodium metal
  (iii) N_2 and O_2

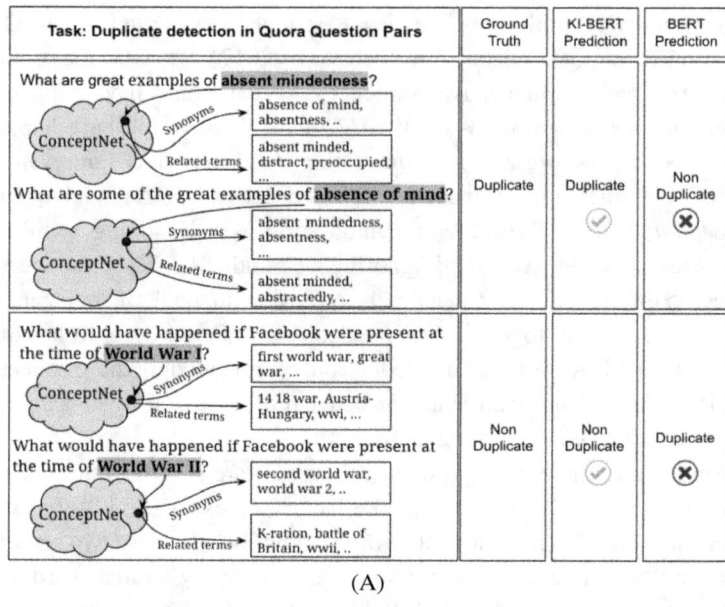

Figure 3.8 Infuse knowledge context to capture conceptual (A) and ambiguous entities (B) for correct classification in the QQP dataset. Picture credit: Faldu et al. (2021a).

(iv) Sodium and nitrogen

(v) Sodium oxide and nitrogen gas (Correct answer)

The entities in the correct answer are not present in the question. To correctly answer the question, we retrieve conjunctive or disjunctive sets of passages using keywords: {sodium azide, airbags, gas, and decomposition}. (*Passage 1*) Sodium azide (NaN_3) reacts in heat and decomposes to *Na and N*. (*Passage 2*) Oxidation-reduction decomposition reactions are redox reactions wherein electrons are transferred from the oxidized atom to the reduced atom. (*Passage 3*) Ionic-compound decomposition, like in NaN_3 occurs when a binary ionic compound is heated. (*Passage 4*) Airbags contain sodium azide and other gas to prevent sodium hyperoxide. Passages 2 & 3 are semantically related by the term "decomposition," and Passage 3 directly informs Passage 1 using "decompose" and "heat" as the concepts. Since Nitrogen (N) undergoes oxidation or reduction, it is related to Passage 2. Finally, Passage 4 logically follows Passage 1 with the term "sodium hyperoxide." This yields sodium oxide and nitrogen gas as correct answers. The order {Passage 2 & 3} → Passage 1 → Passage 4 is possible by exploring the relationships between passages, for which KGs are required (Roy et al., 2022a). Table 2.9 illustrates the importance of context sensitivity in other domains of social impact.

These challenges upscaled the evaluation of LMs from primitive natural language understanding tasks (GLUE (Bowman-Grieve and Conway, 2012) and SuperGLUE (Wang et al., 2019a)) to knowledge-intensive language tasks (KILT; Petroni et al. (2020)).

GLUE tasks do not test if the model can leverage knowledge; the explanations generated are of limited utility to humans (Wang et al., 2019a). Conversely, KILT has focused on building retrieval-augmented LMs to better understand natural language with support from passages that can capture the context in the user's input Petroni et al. (2021). In parallel, "knowledge intensive language understanding"(KILU) tasks are, as of now, focused on making LMs usable in mental healthcare settings. Table 3.1 enumerates the tasks in KILU that require external knowledge to match human-level performance. Further, there are task-specific metrics to evaluate the performance of models built to solve KILU tasks.

Essentially, KILT or KILU induce another set of capabilities in AI models to capture information similar to how a human does (see Table 3.1). These are:

- **Abstraction:** The task of mapping low-level features to higher-level human-understandable abstract concepts is known as abstraction. Humans often use higher-level abstract concepts when explaining their decisions to a user.

Table 3.1 *GLUE tasks are classification or prediction tasks taking a sentence or pair of sentences as input. They are not meant for generation or structured prediction. On the other hand, KILU tasks subsume GLUE tasks and challenge DL models on user-level explainability and interpretability. To provide explanations to KILU tasks, the model should leverage a variety of explicit knowledge to capture context and learn necessary abstraction for human comprehension. EM: Evaluation metrics used in GLUE and KILU.*

GLUE tasks	EM-GLUE	KILU	EM-KILU	Knowledge source
Corpus of Linguistic Acceptability (CoLA)(Warstadt et al., 2019)	Mathew's correlation	Summarization of conversational data (Manas et al., 2021)	Thematic overlap, Flesch reading scale, Jensen Shannon divergence, and Rouge-L	Structured clinical interviews, PHQ-9
Stanford Sentiment Treebank (STB) (Socher et al., 2013)	Accuracy	Predicting severity class of suicide on Reddit (Gaur et al., 2019b)	Precision, recall, ordinal Error, and perceived Risk measure	DSM-5 and drug abuse ontology (Lokala et al., 2020)
Microsoft Research Paraphrase Corpus (Dolan and Brockett, 2005)	F1-score and accuracy	Information disguise (Reagle and Gaur, 2022) using the User-Language Paraphrase Corpus and Reddit data	Word mover distance (Kusner et al., 2015), BLEURT (Sellam et al., 2020)	ConceptNet (Speer et al., 2017), WordNet (Miller, 1995)
Semantic Textual Similarity Benchmark (Cer et al., 2017)	Pearson Spearman correlation	Text-based emoji sense disambiguation (Tatman, 2023)	Average accuracy	EmojiNet (Wijeratne et al., 2017)

Quora Question Pairs (Iyer et al., 2017) MultiNLI Matched/ Mismatched (Williams et al., 2018a)	F1-score and accuracy	—	—
	Accuracy	Mediator to link user with diverse roles (need-resource) (Gaur et al., 2021e)	Time-to-good match, precision, recall, F1-score, and human evaluation	Psycholinguistics, mental health lexicon (for a use-case), domain-specific, & event-specific features
Question NLI (Rajpurkar et al., 2018)	Accuracy	Information seeking question generation for conversational assistance (Gaur et al., 2021b)	BLEURT, semantic relations, logical coherence, Rouge-L	Wikipedia (Rodriguez et al., 2020), WikiNews (Pyatkin et al., 2020), MS-MARCO (Dalton et al., 2020)
Recognizing Textual Entailment (Dagan et al., 2010)	Accuracy	ProKnow: dataset and method for process-guided, safety-constrained, and explainable mental health diagnostic assistance (Roy et al., 2022a)	BLEU, Rouge-L, avg. num. of unsafe matches (AUM), average knowledge base concept matches (AKCM), average squared rank error (ASRE)	PHQ-9 and GAD-7
Winograd NLI (Levesque et al., 2012)	Accuracy	—	—	—

66   Knowledge-Infused Learning: The Subsumer to NeuroSymbolic AI

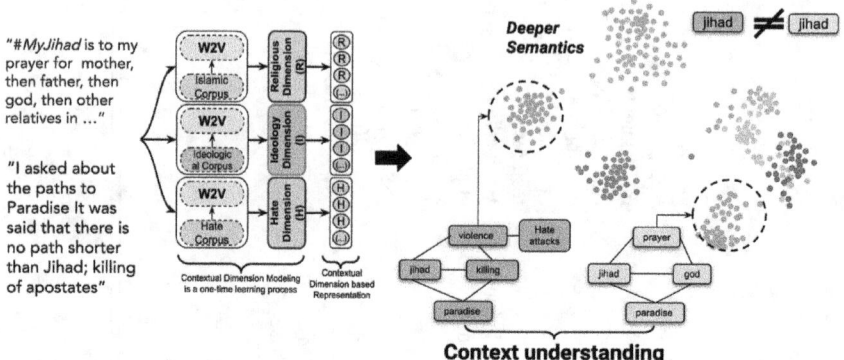

Figure 3.9 An illustration of context modeling in a language model using an external domain-specific corpus. Subsequent clustering manifests the pairing of concepts that co-occur in a domain-specific corpus. The clusters are explainable using the relationships between these concepts. This figure illustrates deeper semantics in a computational social science problem of detecting radicalization behaviors in the dynamic stream of X posts. The word *jihad* occurs in two connotations and is clearly separable using domain-specific knowledge.

AI systems must also explain decisions to the end-users using abstract domain-relevant concepts constructed from low-level features and external knowledge in a KG.

- **Contextualization**: This is defined as interpreting a concept with reference to relevant use or application. Humans contextualize by processing the information through various knowledge sources (e.g., syntactic, structural, linguistic, common-sense and domain-specific). Contextualization is a necessity in the domain of social good, wherein misclassification can have severe consequences. For example, to classify if X posts are from *extremists* or *non-extremists* requires various forms of contextual knowledge to ensure precise classification (Kursuncu et al., 2019). Posts in the domain of radicalization represent a mixed context of religion, ideology, and violence/hate. Thus, modeling user content independently from these domain contexts is important for better clustering and classification (see Figure 3.9).

- **Personalization:** Identifying data point-specific information and integrating it with external knowledge to construct a personalized knowledge source is known as personalization. For example, a person's depressive disorder can be due to family issues, relationship issues, or clinical factors. All of these affect the context specific to the individual and consequently affect their symptoms and medications differently than those for another person.

3.7 Recommender Systems

Data-driven statistical AI-based techniques are effective for recommending the right product or content or connecting people to enhance the user experience. These recommendation methods rely on understanding a user and product/content to recommend based on successful recommendations from the past and aim to evolve the recommendation system based on interaction data. While such purely data-driven techniques can improve success measures, they often lack an inherent understanding of the user and the product/content to recommend. Hence, the recommendations may not be personalized.

Developing and utilizing knowledge bases to augment the data in recommendations can help progress toward more personalized recommendations and also help address one of the inherent challenges of recommendations – *cold start recommendations*. Several recent research studies have utilized knowledge to complement the data and provide more enhanced, personalized, and meaningful recommendations (Guo et al., 2020). Organizing and utilizing knowledge beyond the available data has become a promising research area for providing a better user experience with enhanced recommendation systems.

3.8 Computer Vision

The processing of images and videos tries to give human vision capability to machines. Computer vision systems aim to endow machines with human-like visual understanding capabilities for processing images and videos. However, purely data-driven approaches that rely solely on visual features exhibit fundamental limitations in contextual reasoning and common-sense understanding (Kautz, 2020; Marcus, 2020). For instance, while a convolutional neural network may successfully detect both a horse and a human in an image, it lacks the symbolic reasoning capability to infer the typical spatial relationship that humans ride on horses rather than the inverse relationship. This limitation stems from the absence of structured world knowledge and logical reasoning mechanisms in traditional computer vision pipelines. Scene graphs represent a prominent neurosymbolic approach that bridges this gap by providing structured, graph-based representations of visual scenes (Johnson et al., 2015; Krishna et al., 2017). These representations encode objects, their attributes, and inter-object relationships as nodes and edges in a graph structure. To enhance contextual understanding, scene graphs are augmented with semantic knowledge extracted from external knowledge graphs, creating a hybrid symbolic–neural architecture (Kim et al., 2021; Wickramarachchi et al.,

2021; Zhong et al., 2021). This integration enables the system to leverage both learned visual patterns from neural networks and explicit symbolic knowledge from curated knowledge bases, exemplifying the core principles of neurosymbolic AI (Hamilton, 2022). Visual question answering (VQA) has emerged as a critical testbed for neurosymbolic reasoning in computer vision (Antol et al., 2015; Hudson and Manning, 2019). Knowledge graph-enhanced VQA systems demonstrate superior performance by incorporating structured factual knowledge, enabling multi-hop reasoning, and providing interpretable answer generation (Narasimhan et al., 2018; Shah et al., 2019; Monka et al., 2022). These systems typically employ graph neural networks to process both visual scene graphs and textual knowledge graphs, followed by cross-modal attention mechanisms that align visual and symbolic representations for question answering (Teney et al., 2017; Norcliffe-Brown et al., 2018).

4
Shallow Infusion of Knowledge

A major focus in this chapter will be to learn various ways in which datasets can be transformed using external knowledge. Shallow infusion concerns semantic data transformation and provides the following benefits:

- Concept Classes: Suppose the outcome labels predicted by an AI model lack concrete definitions that distinguish one label from another; then, the classification is subject to varied interpretations. Furthermore, such labels are created based on an empirically defined threshold that is inappropriate for high-stakes decision-making problems. It is acceptable in the general-purpose domain; however, it is not affordable in a healthcare setting, where a subsequent decision has to be made on the predicted label. Shallow Infusion brings in the concept of *concept classes*, which are labels with definitions. Figure 4.1 illustrates a map between a not-so-well-defined set of labels and concept classes. These classes are domain specific and can make AI systems capable of capturing context (Gaur et al., 2021a), handling uncertainty and risk associated with ambiguity (Gaur et al., 2019b), and providing system-level explainability and user-level explainability by mapping the model-defined important features to concepts in KGs.
- Entity Normalization (EN): The linguistic variations in online communication raise challenges for the supervised learning algorithm in determining discriminative patterns. For example, consider the following two posts: **(P1)** "I am *sick of loss* and *need a way out*"; **(P2)** "*No way out*, I am *tired of my losses*"; (P3) "Losses, losses, I want to die." The italicized phrases in P1 and P2 are predictors of suicidal tendencies but are expressed differently (Gaur et al., 2021a). Shallow Infusion of knowledge removes these variations through a process called entity normalization that calculates the semantic similarity between n-gram phrases and concepts in a knowledge source (e.g., KGs, Lexicons). To perform EN, we generate vectors of words in the input using an embedding model (e.g., Word2Vec (Mikolov et al., 2013),

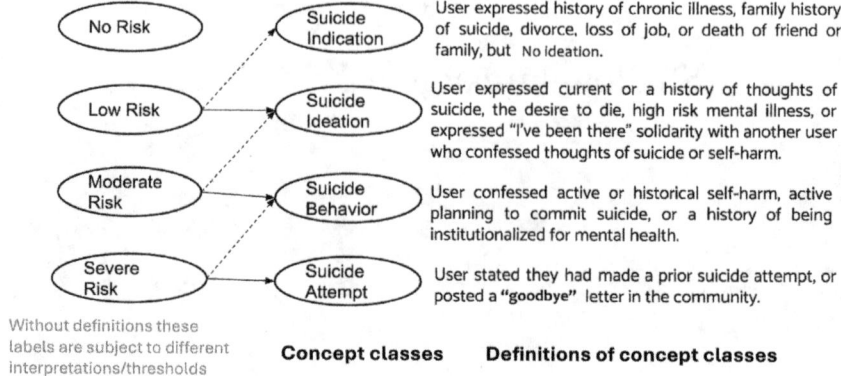

Figure 4.1 An illustration of concept classes to assess suicide risk. These concept classes are obtained from the Columbia Suicide Severity Rating Scale (Posner et al., 2010). A dotted arrow from a "not-so-well-defined" label to a well-defined concept class shows that the label **can** resemble this class if the predicted probability for a solid arrow is lower than for a dotted arrow. A solid arrow from "not-so-well-defined" labels to well-defined concept classes shows that these labels certainly resemble this class if the predicted probability for the solid arrow is higher than for a dotted arrow. This dichotomy on the part of "not-so-well-defined" labels is removed using concept classes.

ConceptNet Numberbatch (Speer et al., 2017)) and computer similarity (e.g., Word Mover Distance (Kusner et al., 2015), Cosine Similarity, BERTScore) with concepts in various knowledge sources. If we perform EN, then P1, P2, and P3 transform to "depress, suicide ideation," "suicide ideation, depress," and "depress, suicide attempt," respectively. This clearly shows that P1 and P2 are related and distinct from P3.

- System-level Explainability: System-level explainability (SysEx) has been developed under the purview of post-hoc explainability techniques that aim to interpret the attention mechanism of LMs/LLMs without affecting their learning process. These techniques establish connections between the LM's attention patterns and concepts sourced from understandable knowledge repositories. Within this approach, two methods have emerged: (a) attribution scores and LM tuning (Slack et al., 2023) and (b) factual knowledge-based scoring and LM tuning (Sun et al., 2023; Yang et al., 2025). The latter method holds particular significance in the domain of health and well-being because it focuses on providing explainability for clinicians as users. This method relies on KGs or knowledge bases like the Unified Medical Language System (UMLS) (Bodenreider, 2004), SNOMED-CT (Donnelly et al., 2006), or RXNorm (Nelson et al., 2011) to enhance its functionality.

While the post-hoc method can provide explanations (by modeling it as a dialogue system (Lakkaraju et al., 2022)), it does not guarantee that the model consistently prioritizes essential elements during training (Jiang et al., 2021). Its explanations may be coincidental and not reflect the model's actual decision-making process.

- User-level Explainability (UseEx): UsEx refers to an AI system's ability to explain to users when requested. The explanations are given once the AI system has made its decisions or predictions. They are intended to assist users in comprehending the logic behind the decisions. Figure 3.6 shows the difference between system-level explainability and user-level explainability in natural language processing applications involving neural attention models (Vaswani et al., 2017a; Sarkar et al., 2023).

4.1 What Is Shallow Infusion?

Shallow infusion, the initial category of knowledge infusion, involves transforming knowledge into a simplified intermediate form suitable for integration with deep learning models. This approach enables the incorporation of external information without requiring significant modifications to the underlying learning model. Specifically, shallow infusion enhances deep network representations using techniques like word embeddings for textual data or graph embeddings for structured information (see Figure 4.2). These methods excel at breaking down inputs into smaller units, such as phrases, which enhances their ability to handle challenges like misspellings, abbreviations, and text with similar linguistic roots. However, they do not capture the full semantic relationships between entities in external knowledge. As a result, their applicability is limited in domains in which precise contextualization from external knowledge is crucial.

To see how shallow infusion can be applied in current state-of-the-art models, we note that recent advances in deep networks employ language models that use an attention mechanism to define the context of words given their neighborhood in the input dataset. The current state-of-the-art Transformer models, such as BERT, broke records for several NLP tasks and learned to capture long-term dependencies and context by training on large amounts of text. Several other works have seen ground-breaking results with several Transformer-based successors of BERT (e.g., RoBERTa, XLNet, and Transformer-XL). However, context sensitivity and handling uncertainty and risk have not been resolved in spite of scaling the parameters of these models from millions to billions. This has a consequence: A large-scale model

Shallow Infusion of Knowledge

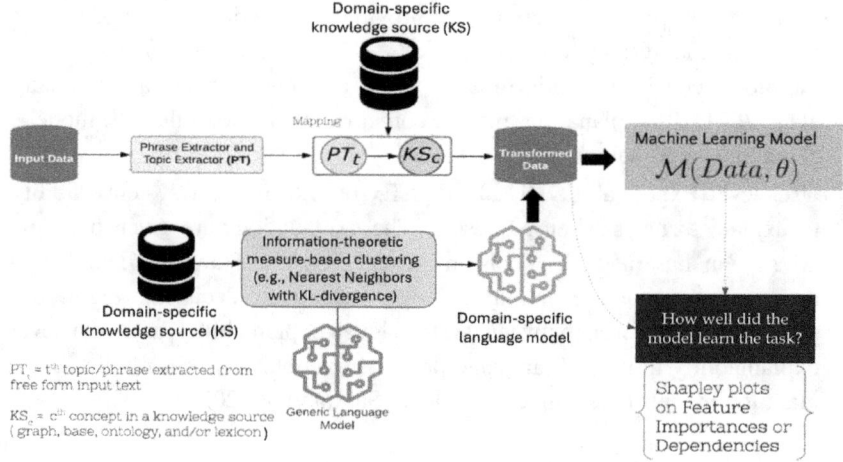

Figure 4.2 A generic architecture of `Shallow Infusion`.

memorizes the patterns in the dataset on which it is trained and tested, and it is difficult to adapt the model to similar or related tasks. For instance, a model trained to identify and classify harassment on social media with simple scaling of parameters is prone to misclassification on a near-related problem of "radicalization in social media." Kursuncu et al. (2019) leveraged multiple domain-specific perspective models in enriching the representation of extremist communication on social media (see Figure 4.3). The approach provided the necessary knowledge required by a model to minimize false alarms. In the context of "harassment on social media," a potential improvement in a machine learning model was made through the infusion of cyberbullying vocabulary knowledge (Wijesiriwardene et al., 2020).

4.2 Methods of Shallow Infusion

Following are some of the well-known methods of shallow infusion that are well studied and used by the NLP community. There is a long list of methods that are classified under `Shallow Infusion`; these are mentioned in Table 4.1.

Word Embeddings: This is the simplest form of shallow infusion. Here, the objective is to provide the model with additional background information that the training data alone cannot provide. This background information

4.2 Methods of Shallow Infusion

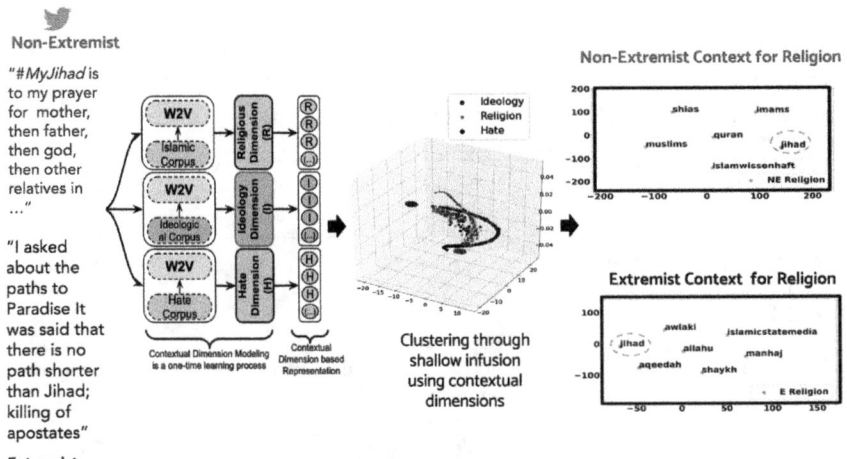

Figure 4.3 A shallow infusion process using contextual dimensions from the radicalization literature. The visualization is performed using the T-SNE method (Van der Maaten and Hinton, 2008).

is available as large text corpora. A shallow neural network or a statistical model is then trained in an unsupervised setting to capture the domain-specific meanings of words. Popular examples include Word2Vec (using skip-gram and CBOW algorithms) and GloVe. Words are represented as n-dimensional vectors (e.g., $n = 300$), making them easily transferable and task-agnostic within a particular domain. As a result, numerous pre-trained word embeddings are available for many languages and domains (Gupta et al., 2022).

Enriched Word Embeddings: In this class of algorithms, the pre-trained word embeddings are enriched using additional information such as domain-specific lexicons/ taxonomies and morphology of words. As a post-processing technique, **retrofitting** leverages semantic lexicons such as WordNet in modifying the embeddings (Faruqui et al., 2015). For example, retrofitting enforces the embedding of the word *incorrect* to be in a similar vicinity to other related words such as *wrong*, *flawed*, and *false* in the embedding space. **Counter-Fitting**, an approach similar to retrofitting, introduces synonymy and antonymy constraints to the word-relatedness when refining word embeddings (Mrkšić et al., 2016). As a result, it prevents the word *inexpensive* from being closer to words such as *pricey* and *costly* even though they are related via an antonymy relation. **FastText** leverages information within the text to improve the learned embeddings (Bojanowski et al., 2017). It considers the morphology of words – particularly,

Table 4.1 *Other methods that are classified under shallow infusion. However, not all of them support system-level explainability (SysEx). Methods such as SysEx are also capable of user-level explainability with manual effort comprising search and retrieval over related knowledge sources.*

Methods	Approach	Type of explainability
Term frequency and inverse document frequency (TF-IDF)	Bag of words	✗ (SysEx)
Retrofitting	Bag of concepts	✓ (SysEx)
	Verb phrase/ noun phrase	✓ (SysEx)
	Sentiments and emotion lexicons	✓ (SysEx)
	Topic modeling	✗ (SysEx)
Latent Dirichlet allocation	Semantic role labeling	✓ (SysEx)
	Predict than explain	✓ (SysEx)
	Explain than predict	✓ (SysEx)
Embeddings	Word2Vec/ GLoVE	✓ (SysEx)
	FastText	✗ (SysEx)
	ELMo	✓ (SysEx)
	BERT/ RoBERTa	✓ (SysEx)
Transformers	GPT-2, GPT-3, XLNet, ProphetNet, and variants	✗ (SysEx)
	T5 and Longformers	✓ (SysEx)
Reinforcement learning	Neural Policy Gradient methods using GLUE-based rewards	✓ (SysEx)
Multirelational reinforcement learning	Functional policy gradient methods	✓ (SysEx)
Reinforcement learning with deterministic search	Combining search and value iteration or policy gradients	✓ (SysEx)

sub-word information – and represents a word as a bag of character n-grams in learning the embeddings. This allows misspelled words, rare words, and abbreviations to have similar meanings to their original forms. Moreover, this enables deriving embeddings for words that did not appear in the training data.

Deep Neural Language Models: The primary difference in this class of models is the use of deep neural architectures with language modeling objectives – that is, learning to predict the next word conditioned on the given context by probabilistically modeling words in a language. ELMo (also ULMFiT (Howard and Ruder, 2018)) marks a significant step in this direction by capturing the *context* in which a word is used in a sentence (Peters et al., 2018). By training a task-specific Bi-LSTM network to model

4.2 Methods of Shallow Infusion

the language from both forward and backward directions, ELMo represents a particular word as a combination of corresponding hidden layers. The current state-of-the-art neural language modeling is inspired by the advent of Transformers – a simple, solely attention-based mechanism that disregards the need to use recurrent and convolutional neural networks. Transformer-based BERT, a model that broke records for several NLP tasks, learns to capture long-term dependencies and context by training on large amounts of text. It further fine-tunes the knowledge gained by specifically training on a supervised-learning task. Last year saw ground-breaking works with several Transformer-based successors to BERT (e.g., RoBERTa (Liu et al., 2019a), XLNet (Yang et al., 2019), and Transformer-XL (Dai et al., 2019)) coming to light, steering modern NLP in new directions.

The combination of these Shallow Infusion methods along with strategies that bring out the benefits of Shallow Infusion sees applications in public health (Gaur et al., 2019b, Gaur et al., 2021a), crisis management (e.g. natural disasters (Arachie et al., 2020), pandemics (Gaur et al., 2021e)), autonomous driving (Chowdhury et al., 2021; Wickramarachchi et al., 2021), epidemiology (Kursuncu et al., 2018; Kumar et al., 2020; Lokala et al., 2020), sports (Bhatt et al., 2018), and others.

We want to focus on social media, an area that is a sore point of information in terms of actionable insights it can provide to stakeholders (e.g., emergency responders and healthcare providers) and the challenges involved in extracting insights, such as semantic ambiguity and negation in the sentences. **Negation detection** is a crucial capability, as the presence of negated sentences can confound a classifier. For example, *I am not going to end my life because I failed a stupid test* is not suicidal, whereas *My daily struggles with depression have driven me to alcohol* reflects the user's mental health. The former sentence can give a false positive if we just extract "going to end my life" as a precursor to a suicide attempt. Gaur et al. employed a negation detection tool and probabilistic context-free grammar to support negation extraction and negation resolution to improve classifier performance (Gaur et al., 2018).

Among various social media platforms, we will be focusing on Reddit. Reddit is one of the largest social media platforms with around 430 million subscribers and 21 billion average screen visits per month across >130,000 subreddits. On a per-month average, around 1.3 million subscribers anonymously post mental health-related content in 15 of the most active subreddits pertaining to mental health (MH) disorders (42K posts on r/SuicideWatch) (Gaur et al., 2019b). The analysis of Reddit content is demanding for a number of reasons, including interaction context, language variation, and the technical determination of clinical relevance. Correspondingly, the potential rewards of greater insight into mental illness in general, and suicidal thoughts and behavior specifically, are great. The Reddit platform enables free, unobtrusive, and honest sharing of mental health concerns because a patient is completely anonymous and so can open up without worrying about any social stigma or other consequences; thus, the content is less biased and of high quality compared to the content shared in survey questionnaires and interviews (Jamnik and Lane, 2017).

Through Shallow Infusion we seek answer to the following questions:
(a) Can *concept classes* and *entity normalization* procedures help AI algorithms to adapt to the task of assessing the severity of suicide risk at an individual level?
(b) Knowing that suicide is a terminal mental illness and patients drift in time across the spectrum of mental health disorders, what architectural choices need to be made to study suicide risk in *time-variant* and *time-invariant* manners?

4.3 Shallow Infusion for Mental Health

Current AI models that predict suicide risk are not clinically grounded and explainable, as the labels used to label samples are not well defined (Gaur et al., 2021d) (see Figure 4.1). Let us see this with an example, starting with Figure 4.4. It illustrates how annotators see posts and provide labels, and how an AI model sees a post through the lens of feature importance weights. This example is taken from the Reddit C-SSRS Suicide dataset, comprising 500 posts labeled with the following labels: *Supportive, Suicide Indication, Suicide Ideation, Suicide Behavior,* and *Suicide Attempt* (Gaur et al., 2019b). C-SSRS stands for Columbia Suicide Severity Rating Scale, a clinical questionnaire used to quantify severity of suicide. Through visual inspection, it is evident that the phrases/tokens that seem important to an expert are not given relatively close importance scores by the model. Scaling over the 500 posts, the model yielded a score of 53% recall.[1] As a next step, we replaced the simple AI model, the support vector machine, with a large model, the convolutional neural network (CNN) (see Figure 4.5).

Although the CNN highlighted more phrases and tokens, it did not significantly improve the severity level predictions. It increased the recall rate from 53% to 57% but struggled with this type of data. A more effective approach involves having the model predict both severity and a confidence score.

---

[1] In order of severity levels: Suicide Indication → Suicide Ideation → Suicide Behavior → Suicide Attempt; if a model predicts a lower severity level than ground truth, it is counted in the recall.

4.3 Shallow Infusion for Mental Health

I do have a potential to live a decent life but not with people who abandon me. Hopelessness and feelings of betrayal have turned my nights to days. I am developing insomnia because of my restlessness.
I just can't take it anymore. Been abandoned yet again by someone I cared about. I've been diagnosed with borderline for a while, and I'm just going to isolate myself and sleep forever.

Input Raw Text

I do have a potential to live a decent life but not with people who abandon me. Hopelessness and feelings of betrayal have turned my nights to days. I am developing insomnia because of my restlessness.
I just can't take it anymore. Been abandoned yet again by someone I cared about. I've been diagnosed with borderline for a while, and I'm just going to isolate myself and sleep forever.

Annotated by Expert
(Label: Moderate Risk)

I do have a potential to live a decent life but not with people who abandon me. Hopelessness and feelings of betrayal have turned my nights to days. I am developing insomnia because of my restlessness.
I just can't take it anymore. Been abandoned yet again by someone I cared about. I've been diagnosed with borderline for a while, and I'm just going to isolate myself and sleep forever.

 **Annotated by SVM**
(Label: Low Risk)

Figure 4.4 Comparison of annotator and SVM model analysis of a user's post. The annotator manually identifies key concepts, while the SVM model uses feature attribution to highlight important words or phrases. This often leads to discrepancies, with the model potentially missing crucial concepts, a common issue visible in current domain-specific language models, as described by Dalal et al. (2023).

I do have a potential to live a decent life but not with people who abandon me. Hopelessness and feelings of betrayal have turned my nights to days. I am developing insomnia because of my restlessness.
I just can't take it anymore. Been abandoned yet again by someone I cared about. I've been diagnosed with borderline for a while, and I'm just going to isolate myself and sleep forever.

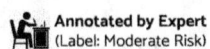 **Annotated by Expert**
(Label: Moderate Risk)

I do have a potential to live a decent life but not with people who abandon me. Hopelessness and feelings of betrayal have turned my nights to days. I am developing insomnia because of my restlessness.
I just can't take it anymore. Been abandoned yet again by someone I cared about. I've been diagnosed with borderline for a while, and I'm just going to isolate myself and sleep forever.

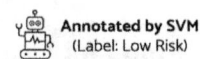 **Annotated by SVM**
(Label: Low Risk)

I do have a potential to live a decent life but not with people who abandon me. Hopelessness and feelings of betrayal have turned my nights to days. I am developing insomnia because of my restlessness.
I just can't take it anymore. Been abandoned yet again by someone I cared about. I've been diagnosed with borderline for a while, and I'm just going to isolate myself and sleep forever.

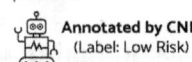 **Annotated by CNN**
(Label: Low Risk)

Figure 4.5 Despite the CNN's ability to capture spatial features, there is no significant improvement over the SVM in determining importance scores.

If the confidence score falls below a certain threshold, the prediction is ignored, and the sample is sent to an expert for verification. This method achieved an 85% recall but only covered 50% of samples, necessitating expert review for the remaining half. While suitable for small datasets, scaling this method to millions of samples would overwhelm experts (Liu et al., 2019b; Sawhney et al., 2022).

Concept classes play a crucial role in reducing uncertainty and capturing context. They involve changes at both the data and model levels. At the data

Table 4.2 *Suicide risk severity lexicon. It can be downloaded from https://github.com/AmanuelF/Suicide-Risk-Assessment-using-Reddit/tree/master*

Suicide risk severity class	Number of concepts per class	Examples
Suicide indication	1535	Pessimistic character, suicide of relative, family history of suicide
Suicide ideation	472	Suicidal thoughts, feeling suicidal, potential suicide care
Suicide behavior	146	Planning on cutting nerve, threatening suicide, loaded gun, drug abuse
Suicide attempt	124	Previous known suicide attempt, suicidal deliberate poisoning, goodbye attempted suicide by self-administered drug, suicide while incarcerated.

level, phrases (or n-grams) are extracted from the input text if they overlap with or are semantically similar to definitions or concepts that describe severity levels (refer to Table 4.2). This process includes:

(a) Using Dependency parsing or constituency parsing to extract nouns or verb phrases, then checking their presence in lexicons and definitions.

(b) Computing sentence or phrase embeddings using Sentence BERT or ConceptNet, and measuring semantic similarity with severity level definitions or concepts in the lexicon.

This approach identifies and highlights concept phrases within the text, which are phrases substantially similar to definitions and lexicons, as illustrated in Figure 4.6

4.4 Explainable Data Creation and Use in Suicide Context

By definition, "explainable data" is a resource created after processing the raw textual input using expert-curated knowledge sources with the purpose of understanding an AI model's behavior in classification or generation. An example illustration of explainable data is shown in Figure 4.6, where an input text is pre-processed by identifying parts of the sentence that are similar to concepts in a related knowledge source (e.g., Lexicons, KGs). The bracketed tokens in Figure 4.6 are considered to be key phrases and are termed concept phrases after checking their presence or similarity with concepts in the knowledge source. Among various ways to extract the key phrases from the sentences, we considered constituency parsing to be a ubiquitous method across all NLP applications (Hasan and Ng, 2014). Figure 4.7 shows a parse tree of the first sentence in Figure 4.6.

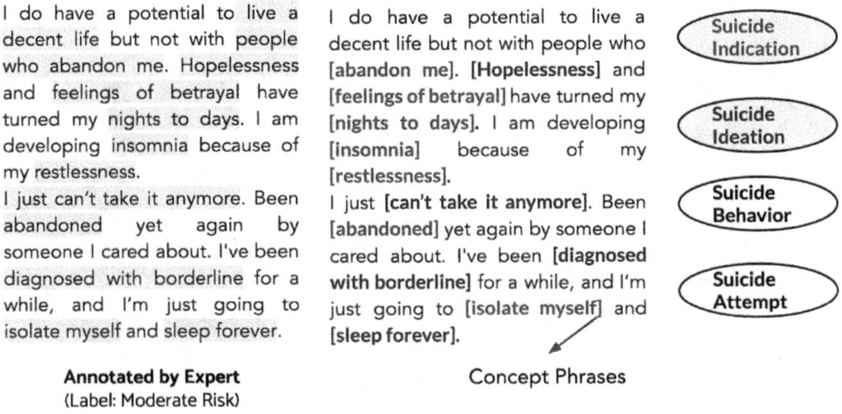

4.4 Explainable Data Creation and Use in Suicide Context

I do have a potential to live a decent life but not with people who abandon me. Hopelessness and feelings of betrayal have turned my nights to days. I am developing insomnia because of my restlessness.
I just can't take it anymore. Been abandoned yet again by someone I cared about. I've been diagnosed with borderline for a while, and I'm just going to isolate myself and sleep forever.

Annotated by Expert
(Label: Moderate Risk)

I do have a potential to live a decent life but not with people who [abandon me]. [Hopelessness] and [feelings of betrayal] have turned my [nights to days]. I am developing [insomnia] because of my [restlessness].
I just [can't take it anymore]. Been [abandoned] yet again by someone I cared about. I've been [diagnosed with borderline] for a while, and I'm just going to [isolate myself] and [sleep forever].

Concept Phrases

— Suicide Indication
— Suicide Ideation
— Suicide Behavior
— Suicide Attempt

Figure 4.6 The text that contains some bracketed tokens is the transformed input text. The bracketed tokens are either similar to the concepts in the lexicon or definitions of the concept classes or present within them. Thus, we call them concept phrases. The elliptical shapes are an illustration of concept classes. Suicide Indication and Suicide Ideation are highlighted because the bracketed concept phrases are significantly similar to these classes. This transformed input text is input to a model described in Section 4.8.

Parsing the constituency parse tree would yield noun phrases (NPs) and verb phrases (VPs) that are potential keyphrases reflecting on the topics of the user's focus. "people who abandon me," and "hopelessness," "feelings of betrayal" are some examples of NPs and VPs that are very similar to phrases identified by the annotators while annotating the post. After identification of the phrases, the next task is to check their similarity to the concepts in the knowledge source. Let us consider that we have two sources of knowledge – Lexicon (L) and Definitions (D) – suitable for capturing cues that describe the suicide risk severity of an individual, and the individual makes **P** posts, where their ith post is represented as p_i. Then the method of identifying **concept phrases** using a lexicon (L) can be formulated as follows:

$$\text{Concept Phrases}_L(p_i) = \begin{array}{l} \{\cos(NP_{p_i}, L)\}, \ NP_{p_i}, VP_{p_i} \in \text{constituency parse}(p_i) \\ \cup \\ \{\cos(VP_{p_i}, L)\}, \ \text{NP: Noun Phrase, VP: Verb Phrase}, p_i \in \mathbf{P} \\ \cup \\ \{NP_{p_i} \cap \{w_0, w_1, w_2, \ldots, w_n\}_{\in L}\} \\ \cup \\ \{VP_{p_i} \cap \{w_0, w_1, w_2, \ldots, w_n\}_{\in L}\} \end{array}$$

$$\cos(NP_{p_i}, L) = \text{for NP} \in NP_{p_i} \text{ and } w \in L, \text{if } \cos(\vec{np}, \vec{w}) > \delta,$$

$$\cos(VP_{p_i}, L) = \text{for VP} \in VP_{p_i} \text{ and } w \in L, \text{if } \cos(\vec{vp}, \vec{w}) > \delta,$$

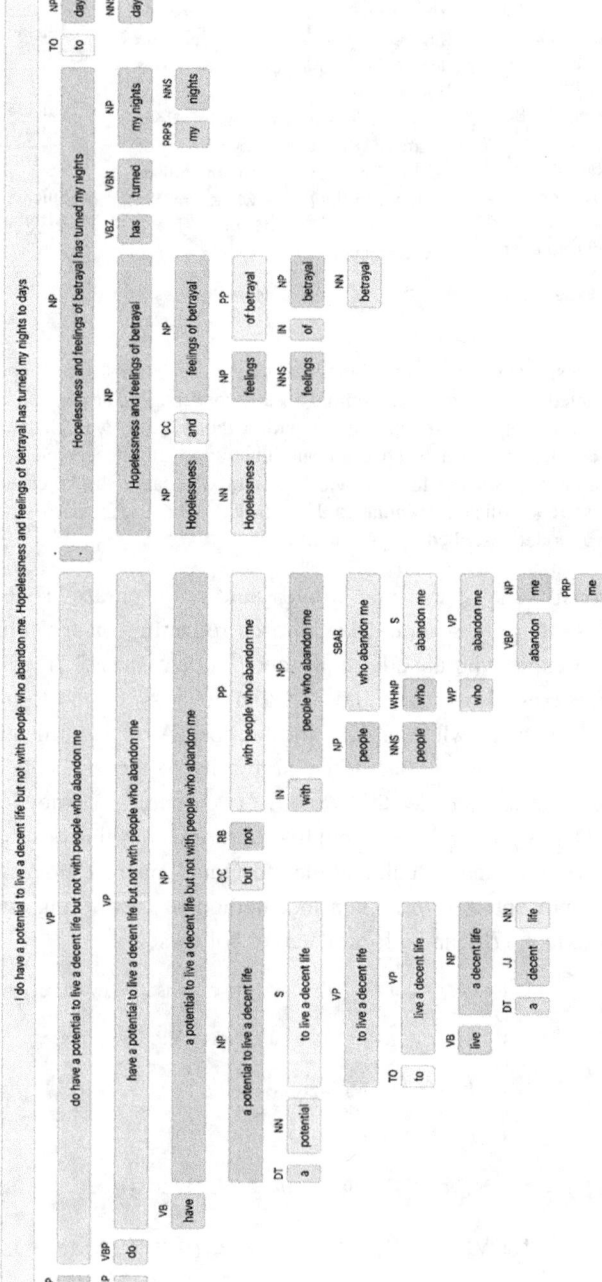

Figure 4.7 An example of the constituency parse tree for the first sentence in Figure 4.6. The image is created using the Berkeley Neural Constituency Parser, available online at https://parser.kitaev.io/.

4.4 Explainable Data Creation and Use in Suicide Context

where $\cos(\vec{np}, \vec{w})$ represents the computation of cosine similarity between vector embeddings of the noun phrase from a post p_i and a word from the lexicon L. Similarly, the method for identifying **concept phrases** using definitions (D) of concept classes can be formulated as follows:

$$\text{Concept Phrases}_D(p_i) = \begin{array}{l} \{\cos(NP_{p_i}, \vec{D})\}, \; NP_{p_i}, VP_{p_i} \in \text{constituency parse}(p_i) \\ \cup \\ \{\cos(VP_{p_i}, \vec{D})\}, \; \text{NP: Noun Phrase, VP: Verb Phrase}, p_i \in \mathbf{P} \\ \cup \\ \{NP_{p_i} \cap \{w_0, w_1, w_2, \ldots, w_n\}_{\in D}\} \\ \cup \\ \{VP_{p_i} \cap \{w_0, w_1, w_2, \ldots, w_n\}_{\in D}\} \end{array}$$

$$\cos(NP_{p_i}, \vec{D}) = \text{for NP} \in NP_{p_i} \text{ if } \cos(\vec{np}, \vec{D}) > \delta,$$

$$\cos(VP_{p_i}, \vec{D}) = \text{for VP} \in VP_{p_i} \text{ if } \cos(\vec{vp}, \vec{D}) > \delta.$$

An intersection of Concept Phrases$_L(p_i)$ and Concept Phrases$_D(p_i)$ constitutes the total set of concept phrases in a post p_i. This process should be applied to all user posts $\mathbf{P}$, resulting in a dataset with identified concept phrases alongside other tokens in the input texts. Concept phrases help preserve context as embeddings can lose semantics due to their distributional nature.

Two methods to create embeddings of concept phrases are:

(a) Using pre-trained or fine-tuned sequential language models (e.g., BERT), which generate representations by processing the concept phrases in either uni-directional (e.g., RNN, LSTM) or bi-directional (e.g., Bi-LSTM, BERT) ways.

(b) Using word-embedding models to generate embeddings for individual words within a concept phrase, then concatenating these embeddings and applying dimensionality reduction techniques (e.g., singular value decomposition, T-SNE) to align with the dimensions required by the AI model for classification (Vaswani et al., 2017a; Rücklé et al., 2018; Goldstein et al., 2022).

After creating embeddings for concept phrases, the remaining tokens in the text are represented using word embedding models. The final input representation is formed by concatenating token embeddings with concept phrase embeddings and then applying dimensionality reduction. Dimensionality reduction after shallow infusion helps by reducing the complexity of the model, enhancing computational efficiency, and retaining the most critical semantic information. This ensures that the model processes a more manageable and informative set of features, improving its ability to understand and classify the input accurately.

This forms the method for creating a numerical representation of the transformed input text, as shown in Figure 4.8. With this approach, an AI model treats the concept phrases as single units, preserving their semantics. To

Table 4.3 *Shallow infusion improves recall when the model is tasked to predict the suicide risk severity of a user. In such a scenario, Recall is the judge of the model's performance, as high false negatives would result in a wrong care plan for a patient with high levels of suicide risk tendencies.*

Model	Method	Recall
SVM with linear kernel	–	53%
CNN	–	57%
CNN (Sawhney et al., 2022)	Gambler loss	62%
CNN (Gaur et al., 2019b)	Concept phrases	74%
CNN (Gaur et al., 2021a)	Semantic embedding loss	84%

classify the suicide risk severity of an individual, we need to infuse knowledge into the AI model. As shown in Table 4.3, transforming the input alone yields satisfactory improvements over baselines. However, significant gains were achieved by implementing a shallow infusion of knowledge. This was done by introducing a new loss function, termed *semantic embedding loss*, which calculates the difference between the model's outermost layer representations and various concept class representations created using embedding models. This can be formulated as follows:

$$\mathcal{L}_{se} = \min_{j} ||\vec{h}^o - \vec{v}_j||^2,$$

where $\vec{h}^o$ is the outermost representation of the AI model, and $\vec{v}^j$ is the jth label among $\{\vec{v}_{SIn}, \vec{v}_{SId}, \vec{v}_{SB}, \text{ and } \vec{v}_{SA}\}$. The results in Table 4.3 are recorded using ConceptNet (vocabulary = 417193, dimension = 300), a multilingual knowledge graph created from expert sources, crowd-sourcing, DBpedia, vocabulary derived from Word2Vec, and GLoVE. The recall score reported in Table 4.3 is computed in the following way:

$$FP = \frac{\sum_{i=1}^{N_T} I(r'_i > r^o_i)}{N_T}, \quad FN = \frac{\sum_{i=1}^{N_T} I(r^o_i > r'_i)}{N_T},$$

where $\Delta(r^o_i, r'_i)$ is the difference between r^o_i and r'_i; r'_i and r^o_i are the predicted and actual responses for i^{th} test sample.

Longitudinal and Cumulative Study of Suicide Risk: Introducing concept classes and their infusion into the AI model opens up avenues for wider applications of AI in suicide risk severity. Prediction of a suicide risk severity level is not always cumulative of the posts made by a user but can also be longitudinal. In the absence of concept classes, it is hard to capture whether a post made by a user is informative for predicting suicide risk severity or should

4.4 Explainable Data Creation and Use in Suicide Context

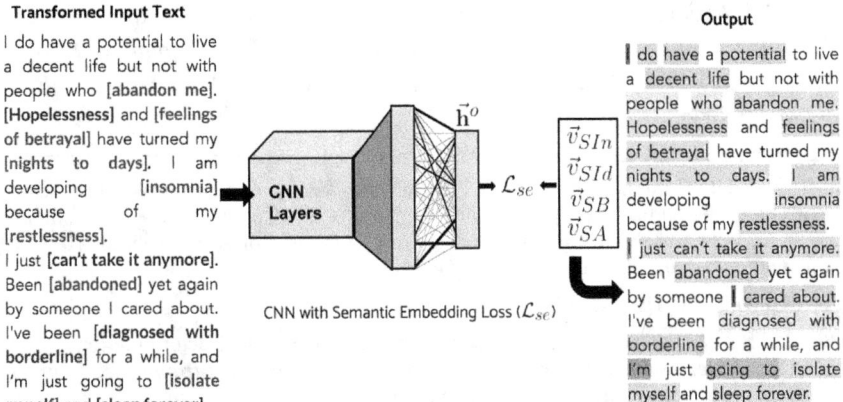

Figure 4.8 The transformed input text is the input to the CNN model that learns by computing semantic embedding loss ($\mathcal{L}_{se}$). This loss is defined because the concept classes have a representation form as vectors. $\vec{v}_{SIn}$ representing the vectorized form of the definition and concepts that describe suicide indication. Likewise, $\vec{v}_{SId}, \vec{v}_{SB}$, and $\vec{v}_{SA}$ represent the vectorized forms of the suicide ideation, suicide behavior, and suicide attempt, respectively. $\mathcal{L}_{se}$ computes the Euclidean distance between the representation of the input text and the vectorized form of the concept classes. The output shows that by identifying concept phrases, the model learns their combined representation, resulting in an increase in their importance scores.

perform a cumulative prediction using the entire posts of the user or consider it length-wise and time-wise. Table 4.4 illustrates time-variant prediction of the AI model with semantic embedding loss, adapted to support temporal learning using long short-term memory (LSTM) networks (Gaur et al., 2021a). The italicized text is phrases that contributed to the representation of each post. These phrases had similarities to the concepts suicide risk severity lexicon (Gaur et al., 2019b). Likewise, Table 4.5 shows the predictions of the CNN model with semantic embedding loss by cumulatively learning over the user's post.

Through concept classes, we were able to explore the time-variant (TvarM) and time-invariant (TinvM) nature of suicide risk. There is a case in the real world where a patient diagnosed with a suicide risk level commits suicide after months of treatment. A known reason is associated with a patient's abrupt discontinuity from clinician meetings because the patient either switches clinicians or conceals the truth regarding suicide risk-related developments between two different suicide risk levels. With the use of concept classes, we were able to reduce suicide risk passively, in longitudinal and cumulative ways.

Table 4.4 *Example posts from a user ordered by timestamp (TS) and prediction from LSTM with semantic embedding loss. These examples illustrate the longitudinal efficiency brought into statistical LSTMs through shallow infusion.*

Post 1 (TS 1): "Homie,... Im 27 yo,... the *job is underpaying* - 700 euros per month... too afraid to search for a new job.... fuck me, I guess?... had these *thoughts of suicide* and these *fears* to *take charge of my life* from like the end of a high school. 10 years same *feelings of dread*, same *thoughts of killing myself*."
Predicted suicide risk severity: Suicide ideation

Post 2 (TS 2): "One day.... sudden realization... I gonna gather determination... *roll over the bridge*. And my parents, or have a nice *heart attack! feel trapped....* nothing gonna change. You will *end up* just like me. I will *roll over the bridge*"
Predicted suicide risk severity: Suicide behavior

Post 3 (TS 3): "No wife, no house, no car, *no decent job*. Every single day... *hating myself* at work.... Im going to *kill myself today* or tomorrow. Probably... middle of next week, but the chances are... *going to sleep forever*"
Predicted suicide risk severity: Suicide behavior

Post 4 (TS 4):) "I dont even go to the *exams*... I might pass those exams... will *not graduate*.... playing some kind of a *Illness joke ...my poor family*."
Predicted suicide risk severity: Uninformative

User-level predicted suicide risk severity: Suicide ideation

Table 4.5 *Example posts from a user (u_i) and prediction from TinvM. The italicized text are phrases that contributed to the representation of the post. These phrases had similarities to the concepts in medical knowledge bases.*

User Post: "Homie,... Im 27 yo,... the job is underpaying - 700 euros per month... too afraid to search for a new job.... fuck me, I guess?... had these *thoughts of suicide* and these *fears* to *take charge of my life* from like the end of a high school. 10 years same feelings of dread, same *thoughts of killing myself*." "One day.... sudden realization... I gonna gather determination... roll over the bridge. And my parents, or have a nice heart attack! *feel trapped....* nothing gonna change. You will end up just like me, *roll over the bridge*" "No wife, no house, no car, no decent job. Every single day... hating myself at work.... Im going to *kill myself today* or tomorrow. Probably... middle of next week, but the chances are... *going to sleep forever*". "I dont even go to the exams... I might pass those exams... will not graduate.... playing some kind of a *Illness joke ...*my poor family."
User-level Predicted Suicide Risk Severity: Suicide Behavior

Edge Cases – Supportive Users: Since we are using social media posts, one unforeseen challenge is the context overlap between users who are actually showing suicidal tendencies and users who are sharing their past experiences. The latter category of users is what we call "supportive users," and considering them as another concept class (e.g., no risk) can minimize the chances of false

4.4 Explainable Data Creation and Use in Suicide Context

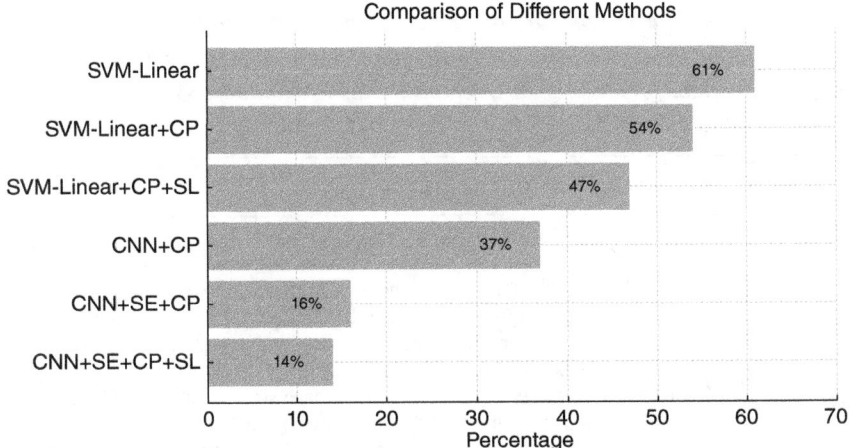

Figure 4.9 Results showing a reduction in Perceived Risk Measure through ablation of Concept Phrase (CP), Supportive Label (SL), and Semantic Embedding Loss (SE).

positives or false negatives. This can be seen by the reduction in perceived risk measures shown in Figure 4.9. In the following, we enumerate the key takeaways from the ROC plots created for each concept class, as shown in Figure 4.10. Qualitative inspection of the AI model with semantic embedding loss can be seen in Table 4.6.

(i) The TinvM model identified 25% more suicide attempters compared to TvarM. Fewer oscillations in suicide risk severity cause TinvM to be less vulnerable to false positives than TvarM. The solid lines in the ROC curves in Figure 4.10 show a significant improvement in recall for TinvM (40% TPR at 20% FPR) compared to TinvM. On the weak side, the TinvM showed a modest performance compared to a random and simple model due to difficulty separating supportive users from suicide attempters, which accounts for many false negatives.

(ii) One level less in suicide risk severity, the suicidal behavior users also did not show a significant change in suicide-related words (e.g., "loaded gun," "alcoholic parents," "slow poisoning," "scars of abuse," etc.) causing the TinvM model to identify 12.5% more users compared to TvarM. Further, TinvM predicted 20% of suicidal behavior users as supportive compared to 42% by TvarM, making it time-sensitive modeling susceptible to ignoring care for users with severe mental illness.

(iii) In contrast to users with suicide behaviors and attempt tendencies, users with ideations show high oscillations in suicidal signals, making TvarM capable of correctly capturing 65% of the users, while 20% of the users were predicted with high severity levels. The false positives are due to

Table 4.6 *Qualitative comparison of TinvM and TvarM models' representative posts from users who are either supportive or showing signs of suicide ideations, behaviors, or attempt. Pred.: Predictions, SW: r/SuicideWatch.*

TinvM Pred.	TvarM Pred.	SW Reddit post or comments
\multicolumn{3}{c}{(a) *true label: Support*}		
Ideation	Support	"Of many experiences of paranoia, anxiety, guilt, forcing me to jump into a death pithole, ... I realized how worthy I m of many things ... would be giving you my experience on this subreddit."
	Support	"I was a loner, facing increase strokes of anxiety and paranoia, that I went on driving myself into a pithole. I was missing one person who I cared the most .... I feel tired and careless towards anything... Guilt of not saving her."
\multicolumn{3}{c}{(b) *true label: Behavior*}		
Behavior	Behavior	"Please listen, I doubt myself and think commiting suicide to escape my situation. Patience, I heard countless times but dying is still a bold decision for me."
	Attempt	"This may be my last appearance. A thoughtful attempt to take my life is what I left with. I have ordered the materials required for my Suicide this evening. I also have a backup supplier in case my primary source sees through my lies and refuses sale."
\multicolumn{3}{c}{(c) *true label: Ideation*}		
Behavior	Ideation	"Thank you. I actually am not on any medication. I was on Zyprexa and then Seroquel for quite a while but stopped taking the anti-psychotics about a year ago."
	Ideation	"Anyway, Ive been thinking about seeing my shrink for a while. Maybe get back on the anti-depressants or something. Thank you though for the thoughtful post. It actually means a lot to me since I dont have many friends."
\multicolumn{3}{c}{(d) *true label: Attempt*}		
Attempt	Ideation	"My dad asked to step out of the house. I feared the ugly look and how disgusting I am looking. I tried therapy, talked to strangers. Everday is a torture for me. I like crafts but feel lack of energy in my self."
	Ideation	"Dark overwhelming sadness and hyperactive behavior is what describes me. I am trying to live my time to see if something changes for me."

4.4 Explainable Data Creation and Use in Suicide Context

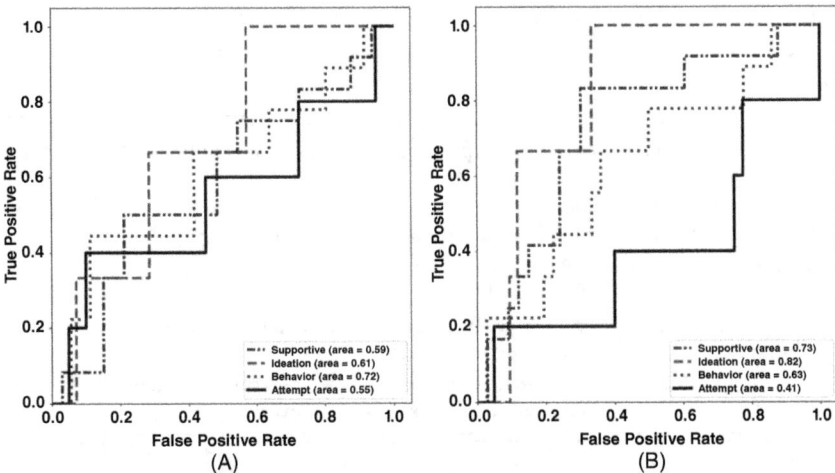

Figure 4.10 The ROC plots illustrate the effectiveness of different approaches in detecting users with varying levels of suicide risk severity based on their behavior over time on the SW subreddit. TvarM (B) excels at identifying supportive and ideation users, while TinvM (A) is effective at detecting behavior and attempt users. A hybrid approach combining TinvM and TvarM is necessary for accurately detecting users exhibiting suicidal behaviors.

overlap in content with behavior and attempt users because users with ideation explain behavior signs in the future tense. For example, in the following sentence, "*For not able to make anything right, getting abused, I would buy a gun and burn my brain*," the user used a future tense to describe his ideations, developing a reasonable probability for false positives. A significant improvement of 26% in AUC for TvarM shows low sensitivity and high specificity compared to TinvM.

(iv) Supportive users on Reddit account for the high levels of false positives in the prediction of suicide assessment because of the substantial overlap in the content with users having ideation, behavior, and attempts. The time-variant methodology discreetly identifies semantic and linguistic markers that separate supportive users from users with a high risk of suicide. The use of the past tense, words like "experience," "sharing," "explain," "been there," "help you," and subordinate conjunctions were consistent in temporal learning; however, their importance is overridden by suicide-related words in TinvM, leading to high levels of false positives. From the ROC curves in Figure 4.10, TvarM is more specific than and less sensitive than TinvM with 20% improvement in AUC and TPR = 1.0 at FPR = 0.38 compared to TPR = 1.0 at FPR = 0.6.

Table 4.7 *Paraphrased posts from potential suicidal Reddit users and their associated suicide risk severity levels are presented. SU: Supportive users or no-risk users.*

Always time for you to write your happy ending .... doesnt need to be spelled out with alcohol and Xanax.... keep an open mind	SU
Ive never really had a regular sleep schedule....no energy to hold a conversation....no focus on study....barely eat and sleep....fluffy puppy dog face	IN
Sometimes I literally cant bear to move....my depression....since I was 14....suffering rest of my life....only Death is reserved for me.	ID
Driving a sharp thing over my nerve. Extreme depression and loneliness.... worthless excuse for a life....used everything from wiring to knife blades	BR
I am going to off myself today...loaded gun to my head..determined....huge disappointment....screwed family life....breaks my heart everyday.	AT

4.5 Description of Explainable Data

For the purpose of annotation, we randomly picked 500 users from a set of 2181 potential suicidal users. In the annotated data, each user, on average, has 31.5 posts within the timeframe of 2005 to 2016. The dataset is publicly available at https://zenodo.org/records/4543776.

The annotated data comprises 22% supportive users, 20% users with some suicidal indication but who cannot be classified as suicidal, 34% users with suicidal ideation, 15% users with suicidal behaviors, and 9% users who have made an attempt (success or failure) to commit suicide. Supportive users constitute 1/5th of the total data volume, and prior studies have ignored them.

Table 4.7 shows posts from Redditors and their associated suicide risk severity level. To identify which mental health subreddits (except SW) contributed most to suicidality, we mapped potential suicidal Redditors to their subreddits (see Figure 4.11).

Evaluation of Annotation

Four practicing clinical psychiatrists were involved in the annotation process. Each expert received a 500-user dataset comprising 15,755 posts. We perform two annotation analyses defined for ordinal labels: (1) a pairwise annotator agreement using Krippendorff metric (α) to identify the annotator with the highest agreement with others; (2) an incremental groupwise annotator agreement to find the robustness of the earlier annotator (Soberón et al., 2013). For groupwise agreement, we denote a set of annotators as G with cardinality

4.5 Description of Explainable Data

Table 4.8 *(Left) Pairwise annotator agreement; (Right) Groupwise annotator agreement. A,B,C,and D are annotators.*

	B	C	D
A	0.79	0.73	0.68
B	–	0.68	0.61
C	–	–	0.65

	B	B&C	B&C&D
A	0.79	0.70	0.69

($|G|$) ranging from 2 to 4. α is calculated as $1 - \left(\frac{D_o(A_j,S)}{D_e}\right)$, where $D_o(A_j,S)$ is observed disagreement, and D_e is expected disagreement. The pairwise annotator agreement is a subset of groupwise, and we formally define it as

$$D_o(A_j, S) = \frac{1}{N.|S|} \sum_{i=1}^{N} \sum_{m \in S} |A_j^i - S_m^i|^2, S \subset G \setminus \{A_j\}, \quad (4.1)$$

$$D_e = \frac{2}{N \cdot |G|(|G|-1)} \sum_{i=1}^{N} \sum_{m,q \in G, m \neq q} |G_m^i - G_q^i|^2, \quad (4.2)$$

where A_j is the annotator having a highest agreement in pairwise α. S is the subset of a group of annotators G that excludes A_j. G_m^i and G_q^i represent the two annotators m and q within the group G^i. i is the index over all the users in the dataset. Results of pairwise and groupwise annotators' agreement are in Table 4.8. We observe a substantial agreement between the annotators.

Extension of the Dataset to Study Longitudinal and Transverse Suicide Risk

To assess which of the suicide risk levels are time-variant and which are time-invariant, we utilize the aforementioned dataset of 500 Reddit users. The created dataset allows time-invariant suicide risk assessment of an individual on Reddit, ignoring time-based ordering of posts. For time-variant suicide risk assessment, the posts needed to be ordered with respect to time and be independently annotated. Following the annotation process highlighted in (Gaur et al., 2019b) using a modified C-SSRS labeling scheme, the same four psychiatrists performed post-level annotation with an inter-rater agreement of 0.88 (Table 4.9 (left)) and a groupwise agreement of 0.76 (Table 4.9 (right)). The annotated dataset of 448 users comprises 1170 supportive (throwaway account: 421, non-throwaway account: 437) and uninformative(throwaway account: 115, non-throwaway account: 197) posts. For throwaway accounts,

Table 4.9 *(Left) Pairwise reliability agreement; (Right) Groupwise reliability agreement. A,B,C,and D are annotators. Inter-rater reliability agreement using Krippendorff metric. A,B,C,and D are mental healthcare providers(MHPs) as annotators. The annotations provided by MHP "B" showed the highest pairwise agreement and were used to measure incremental groupwise agreement for the robustness in the annotation task.*

	B	C	D
A	0.82	0.79	0.80
B	–	0.85	**0.88**
C	–	–	0.83

	A	A&C	A&C&D
B	0.82	0.78	**0.76**

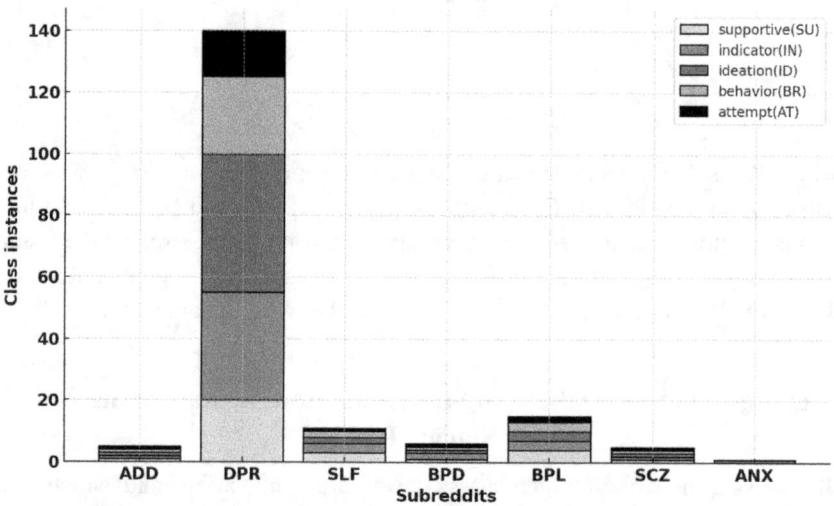

Figure 4.11 Distribution of 500 annotated users in different mental health subreddits. ADD: Addiction, DPR: Depression, SLF: Self Harm, BPD: Borderline Personality Disorder, BPL: Bipolar Disorder, SCZ: Schizophrenia, and ANX: Anxiety.

the dataset had 37 supportive users (S), 63 users with suicide ideation (I), 23 users with suicide behavior (B), and 17 users with past experience with suicide attempts (A). User distribution within non-throwaway accounts is as follows: 85 S users, 115 I users, 76 B users, and 33 A users.

4.6 Explainability as a Metric: Perceived Risk Measure (PRM)

This is defined to better characterize the difficulty in classifying a data item while developing a robust classifier in the face of *difficult to unambiguously annotate* datasets. It captures the intuition that if a data item is difficult for human annotators to classify unambiguously, it is unreasonable to expect a machine algorithm to do it well, or in other words, misclassifications will receive reduced penalties. Conversely, if the human annotators are in strong agreement about the classification of a data item, then we would increase the penalty for any misclassification. This measure captures the biases in the data using disagreement among annotators. Based on this intuition, we define PRM as the ratio of disagreement between the predicted and actual outcomes summed over disagreements between the annotators multiplied by a reduction factor that reduces the penalty if the prediction matches any other annotator. We formally define it as

$$\text{PRM} = \frac{1}{N_T} \sum_{i=1}^{N_T} \left(\frac{1 + \Delta(r_i', r_i^o)}{1 + \sum_{m,q \in G^i, m \neq q} \Delta(G_m^i, G_q^i)} \cdot \frac{\sum_{m \in G^i} I(r_i' = G_m^i)}{|G^i|} \right), \tag{4.3}$$

where the denominator is the disagreement between G_m^i and G_q^i annotators summed over all annotators in a group $\mathbf{G^i}$. $\frac{\sum_{m \in G} I(r_i' = G_m^i)}{|\mathbf{G^i}|}$ is the risk-reducing factor calculated as the ratio of agreement of prediction with any of the annotators over the total number of annotators. In cases where r' disagrees with all the annotators in $\mathbf{G}$, the risk-reducing factor is set to 1.

Influence of Concept Classes on PRM: On analyzing models' behavior using PRM, Figure 4.9 illustrates that concept phrases showed a reduction of 11.4% from SVM-Linear (the baseline) to SVM-Linear working on data with concept phrases. The CNN model provides an opportunity to learn through a new semantic embedding loss method, which reduces the uncertainty in classification. It is noticeable in Figure 4.9 that CNN working on the transformed dataset with concept phrases benefits further if the model learns with semantic embedding loss wherein the predicted outcome is compared with concept classes (↓ 57%). Suppose we extend the set of concept classes by modeling users who show supportive behavior online and characterize it with keywords similar to the ones shown in Table 4.2. In that case, the model better distinguishes between suicide risk classes and no-risk classes. This results in further minimizing risk (↓ 13% from SVM-Linear+CP to SVM-Linear+CP+SL; ↓ 12.5% from CNN+SE+CP to CNN+SE+CP+SL).

92   *Shallow Infusion of Knowledge*

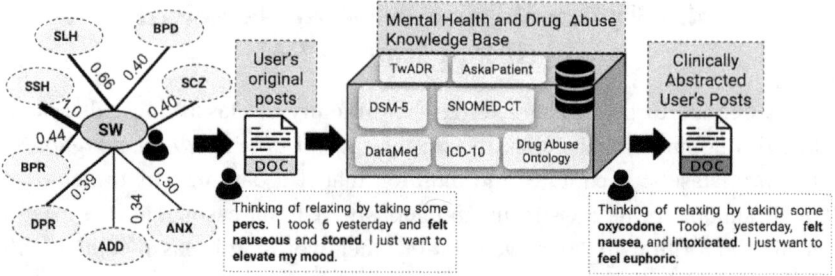

Figure 4.12 The transient posting of potential suicidal users in other subreddits requires careful consideration to predict their suicidality appropriately. Hence, we analyze their content by harnessing their network and bringing their content if it overlaps with other users within r/SuicideWatch (SW). We found Stop Self Harm (SSH) > Self Harm (SLH) > Bipolar (BPR) > Borderline Personality Disorder (BPD) > Schizophrenia (SCZ) > Depression (DPR) > Addiction (ADD) > Anxiety (ANX) to be the most active subreddits for suicidal users. After aggregating their content, we perform MedNorm using Lexicons to generate clinically abstracted content for effective assessment.

4.7 Summary

We presented the notion of *concept classes* as one of the many methods of shallow knowledge infusion to bridge the gap between observational input and expected output. This chapter mainly uses external knowledge to make AI context sensitive and user-level explainable in high-consequence applications. Specifically, we show how the suicide severity lexicon can transform the observational data and outcome labels so that the model's learning behavior can be gauged for uncertainty and context sensitivity. We introduce a perceived risk measure metric to quantify uncertainty in the presence of annotators' agreements and disagreements among themselves and with the model's outcome over a data sample.

There are certain limitations of shallow infusion:

Model Interpretability: The approaches described in this chapter are large concerns with explainable data creation and semantic labels so that a model's learning can be grounded in the domain. We haven't inspected the internal mechanics of the model and methods for knowledge infusion.

Domain Specific: Approaches under shallow knowledge infusion, which are essentially embedding based, are highly domain specific or task specific. Thus, their transferability is a challenge because of the rigid parametric knowledge learned by the model. Further, the concept classes required to make the model explainable and adaptive in a domain can hurt transferability

4.7 Summary

across multiple domains. This is because not all domains have concept classes.

Modeling Uncertainty: We discussed PRM as a metric to assess uncertainty in predictions; however, we did not enforce "uncertainty handling" within the model's learning behavior. We also touched upon the gambler's loss function as a method to model uncertainty, but its statistical nature removes many samples (Sawhney et al., 2022). Thus, we need an approach at the intersection of semantics and statistics.

Cost and User-explainability trade-off: There is a tradeoff between the cost involved in creating explainable data and the need for user-level explainability in the application. Recent datasets have spent thousands of dollars on annotation, but still, the model shows a vast gap between its prediction and human-level performance. So, to employ shallow infusion methods, the tradeoff requires a nudge.

For clarity, we restricted the application of shallow infusion to mental health, particularly suicide risk classification. Figure 4.12 shows an architecture to scale the explainable data creation approach described in this chapter using a wide variety of domain-specific knowledge sources. Shallow knowledge infusion is applicable in various other applications, such as sub-event detection in dynamic tweet streams (Arachie et al., 2020), asking better followup questions in mental health (Gupta et al., 2022), explainable clustering to study patients' discourse in social media and clinical notes (Thiruvalluru et al., 2021), infusing cognitive theories (Purohit et al., 2020), crisis informatics (Senarath et al., 2021), and others.

5
Semi-deep Infusion Learning

Compared to *shallow infusion, semi-deep infusion* concerns opening the blackbox of AI systems using knowledge sources. This chapter will provide a detailed grounding of model interpretability, highlighting the state-of-the-art methods that promise interpretable AI, the limitations of these methods, and how knowledge infusion in AI can help make models interpretable without sacrificing uncertainty while handling context sensitivity, and user-level explainability.

> **Significance**
>
> Semi-deep infusion retains the representational richness of knowledge representation and allows the use of a range of knowledge in the infusion process. It develops strategies to augment knowledge representation with latent representations to make statistical models interpretable. It also introduces methods wherein the model learns to balance between knowledge and data (please refer to Figure 5.1 for architecture of semi-deep infusion).

5.1 Benefits of Semi-deep Infusion

The methods concern innovation in loss functions and optimization functions for knowledge infusion.

Optimization Function: The deep learning model learns by computing the correlation between words or sentences, which is analogous to self-attention matrices (Schlag et al., 2021). This chapter seeks to leverage self-attention to learn a cross-correlation matrix between input words or sentences and concept classes in a knowledge source. The matrix in Figure 5.2C is the target

5.1 Benefits of Semi-deep Infusion

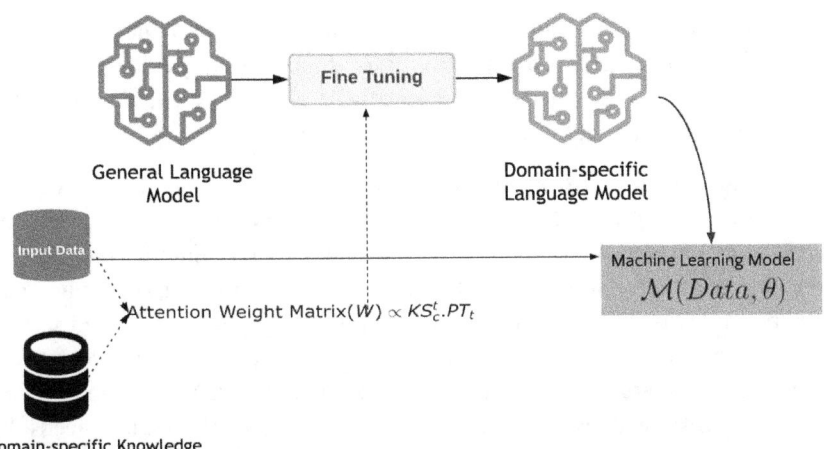

Figure 5.1 A general architecture of semi-deep infusion. KS_c^t: cth concept in a knowledge source (KS) that is similar to a tth topic or phrase extracted from free-form input text. Semi-deep infusion concerns making an AI model that learns a weight matrix that intersects with input observational data and expert knowledge.

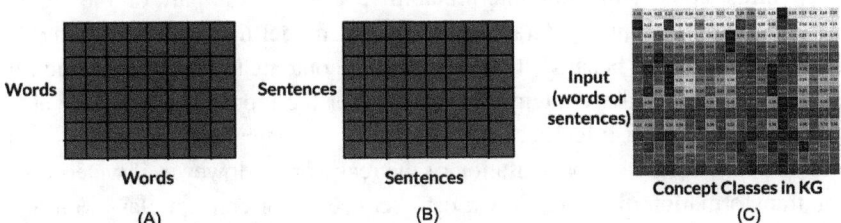

Figure 5.2 Conventional representations include: (A) a word-to-word mapping matrix and (B) a sentence-to-sentence mapping matrix. The desired representations, leveraging a knowledge graph, involve (C) mapping inputs (whether words or sentences) to concept classes within the knowledge graph.

matrix we want the model to learn. The intuition behind this is to achieve interpretability in the model. One can use the matrix, visualize it using T-SNE (T-distributed stochastic neighbor embedding Van der Maaten and Hinton, 2008) or study the mapping scores to confirm whether the model could align words/sentences in the input with correct concept classes. From Chapter 4, concept classes give an understandable representation of the domain (e.g., the mental health domain's concept classes are disorders mentioned in DSM-5(Diagnostic and Statistical Manual of Mental Disorders - 5th edition)), and mapping of independent words/sentences in the input allows us to judge the model's interpretation of the input. We will discuss a semantic encoding- and decoding-based optimization scheme that will enable the model to generate contextual feature vectors irrespective of the domain as long as the knowledge source supports the scheme. Additionally, this process enables zero-shot learning using external knowledge (Gaur et al., 2018).

Constraints-Based Loss Function: Such loss functions became important for summarization in natural language processing. The constraints are placed on picking a sentence with the desired characteristics for summary generation. Integer linear programming, inductive logic programming, planning, and others are areas where constraints-based loss functions have proved useful. In this chapter, we will describe a novel use-case of constraints-based loss functions, which is to enforce a logical order and maintain semantic relations in a conversational agent tasked to fulfill a user's information needs by asking information-seeking questions in a conceptual flow. We will see how such a loss function in conjunction with knowledge graphs can improve the generation quality of a conversational agent and be safe when used in sensitive areas, like mental healthcare.

Model Interpretability: Figure 5.3 illustrates the complete pipeline of semi-deep infusion in achieving interpretability. The top-left part of the figure describes the working of a traditional ML/DL model that ends up giving an incorrect prediction because it fails to capture contextual cues responsible for correct prediction. If we attempt to reason over the model, we won't be able to make meaningful inferences because of the statistical feature vectors that provide an inaccurate representation of the real world. However, if we enforce the transformation of the input text using concepts (or concept classes) in the knowledge graph within the model's functional part (optimization function, loss function, or activation function), then we achieve model interpretability. The resultant feature vector would be dominated by phrases mapped to a set of concepts (or concept classes) in knowledge graphs with high scores. It can be visualized as a heat map as shown in Figure 5.2C. This process yields two benefits: (a) reduction in misclassification because the feature space is less varied and contextual, and (b) reasoning over the model is possible.

User-Level Explainability: A semi-deep knowledge-infused model provides user-level explainability by querying the knowledge graph using the concept (or concept class) and the word or phrase in the input having a maximum correlation with the concept (or concept class). For example, this can be seen in Figure 5.3 (bottom-right), which illustrates the multi-hop traversal in a knowledge graph using words or phrases identified as important by a semi-deep knowledge-infused model. Another benefit from multi-hop or single-hop traversal is retrieving information that might overlap with or inform the target

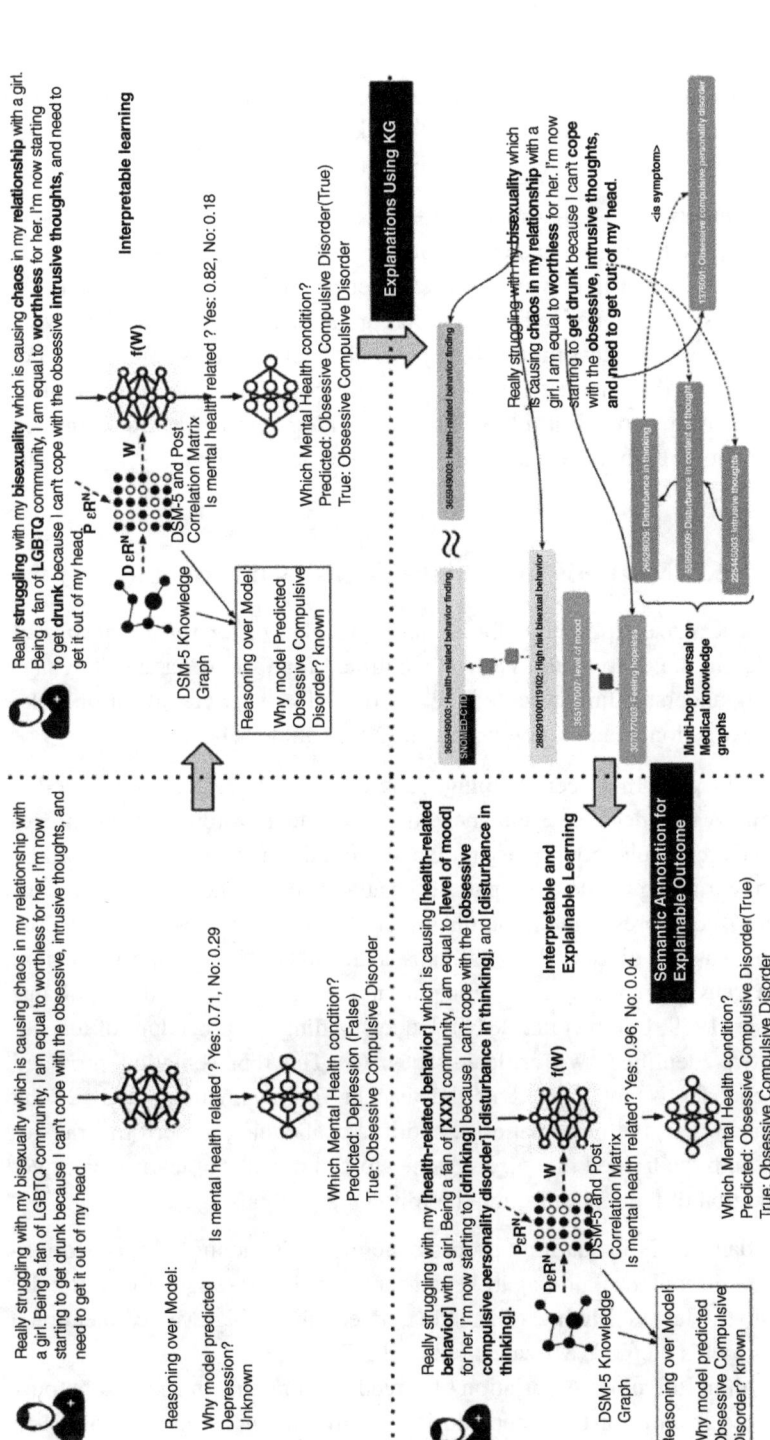

Figure 5.3 An overall pipeline illustrating the benefit of Semi-Deep Infusion in making ML/DL explainable and interpretable.

label the model should predict. As a result, through user-level explainability, one can associate the traversed part of the knowledge graph with the target label to measure the correctness of the model.

Context Sensitivity: A semi-deep knowledge-infused model is context sensitive. It semantically annotates the input context while learning using a cross-correlation matrix between words/sentences in the input and concept (or concept class) in the knowledge graph. It can be defined as either identifying *concept phrases* or substituting them with abstract concepts/categories. For instance, in the bottom-left section of Figure 5.3, the words "bisexuality" and "relationship" are substituted with *health-related behavior*. Such implicit transformation of input text makes the model context sensitive.

5.2 Methods to Achieve Semi-deep Infusion

Here we categorize different methods and approaches of *semi-deep infusion* of knowledge in the deep neural networks outlined for various natural language processing/understanding tasks (e.g., event detection, user classification, relationship extraction, reading comprehension) (see Table 5.1).

Teacher Forcing: In a deep learning framework comprising an autoencoder, the capability of a decoder is enhanced through teacher forcing. In this procedure, the target labels (non-binary rather structured sentences) are fed word by word while training the decoder part of the autoencoder. The encoder provides the vectorized representation of the input the decoder tries to learn. The procedure was first discussed by Williams et al. and has shown improvement in machine translation, entity extraction, and negation detection tasks (Williams and Zipser, 1989; Lamb et al., 2016). Understanding the procedure of teacher forcing, we identified two critical issues: (1) The representation provided by the encoder is not gauged in the teacher forcing method, and (2) the model memorizes the input patterns, and it is challenging to perform transfer learning with the trained model. A teacher-forced model can learn the correct representation of the input through the following methods:

- Redundancy: In this learning process, the model is monitored for information loss through backpropagation and is replenished through replicating the input to the layers. Methods like skip connections or highway connections, follow such a method (Mirzadeh et al., 2022).
- Curriculum Learning: A variation of forced learning that introduces outputs generated from prior time steps during training to encourage the model to correct its own mistakes (Bengio et al., 2009).

Table 5.1 *Existing methods and approaches that are classified based on whether they provide user-level explainable and knowledge-based interpretability. DLMs: deep language models.*

Method	Approach	Explainability	Knowledge-based interpretability
Fine-tuning, Mosbach et al. (2020)	Any DLMs	User-Ex (✗), Sys-Ex (✓)	✗
Teacher forcing, Williams and Zipser (1989)	Any DLMs	User-Ex (✗), Sys-Ex (✓)	✗
Professor forcing, Lamb et al. (2016)	Any DLMs	User-Ex (✗), Sys-Ex (✓)	✗
LSTMs	KG-LSTMs, Annervaz et al. (2018)	User-Ex (✗), Sys-Ex (✓)	✓
	KB-LSTMs, Cai and Wang (2018)	User-Ex (✗), Sys-Ex (✓)	✓
GANs	KG-GANs Chang et al. (2019)	User-Ex (✗), Sys-Ex (✗)	✓
Attention	Self-attention, Shaw et al. (2018); Zhang et al. (2019a)	User-Ex (✗), Sys-Ex (✓)	✓
	KG-guided attention, Yang and Mitchell (2017)	User-Ex (✗), Sys-Ex (✓)	✓
	CAGE, Bose et al. (2021)	User-Ex (✗), Sys-Ex (✓)	✗
	ERNIE v1.0, Zhang et al. (2019d)	User-Ex (✗), Sys-Ex (✓)	✗
	ERNIE v2.0, Sun et al. (2020)	User-Ex (✗), Sys-Ex (✓)	✗
	ERNIE v3.0, Sun et al. (2021)	User-Ex (✗), Sys-Ex (✓)	✗
	Human parity, Xu et al. (n.d.)	User-Ex (✓), Sys-Ex (✓)	✗
	K-BERT, Liu et al. (2020)	User-Ex (✗), Sys-Ex (✓)	✗
	K-Adapter, Wang et al. (2021a)	User-Ex (✗), Sys-Ex (✓)	✗
	SenseBERT, Levine et al. (2020)	User-Ex (✗), Sys-Ex (✓)	✗
	KI-BERT, Faldu et al. (2021a)	User-Ex (✗), Sys-Ex (✓)	✗

continued

Table 5.1 (*cont.*)

Method	Approach	Explainability	Knowledge-based interpretability
Integrated gradients, Sundararajan et al. (2017)	–	User-Ex (✗), Sys-Ex (✓)	✗
Integrated Hessians, Janizek et al. (2021)	–	User-Ex (✗), Sys-Ex (✓)	✗
Autoencoders	Semantic encoding and decoding, Gaur et al. (2018)	User-Ex (✓), Sys-Ex (✓)	✓
Reinforcement learning	Deep reinforcement learning methods with GLUE-based rewards, Dehghani et al. (2021)	User-Ex (✗), Sys-Ex (✓)	✗
Multi-relational reinforcement learning	Relational functional policy gradient methods, Roy et al. (2021)	User-Ex (✓), Sys-Ex (✓)	✓
Reinforcement	Combining search with value iteration, policy gradient, and Monte-Carlo tree search, He et al. (2017)	User-Ex (✗), Sys-Ex (✓)	✓
Search and learning	ISEEQ, Gaur et al. (2021b)	User-Ex (✓), Sys-Ex (✓)	✓
	AlphaGo, Silver et al. (2016)	User-Ex (✗), Sys-Ex (✓)	✗
	PKiL, Roy et al. (2022a)	User-Ex (✓), Sys-Ex (✓)	✓

5.2 Methods to Achieve Semi-deep Infusion

In the teacher-forcing paradigm, during inference, the conditioning context may diverge during training when ground truth labels are given as input. As the encoder acts as a generator and the decoder behaves like a discriminator, their independent functioning affects model performance. Further, knowledge incorporation is on the decoder side, independent of the encoder. Hence, it is challenging to quantify the loss of information incurred on the encoder side. Our proposed approach on deep infusion regulates (1) where in a model the latent weights are wrongly enforced and (2) how to adjust the weights leveraging external human-curated graphical knowledge sources.

Neural Attention Models (NAMs): Attention models highlight important features for pattern recognition/classification based on a hierarchical architecture of the content. The manipulation of attentional focus effectively solves real-world problems involving massive data (Sun et al., 2017). In contrast, some applications demonstrate the limitation of attentional manipulation in problems such as sentiment (mis-)classification and suicide risk (Gaur et al., 2019b), where feature presence is inherently ambiguous, just as in the radicalization problem. For example, in the suicide risk prediction task, references to suicide-related terminology appear in the social media posts of both victims and supportive listeners, and the existing NAMs fail to capture semantic relations between terms to help differentiate a suicidal from a supportive user. To overcome such limitations in a sentiment classification task, Vo et al. (2017) have augmented sentiment scores in the feature set for enhancing the learned representation and modified the loss function to respond to the values of the sentiment score during learning. However, Sheth et al. have pointed out the importance of using domain-specific knowledge, especially in cases where the problem is complex (Sheth et al., 2017). In an empirical study, Bian et al. showed the effectiveness of combining richer semantics from domain knowledge with morphological and syntactic knowledge in the text by modeling knowledge assistance as an auxiliary task that regularizes learning of the main objective in a deep neural network (Bian et al., 2014).

Professor Forcing and Learnable Knowledge Constraints: Professor forcing creates a setup where the encoder (generator) and decoder (discriminator) compete to improve the results, forming an adversarial network. This approach enhances learning by acting as a posterior regularizer and incorporating rich structured domain knowledge. If knowledge constraints are needed in professor forcing, they must be added before learning, not during the process. A recent study by Hu et al. focuses on incorporating knowledge as constraints in an adversarial network by optimizing the Kullback–Leibler (KL) divergence (Hu et al., 2018). However, the study uses knowledge from the dataset, not a curated knowledge graph. While the study monitors KL divergence, it lacks a suitable method for adding relevant knowledge based on the KL score. Our deep infusion paradigm aims to define and include relevant knowledge in deep models to reduce learning time and false alarms.

Graph Neural Network: The graph neural network (GNN) is a type of neural network that directly operates on the graph structure (Scarselli et al., 2008). A typical application of the GNN is node classification. Essentially, every node in the graph is associated with a label, and we want to predict the nodes' labels without ground truth. In this process, the model generates an importance score for each node, and the connection weights form the relationship weights between the nodes. Marino et al. utilize knowledge graphs for multi-label classification of images using a knowledge graph (Marino et al., 2017). In this and a similar study by Wang et al., the GNN framework can be seen as leveraging the structural property of the knowledge graph and quantifying itself using the input data (Wang et al., 2019b). However, the framework is restricted to the labels in the input dataset and their inter-relationships. Further, the GNN does not exploit the structural property and taxonomic relationships of the knowledge graph to identify the relevant knowledge that can be applied to the learning of the neural network. Further, the hidden nodes in a GNN are not abstractions corresponding to stratified knowledge in a knowledge graph; thus, the relationships between the labels are not well contextualized.

Neural Language Models: NLMs are a category of neural networks capable of learning sequential dependencies in a sentence and preserving such information while learning a representation. In particular, LSTM (long short term memory) networks have emerged from the failure of RNNs (recurrent neural networks) in remembering long-term information (Hochreiter and Schmidhuber, 1997). Concerning the loss of contextual information while learning, Cho et al. proposed a context feed-forward LSTM architecture in which the previous layer learns context merged with forgetting and modulation gates of the next layer (Cho et al., 2014). However, if erroneous contextual information is learned in previous layers, it is difficult to correct (Masse et al., 2018), a problem magnified by noisy data and content sparsity (e.g., X, Reddit, blogs). As the inclusion of structured knowledge (e.g., knowledge graphs) in deep learning improves information retrieval (Sheth and Kapanipathi, 2016), prior research has shown the significance of knowledge in the pursuit of improving NLMs, such as in commonsense reasoning (Liu and Singh, 2004). The transformer NLMs, such as BERT (including its variants BioBert and SciBERT) are still data dependent (Devlin et al., 2019). BERT has been utilized in hybrid frameworks such as creating sense embeddings using BabelNet and

NASARI (Scarlini et al., 2020). Liu et al. proposed K-BERT, which enriches the representations by injecting the triples from knowledge graphs into the sentence (Liu et al., 2020). As this incorporation of knowledge for BERT takes place in the form of attention, we consider K-BERT as a semi-deep infusion (Sheth et al., 2019c). Similarly, ERNIE incorporated external knowledge to capture lexical, syntactic, and semantic information, enriching BERT (Zhang et al., 2019d).

Tree LSTMs: Long short-term memory (LSTM) models are sequential models, whereas the sentences in the input corpus follow a grammatical tree structure (dependency or constituency). Hence, it is important to learn the contextual representation of the input following the same tree structure. Tree LSTMs replace the nodes in the graph with LSTMs cells, and a vector representation of the words/phrases is given as input (Tai et al., 2015). This model considers the structural (syntactic) property of the input, but the domain knowledge is ignored. A recent study from Yang et al. utilizes external knowledge bases (e.g., WordNet, NELL) to improve the performance of BiLSTMs by minimizing task-specific feature engineering (Yang and Mitchell, 2017). The study focused on improving entity and event extraction. The knowledge-based LSTM proposed in the study comprises an attention mechanism that acts as a sentinel to guide the model in deciding whether to use external knowledge and adaptively decide the level of abstractness in the information. Though the proposed architecture uses an external knowledge base as a separate component for each LSTM cell, it is uncertain how much of the external knowledge needs to be incorporated and to what level of abstraction the traversing of the knowledge base needs to be done to fulfill the information loss in the learning process.

Knowledge-Based Neural Networks: Yi et al. introduced a knowledge-based, recurrent attention neural network (KB-RANN) to improve model generalization by modifying the attention mechanism using domain knowledge. However, their domain knowledge is statistically derivable from the input data itself and is analogous to merely learning an interpolation function over the existing data. Dugas et al. proposed a modification in the neural network by adopting Lipschitz functions for its activation function (Dugas et al., 2009). Hu et al. proposed a combination of deep neural networks with logic rules by employing a knowledge distillation procedure of transferring the learned tacit knowledge from the larger neural network to the weights of the smaller neural network in data-limited settings (Hinton et al., 2015; Hu et al., 2018).

These studies for incorporating knowledge in a deep learning framework have not explored declarative knowledge structures in the form of knowledge graphs (e.g., DBpedia, BabelNet, UMLS, Wikidata). However, Casteleiro et al. recently showed how the Cardiovascular Disease Ontology (CDO) provided context and reduced ambiguity, improving performance on a synonym detection task (Arguello Casteleiro et al., 2018). Shen et al. employed embeddings of entities in a knowledge graph, derived through Bi-LSTMs, to enhance the efficacy of NAMs (Shen et al., 2018). Sarker et al. presented a conceptual framework for explaining artificial neural networks' classification behavior using background knowledge on the semantic web (Sarker et al., 2017). Makni et al. explained a deep learning approach to learning RDFS (resource description framework schema) rules from both synthetic and real-world semantic web data. They also claimed that their approach improves the noise-tolerance capabilities of RDFS reasoning (Makni and Hendler, 2019). All of the frameworks in the above subsections utilized external knowledge before or after the representation has been generated by NAMs, rather than within the deep neural network, as in our approach (Sheth et al., 2019c). We propose a learning framework that infuses domain knowledge within the latent layers of neural networks for modeling.

Semi-deep Infusion in Mental Health

We introduce a zero-shot unsupervised method to enhance mental health disorder classification, eliminating the need for additional annotated data. We will delve into its application within the mental health context, specifically the classification of users' mental health conditions on Reddit using the DSM-5.

5.3 Semantic Encoding and Decoding Optimization (SEDO)

We explain our semantic weighting algorithm, called SEDO, and its role in the DSM-5 multi-class classification, as illustrated in Figure 5.4.

SEDO is an approach for obtaining a *discriminative weight* matrix between the DSM-5 lexicon and Reddit word embedding space after optimization utilizing the Sylvester equation (Agovic and Banerjee, 2012). Although the Sylvester equation has been used in computer vision within the context of zero-shot learning (Kodirov et al., 2017), its utilization in creating a *discriminative weight* matrix between unstructured(e.g., Reddit) and structured data (DSM-5 lexicon) has not been investigated.

According to Kodirov et al. (2017), **zero-shot learning** is the task of recognizing instances from unseen classes by transferring knowledge learned from seen classes through a shared semantic embedding space.

SEDO requires (1) embedding space for each category in the DSM-5 lexicon and (2) embedding space for each word in the Word2Vec vocabulary

5.3 Semantic Encoding and Decoding Optimization (SEDO)

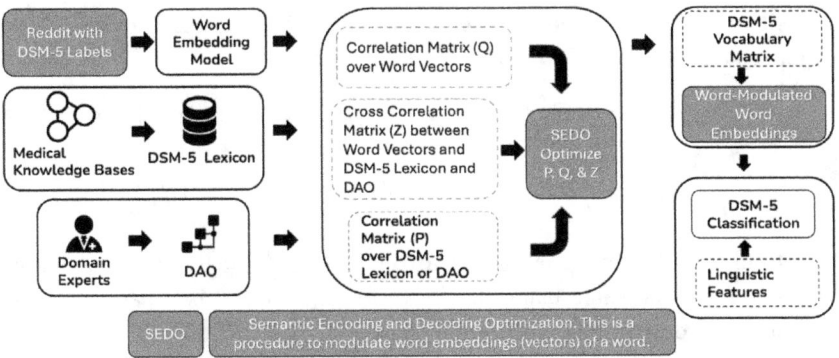

Figure 5.4 Proposed approach to DSM-5 classification using SEDO-based word-vector modulation together with horizontal linguistic features (HLF), vertical linguistic features (VLF), and fine-grained features (FGF). HLF includes *number of definite articles, number of words per Reddit post, first-person pronouns, number of pronouns, and subordinate conjunction*. VLF includes *number of POS tags, similarity between Reddit posts made by a user, intra-subreddit similarity, and inter-subreddit similarity*. FGF includes *sentiment scores, emotion scores, and readability scores*. These **linguistic features** are specific to mental health, for which SEDO was used. Details of these features are presented in Gaur et al. (2018).

created from Reddit data. Creating a link between the embedding spaces of DSM-5 categories and Reddit data requires an energy function that will semantically maximize the number of matches while reducing the number of mismatches. As we utilize the methodology of min-max separability Bagirov and Ugon (2005) that provides precise differentiation between categories, we model our problem as the minimization of the semantic mismatch. SEDO formulates the function $E(\mathbf{R}, \mathbf{D})$ as minimizing the Frobenius norm of the difference between the Reddit and DSM-5 embedding spaces:

$$E(R, D) = \min_W \{||R - W^T D||_F^2 + \delta ||WR - D||_F^2\}, \quad (5.1)$$

where R represents the Reddit word embedding space, D the DSM-5 embedding space, and W the weight matrix to be minimized.

As we are mapping the Reddit (unstructured) embedding space to the DSM-5 (structured) embedding space, we call this process decoding and the one from DSM-5 to Reddit data encoding. In Equation 5.1, the part before the "+" represents the encoding of DSM-5 categories to the Reddit data embedding space, while the part after the "+" represents the decoding of Reddit data to DSM-5 categories. Furthermore, Equation 5.1 is a convex function; hence, we can expect a globally optimal solution. Differentiating Equation 5.1 with respect to W for minimization involves the following properties: $\mathbf{Tr}(\mathbf{W^T D}) = \mathbf{Tr}(\mathbf{D^T W})$ (cyclic property of trace) (McCullough, 2010) and $\mathbf{Tr}(\mathbf{R}) = \mathbf{Tr}(\mathbf{R^T})$.

A positive, symmetric, and quasiseparable (Massei et al., 2018) matrix show such properties. Hence, Equation 5.1 is transformed to

$$E(R, D) = \min_w \{||R^T - D^T W||_F^2 + \delta ||WR - D||_F^2\}, \quad (5.2)$$

$$\frac{d(E(R, D))}{d(W)} = -2(D)(R^T - D^T W) + 2\delta(WR - D)(R^T). \quad (5.3)$$

Setting the LHS of Equation 5.3 to zero, $\frac{d(\mathbf{E}(\mathbf{R},\mathbf{D}))}{d(\mathbf{W})} = \mathbf{0}$, will result in an equation that is solvable using the Sylvester equation. δ is a parameter for regularization during the optimization phase:

$$-DR^T + DD^T W + \delta WRR^T - \delta DR^T = 0, \quad (5.4)$$

$$(DD^T)W + W(\delta RR^T) = (1+\delta)DR^T; 0 < \delta < 1. \quad (5.5)$$

Equation 5.5 represents the Sylvester equation form: $\mathbf{PX} + \mathbf{XQ} = \mathbf{Z}$ where $\mathbf{P}$ is $\mathbf{DD^T}$ and $\mathbf{Q}$ is $\mathbf{RR^T}$, which represents self-correlation between the DSM-5 and Reddit embedding spaces, respectively, and $\mathbf{Z}$, which is $\mathbf{DR^T}$, represents cross-correlation between DSM-5 and Reddit embeddings. The δ controls the knowledge infusion. A decrease in δ increases the infusion of knowledge in DSM-5 (D) to balance the left-hand side of Equation 5.5 with the right-hand side. Figure 5.5 demonstrates the effect of δ.

Figure 5.5 δ controls the amount of knowledge infusion in SEDO for acceptable classification of mental health disorder given a user's profile in the form of posts. Upon 34% knowledge infusion, the model's recommendations matched five MHPs and provided labels 84% of the time (Gaur et al., 2018).

5.3 Semantic Encoding and Decoding Optimization (SEDO)

DSM-5 Embedding Space: Each category in the DSM-5 lexicon is represented by a set of concepts. These concepts can be U, B, or T. We created embeddings of each category of DSM-5 using a trained Word2Vec model on the Reddit corpus. We performed summation over concept vectors to 300 dimensions of embedding for each DSM-5 lexicon. Hence, the DSM-5 embedding space is of dimensions 20 X 300. Self-correlation of the DSM-5 embeddings ($\mathbf{DD^T}$) is performed using Pearson correlation and creates a matrix of dimensions 20 X 20. Similarly, self-correlation of the Reddit word-embedding space ($\mathbf{RR^T}$) creates a matrix of dimensions 12,808 X 12,808. Cross-correlation between $\mathbf{RR^T}$ and $\mathbf{DD^T}$ creates a matrix of dimensions 20 X 12,808.

Evaluation: The assessment of SEDO establishes it as a method that can utilize social media behaviors to estimate psychiatric diagnostic categories in a user. For the sake of simplicity, we replaced random forest's weighting function with SEDO, thus allowing semi-deep infusion. Likewise, with CNNs, we employed a CNN autoencoder with an optimization function defined using SEDO. Figure 5.6 demonstrates a significant reduction in false alarms from

Figure 5.6 Results showing a reduction in false alarms by replacing statistical features with knowledge and its subsequent ablations of various forms of knowledge. CC: Concept Classes; DSM-5: Diagnostic Statistical Manual for Mental Health Disorders, a knowledge source for mental healthcare practitioners; K_{onto}: Drug Abuse Ontology, a domain-specific ontology for substance use and addictive disorders; RF: Random forest; CNN: Convolutional neural network. **Model(Features or Knowledge):** This represents that either statistical features or concepts from knowledge sources are given as input to the model.

SEDO. With knowledge infusion through SEDO, not only was the feature set reduced, but the ML/DL model also became capable of working with different forms of knowledge.

5.4 TDLR: Top (Semantic)-Down (Syntactic) Language Representation

The top-down language representation (TDLR) framework addresses the limitation that while language models capture syntactic patterns effectively, they do not explicitly leverage human-understandable semantics from external knowledge sources. TDLR operates through three sequential steps to infuse semantic knowledge into language models:

(i) **Embedding Knowledge and Data at the Syntactic Level**: Create syntactic representations for both knowledge graphs and input data.
(ii) **Encoding Knowledge Graph Semantics**: Explicitly incorporate desired semantics from knowledge graphs into the self-attention mechanism of language models.
(iii) **Knowledge Graph Semantics-Driven Syntax Processing**: Train the language model using standard procedures while enabling semantics-driven processing of syntactic information.

To illustrate these steps, we use the following example: "The World Wars have had a significant impact on 21st-century technology. The Great War introduced tanks in battle, and the Second World War introduced sophisticated and encrypted radio communications. The resource demands of these technologies propelled the advancement of modern transistor technology."

5.4.1 Embedding Knowledge and Data at the Syntactic Level

The framework begins by creating comprehensive representations that combine both linguistic and semantic information. For each word in the input sentence, we obtain embeddings from multiple sources and concatenate them to form a unified representation.

Specifically, we derive word embeddings using a standard word embedding model (Mikolov et al., 2013) and encode knowledge concepts using knowledge graph embedding techniques. For example, the term "war" in our example sentence receives representations from three sources: word2vec (providing syntactic context), ConceptNet Numberbatch embedding (capturing relational knowledge), and WordNet embedding (encoding lexical relationships). These three representations are concatenated to create the final representation for "war."

This process is repeated for all words, and the individual word representations are then concatenated to form the complete sentence representation. This approach ensures that our representations contain both syntactic information from traditional embedding models and semantic knowledge from structured knowledge sources.

5.4.2 Encoding Knowledge Graph Semantics

While knowledge graphs like ConceptNet contain rich semantic relationships, traditional embedding models often aggregate multiple contexts into single representations, potentially losing specific meanings. For instance, the word "war" appears in various contexts, such as "civil war," "drug war," and "proxy war." Although these concepts exist within the same graphical neighborhood in ConceptNet, standard embedding approaches may not capture the specific meaning of "world war."

To address this limitation, we construct knowledge graph masks that encode particular contexts of interest, representing the semantics that will guide the processing of syntactic input and knowledge representations.

Using our running example, consider the words "great" (denoted as e_{11}) and "war" (denoted as e_{12}) as shown in Figure 5.7. Without explicit semantic encoding, a language model trained on data where "war" frequently appears with "civil," "drug," and "proxy" contexts might not adequately capture the "great war" meaning. To ensure proper attention, we set the corresponding entry in our knowledge mask to 1 for the "great"–"war" relationship while masking other entries with 0.

This masking approach explicitly encodes the semantic context, ensuring that "war" applies to "great" and vice versa. After constructing the knowledge semantics mask, we apply it to obtain a semantics-encoded self-attention matrix.

Bayesian Perspective

The application of knowledge masks can be understood through a Bayesian framework. While the masked self-attention matrix loses its strict probabilistic interpretation (row and column sums no longer equal 1), we can view this as a natural application of Bayes' rule:

$$P(A|K, \text{data}) = \frac{P(\text{data}|A) \cdot P(A|K)}{Z}, \tag{5.6}$$

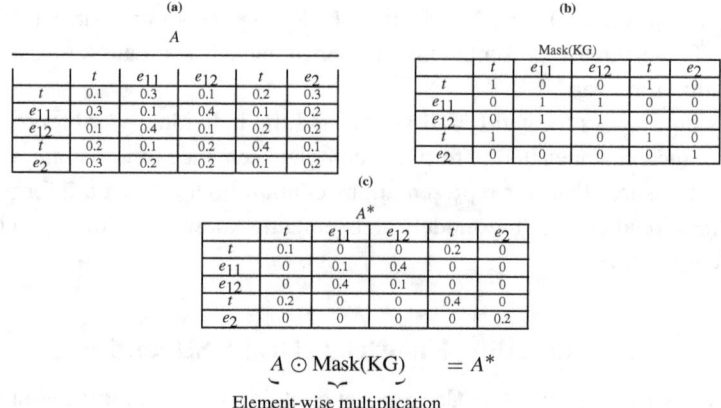

Figure 5.7 Shows how TDLR applies knowledge graph masks to the self-attention mechanism. (a) Self-attention matrix, (b) Knowledge semantics encoder mask, (c) Knowledge semantics encoded self-attention matrix. The original self-attention matrix is element-wise multiplied with the knowledge graph mask to produce the knowledge-encoded self-attention matrix. Notation: e_{11} and e_{12} are constituent bigram words from the knowledge graph (e.g., "great" and "war" from "great war"), and e_2 is a unigram word from the knowledge graph (e.g., "war").

where A represents self-attention, K represents knowledge, and Z is the normalizing constant. The knowledge mask encodes a prior probability distribution (unnormalized), while the self-attention matrix encodes data-likelihood probabilities. The mask application thus corresponds to a likelihood-prior product proportional to the posterior probability.

5.4.3 Knowledge Graph Semantics-Driven Syntax Processing

With the desired knowledge semantics encoded in the self-attention matrix, we proceed with standard forward-backward training passes in the language model as illustrated in Figure 5.8. The framework's flexibility allows for expanding the scope of knowledge semantics by adding multiple attention masks at different layers, enabling more sophisticated top-down semantic processing.

5.4.4 Example of TDLR

We recall that, fundamentally, an LM learns distributed representations of text fragments tending to the "normal" distribution contained in the training corpora. That is, for a fragment $x_i \in \mathbf{T}(\mathbf{x})$, where $\mathbf{x}$ is a whole text segment (e.g., an input sentence), $\mathbf{T}(\mathbf{x})$ is the set of fragments that $\mathbf{x}$ is decomposed into (e.g., words or phrases), and $x_i \in \mathbf{T}(\mathbf{x})$. A LM induces a probability

5.4 TDLR: Top (Semantic)-Down (Syntactic) Language Representation

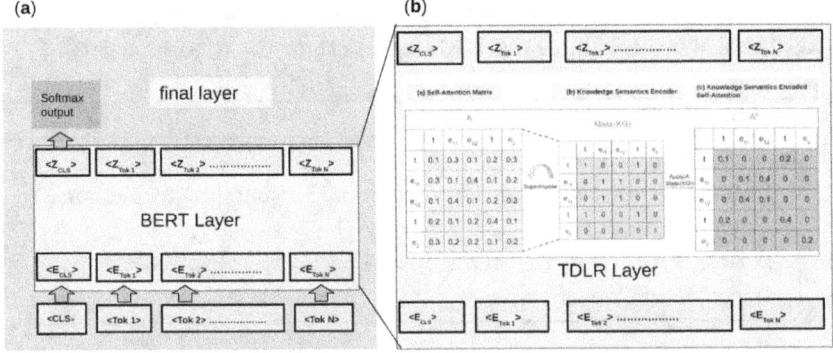

Figure 5.8 (a) A Transformer LM layer – BERT Layer; (b) shows the BERT layer with the knowledge semantics-encoded self-attention computation.

distribution $\mathbf{P(x)_{LM}}$ that assigns a probability of co-occurrence between each pair $(\mathbf{x_i}, \mathbf{x_j}) \in \mathbf{T(x)}$. Thus, we might interpret the infusion of common-sense knowledge from a set of KGs denoted by **KG** as computing the posterior probabilities of co-occurrence between each pair $(\mathbf{x_i}, \mathbf{x_j}) \in \mathbf{T(x)}$, where $\mathbf{P(x)_{LM}}$ is the data likelihood (induced from the training corpora), and each KG in the set **KG** assigns a prior probability of co-occurrence between each pair $(\mathbf{x_i}, \mathbf{x_j}) \in \mathbf{T(x)}$. To capture this behavior, we define attention masks for each $KG \in \mathbf{KG}$ as:

$$Mask(KG) = \left\{ \begin{array}{ll} 1, & \text{if } cossim(z_{\mathbf{x_i}}^{KG}, z_{\mathbf{x_j}}^{KG}) \geq \theta \\ 0, & \text{if } cossim(z_{\mathbf{x_i}}^{KG}, z_{\mathbf{x_j}}^{KG}) < \theta \end{array} \right\}, \quad (5.7)$$

where *cossim* denotes cosine similarity, θ denotes an acceptable similarity threshold capturing presence or absence of the pair $(\mathbf{x_i}, \mathbf{x_j})$ in the same graphical neighborhood, and $z_{\mathbf{x_i}}^{KG}$ and $z_{\mathbf{x_j}}^{KG}$ denote KG embedding representation of $\mathbf{x_i}$ $\mathbf{x_j}$, respectively.

We define an operation $Apply(A, Mask(KG))$ as:

$$Apply(A, Mask(KG)) = A^* \quad (5.8)$$

to obtain the transformed attention matrix A^*, where $A = \frac{QK^T}{\sqrt{d_k}}$, where all terms mean the same as in Vaswani et al. (2017a). Since $A = \frac{QK^T}{\sqrt{d_k}}$ can be interpreted as the likelihood probability of co-occurrence between each pair $(\mathbf{x_i}, \mathbf{x_j}) \in \mathbf{T(x)}$ learned from the data, application of the mask has the effect of inducing a posterior potential function (*not yet a distribution, as it is unnormalized*) that is proportional to the posterior distribution. The normalization constant neither has an analytical form nor is computationally tractable to compute. Therefore, we leave the posterior potential intact for further computation. The **TDLR** learning framework for an input **x** using an LM of choice involves three repeated steps, as shown in Algorithm 5.1.

Algorithm 5.1: TDLR
---
1 **for** *each $KG \in$* **KG do**
2   Execute *forward-backward pass* for input **x** using the LM of choice
3   Compute: $Mask(KG)$
4   Perform: $Apply(A, Mask(KG)) = A^*$
5   Repeat until Convergence

5.5 Ensemble Learning

The NLP community is growing by developing new LMs and datasets catering to a wide range of domains, including general-purpose (Wang et al., 2019a) and domain-specific (Xiao et al., 2021). Concurrently, there is an emergent unease about the ability of these new LMs to emulate the performance derived from human annotations in such datasets, which is typically assessed via inter-annotator agreement scores, for instance, Cohen's kappa (κ). However, performance assessment predominantly hinges on conventional metrics, which do not adequately reflect the reliability of LMs (Liang et al., 2022). Nonetheless, every new LM to achieve acceptance within the NLP community has to demonstrate effectiveness in understanding natural language through simple and effective GLUE benchmarks (Wang et al., 2018b). GLUE benchmarks have established prominence in NLP because of high annotator agreement, thus defining a high threshold for new LMs to break through. Interestingly, since the inception of the GLUE benchmarks, no prior work has emphasized the use of an annotation agreement as a proxy measure for reliability in LMs. As a countermeasure, researchers have been increasingly allocating resources to advance LMs. Still, this approach has inadvertently compromised the model's ability to surpass simpler LMs or human performance, especially when the models are trained on datasets aggregated via crowdsourcing. We present an ensembling of LMs, taking inspiration from *Cohen's kappa*, which states that if an annotation agrees with two annotators, it is sufficiently reliable (McHugh, 2012). Ensembling LMs presents a synergistic collaboration among simpler models, culminating in a system that is more resilient and effective than individual models. We emphasize that the ensemble's collective strength enables it to compensate for the inadequacies of an individual model under specific conditions and bolster its decision-making confidence. Their performance needs to be assessed for the ensembling of LMs to be functional and reliable.

In this section, we aim to conceptualize, devise, and evaluate the ensembling of LMs by addressing three research questions. **RQ1:** Can we employ κ to evaluate the reliability of LMs trained on GLUE benchmarks? **RQ2:** Considering the language models as annotators, is it possible to enhance κ by strategically ensembling LMs? **RQ3:** Given that crowd workers frequently resort to external knowledge to augment the quality of annotations, can the infusion of external knowledge during ensembling improve overall reliability? To answer these questions, we make two contributions. (a) We propose three ensembling techniques: aggregation ensemble (AE), interpolation ensemble (IE), and knowledge ensemble (KE), where KE is characterized as a knowledge-guided ensembling method that integrates LMs with knowledge from ConceptNet (Speer et al., 2017) and Wikipedia (Yamada et al., 2020) through reinforcement learning. (b) We evaluate the reliability of the ensemble models using κ across nine GLUE tasks.

5.5.1 Ensemble Methods

Let $\mathcal{D} = \{S^{(i)}, y^{(i)} : i = 1, \ldots, m\}$ be the given dataset, where $S^{(i)}$ is the text sentence and $y^{(i)}$ is the observed class for the ith sentence. $y^{(i)}$ can take values from 1 to c. Let $\mathcal{M} = \{M_\ell : \ell = 1, \ldots, n\}$ be a collection of n LMs. $S^{(i)}$ is transformed to a feature vector as

$$Z_{S_i}^{M_l} = \text{SBERT}(S_i, M_l), \tag{5.9}$$

where SBERT represents the sentence transformer of Reimers and Gurevych (2019). We take the embeddings generated using SBERT because it outperforms individual BERT embeddings (Devlin et al., 2019).

1. Aggregation Ensemble (AE): For each $Z_{S_i}^{M_l}$, the estimated probability of it belonging to a certain category k using model M_ℓ is denoted as $\text{Prob}_\ell\left(y_i = k | Z_{S_i}^{M_l}\right)$. Given weights $\alpha_1, \ldots, \alpha_n$ such that $\alpha_\ell \in [0, 1]$ and $\sum_{\ell=1}^{n} \alpha_\ell = 1$, the probabilities are combined as $\sum_{\ell=1}^{n} \alpha_\ell \cdot \text{Prob}_\ell(y_i = k | x_i)$, as shown in Figure 5.9A. The predicted class is obtained as

$$\hat{y}_i(\alpha) = \arg\max_k \left[\sum_{\ell=1}^{n} \alpha_\ell \cdot \text{Prob}_\ell\left(y(i) = k | Z_{S_i}^{M_l}\right) \right]. \tag{5.10}$$

The loss is defined as a function of α as $L(\alpha) = \sum_{i=1}^{m} \mathbb{I}[y_i \neq \hat{y}_i(\alpha)]$. The objective is to minimize the loss for better performance. IE uses a statistical approach of averaging the predicted probabilities.

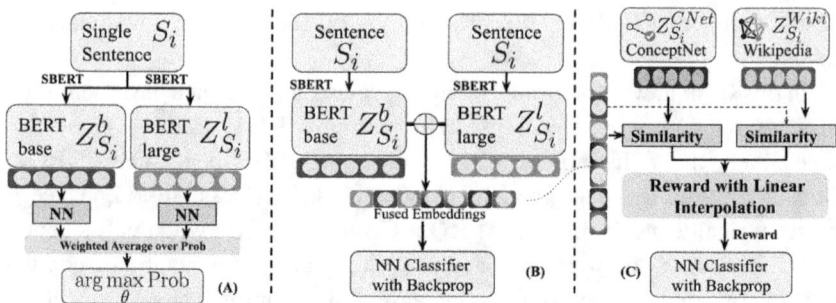

Figure 5.9 Illustration of the three proposed ensemble methods on two variants of the BERT model: (A) A weighted average-driven aggregation ensemble (AE) method, (B) an embedding fused interpolation ensemble (SE) method, and (C) A knowledge-infused ensemble (KE) method that uses external knowledge from Wikipedia and the ConceptNet knowledge graph.

2. Interpolation Ensemble (IE): We define a new feature vector $Z_{S_i}^{\prime M_l}$ as $Z_{S_i}^{\prime M_l} = Z_{S_i}^{M_1} \oplus Z_{S_i}^{M_2} \oplus \cdots \oplus Z_{S_i}^{M_l}$, which represents the fused embeddings obtained from M_l models as described in Figure 5.9B. These fused embeddings leverage the combined strength of individual models. These embeddings are then fed into a neural network (NN). The objective is to minimize the binary cross-entropy loss function defined by L as

$$L = -\frac{1}{N} \sum_{i=1}^{N} y_i \log(\hat{y}_i) + (1 - y_i) \log(1 - \hat{y}_i),$$

where N is the total number of samples, y_i represents the ground truth label for the ith sample, and $\hat{y}_i$ represents the predicted probability output by the NN for the ith sample.

3. Knowledge Ensemble (KE): We incorporate external knowledge using two general-purpose knowledge graphs, ConceptNet (CNet) and Wikipedia(Wiki) (as shown in Figure 5.9C), to improve the IE ensemble model. This addition helps in the contextual understanding of LMs. For each S_i, we denote the embeddings from CNet and Wiki as $Z_{S_i}^{CNet}$ and $Z_{S_i}^{Wiki}$, respectively. Using the fused embeddings $Z_{S_i}^{\prime M_l}$, the reward of the RL policy is computed as

$$R(\beta)_i := \beta \operatorname{CS}\left(Z_{S_i}^{\text{CNet}}, Z_{S_i}^{\prime M_l}\right) + (1 - \beta) \operatorname{CS}\left(Z_{S_i}^{Wiki}, Z_{S_i}^{\prime M_l}\right), \quad (5.11)$$

5.5 Ensemble Learning

Table 5.2 *A comparison of AE, IE, and KE Ensemble.*

Functionalities	AE	IE	KE
Knowledge graph	✗	✗	✓
Fused BERT embeddings	✗	✓	✓
Weighted average	✓	✗	✓
Reinforcement learning	✗	✗	✓

where $\beta_i \in [0, 1]$ for $i = 1, 2, \ldots, n$, $\sum_{\ell=1}^{n} \beta_\ell = 1$, and CS denotes cosine similarity. The loss is defined as a function of β as

$$L(\beta) = \frac{1}{N} \sum_{i=1}^{N} \left(y_i \log(\hat{y}_i) + (1 - y_i) \log(1 - \hat{y}_i) \right) \cdot R(\beta)_i, \qquad (5.12)$$

where N is the total number of samples, y_i is the ground truth label, and $\hat{y}_i$ represents the predicted probability output by the NN for the ith sample. The objective is to minimize the loss by maximizing $R(\beta)$. Table 5.2 describes the different components of the three ensemble methods.

5.5.2 Experiments

Datasets: In our study, we employ nine benchmark classification datasets from the GLUE suite. The datasets are categorized INTO three categories of NLU: (a) Single Sentence (b) Inference (c) Similarity and Paraphrase. These include: (1) **CoLA** (Warstadt et al., 2019) for assessing grammatical correctness in English sentences, (2) **SST-2** (Socher et al., 2013) for evaluating movie review sentiments, (3) **MRPC** (Madnani et al., 2012) for determining whether two sentences are paraphrases, (4) **STS-B** (Conneau and Kiela, 2018) for rating the similarity between two sentences, modified in our study to binary labels, (5) **QQP** (Sharma et al., 2019) for comparing similarity in pairs of Quora questions, (6) **MNLI** (Williams et al., 2018b) addresses tasks involving pairs of sentences (Hypothesis and Premise) with labels entailment, contradiction, and neutral. (7) **RTE** (Dagan et al., 2005) aids in determining textual entailment within sentence pairs, (8) **QNLI** (Wang et al., 2018b) involves a context sentence and a question to determine if the answer lies within the context, and (9) **WNLI** (Levesque et al., 2012; Wang et al., 2018b) handles sentence coreference by discerning if an ambiguous pronoun refers to a designated target word. Datasets 1 and 2 consist of individual sentences, while Datasets 3–5 involve tasks related to measuring similarity and paraphrasing between a pair of sentences. Datasets 6–9 consist of natural language inference tasks. The ensemble methods (i.e., AE, IE, and KE) take sentence S_i as input. However, datasets 3–7 comprise a pair of sentences – S_{i1} and S_{i2}. We process these sentences into a single input $S_i = S_{i1} \oplus S_{i2}$.

Metrics: We assess our ensemble techniques using accuracy and the interrater reliability metric, Cohen's kappa (κ). While accuracy is standard in GLUE tasks, κ focuses more on reliability, which is a better measure of prediction uncertainty, specifically considering the chance behavior of LMs (McHugh, 2012). κ is defined as $\kappa = \frac{p_o - p_e}{1 - p_e}$. In our study, we denote p_e as the ground truth and p_o as the class predicted by the model M. Since κ considers outcomes from two annotators, we consider the outcomes of p_o and p_e as our two annotators. According to McHugh (2012), interrater reliability is directly proportional to κ. Consequently, κ is directly proportional to the reliability of language models. This provides an answer to our first research question **RQ1:** *Can we employ κ to evaluate the reliability of LMs trained on GLUE benchmarks?*

Experimental Setup: We employ the BERT model to present our findings, as BERT is a streamlined model composed of a few million parameters, making it relatively simple and efficient. We consider the two variants of the BERT model, that is, BERT$_{base}$ and BERT$_{large}$, as our ***baselines***. We first compute $Z_{S_i}^{\text{BERT}_{base}}$ and $Z_{S_i}^{\text{BERT}_{large}}$ using Equation (5.9), and then train using an NN classifier.

Reduced Embeddings: To ensure an equitable comparison during the assessment of LMs, we employ principal component analysis on $Z^{M_l} S_i$. The embedding dimensions of BERT$_{base}$ and BERT$_{large}$ are originally 768 and 1024, respectively, but we transform them into 100 dimensions each. AE uses the condensed dimensions of BERT$_{base}$ and BERT$_{large}$. Initially, SE combines the embeddings of BERT$_{base}$ and BERT$_{large}$, resulting in an embedding dimension of 768 + 1024 = 1792, which is then further reduced to 100 dimensions. KE utilizes this fused embedding in conjunction with Wikipedia and ConceptNet embeddings. The embeddings from Wikipedia and ConceptNet initially have 500 and 300 dimensions, respectively, but are also reduced to 100 dimensions.

Parameter Settings: To ensure reproducibility, we partitioned the datasets using a random seed of 42. For AE, IE, and KE, an NN was trained with a batch size of eight. Each model was tested on five different partitions (10%, 15%, 20%, 25%, and 30%). The accuracy and κ values presented in Table 5.3 represent the average performance across these partitions. We utilized the AdamW optimizer for batch normalization (Loshchilov and Hutter, 2019). We maintained a small learning rate of $2e^{-5}$ and weight decay of $1e^{-6}$ to ensure a stable model-building process.

Table 5.3 *Performance metrics – the accuracy and Cohen's kappa (κ) for individual BERT models are compared with three variations of ensembles: AE and IE – both without incorporating knowledge and KE, which includes knowledge. These models were assessed on the GLUE benchmark. The reported accuracy and κ values are averages derived from five different data splits, as elaborated in Section 3.3. In every instance, the ensembles outperformed the baseline models. Among them, KE has the **best** results in four tasks and impressively attains the second best performance in the remaining five tasks.*

Dataset	BERT_{base}		BERT_{large}		AE		IE		KE	
	Accuracy	κ	Accuracy	κ	Accuracy	κ	Accuracy	κ	Accuracy	κ
CoLA	62.0	0.18	64.5	0.24	67.34	0.28	**79.04**	**0.42**	72.88	0.38
MRPC	56.0	0.11	52.3	0.02	59.08	0.16	**73.08**	**0.35**	64.4	0.28
QNLI	67.33	0.34	66.00	0.32	**68.62**	**0.37**	67.34	0.35	67.65	0.35
MNLI	48.64	0.22	49.47	**0.25**	50.52	**0.25**	49.9	**0.25**	50.0	**0.25**
QQP	73.92	0.47	73.35	0.46	74.80	0.49	75.12	0.50	**75.66**	**0.51**
SST-2	85.16	0.70	86.62	0.72	87.5	0.74	87.9	**0.75**	**88.12**	**0.75**
RTE	52.45	0.04	48.86	0.00	51.76	0.03	55.5	**0.12**	**56.03**	**0.12**
STS-B	63.01	0.25	62.31	0.24	66.86	0.33	**76.6**	**0.52**	73.52	0.47
WNLI	49.93	0.006	51.72	0.03	50.06	0.002	33.5	0.1	**57.07**	**0.14**
GLUE avg	62.04	0.26	61.68	0.25	64.06	0.29	66.44	0.37	**67.25**	0.36

5.5.3 Results

This section describes the experimental outcomes and addresses **RQ2** and **RQ3**.

Overall Performance: As outlined in Table 5.3, we showcase accuracy and κ of our ensemble techniques across nine GLUE datasets. The results clearly indicate that: (1) Our ensemble models uniformly outperform the baselines (individual BERT models) across all nine GLUE tasks. (2) AE is the highest-performing model in two GLUE tasks. (3) IE claims the lead in three GLUE tasks. (4) KE excels in four GLUE tasks, the highest among the baselines and other ensembles (AE and IE). KE's average accuracy surpasses BERT$_{base}$ by 5.21% and BERT$_{large}$ by 5.57% in the GLUE tasks, solidifying its position as the best-achieving model compared to the baselines (see Table 5.3).

RQ2: *Considering the language models as annotators, is it possible to enhance κ by strategically ensembling LMs?* Table 5.3 reveals that all ensemble models experience an increase in κ score. It shows that IE achieves the highest κ, with KE also making significant strides. On average, there is a 0.12 increment in the κ score compared to the baselines. Individual models often exhibit uncertainty in their predictions (Zhou et al., 2023). However, by strategically combining these models (i.e., AE, IE, and KE), their weaknesses are counterbalanced by focusing on confident outcomes, elevating the κ values.

RQ3: *Given that crowd workers frequently resort to external knowledge to augment the quality of annotations, can the infusion of external knowledge during ensembling improve overall reliability?* KE incorporates knowledge from external sources. Table 5.3 demonstrates that KE achieves the best accuracy results compared to baselines and also sees an average increase in κ score by 0.11, indicating that adding knowledge boosts the model's overall reliability. However, it's noteworthy that IE records a marginally superior κ score than KE. *This observation emphasizes that while increased accuracy often implies enhanced reliability, this isn't necessarily a universal truth.*

Ablation Study: This section entails ablation for the ensembles. **(1) AE –** We compare $\alpha \in [0, 1]$ as shown in Figure 5.10. $\alpha = 1$ shows the performance of BERT$_{base}$, whereas $\alpha = 0$ represents BERT$_{large}$ as described in Equation 5.10. For single-sentence tasks, it is observed that the model performs best when there is an equal mixture ($\alpha \in [4, 5]$) from both BERT variants In similarity tasks, for QQP and STS-B datasets, the model's performance is influenced by BERT$_{base}$ since $\alpha = 0.6$, whereas for MRPC it is more influenced by BERT$_{large}$ as $\alpha = 0.4$. In inference tasks, for QNLI and RTE datasets, the model's performance is influenced by BERT$_{base}$ since $\alpha = 0.6$ whereas, for WNLI, it is influenced by BERT$_{large}$ as $\alpha = 0.4$. MNLI performs

5.5 Ensemble Learning

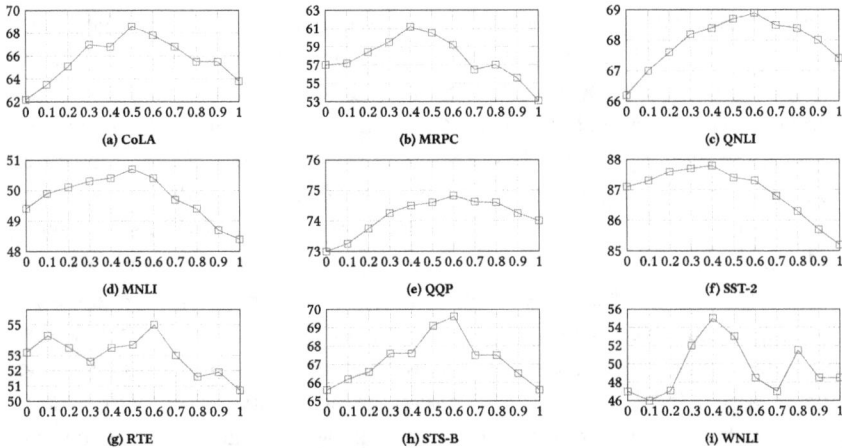

Figure 5.10 Ablation Study of AE for GLUE datasets. The x-axis represents $\alpha \in [0, 1]$. The y-axis represents the accuracy. $\alpha = 0$ denotes the performance of $\text{BERT}_{\text{large}}$ and $\alpha = 1$ denotes the performance of $\text{BERT}_{\text{base}}$.

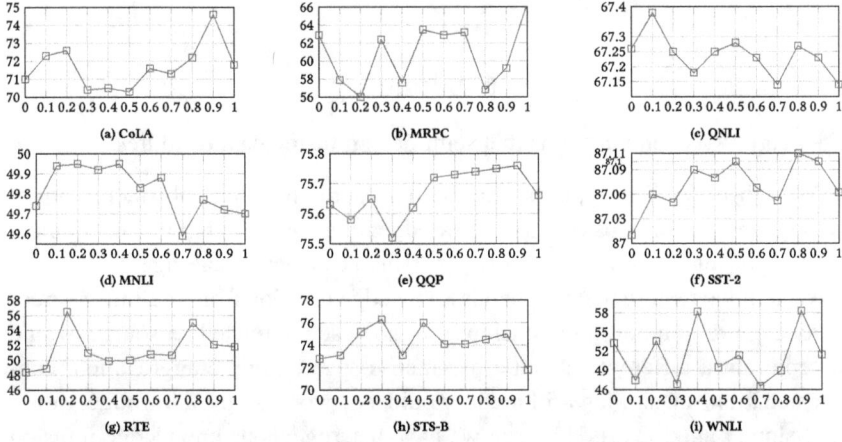

Figure 5.11 Ablation Study of KE for GLUE datasets. The x-axis represents $\beta \in [0, 1]$. The y-axis represents the accuracy. $\alpha = 0$ represents the knowledge infusion from CNet and $\alpha = 1$ represents the knowledge infusion from Wiki.

best when there is an equal contribution from both BERT variants. These results show that a model trained on lesser parameters ($\text{BERT}_{\text{base}}$) sometimes tends to perform better than a model trained on more parameters ($\text{BERT}_{\text{large}}$). **(2) IE** – No ablation study exists for IE because this ensemble consisted of a fusion of embeddings. **(3) KE** – Figure 5.11 displays the outcomes of KE for

β. β regulates the extent of knowledge integration from the knowledge graphs (Section 2). From Equation 5.11, $\beta = 1$ denotes the knowledge infusion of Wiki, whereas $\beta = 0$ considers the knowledge infusion from CNet. For single-sentence tasks, the model is highly influenced by adding knowledge from Wiki because the model gives the best performance at $\beta = 0.9$. There is an equal mixture ($\beta \in [4,5]$) from BERT$_{base}$ and BERT$_{large}$. In similarity tasks, it is found that for QQP and MRPC, the model's performance is highly influenced by Wiki because $\beta = 0.9$ and 1.0, respectively. In the case of STS-B, the model performs better when there is an equal mixture of both knowledge graphs. It performs equally well with CNet at $\beta = 0.3$. For inference tasks, it can be seen that for all four datasets, the model's performance is highly influenced by CNet since $\beta \in [0.1, 0.4]$. For WNLI, the model performs equally well with Wiki as $\beta = 0.9$. The results for single sentence tasks and similarity tasks show that adding Wiki is crucial in improving the model. However, its addition yields a contrasting outcome for inference tasks, where CNet significantly enhances model improvement. This is because inference tasks rely on common-sense knowledge, effectively captured by CNet (Wang et al., 2019c).

5.6 Summary

There are two open questions that semi-deep infusion cannot address:

- What if the human input has an implicit hierarchical and abstract relationship, and one-shot parametric knowledge infusion at the input is insufficient in capturing and leveraging it for explainable decision making?
- What if we require heterogeneous knowledge infusion from multiple sources to capture implicit relationships? If so, each knowledge source would represent a different semantic parametric space. Simple aggregation, concatenation, or similar arithmetic would not work as they introduce noise (Faldu et al., 2021a). How can we have heterogeneous knowledge infusion in a stratified manner, and how can we control the amount of heterogeneous knowledge infusion?

6
Deep Knowledge-Infused Learning

We define the third category of knowledge infusion, that is, deep infusion of knowledge, as a paradigm that couples the latent representation learned by deep neural networks with KGs exploiting the semantic relationships between entities. This chapter will provide a theoretical background to achieve deep infusion, as illustrated in Figures 6.1 and 6.2. We aim to:

- quantify the information loss;
- identify the relevant knowledge at an appropriate level of abstraction;
- appropriately combine identified concepts in KGs with a latent data representation.

> **Significance**
>
> Deep infusion supports the stronger weaving of different forms of knowledge at different levels of abstraction that typically map to different layers in a deep neural network architecture.

Recent research that is in line with the general theme of KiL leverages what is called parametric knowledge (Lewis et al., 2020). For instance, Dai et al. define a term called "knowledge neuron" within the deep neural network, which is described as a hidden node that represents the knowledge infused at the input (Dai et al., 2022). Further, we argue that there is a subtle difference between the terms *knowledge infusion* and *knowledge injection* (Yang et al., 2021). Methods under the latter theme are similar to *shallow infusion and semi-deep infusion* categories, whereas *knowledge infusion* is about the use of stratified representation of knowledge representing different levels of abstraction that would be merged at various layers of a deep neural network and not just at the input. As we understand the levels of abstraction represented by different layers in a deep neural network, we can look to

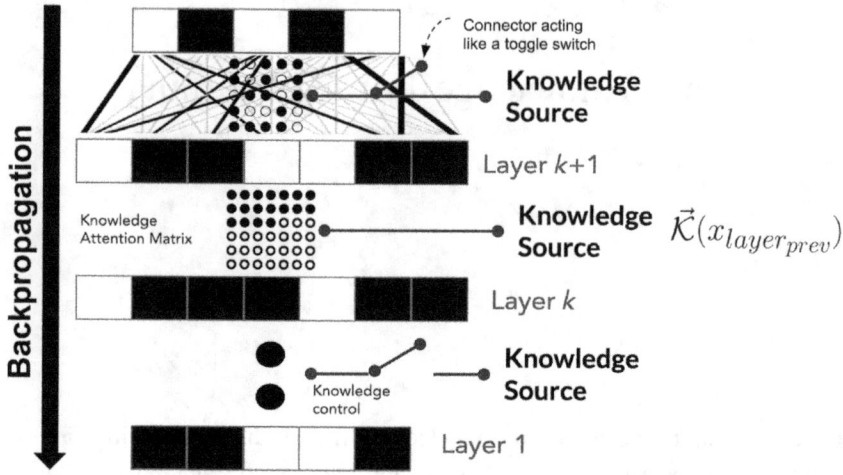

Figure 6.1 An illustration of deep knowledge infusion. The procedure provides an improvement over existing DL architectures by including (a) layer-wise knowledge augmentation ($\mathcal{K}$) and (b) monitoring correct infusion through a knowledge attention matrix. The latter component controls the information flow between the previous layer ($x_{layer_{prev}}$) and the next layer ($x_{layer_{next}}$).

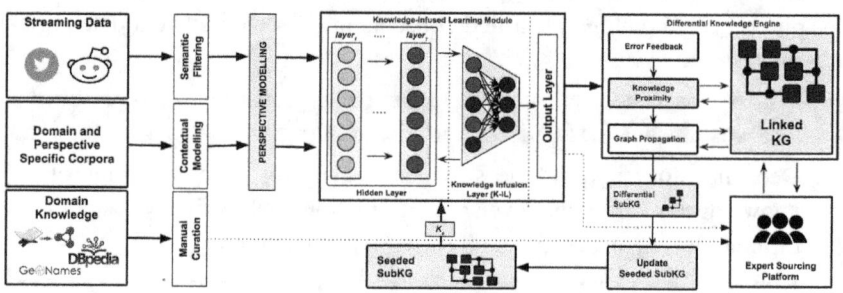

Figure 6.2 Overall architecture: Contextual representations of data are generated, and domain knowledge amplifies the significance of important concepts missed in the learning model. Classification error determines the need for updating a seeded subKG with more relevant knowledge, resulting in a seeded subKG that is more refined and informative to our model.

transfer knowledge that aligns with the corresponding layer in the layer-wise learning process in DL. We argue that deep infusion within the latent layers of neural networks will boost the performance of neural networks as an integral component of AI models deployed in applications. A deep infusion of such structured knowledge will reveal patterns missed by shallow and semi-deep infusions because of sparse feature occurrence, ambiguity, and noise. At the same time, deep infusion would retain the explainability, interpretability, and uncertainty handling aspect of ML/DL. In this chapter, we will lay down the theoretical positioning of deep infusion and discuss novel technological components required for knowledge infusion in the current most widely used neural language models.

6.1 Deep Infusion Module

In a neural network, each layer creates a hidden input representation. The network comprises an input layer, hidden layers, and an output layer, with external information integrated both before and after the output. However, the infusion of knowledge has not been explored in the layers after the input, within the hidden layer, or before the output. Our approach involves infusing knowledge into the neural network while the hidden representation is transferred across layers, including the hidden layers. This infusion of knowledge during the learning phase raises important research questions: (i) *Knowledge-aware loss function (K-LF):* How do we determine when and how to infuse knowledge during learning between layers, and how do we measure the extent of knowledge integration? (ii) *Knowledge modulation function (K-MF):* How can we combine latent representations with knowledge representations, and how do we effectively propagate knowledge through the learned representation?

Configurations of neural networks can be designed in various ways depending on the problem. As our aim is to infuse knowledge within the neural network, such operation can take place (i) before the output layer (e.g., SoftMax), or (ii) between hidden layers (e.g., reinforcing the gates of an NLM layer, modulating the hidden states of NLM layers, knowledge-driven NLM dropout, and recurrent dropout between layers). To illustrate (i), we describe our initial approach to neural language models that fuses knowledge before the output layer.

Following the Figure 6.2, in the subsequent subsections, we explain (a) the creation of knowledge representations (e.g., knowledge embeddings, K_e), (b) how the knowledge infusion layer is responsible for the two proposed functions. In these subsections, we provide an initial approach that, we believe, will shed light on reliable and robust solutions following more research and rigorous experimentation.

K_e – **Knowledge Embedding Creation:** We generate a representation of knowledge in the seeded subKG as embedding vectors. We create an embedding of each concept and their relations in the seeded subKG using the perspective models (R, I, V), and merge these embeddings through the proximity

Algorithm 6.1: Routine for infusion of knowledge in NLMs
---
1 Data: $NLM_{type}, \#Epochs, \#Iterations, K_e$
2 Output: $\vec{M_T}$
3 **for** $ne=1$ to $\#Epochs$ **do**
4 $\quad$ Compute $\vec{h_T}, \vec{h_{T-1}} \leftarrow$ TrainingNLM($NLM_{Type}, \#Iterations$)
5 $\quad$ **while** $(D_{KL}(\vec{h_{T-1}}||\vec{K_e}) - D_{KL}(\vec{h_T}||\vec{K_e}) > \epsilon)$ **do**
6 $\quad\quad$ $\triangleright$ ϵ: acceptance threshold
7 $\quad\quad$ Compute $h_T \leftarrow \sigma(W_{hk} * (\vec{h_T} \oplus \vec{K_e}) + b_{hk})$ $\quad\triangleright$ σ: sigmoid activation
8 $\quad\quad$ Compute $W^{hk} \leftarrow W^{hk} - \eta_k \nabla(\text{K-LF})$ $\quad\triangleright$ η: learning rate
9 $\quad\quad$ Compute $\vec{M_T} \leftarrow \vec{h_T} \odot W^{hk}$
10 **return:** $\vec{M_T}$

of their concepts and relations in the graph. Unlike traditional approaches that compute the representation of each concept in the KGs by simply taking the average of embedding vectors of concepts, we leverage the existing structural information of the graph. This procedure is formally defined as follows:

$$K_e = \sum_{ij}[C_i, C_j] \bigotimes D_{ij}, \tag{6.1}$$

where K_e is the representation of the concepts enriched by the relationships in the seeded KG, (C_i, C_j) is the relevant pair of concepts in the seeded KG, $\mathbf{D_{ij}}$ is the distance measure (e.g., least common subsumer; Baader et al. (2007)) between the two concepts C_i and C_j. We will further examine novel methods building upon our initial approach above as well as existing tools that include TRANS-E (Bordes et al., 2013), TRANS-H (Wang et al., 2014), and HOLE (Nickel et al., 2016) for the creation of embeddings from KGs.

Knowledge Infusion Layer: In a many-to-one NLM (Shivakumar et al., 2018) network with **T** hidden layers, the **T**th layer contains the learned representation before the output layer. The NLM model's output layer (e.g., SoftMax) will estimate the error to be back-propagated. As discussed above, knowledge infusion can occur between hidden layers or just before the output layer. We will explore techniques for both scenarios. This subsection explains the knowledge infusion layer (*Ki-layer*), which takes place just before the output layer.

Algorithm 6.1 takes the type of NLM, number of epochs, iterations, and the seeded knowledge graph embedding K_e as input and returns a knowledge-infused representation of the hidden state $\mathbf{M_T}$. In line 4, the infusion of

6.1 Deep Infusion Module

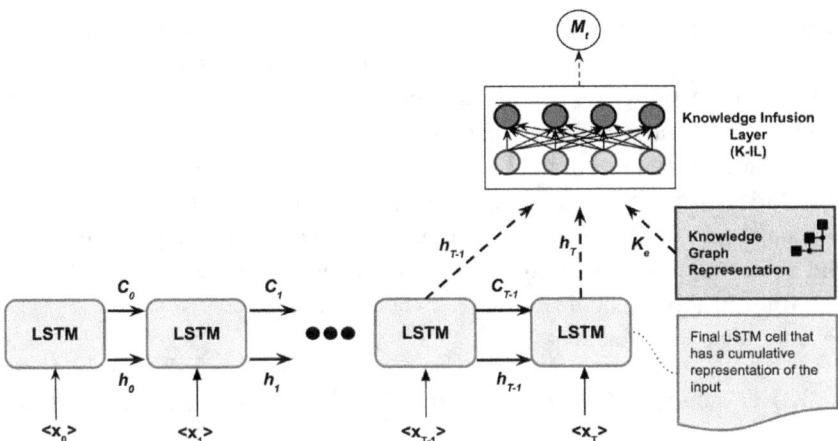

Figure 6.3 Inner mechanism of the knowledge infusion layer in an LSTM network.

knowledge takes place after each epoch without obstructing the learning of the vanilla NLM model, which is explained in lines 5–10. Within the knowledge infusion process (lines 7–9), we optimize the loss function in Equation 6.2 with a convergence condition defined as the reduction in the difference between the $\mathbf{D}_{KL}$ of h_T and h_{T-1} in the presence of K_e. Considering the vanilla structure of an NLM, $\mathbf{M_T}$, the fully connected layer is utilized for classification.

To illustrate an initial approach in Figure 6.3, we use LSTMs as NLMs in our neural network. *Ki-layer* functions add a layer before the output layer of our proposed neural network architecture. This layer takes the latent vector (h_{T-1}) of the penultimate layer, the latent vector of the last hidden layer (h_T), and the knowledge embedding (K_e) as input. In this layer, we define two functions that will be critical for merging the latent vectors from the hidden layers and the knowledge embedding vector from the KG. Note that the dimensions of these vectors are the same because they are created from the same models (e.g., contextual models), which makes the merge operation of those vectors possible and valid.

Knowledge-Aware Loss Function (K-LF): In neural networks, hidden layers may de-emphasize important patterns due to the sparsity of certain features during learning, which causes information loss. In some cases, such patterns may not even appear in the data. However, such relations or patterns may be defined in KGs with even more relevant knowledge. We call this information gap between the learned representation of the data and knowledge representation *differential knowledge*. Information loss in a learning process is relative to the distribution that suffered the loss. Hence, we propose a measure to determine the differential knowledge and guide the degree of knowledge infusion in learning. As our initial approach to this measure, we developed a two-state regularized loss function by utilizing Kullback–Leibler (KL) divergence. Our choice of the KL divergence measure is largely influenced by the Markov assumptions made in language modeling and has been highlighted in Longworth (2010). The K-LF measure estimates the divergence between the hidden representations $(\mathbf{h_{T-1}}; \mathbf{h_T})$ and knowledge representation (K_e), to determine the differential knowledge to be infused.

Formally, we define it as

$$\mathbf{K\text{-}LF} = \min \mathbf{D}_{KL}(\vec{h_T}||\vec{K_e}); \text{ s.t. } \mathbf{D}_{KL}(\vec{h_T}||\vec{K_e}) < \mathbf{D}_{KL}(\vec{h_{T-1}}||\vec{K_e}), \quad (6.2)$$

where $\mathbf{h_{T-1}}$ is an input for convergence constraint.

We minimize the *relative entropy* for information loss to maximize the information gain from the knowledge representation (e.g., K_e). We will compute differential knowledge ($\nabla \mathbf{K\text{-}LF}$) through such an optimization approach; thus, the computed differential knowledge will also determine the degree of knowledge to be infused in the *Ki-layer*. $\nabla \mathbf{K\text{-}LF}$ will be computed as embedding vectors, and the dimensions from K_e will be preserved.

Knowledge Modulation Function (K-MF): We need to merge the differential knowledge representation with the learned representation. However, such an operation cannot be done arbitrarily. We explain an initial approach for the K-MF to modulate the learned weight matrix of the neural network with the hidden vector through an appropriate operation (e.g., Hadamard pointwise multiplication). This operation at the **T**th layer can be formulated as follows.

The equation for $W^{hk} = W^{hk} - \eta_k * \nabla \mathbf{K\text{-}LF}$, where W^{hk} is the learned weight matrix infusing knowledge, η_k is learning momentum (Sutskever et al., 2013), and $\nabla \mathbf{K\text{-}LF}$ is differential knowledge. The weight matrix (W^{hk}) is computed through the learning epochs utilizing the differential knowledge embedding ($\nabla \mathbf{K\text{-}LF}$). Then we merge W^{hk} with the hidden vector $\mathbf{h_T}$ through the K-MF. Considering that we use Hadamard pointwise multiplication as our initial approach, we formally define the output $\mathbf{M_T}$ of K-MF as

$$\vec{M_T} = \vec{h_T} \odot W^{hk}, \quad (6.3)$$

where M_T is a knowledge-modulated representation, h_T is the hidden vector, and Whk is the learned weight matrix infusing knowledge. Further investigations of techniques for K-MF constitutes a central topic for the research community.

6.2 Differential Knowledge Engine

In deep neural networks, each epoch generates a back-propagated error until the model reaches a saddle point in the local minima, and the error is reduced in each epoch. The error indicates the difference between probabilities of actual and predicted labels, and such differences can be used to enrich the seeded subKG in our proposed knowledge-infused deep learning framework.

In this section, we discuss the sub-knowledge graph operations that are based on the difference between the learned representation of our knowledge-infused model (M_T) and the representation of the relevant sub-knowledge graph from the R-KG, which we call a differential sub-knowledge graph. We define a *knowledge proximation function* to generate the *differential sub-knowledge graph*, and *update seeded subKG* to insert the differential sub-knowledge graph into the seeded subKG.

Knowledge Proximity: Upon arriving at the learned representation from the knowledge-infused learning model, we query the KG to retrieve information related to the respective data point. In this particular step, finding the optimal proximity between the concept and its related concepts is important. For example, from the "South Carolina" concept, we may traverse the surrounding concepts with varying hops (empirically decided). Finding the optimal number of hops each direction from the concept is still an open research question. As we find the optimal proximity of a particular concept in the KG, we propagate the KG based on the proximity starting from the concept in question.

Differential SubKG: Once we obtain the subKG from the graph propagation, we create a differential subKG that will reflect the difference in knowledge from the seeded subKG. For this procedure, we plan to carry out research formulating the problem using variational autoencoders to extract such sub-KGs, which we call the *differential subKG* ($\mathbf{D_{kg}}$); we believe it will provide the missing information in the seeded-KG.

Update Function: The differential subKG generated due to minimizing knowledge proximation is considered an input factual graph to the update procedure. As a result, the procedure dynamically evolves the seeded subKG with missing information from the differential subKG. We plan to utilize the *Lyapunov stability theorem* (Liu et al., 2014) and *zero shot learning* to update the seeded-KG using D_{kg}. D_{kg} and the seeded-KG represent two knowledge structures requiring transferring the knowledge from one structure to another (Hamaguchi et al., 2017). We define it as generating semantic mapping weights that encode and decode the two semantic spaces. We plan to utilize the Lyapunov stability constraint and Sylvester optimization approach: Given two semantic spaces belonging to a domain D, we tend to attain an equilibrium position defined as

$$||S_{kg} - W * D_{kg}||_F = \alpha * ||W * S_{kg} - D_{kg}||_F, \qquad (6.4)$$

where $||.||_F$ represents the Frobenius norm, and α is a proportionality constant belong to $\mathbb{R}$. Equation 6.4 reflects the Lyapunov stability theorem, and to achieve such a stable state, we define our optimization function as follows:

$$\mathcal{L} \equiv \min(||S_{kg} - WD_{kg}||_F - \alpha * ||WS_{kg} - D_{kg}||_F), \alpha > 0, W \in \mathbb{R} \, X \, \mathbb{R}. \quad (6.5)$$

Equation 6.5 is solvable using Sylvester optimization, and its derivation is defined in a recent study (Gaur et al., 2018).

Let us investigate how **deep infusion** can happen in deep neural language models that are gaining popularity in various application areas like computational social science, conversational artificial intelligence, multi-agent systems, and others.

Deep Infusion in Neural Language Models Neural language models (NLMs) are designed to gather parametric knowledge after pre-training over a large-scale natural language corpus. This parametric memory is utilized in downstream applications in the following forms: (a) fine-tuning of NLMs on domain-specific tasks (Wolf et al., 2019a), (b) augmenting the NLMs with external knowledge at the input layer and tuning it end-to-end (Faldu et al., 2021a), (c) leveraging a pre-trained NLM and passing the generated representation through the knowledge-aware generative model for contextualized representation learning (Zhang et al., 2019d), and (d) probing (edge and structured) the NLMs at each layer for checking the accuracy of parametric memory (Tenney et al., 2018; Arps et al., 2022). These state-of-the-art methods are consistent with our definition of shallow infusion and semi-deep infusion but can be improved toward deep infusion. We provide a positive direction for deep infusion as answers to the following questions:

When Does an NLM Require Non-parametric Knowledge? An intermediate representation between two hidden layers, denoted by h_{out}^{l-1} and h_{in}^{l}, is often studied as the model attention in current transformer models. These representations can be used to inquire about the model's learning behavior. A distributional drift (also known as variational inference) between a *gold representation* (also known as knowledge representation) and h_{output}^{l-1} can be considered as a signal for non-parametric knowledge infusion. Of the various methods to measure variational inference, KL divergence is the most widely used (Group, 2023).

How To Infuse Non-parametric Knowledge Seamlessly? Let us consider the most widely used multi-lingual KG, ConceptNet, created by Speer et al. (2017), as the source for *knowledge representation*. Since it would be tedious and error-prone to measure the variational inference between every node in ConceptNet and h_{out}^{l-1}, we construct a subKG of ConceptNet (S^{kg}) by computing exact and cosine similarity between input and concepts in S^{kg}. Now, we use h_{out}^{l-1} to traverse each node in S^{kg} by computing a distance score measured using KL divergence. We formally define it as

$$KL(h_{out}^{l-1}, S^{kg}) = \left\{ h_{out}^{l-1} \log \frac{h_{out}^{l-1}}{S_i^{kg}} \right\}_i ; \text{where} \quad i \in \text{Nodes in } S^{kg}.$$

$KL(h_{out}^{l-1}, S^{kg})$ yields a set of nodes with their KL divergence scores. The nodes with scores above a threshold (δ, often defined empirically) are recorded as visited nodes, and their representations are used in infusion. The infusion of knowledge happens following Equation 6.3, which can be formalized as

$$\tilde{h}_{out}^{l-1} = h_{out}^{l-1} \odot S_0^{kg} \odot S_1^{kg} \odot S_2^{kg} \cdots \odot S_{j-1}^{kg},$$

where $j \in \{S^{kg}\}_i$ is the set of nodes with acceptable KL scores. After the infusion of external knowledge, the model needs to be regularized, which is done by updating the back-propagation update of weights and dropout strategies. We leverage the dual form of deep neural network for updating the neurons' weights. The dual form focuses on attention, thus informing us about the importance of each neural connection between two hidden layers. The dropout is made deterministic by thresholding over the attention matrix created between $\tilde{h}_{out}^{l-1}$ and h_{in}^{l}, as described by Faldu et al. (2021a). To appreciate the importance of the dual form of the neural network, I would direct the reader to a recent study by Irie et al. (2022).

Due to deep knowledge infusion, the model's predicted outcome would differ from gold truth by some margins. However, this would show the model's thoughtful prediction (or classification), where the end-user would notice the likelihood of predicting other labels or generations (if it is a language generation model) that seem similar to ground truth. This would happen because, in deep infusion, the model would be trained end-to-end with marginalized loss. This can be seen as beam search optimization (Wiseman and Rush, 2016), defined as

$$P(X) = \sum_y P(X, Y = y) = \sum_y P(X|Y = y) * P(Y = y),$$

where X is input, and Y is a class label or a natural language generation from the deep neural network. This loss would enable the model to preserve the input semantics ($P(X)$) by generating its probabilities from the model's prediction or generation.

How to Leverage External Knowledge's Inherent Abstraction in Enhancing It? The reason for having S^{kg} is to allow the hierarchical concepts in KG to be infused into the upper layers of the deep neural network. Maintaining a set of visited nodes, starting from the lowermost layers, supports traversing higher-order concepts in a KG when representations from this and above are generated through non-linear activation. This structuring of knowledge infusion is based on the assumption that (a) non-linear activation allows the neural network to exploit all possible syntactic combinations of input tokens, which might yield a representation of concepts in the KG (not present in the input), and (b) these combinations represent a closed world that can be studied with input and semantically related concepts in S^{kg} (Acunzo et al., 2022).

Such a training methodology (a) introduces explainability intrinsically into the model's behavior; (b) the trace over the S_{kg} created during the model's training provides a clue to the model's interpretations of the input; (c) the deterministic nature of dropout, governed by knowledge-infused attention matrices, enables uncertainty handling; and (d) the context capture is always the centric component in knowledge infusion, which in deep infusion is achieved by computing variational inference between the latent, hidden representation and knowledge nodes in the KG.

6.3 Summary

Combining deep learning and knowledge graphs in a hybrid neural–symbolic learning framework will further enhance performance and accelerate the convergence of the learning processes. Specifically, the impact of this improvement in susceptible domains such as health and social science will be significant in terms of their implications for real-world deployment. Furthermore, adopting tools that automate tasks that require knowledge and intelligence and are traditionally done by humans will improve with the help of this framework that marries deep learning and knowledge graph techniques. Specifically, we envision that the infusion of knowledge described in this framework will capture information for the corresponding domain in finer granularity of abstraction. We believe that this approach will provide reliable solutions to the problems faced in deep learning. Hence, in real-world applications, resolving these issues with knowledge graphs and deep learning in a hybrid neurosymbolic framework will significantly contribute to fulfilling AI's promise (Faldu et al., 2021b).

7
Process Knowledge-Infused Learning

Process knowledge is an ordered set of information that maps to evidence-based guidelines or categories of conceptual understanding to experts in a domain. For instance, The American Academy of Family Physicians (AAFP) develops clinical practice guidelines (CPGs) that serve as a framework for clinical decisions and supporting best practices. CPGs allow systematic assessment to optimize patient care. In addition, the US Departments of Agriculture (USDA) and Health and Human Services (HHS) develop dietary guidelines for Americans that serve as a recommendation for meeting nutrient needs, promoting health, and preventing disease. An AI system adapted to process knowledge can handle uncertainty in prediction, and the predicted outcomes are safe and user-level explainable. Further, an AI system can consider process knowledge as meta-information to capture the sequential context necessary for carrying out a structured conversation. Also, it allows the developer of the AI system to probe its internal decision making using application-specific guidelines or specifications that inform the synchrony between the end-user's thought process and the model's functioning.

This unique form of knowledge differs from other forms of knowledge in the following manner: (a) Knowledge graph: This is structured but not ordered; knowledge graphs can support context capture but cannot enforce conceptual flow (Gaur et al., 2021c). (b) Semantic lexicon: This is a flattened form of knowledge graph that makes deep language models contextsensitive and adds constraints but cannot enforce conceptual flow (Libben, 2021). (c) Ontologies: These are curated schematic forms of knowledge graphs with classes, instances, and constraints. Thus, ontologies can provide stricter control over context and constraints. If defined, an ontology can enforce order in question generation using deep language models (Stasaski and Hearst, 2017).

Process knowledge is represented differently for different applications. For instance, to assess the severity of suicide risk, the process knowledge used is

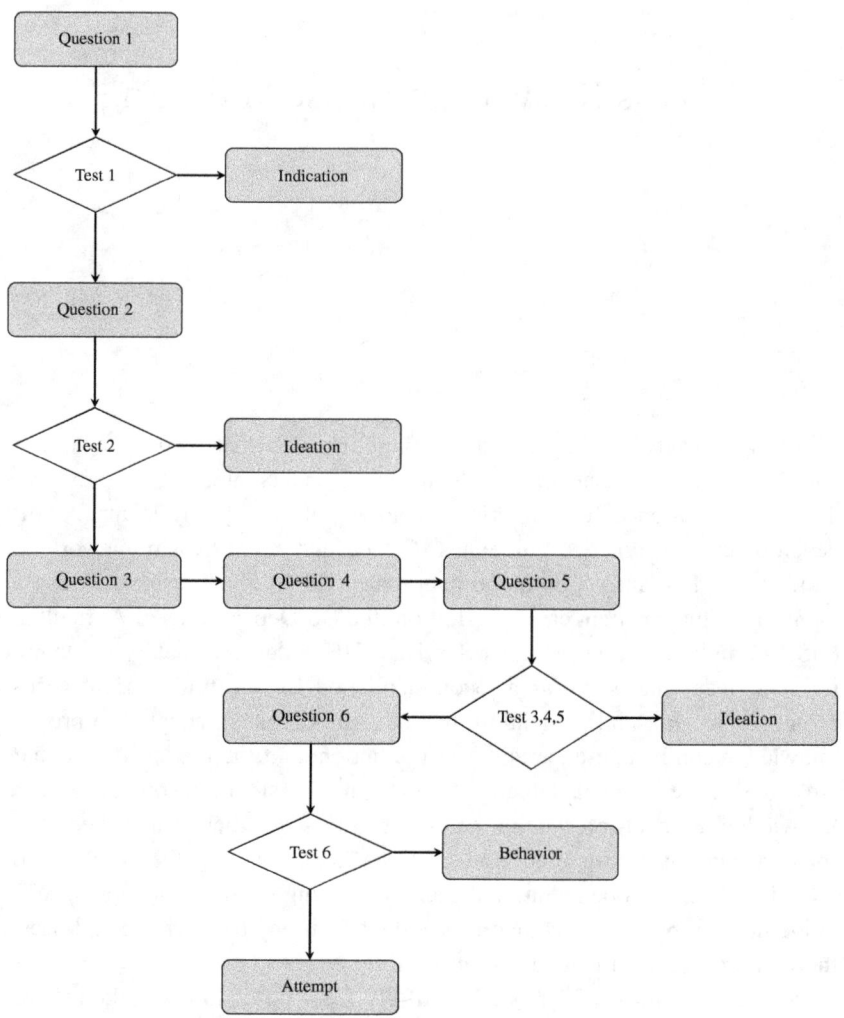

Figure 7.1 Process knowledge in the Columbia Suicide Severity Rating Scale (C-SSRS) in the form of six questions having a conditional structure.

C-SSRS, which is similar to a flow chart (see Figure 7.1). In contrast, GAD-7-based process knowledge is used to assess anxiety severity, which has a flattened structure (see Figure 7.2). NIH's DASH Diet Plan is another example of process knowledge that can be used to assess the dietary intake of hypertension patients and also recommend meals (Siervo et al., 2015). These characteristic properties of process knowledge and its infusion into statistical AI would yield a new class of neurosymbolic algorithms that would drive the question:

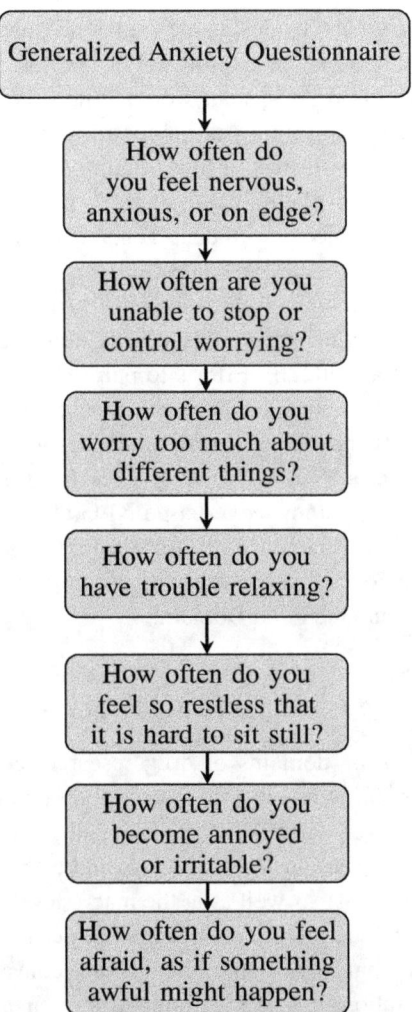

Figure 7.2 Process knowledge for the severity assessment of anxiety disorder. The scale is Generalized Anxiety Disorder 7 (GAD-7), where 7 represents the number of questions.

What if we could explicitly guide a model's learning process using the annotator's labels (e.g., concept classes) and the guidelines or processes they followed, rather than relying on implicit data-driven machine learning?

Such an algorithm would, by design, be explainable and emulate the human model of similarity between data points. For the task of classification, a process knowledge-infused AI system would solicit the use of interpretable machine learning algorithms (e.g., decision trees, random forest) that can enforce structure in decision making over traditional deep language model-based classification (Roy et al., 2022a).

In NLG, the biggest concern with deep generative language models is that they hallucinate when either asking questions or providing responses in a conversational setting. Along with the issue of hallucination, there has been an extensive study about the inappropriate and unsafe risk behaviors of language models (Thoppilan et al., 2022b). Efforts to pair these language models with passage retrievers and rankers have been proposed to control incoherent, irrelevant, and factually incorrect responses and questions; however, the order, like the one defined in process knowledge, is far from being realized (Glass et al., 2022). Such process knowledge-based NLG is even more crucial in the field of healthcare NLP, where each response from the agent can have severe consequences. These concerns are further discussed with the help of two use cases: Mental Health and the Food Domain.

7.0.1 Mental Health Use-Case

AI has contributed to the domains of drug research, customized medicine, and patient care monitoring and has the potential to aid physicians in making better diagnoses. However, when AI is used in health care, various dangers and problems might arise at the individual, macro, and technological levels (e.g., awareness, education, trust), as well as at the macro level (e.g., legislation and rules risk of accidents due to AI faults, usability, performance, data privacy, and security). In the context of mental healthcare, conversational agents are prone to unsafe generations that can harm the user or engage in a conversation involving escalation in the severity of medical conditions.

Figure 7.3 illustrates a pipeline wherein (A) the deep statistical language model pre-trained on an open domain corpus when tasked to converse with a user in a mental healthcare setting generates questions that it sees online. (B) Such questions are not what a mental healthcare provider would ask. If we utilize a clinical guideline, in this case, C-SSRS, the model can measure the safety of the generated question before asking it. (C) Figure 7.4 shows a process over the detailed process knowledge that an AI agent followed to control its question generation and ask medically correct questions. A recent study from Roy et al. details this approach using C-SSRS, and Gupta et al. detail this approach using GAD-7 and PHQ-9, which are clinical guidelines to

Process Knowledge-Infused Learning 135

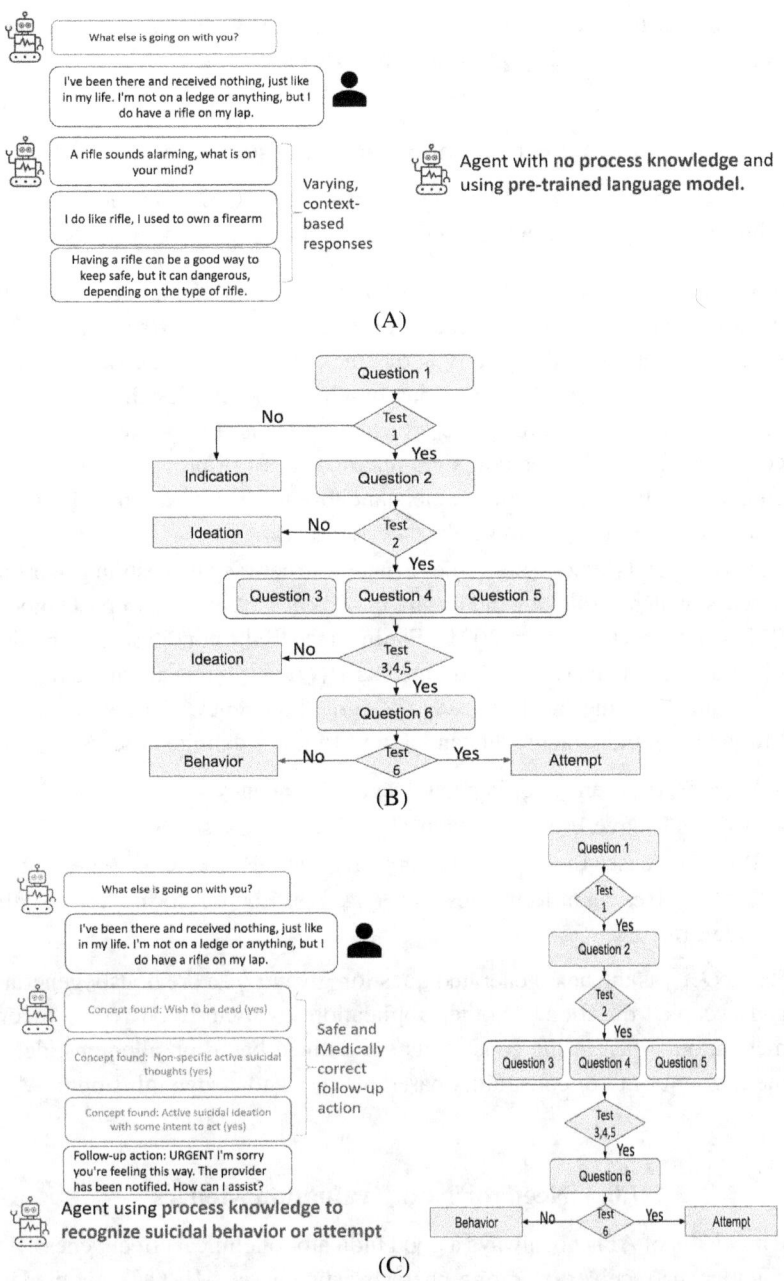

Figure 7.3 An illustration of safety in conversational artificial intelligence. It explains why process knowledge is needed to avoid unsafe conversations and make models interpretable and explainable. (A) Extreme behavior detection; (B) Process knowledge to assess suicide risk severity; (C) Model utilizes process knowledge for safe and medically correct follow-up question generation.

check whether the user is a patient of an anxiety disorder (GAD-7) or clinical depression (Patient Health Questionnaire – PHQ-9).

7.0.2 Process Knowledge as Constraints

Some more ways in which process knowledge can be infused to add constraints and improve the NLG of the current AI methods are:.

- Textual entailment constraints (TEC) provide a directional relationship between sentences in a response or questions. If two sentences share semantic relations and logically agree, they are entailed. The two sentences are neutral if they are synonymous based on the entities they contain. If the second sentence refutes the information in the first sentence, they are contradictory. Such constraints are manifestations of process knowledge in clinical practice. In machine-understandable form, we can model them as Rules containing Tags and Ranks (see Table 7.1).
- Rules (Tag and Rank): These rules can help structure the question generation process, which is random and unsafe in current state-of-the-art NLG models (Srivastava and Goodman, 2021). For instance, if the conditional probability function within an AI model, defined as $P(\hat{Q}_{k+1}|\hat{Q}_k)$, is augmented with a Tag containing the labels {Yes/No, Degree/Frequency, Causes, Treatment/Remedies}, then the model can learn to follow a definite process:
    - If $\hat{Q}_k$ is Yes then $\hat{Q}_{k+1}$ is about Degree/Frequency
    - If $\hat{Q}_k$ is Degree/Frequency then $\hat{Q}_{k+1}$ is about Causes
    - If $\hat{Q}_k$ is Causes then $\hat{Q}_{k+1}$ is about Treatment/Remedies
    - If $\hat{Q}_k$ is Treatment/Remedies then $\hat{Q}_{k+1}$ ask about Information on Other Side Effects

Here, $\hat{Q}_{k+1}$ is the next generated question given $\hat{Q}_k$, a previously generated and accepted question. Another application involving food recipe recommendation, wherein the constraints are defined based on allergens, details the further utility of constraints-based process knowledge infusion in AI.

7.0.3 Need for New Evaluation Metrics

The precision of AI is not always a good indicator of clinical effectiveness. The area under the receiver operating characteristic curve (AUROC), another frequent metric, is also not always the ideal indicator for clinical application. Such AI measures may be complex for physicians to comprehend or may not be

Table 7.1 *This is an example of how a process knowledge-integrated dataset is constructed in collaboration with mental healthcare providers. The leftmost column presents example questions mental healthcare providers (MHPs) asked. The MHPs provided Tag and Rank, which are shown in the rightmost columns and represent process knowledge. The middle column provides a series of questions gathered using Google SERP API SerpAPI (2023) and Bing Search API Microsoft (2023), logically ordered by MHPs. (Deg./freq.): degree/frequency.*

GAD-7 Questions (x)	Paraphrases (Y)	Process knowledge (P) (Tag, Rank)
Feeling nervous, anxious, or on edge	• Do you feel nervous anxious or on edge • How likely are you to feel this way • Any ideas on what may be causing this • Have you tried any remedies to feel less nervous • Are you also feeling any other symptoms, such as jitters or dread	• (Yes/No,1) • (Deg./freq.,2) • (Causes,3) • (Remedies,4) • (OSI, 5)
Not being able to stop or control worrying	• Do you feel unable to stop or control worrying • How likely are you to feel this way • Any thoughts on what may be causing this • Have you tried any remedies to stop worrying • Are you also feeling any other symptoms	• (Yes/No,1) • (Deg./freq.,2) • (Causes,3) • (Remedies,4) • (OSI, 5)
Trouble falling or staying asleep	• Do you have difficulty falling or staying asleep • How often do you experience sleep problems • What do you think might be affecting your sleep • Have you tried any sleep improvement techniques • Are you experiencing any related symptoms like fatigue	• (Yes/No,1) • (Deg./freq.,2) • (Causes,3) • (Remedies,4) • (OSI, 5)

clinically relevant. Furthermore, AI models have been assessed using a range of indices, including the F1 score, accuracy, and false-positive rate, which are indicators of distinct elements of AI's analytical ability. Understanding how complicated AI works necessitates a level of technical understanding not commonly seen among physicians.

AI models with process knowledge infusion require specialized metrics for evaluating their performance concerning safety uncertainty and risk handling. For instance, the Stanford Natural Language Inference, Multi-genre Natural Language Inference, and other similar datasets can be used to create a learned evaluation metric to assess safety in generation by comparing the generated hypothesis with a premise (Papers With Code, 2023). In essence, safety, uncertainty, and risk handling would require human evaluation, which is a mandate; these metrics are also equally important as they either involve: (a) annotators' agreements/disagreements, (b) knowledge sources, or (c) training deep language models on datasets that have data samples ordered by some relationships (Williams et al., 2018a; Camburu et al., 2018).

(a) *Average Number of Unsafe Matches:* This represents the average number of matches across all model-generated questions against a set consisting of utterances, lexical content, or ontology concepts used to describe harmful communication. Such a measure provides a range of means to impose safety checks that can be extracted from unstructured, semi-structured, and structured sources and domain experts. For example, named entities in the generated content could match harmful concepts in a knowledge base or in a lexicon set containing harmful phrases (unigrams, bigrams, and trigrams).

(b) *Perceived Risk Measure:* This is an annotator-in-the-loop metric to judge the model's stability in light of agreement and disagreement between the annotators, a notion of uncertainty and safety. It is composed of two components: (a) Penalty: – a ratio of the count of misclassified samples over the count of those samples where the annotators disagree with each other; (b) Benefit – a ratio of the count of samples where the model's predicted label agrees with some annotators (ignoring the disagreement between them) over the total number of annotators. Such a metric is efficient for controlling unsafe predictions as opposed to using statistical loss functions that quantify uncertainty in predictions and overwhelm the experts in the loop with re-annotations (Sawhney et al., 2022).

(c) *Semantic Relations and Logical Agreement Measures:* These are trained metrics constructed using the RoBERTa model, a deep language model trained independently on sentence similarity and natural language inference GLUE tasks. These metrics have been introduced in a recent study by Gaur et al. that unites meta-information-guided passage retrievers and TEC for inducing logical ordering in the generations and preventing retrieval-augmented language models from hallucinations (Gaur et al., 2021b). Semantic relation is a metric that counts the number of generations semantically similar to a user query over the total number of generations. The logical agreement score records the count when the currently generated question entails a previously generated question. The score takes the sum of such counts and divides them by the number of generations.

7.1 PKiL for Safety Constrained and Explainable Question Generation in Mental Health

7.1.1 ProKnow-data Construction

ProKnow-data is a large-scale dataset of diagnostic questions for assessing major depressive disorder (MDD) and anxiety disorder (AD). The process of creating the dataset starts with the existing questionnaires used by clinicians to judge the severity of MDD and AD in patients. These were the Patient Health Questionnaire (PHQ-9) and Generalized Anxiety Disorder (GAD-7). PHQ-9 has nine questions, and GAD-7 has seven questions. We leverage Google SERP API and Microsoft BING API to extract people also ask (PAA) questions. People ask these questions on Google Search or the Microsoft Bing search engine. The naturalness of these questions drives our motivation to enhance the sensitivity and specificity of the PHQ-9 and GAD-7 scales. The challenges concerning the safety and explainability aspects of PAA questions urged the need for domain experts to curate the list of potential questions extracted from PAA. Therefore, for each question in either PHQ-9 or GAD-7, a list of 120 additional questions (16*120: 1920 questions) was extracted, out of which 40 on average per PHQ-9/GAD-7 questions were kept for evaluation and further curation by domain experts. The first step of filtering was performed by students having research experience in mental healthcare. Approximately 640 questions were sent to domain experts, a group of three personnel: one senior psychiatrist (SP) and two resident psychiatrists (RPs). The annotation task was designed so that two RPs (RP1 and RP2) would annotate the questions for relevance and the order in which they should be asked within a question from PHQ-9/GAD-7. The first phase of annotation yielded agreement scores of 0.72 (SP and RP1) and 0.713 (SP and RP2) (Cohen's kappa), which is below the acceptance threshold defined by mental health professionals. Krippendorff's agreement was 0.68 (SP and RP1) and 0.667 (SP and RP2) when checking the agreement on the ordering of the questions. After that, the SP defines the guidelines for annotation following SCID, which denotes structured clinical interviews for DSM-5. It is a handbook of questions from which questionnaires like PHQ-9 and GAD-7 are created. SCID-defined guidelines exemplify ProKnow and reflect on clinical process knowledge embedded in PHQ-9 and GAD-7. With the use of SCID to streamline the annotation process, the SP and RPs found information pertinent to MDD and AD, which can contextualize the PAA questions better than simply finding PAA questions from PHQ-9 and GAD-7. Hence, we (students involved in this mental health research) repeated the process of extracting PAA questions. This time, we augmented the questions with contextual information provided by SP. We extracted 640 questions across 16 questions in combined PHQ-9 and GAD-7, which were higher in quality. The annotation agreement on these questions measured 0.805 (Cohen's kappa), which is a substantial improvement compared to the first round. The agreement was measured in an independent pairing of SP and RP, giving two agreement scores: 0.805 (SP and RP1) and 0.811 (SP and RP2). In this annotation round, the Krippendorff agreement score went to 0.733 (SP and RP1) and 0.748 (SP and RP2) from 0.68 and 0.667, respectively.

Formal Description of ProKnow-data: We define each data point in our dataset $\mathbf{D}$ to be a triplet $\langle x, \mathbf{Y}, \mathbf{P} \rangle$, where x is a question from a medical questionnaire (PHQ-9 or GAD-7), $\mathbf{Y}$ is a set of questions that elaborate on x (by RPs), and $\mathbf{P}$, the process knowledge, is a set of (*Tag*, *Rank*) tuples corresponding to the elaboration questions in $\mathbf{Y}$ (by an SP). An example triplet $\langle x, \mathbf{Y}, \mathbf{P} \rangle$ is seen in Table 7.2.

We created a sizeable dataset with MDD- and AD-defined questions and information from SCID. However, more is needed to train a convAI agent, which requires large-scale datasets. Hence, we faced two hurdles: (a) How could we create a richer dataset that would enable a convAI to generate information-gathering questions whose responses from patients would be assistive to the psychiatrist? We completed this with support from mental health professionals. (b) How could we scale it to a larger number of samples? To address (b), we expanded this dataset using a T5 paraphrasing model to obtain 800,000 data points that contained conversations similar to the annotated dataset. Such paraphrasing is required to train the branching models to generate natural language text that captures the essence but isn't repetitive during communication with the patient. Table 7.2 shows an example row in ProKnow-data.

7.1.2 Proposed Approach (ProKnow-algo)

The parametric knowledge within pre-trained language models (LMs) has often been exploited in downstream tasks through distillation (Hinton et al., 2015; Sun et al., 2019) or fine-tuning (Howard and Ruder, 2018). However, enforcing conceptual flow in question generation, adherence to prior

7.1 PKiL for Suicidality Assessment

Table 7.2 *Examples of ProKnow-data for GAD-7. OSI: other symptoms or information.*

GAD-7 question (x)	Paraphrases (**Y**)	Process knowledge (**P**) (Tag, Rank)
Feeling nervous, anxious, or on edge	Do you feel nervous, anxious, or on edge	(Yes/No, 1)
	How likely are you to feel this way	(Degree/frequency, 2)
	Any ideas on what may be causing this	(Causes, 3)
	Have you tried any remedies to feel less nervous	(Remedies, 4)
	Are you also feeling any other symptoms such as jitters or dread	(OSI, 5)
Not being able to stop or control worrying	Do you feel not able to stop or control worrying	(Yes/No, 1)
	How likely are you to feel this way	(Degree/frequency, 2)
	Any thoughts on what may be causing this	(Causes, 3)
	Have you tried any remedies to stop worrying	(Remedies, 4)
	Are you also feeling any other symptoms	(OSI, 5)

knowledge, and safety have not been explored. This is because these properties require a specialized dataset and training process. So, to make LMs functional over the ProKnow-data, we propose a search algorithm mounted over pre-trained LMs that explicitly compares the generated question against the ProKnow-data ground-truth questions, *a safety lexicon*, and a knowledge base (**KB**). This introduces an additional loss function along with cross-entropy (CE) loss that promotes **medical knowledge capture** and **safety**. Further, the ProKnow-algo enforces conceptual flow in question generation, thus capturing precise, relevant information using the rank in the **ProKnow-data**. The additional "loss function" is optimized to ensure that the question generation follows ProKnow. It can be seen as choosing the right branch on a process flowchart where the branching decision tests for the number of ProKnow violations per branch (and chooses the minimum one). Thus even if a response is better in terms of achieving a higher gradient on the standard CE loss surface, the nudge in that direction may be unsafe due to distributional semantics improvements not coinciding with what is a clinically correct and safer response.

Thus, at the center of ProKnow-algo is a branch and bound method, which is a conditional probability-based scoring function that takes as input the previous question (Q_k), the tag and rank of Q_k, **KB**, and the safety lexicon (L) to

Algorithm 7.1: ProKnow-algo

(i) *Probability from a deep language model,*
$\hat{Q}_{k+1} = \arg\max_{\hat{Q}_{k+1}} P(\hat{Q}_{k+1}|Q_k)$
(ii) *Score from Tag and Rank heuristic (TR)*
$\hat{Q}_{k+1} = \arg\max_{\hat{Q}_{k+1}} (TR(\hat{Q}_{k+1}) - TR(Q_k))$
(iii) *Score from Knowledge Base concept capture heuristic (KB)*
$\hat{Q}_{k+1} = \arg\max_{\hat{Q}_{k+1}} Sim(\hat{Q}_{k+1}, \mathbf{KB})$
(iv) *Score from Safety Lexicon heuristic (L)* $\hat{Q}_{k+1} = \arg\min_{\hat{Q}_{k+1}} \hat{Q}_{k+1} \cap L$
The $\hat{Q}_{k+1}$ with the highest additive score is selected ((**1**)+(**2**)+(**3**)+(**4**)).

Table 7.3 *Snapshot of safety lexicon used to constrain question generation in depression and anxiety context.*

Lexicon category	Concepts
Anxiety disorder (AD)	Cognitive distortions, panic attacks, hopelessness, physical sensations, depressed mood, dejection, feel no pressure, melancholy, feeling blah, nothing to live for, feeling blue, low spirit
Major depressive disorder (MDD)	Petrified, shaken, terrified, fear, scared, panicky, on edge, with my stomach in knots, fretful, tense, edgy, antsy, troubled, panic attacks, hopelessness, physical sensations

compute a score that reflects the safety (refer to safety lexicon in Table 7.3), medical knowledge capture, and explainability of the generated question. The **KB** comprises comprehensive mental health lexicons that have been built using PHQ-9, GAD-7, and other questionnaires (Yazdavar et al., 2017). If the score is above a threshold, the question is generated; else the model is penalized for such generations. We break down the ProKnow-algo into four components and formalize them in Algorithm 7.1.

Using the ProKnow-algo, we propose two novel architectures:

- **QG-LSTM:** Q^k is passed as input to the LSTM Cell Type 1, which generates the first token for $\hat{Q}_{k+1}$. LSTM Cell Type 2 then generates the remaining tokens of $\hat{Q}_{k+1}$ until the $\langle EOS \rangle$ token is seen. LSTM Cell Type 1 stops generating questions when the *end of list* sentence is seen (the *end of list* sentence is appended to the set **Y** in $\langle x, \mathbf{Y}, \mathbf{P} \rangle$ for all triples) to signify the end of the question set for a query x, similar to a $\langle EOS \rangle$ token. Figure 7.4 illustrates the working architecture of QG-LSTM.

7.1 PKiL for Suicidality Assessment

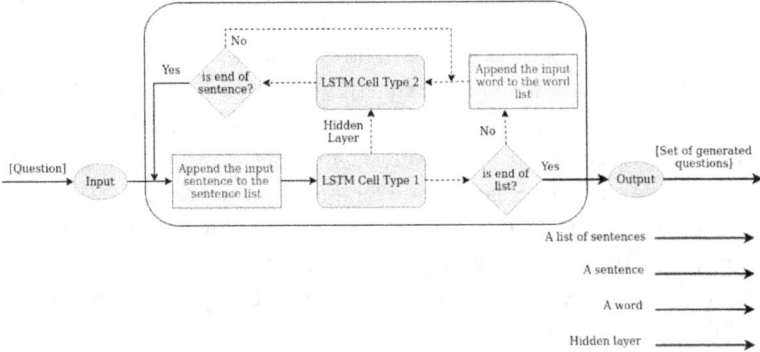

Figure 7.4 An illustration of an LSTM-cell in QG-LSTM. The architecture of QG-T is similar.

- **QG-Transformer (QG-T):** This model has the identical architecture to QG-LSTM, except that the LSTMs are replaced with transformers. Our experiments find that the QG-T and T5-FT (fine-tuned) perform best. Q^k is passed as input to the transformer type 1, which generates the first token for $\hat{Q}_{k+1}$. transformer type 2 then generates the remaining tokens of $\hat{Q}_{k+1}$ until the $\langle EOS \rangle$ token is seen. Transformer type 1 stops generating questions when the *end of list* sentence is seen (the *end of list* sentence is appended to the set **Y** in $\langle x, \mathbf{Y}, \mathbf{P} \rangle$ for all triples) to signify the end of the question set for a query x, similar to a $\langle EOS \rangle$ token.

On the Utility of Algorithm 7.1: Through intersectionality with the knowledge base (KB) shown in **point 3** of ProKnow-algo, we seek *specificity* in the generated questions, as shown in the following examples. The generated question "Do you feel anxious or nervous?" *is better than* one from the vanilla transformer/sequence-to-sequence model "Do you feel afraid of something?" Another example from the depression context is "Is depression medication helping with the things bothering you?" *is better than* "how many antidepressants are you taking for the things that are bothering you?" (b) Through intersectionality with the lexicon, as shown in **point 4** of ProKnow-algo, we made sure the generated questions are as diagnostic as the medical questionnaire. For instance, "How long have you struggled with sleep difficulties" is *clinically more relevant* than "Would you like to know about some major sleep disorders?" Another example of the generated question by including point 4 in ProKnow-algo is "How often did you miss your medication?" This is more information-seeking and relevant than "do you know about prozac?" Through the Tag and Rank heuristic, as shown in **point 2** of ProKnow-algo, we ensured the questions had a conceptual flow that followed the medical questionnaires. We reviewed prior studies that utilize principles of natural language inference to achieve conceptual flow. For instance, RoBERTa trained on Stanford Natural Language Inference (SNLI) and Multi-Genre Natural Language Inference (MNLI) datasets is used in downstream applications requiring flow-in-question generation or response generation (Gaur et al., 2022a). However, RoBERTa's performance on entailment is underwhelming and unstable. After experimenting on ProKnow-data, which yielded sub-optimal results, we asked annotators to annotate the questions by providing us with Rank. Hence, our manuscript reports Cohen's kappa and Krippendorff alpha agreement scores. **Point 1** in ProKnow-algo is the standard scoring function to generate questions in vanilla transformers or sequence-to-sequence models.

To validate the two novel architectures of ProKnow-algo, the QG-LSTM's or QG-T's question generation, we compute the cosine similarity between the context vector (QG-LSTM) or attention matrix (QG-T) with a numerical representation of the concepts in KB.

7.2 PKiL for Suicidality Assessment

In clinical practice, a guideline or process is often detailed by which the clinician can label or assess a patient. For example, to label patients for degrees of suicidal tendencies in a physical clinical setting, a well-known scale, the Columbia Suicide Severity Rating Scale (C-SSRS), created by Bjureberg et al. (2021), is used to determine the right set of labels. The C-SSRS scale is a process that consists of six conditions whose values determine four assessment outcomes from the set {*indication, ideation, behavior, attempt*}.

Similarly, when patients are assessed for depression, clinicians evaluate patient responses using a process or guideline such as the PHQ-9. Traditional DL pipelines do not utilize such process knowledge and instead employ explainable AI methods, like local interpretable model-agnostic explanations (LIME) and Shapley additive explanations (SHAP), to derive explicit explanations for the model's predictions using a simpler surrogate model approximation (Ribeiro et al., 2016; Lundberg and Lee, 2017; Adadi and Berrada, 2018). While explainable AI models are helpful for computer scientists in debugging and improving deep learning models, they offer limited utility to end-users (e.g., psychotherapists) when making decisions. This is due to the absence of an explicit process knowledge model that enables explanations using user-understandable concepts. Additionally, approximating

7.2 PKiL for Suicidality Assessment

very large and complex models, such as language models (LMs), with simpler surrogate models is challenging (Vaswani et al., 2017a).

Crucially, PKiL enables the tracking of concepts in explicit process knowledge structures to provide user-understandable explanations for model predictions. The PKiL learning framework achieves this through a novel training method with the following salient features:

- PKiL utilizes advanced deep learning models with hundreds of millions of parameters, requiring minimal additional parameter training. These additional parameters correspond to the number of process knowledge conditions, enabling the generation of user-explainable model predictions.
- The optimization objective is simple to understand, enabling globally optimal solution discovery through various optimization procedures.

Problem Formulation Let $X_\mathcal{D}$ denote a dataset of input texts and their labels in a domain $\mathcal{D}$. An example of an input post is shown in Table 7.4, and its suicidality assessment label is from the set *indication, ideation, behavior, attempt* in the domain of mental health. Let $Pk_\mathcal{D}$ denote the relevant process knowledge available to us from established literature in the domain $\mathcal{D}$. Let $\Lambda_\mathcal{D}$ be a language model available to us that is fine-tuned on domain-specific data (e.g., BERT fine-tuned on mental health posts from social media). PKiL is a training method that makes combined use of $X_\mathcal{D}$ and $Pk_\mathcal{D}$ to evaluate the conditions in the process knowledge to predict the final label. The evaluated conditions in the process knowledge are familiar to end users and, therefore, enable user-understandable explanations for predictions.

Approach Consider a piece of single-condition process knowledge $Pk_\mathcal{D}$ to predict a binary label L for an input $x \in X_\mathcal{D}^{Pk}$:

Table 7.4 *C-SSRS Classification System for User Text Analysis*

User text (x)	Process Knowledge (PK)	CSSRS Label
[...] a voice telling me to kill myself [...] yes - I think I should do it [...]	1.2 (yes - a voice telling me to kill myself) 2.2 (yes - I think I should do it) 4 (yes - I think I should do it)	Behaviour or Attempt
[...] Rarely is a day where I dont suffer from thoughts of self-harm...	1.1 (yes - Rarely is a day where I dont suffer from thoughts of self-harm) 2 (no - no words indicating active suicidal thought)	Ideation

$$\text{if } (C(x) = 1), L(x) = 1$$
$$\text{else}, L(x) = 0.$$

Here $C(x)$ is a condition evaluation function for the input x that evaluates to 1 if the condition is satisfied and 0 if the condition is not satisfied. $Pk_\mathcal{D}$ can be written algebraically as

$$L(x) = \mathbf{I}(L(x) = 1)(C(x) = 1) \\ + \mathbf{I}(L(x) = 0). \quad (7.1)$$

Here $\mathbf{I}(L(x) = l)$ is the indicator function that evaluates to 1 or 0, indicating whether the value that the label $L(x)$ takes is equal to l. How do we mathematically formulate $C(x) = 1$? We can parameterize $C(x) = 1$ as $S(e_x^{\Lambda_\mathcal{D}}, e_C^{\Lambda_\mathcal{D}}) \geq \theta_C$, where S is a similarity function (e.g., cosine similarity) and θ_C is the similarity threshold. The $e_x^{\Lambda_\mathcal{D}}$ and $e_C^{\Lambda_\mathcal{D}}$ are embeddings of the input and condition obtained using a domain-specific fine-tuned language model $\Lambda_\mathcal{D}$. Thus, we can write a parameterized approximation to Equation 7.1 as

$$\hat{L}(x, \theta_C) = \mathbf{I}(L(x) = 1) S(e_x^{\Lambda_\mathcal{D}}, e_C^{\Lambda_\mathcal{D}}) \geq \theta_C) \\ + \mathbf{I}(L(x) = 0). \quad (7.2)$$

Now we consider a slightly more complex piece of process knowledge $Pk_\mathcal{D}$, a multilabel and multi-conditioned item of process knowledge to predict label $L \in \{1, 2, 3\}$, given conditions $C1, C2, C3$, for an input $x \in X_\mathcal{D}^{Pk}$:

$$\text{if } (C1(x) = 1 \wedge C2(x) = 1), L(x) = 1,$$
$$\text{if } (C1(x) = 1 \wedge C3(x) = 1), L(x) = 2$$
$$\text{else}, L(x) = 3.$$

Similar to Equation 7.1, we can write this $Pk_\mathcal{D}$ algebraically as

$$L(x) = \mathbf{I}(L(x) = 1)(C1(x) = 1)(C2(x) = 1) \\ + \mathbf{I}(L(x) = 2)(C1(x) = 1)(C3(x) = 1) \quad (7.3) \\ + \mathbf{I}(L(x) = 3).$$

Following a similar procedure as the one used to derive Equation 7.2, we obtain

$$\hat{L}(x, \theta_{C1}, \theta_{C2}) = \mathbf{I}(L(x) = 1)(S(e_x^{\Lambda_\mathcal{D}}, e_{C1}^{\Lambda_\mathcal{D}}) \geq \theta_{C1})(S(e_x^{\Lambda_\mathcal{D}}, e_{C2}^{\Lambda_\mathcal{D}}) \geq \theta_{C2}) \\ + \mathbf{I}(L(x) = 2)(S(e_x^{\Lambda_\mathcal{D}}, e_{C1}^{\Lambda_\mathcal{D}}) \geq \theta_{C1})(S(e_x^{\Lambda_\mathcal{D}}, e_{C3}^{\Lambda_\mathcal{D}}) \geq \theta_{C3}) \\ + \mathbf{I}(L(x) = 3).$$
$$(7.4)$$

7.2 PKiL for Suicidality Assessment

Generally, given a piece of multi-condition process knowledge $Pk_\mathcal{D}$ for a multilabel prediction of the form

$$\text{if } \wedge_j (C_j(x) = 1), L(x) = l,$$

we get its algebraic form as

$$L(x) = \mathbf{I}(L(x) = l) \prod_j (C_j(x) = 1). \tag{7.5}$$

Denoting all the parameters as the set $\{\theta_{C_j}\}$, we get the parameterization

$$\hat{L}(x, \{\theta_{C_j}\}) = \mathbf{I}(L(x) = l) \prod_j (S(e_x^{\wedge_\mathcal{D}}, e_{C_j}^{\wedge_\mathcal{D}}) \geq \theta_{C_j}). \tag{7.6}$$

For all $x \in X_\mathcal{D}^{Pk}$, we get a system of equations like Equation 7.6.

Sentiment Analysis The conditions in the process knowledge help the model assess problem issues. However, a complete mental health assessment usually also involves the identification of signs of positivity. Therefore for each θ_{C_j}, we also optimize for a γ_{C_j} term, where the model predicts positive sentiment in the input if $S(e_x^{\wedge_\mathcal{D}}, e_{C_j}^{\wedge_\mathcal{D}}) \leq \theta_{C_j} + \gamma_{C_j}$.

Optimization Problem Formulation For a process knowledge-augmented dataset $X_\mathcal{D}^{Pk}$, we know the ground truths $L(x)$ for all $x \in X_\mathcal{D}^{Pk}$. We want to solve for the unknown parameters θ_{C_j} that yield minimum error between the parameterized approximation $L(x, \{\theta_{C_j}\})$ and the ground truth $L(x)$, that is,

$$\sum_{x \in X_\mathcal{D}^{Pk}} \mathcal{E}(\hat{L}(x, \{\theta_{C_j}\}), L(x)).$$

Here $\mathcal{E}$ denotes the error function. The choice of similarity functions S is a hyperparameter (explore cosine similarity and normalized Gaussian kernels in our experiments).

Projected Newton's method: When one of the $\{\theta_{C_j}\}$ is fixed, setting $\mathcal{E}(\hat{L}(x, \{\theta_{C_j}\}), L(x))$ to be the cross-entropy loss reduces to a strongly convex objective that can be solved by **Newton's method** (with ε corrections for low-determinant Hessians). After each optimization step, we project the θ_{C_j} to the $[-1, 1]$ range.

Grid Search: Since the number of parameters to optimize is small (six for CSSRS 2.0 and nine for PRIMATE), we can perform a grid search over a predefined set of grid values to find the values that yield minimum cross-entropy loss. For S, we choose **cosine similarity and normalized Gaussian kernel**; therefore, grid search candidate values are in the $[-1, 1]$ range.

Optimizing for the γ_{C_j}***:*** To find the optimal γ_{C_j}, we first predict positive and negative sentiment labels using the **Stanford CoreNLP** model for all the inputs. Next, we perform a grid search in the $[-1, 1]$ range and set values for the γ_{C_j} that result in the maximum agreement between $S(e_x^{\Lambda_D}, e_{C_j}^{\Lambda_D}) \leq \theta_{C_j} + \gamma_{C_j}$ and the Stanford CoreNLP model labels (only the positive labels). In our experiments, we try both Newton's method and grid search optimization strategies.

Experiments and Results We demonstrate the effectiveness of PkiL training using PRIMATE and C-SSRS 2.0 combined with several state-of-the-art language models. We also perform experiments with prompting Text-Davinci-003 using the LangChain library.

7.2.1 Process Knowledge-Augmented Datasets

For CSSRS 2.0, the process knowledge is defined as follows:

$$\text{if } ((C1(x), C2(x), C3(x), C4(x), C5(x), C6(x)) = 1),$$
$$L(x) = attempt,$$
$$\text{if } ((C1(x), C2(x), C3(x), C4(x), C5(x)) = 1),$$
$$L(x) = behavior,$$
$$\text{if } ((C1(x), C2(x)) = 1), L(x) = ideation,$$
$$\text{if } (C1(x) = 1), L(x) = indication.$$

The conditions $C1-C6$ in the CSSRS are:

- $C1$: *Wish To Be Dead*
- $C2$: *Non-Specific Active Suicidal Thoughts*
- $C3$: *Active Suicidal Ideation with Any Methods (Not Plan) without Intent to Act*
- $C4$: *Active Suicidal Ideation with Some Intent to Act without Specific Plan*
- $C5$: *Active Suicidal Ideation with Specific Plan and Intent*
- $C6$: *Aborted Attempt or Self-Interrupted Attempt.*

For PRIMATE, the process knowledge is a set of nine conditions. If any of the conditions evaluate to yes, the depression assessment label is 1. This is a binary classification task. We input this process knowledge in the form (we collapse conditions $C3-C8$ for brevity):

7.2 PKiL for Suicidality Assessment

$$\text{if } (C1(x) = 1), L(x) = 1,$$
$$\text{if } (C2(x) = 1), L(x) = 1,$$
$$\ldots$$
$$\text{if } (C9(x) = 1), L(x) = 1,$$
$$\text{else}, L(x) = 0.$$

The conditions $C1-C9$ in the PHQ-9 are:

$C1$: *Little interest or pleasure in doing things*

$C2$: *Feeling down, depressed, or hopeless*

$C3$: *Trouble falling or staying asleep,*
       or sleeping too much

$C4$: *Feeling tired or having little energy*

$C5$: *Poor appetite or overeating*

$C6$: *Feeling bad about yourself,*
       or that you are a failure,
       or have let yourself or your family down

$C7$: *Trouble concentrating on things,*
       such as reading the newspaper or watching television

$C8$: *Moving or speaking so slowly that*
       other people could have noticed
       Or so fidgety or restless that
       you have been moving a lot more than usual

$C9$: *Thoughts that you would be better off dead*
       or thoughts of hurting yourself in some way?

Examples from the PRIMATE dataset can be found at this Github link: https://github.com/primate-mh/Primate2022.

7.2.2 Experimental and Hyperparameter Configurations during Training

(i) **Embedding Models for Input Post and Questions:** We use the models Word2Vec, SBERT, RoBERTa, T5, ERNIE, and Longformer fine-tuned on the training data.

(ii) **Similarity Function:** We explore the cosine similarity and the normalized Gaussian kernel (input vectors are normalized to be unit

```
from langchain.prompts import PromptTemplate
input = "Been there done that, got nothing. I have a gun on lap and I don't know what to do"
template = "Is the input post {input}, exhibiting a {question}? Answer yes or no"
prompt = PromptTemplate(input_variables = ["input","question"],
                        template = template)
print (llm(prompt.format(input=input,
                         question="wish to be dead")))
```

Figure 7.5 Using the LangChain library to prompt Text-Davinci-003 for answers to questions from the process knowledge.

length before plugging into the Gaussian kernel). For the normalized Gaussian kernel, we range the scale parameter between $[-1, 1]$ in increments of 0.001.

(iii) **Parameters for Grid Search:** During grid search optimization, we explore parameters in the $[-1, 1]$ range, again in increments of 0.001.

(iv) **No. of Epochs for Newton's Optimization Method:** We set max epochs of 100 and experiment with batch sizes of 16 and 32 for Newton's method. We train for only 100 epochs as we have far more equations than unknowns and also perform early stopping if the total parameter differences are less than 0.001.

Text-Davinci-003 Experiment Details

We use the LangChain library and write a prompt template to obtain answers to the process knowledge questions from Text-Davinci-003. For example, Figure 7.5 shows the prompt template for the first condition $C1$: *Wish to be dead* from the CSSRS process knowledge. For sentiment analysis, we set the *question* variable in Figure 7.5 to *positive sentiment*. We will call this model Text-Davinci-003$_{PK}$. Once we evaluate all the conditions, we follow the process knowledge pertaining to the evaluated condition values to determine the label.

7.2.3 Quantitative Results and Discussion

Figure 7.6 shows the results of PKiL for various experiment configurations for the CSSRS 2.0 and PRIMATE datasets. The figure also shows results from the Text-Davinci-003$_{PK}$ model.

Quantitative Results for CSSRS 2.0: First, excluding the Text-Davinci-003$_{PK}$ from the analyses, we observe that SBERT trained using PKiL with a normalized Gaussian kernel performs the best in terms of accuracy, and the Word2Vec model performs the best on AUC-ROC scores for the CSSRS 2.0 dataset. In general, we see that PKiL leads to large boosts in performance of up to 14% over the baseline. Analysis of the Text-Davinci-003$_{PK}$ model

7.2 PKiL for Suicidality Assessment

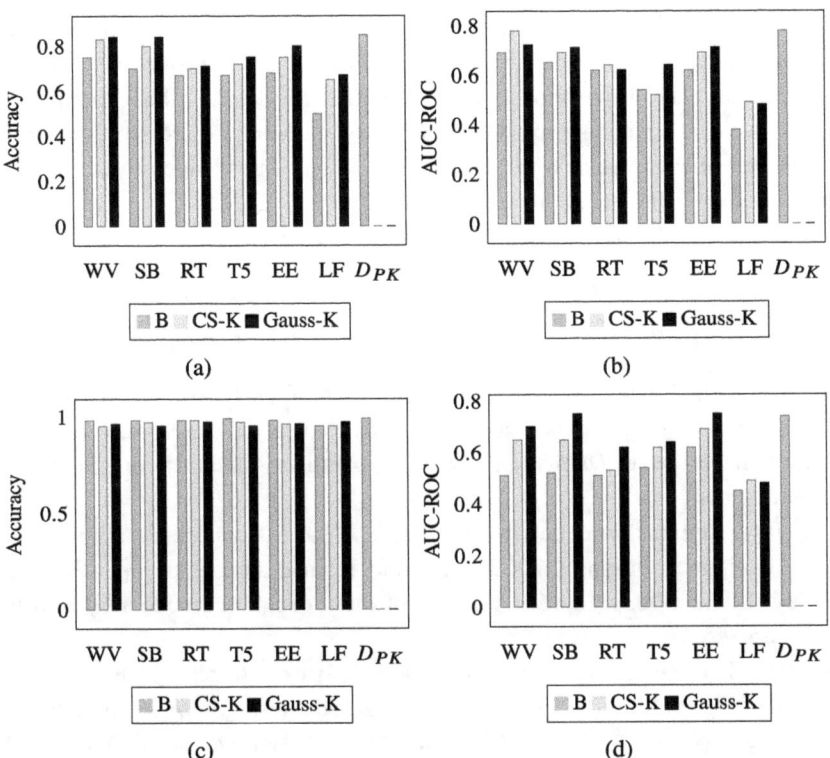

Figure 7.6 (A) and (B) show the results on the CSSRS 2.0 dataset. (C) and (D) show the same for the PRIMATE dataset: The mean accuracy/AUC-ROC, rounded up, of all the language models (LMs) – Baseline fine-tuned model for classification (**B**), PKiL performance with cosine similarity kernel (**CS-K**), and PKiL performance with normalized Gaussian kernel similarity (**Gauss-K**). D_{PK}, being a prompt-based model, does not use either CS-K or Gauss-K method; therefore, there is no associated bar. W2V: Word2Vec, SB: SBERT, RT: RoBERTa, EE: ERNIE, LF: LongFormer.

performance reveals that it is the best performer among all the models for the CSSRS 2.0 dataset. Our experiments show that large language models can significantly increase suicidality assessment performance when leveraging process knowledge structures and process knowledge-augmented datasets.

Quantitative Results for PRIMATE: Again, first excluding the Text-Davinci-003$_{PK}$ from the analyses, we observe that RoBERTa trained using PKiL with a cosine similarity function performs the best in terms of accuracy, and SBERT and ERNIE perform the best on AUC-ROC scores for the PRIMATE dataset. In general, we see that PKiL leads to large boosts in performance of up to 23% over the baseline. Analysis of the Text-Davinci-003$_{PK}$ model performance reveals that it is the best performer in terms of accuracy among all the models for the PRIMATE dataset. Our experiments show that large language models can also significantly increase depression assessment performance when leveraging process knowledge structures and process knowledge-augmented datasets.

7.2.4 Qualitative Results and Discussion

We evaluate PkiL model outputs qualitatively for the following aspects:

- **Mental health disturbance assessment**: The final label predicted by the model, that is, the label *depression* for depression assessment), and a label from the set {*indication, ideation, behavior, attempt*} for suicidality assessment.
- **PHQ-9 depression concepts identified**: A list of concepts resulting from evaluating conditions C1–C9 using the learned thresholds θ_{C_j}. For the Text-Davinci-003$_{PK}$ model, we prompt the model using code as shown in Figure 7.5.
- **CSSRS suicidality concepts identified**: A list of concepts resulting from evaluating conditions C1–C6 using the learned thresholds θ_{C_j}. Similar to the depression case, for the Text-Davinci-003$_{PK}$ model, we prompt the model using code as shown in Figure 7.5.
- **Positive sentiment assessment**: Using the learned θ_j and γ_j to identify input post fragments that convey positive sentiment.

Baseline Model Explanations: We use the bert-viz visualization technique (https://github.com/jessevig/bertviz) to interpret the contributions of the different input post fragments to the prediction outcome (the CLS token). Figure 7.7 shows the output for SBERT. The highlights convey meaningful information from the perspective of depression, which is the correct label. However, it is unclear how the highlights map to user-explainable concepts from process knowledge guidelines for depression assessment. A manual post-processing layer for mapping to user-explainable concepts is needed to verify the prediction.

PKiL Model Explanations: We divide the input post into contiguous fragments of max size three sentences for models and infer the process knowledge condition values using the PKiL-trained models and the parameters θ_{C_j} and θ_{γ_j}. This is done for enhanced user explainability, as simply annotating all the posts with concepts still requires additional post-processing by humans to glean fragments that correspond to problem issues and positive sentiments.

7.2 PKiL for Suicidality Assessment

Mental Health Disturbance Assessment:
Person is showing signs of **Depression**

Attention Highlights from SBERT (highlighted in orange):

Input Post
A book is usually what I do when Im getting down, but it doesnt work when I start getting panicky. Ill try the carbs, the caffeine doesnt work because Ive gotten it in a movie theater and had a soda with me...', 'A few reasons. I feel backed into a corner mostly. And Im Tired of being Tired of everything. If that makes sense.', 'Thank you! I understand its a sad thing. But I also want people to realize that there can be humor in anything and its the best way to deal with this. Its how I would do it. ', 'I really dont want to ask for help. Id rather not let anyone know Im having these kind of issues.

Figure 7.7 Visualization of self-attention-based interpretability for the SBERT baseline model. The prediction output is correct, and the highlights are sensible. However, to a user such as a clinician, it may be unclear how these highlights map to user-explainable concepts from processes they use in practice. Note that the model also highlights *sad* even though the word *sad* is contained in a text fragment conveying positive sentiment. We consistently notice similar failures of baseline language models for capturing negation.

Mental Health Disturbance Assessment:
Person is showing signs of **Depression**

Input Post
(2) A book is usually what I do when Im getting down, but it doesnt work when I start getting panicky. Ill try the carbs, the caffeine doesnt work because Ive gotten it in a movie theater and had a soda with me...', 'A few reasons. **(1)** I feel backed into a corner mostly. **(1)** And Im Tired of being Tired of everything. If that makes sense.', ' Thank you! I understand its a sad thing. But I also want people to realize that there can be humor in anything and its the best way to deal with this. Its how I would do it. ', 'I really dont want to ask for help. Id rather not let anyone know Im having these kind of issues.

PHQ-9 Depression Concepts Identified (highlighted in blue):
C1: Little interest or please in doing things; C2: Feeling down, depressed, or hopeless, [...]

Positive Sentiment Assessment (highlighted in pink):
Person is showing signs of Positivity

Figure 7.8 Explanations from SBERT, trained using PKiL with the normalized Gaussian kernel. We see that leveraging process knowledge imparts a much higher degree of user understandability to the generated explanations. The outcome is annotated with problem concepts that the clinician is familiar with. Additionally, the model parameters obtained after PkiL parameters enable the analysis of fragments conveying positive sentiment.

> **Mental Health Disturbance Assessment:**
> Person is showing signs of **Depression**
>
> **Input Post**
> I wish I could give a shit about what would make it to the front page. **(1)(2)(2)** I have been there and got nothing. **(1)(2)(2)** Same as my life. **(2)** I do have a gun.', 'I thought I was talking about it. **(2)** I am not on a ledge or something, but I do have my gun in my lap.', 'No. I made sure she got an education and she knows how to get a job. I also have recently bought her clothes to make her more attractive. She has told me she only loves me because I buy her things.
>
> **PHQ-9 Depression Concepts Identified (highlighted in blue   ):**
> C1: Little interest or pleasure in doing things; C2: Feeling down, depressed, or hopeless, **[...]**
>
> **CSSRS Suicidality Concepts Identified (highlighted in green   ):**
> C2: Non-specific active suicidal thoughts, **[...]**

Figure 7.9 Explanations from the Text-Davinci-003$_{PK}$ model. Once again, we see that leveraging process knowledge imparts a much higher degree of user understandability to the generated explanations since the outcome is annotated with problem concepts that the clinician is familiar with.

Figure 7.8 shows the output of the SBERT model trained using PKiL with the normalized Gaussian kernel. Figure 7.9 shows the output of prompting the Text-Davinci-003$_{PK}$ as shown in Figure 7.5. We can readily observe that the explanations are more useful to the clinician as they directly explain the outcome in terms of concepts used in everyday practice. Finally, we provided PKiL explanations to the experts who helped construct the CSSRS 2.0 dataset and asked them to provide the percentage of times they found the explanations beneficial. We also provided baseline explanations for comparison. To control for bias, we told them that humans generated the PKiL explanations and deep learning models generated the baseline explanations. PKiL explanations scored 70% vs. 47% for the baseline models. We recorded an inter-annotator agreement of 0.72. We analyzed the 30% that the experts did not find beneficial and observed that models have difficulty distinguishing casual mentions from serious ones. For example, a Reddit user reported wanting to kill themselves out of class boredom before identifying a legitimate clinical issue much further into their post. We leave the investigation of these posts for future work (e.g., by expanding our framework to detect sarcasm).

8
Knowledge-Infused Conversational NLP

Traditional dialog agents in conversational information seeking have repeatedly focused on entities in the user query (Rao and Daumé III, 2018; Zamani et al., 2020). Consequently, the generated questions are redundant and lack diversity, losing user engagement.

Further, the multi-turn conversations to support user engagement often result in irrelevant question generation by the agent. For instance, in Figure 8.1, a traditional dialog agent generated a question, "Do you want to know about economics?" which seems relevant to the user query; however, the user did not find it suitable. This is because economics is a vast subject, and the user is only interested in crucial economics concepts related to the gross domestic product (GDP), inflation, and employment. Hence, capturing the context and adapting the question generation to context is essential. Current conversational agents lack curiosity in question generation, which is critical for cohesive response (Lewis et al., 2020; Guu et al., 2020). Curiosity in a conversational agent is defined by the agent's capability to diversify the user query with triples that are semantically related to entities in the query. Further, the agent retrieves meta-information using the diversified query for question generation. These properties sum up ISEEQ, an information-seeking question generation agent that generates a series of information-seeking questions to gather the context of the user's query. *Another feature of the conversational agent brought into ISEEQ is to force a conceptual flow while generating questions, defined by semantic relations and logical coherence between the generated questions* (Gaur et al., 2021b).

The problem of generating information-seeking questions (ISQs) given an initial user's information-seeking-type (IS) query, in which ISEEQ specializes, has not been addressed in the literature so far. Apart from the general context of economics, illustrated in Figure 8.1, consider the user IS query in mental health: "Bothered by feeling down or depressed. Need advice."

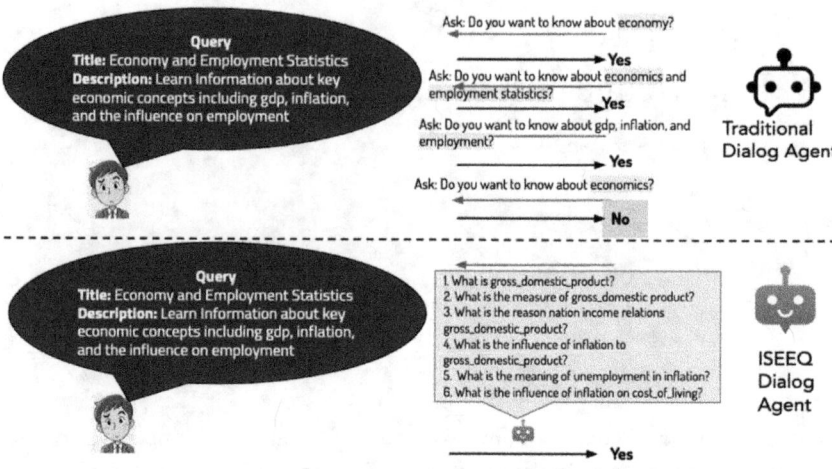

Figure 8.1 ISEEQ's one-shot procedural question generation.

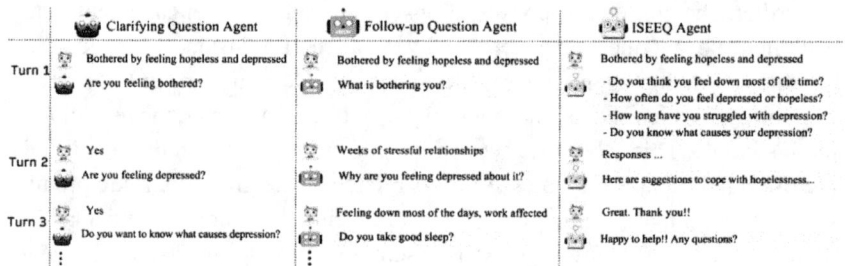

Figure 8.2 ISEEQ's generation of information-seeking questions reduces the number of turns involved in providing the response needed by the end-user, thus improving user engagement.

ISEEQ-generated ISQs are: "How often do you feel depressed or hopeless?", "How long have you struggled with depression?", and others, which can be used either by the Conversational Information Seeking (CIS) Agent CIS or the healthcare provider to generate an appropriate response to the user's needs. Another example is shown in Figure 8.2. ISQs differ from other question types (e.g., clarifying questions, follow-up questions (Rao and Daumé III, 2018; Pothirattanachaikul et al., 2020; Zamani et al., 2020)) by having a structure, covering objective details, and expanding on the breadth of the topic. For such a flow to exist between questions, ISQs require maximizing semantic relations and logical coherence. Semantic relations are synonymous with semantic similarity and can be computed using a variety of metrics, such as cosine similarity, BERTScore (Zhang et al., 2020), Word Mover Distance

(Kusner et al., 2015), Concept Mover Distance (Stoltz and Taylor, 2019), and others. Logical coherence can be considered synonymous with natural language inference or textual entailment, where the next question should entail the previous in order to maintain consistency in the flow of context. Further, Sekulić et al. (2021) describes clarifying questions as simple questions of facts, good to clarify the dilemma and *confined to the entities in the query*. In contrast, ISQs go a step further with expanding the query context by *exploring relationships between entities in the query and linked entities in a KG*. Thus, retrieving a diverse set of passages (or meta-information) would provide a proper solution to a user query.

ISEEQ as a tool can automatically generate curiosity-driven and conceptual flow-based ISQs from a short user query. There are two major components in ISEEQ:

Dynamic Knowledge-Aware Passage Retrieval: ISEEQ infuses IS queries with semantic information from knowledge graphs to improve unsupervised passage retrieval. Passages serve as meta-information for generating ISQs.

Reinforcement Learning for ISQs: To improve compositional diversity and legibility in QG, we allow ISEEQ to self-guide the generations through reinforcement learning in a generative-adversarial setting that results in ISEEQ-RL. I introduce entailment constraints borrowed from natural language inference (NLI) guidelines to expand ISEEQ-RL to ISEEQ-ERL to yield smooth topical coherent transitions in the questions, achieving conceptual flow. ISEEQ-RL is a variant with a reward on semantic relations, whereas, in ISEEQ-ERL, the reward is on both semantic relations and logical coherence.

This structure of ISEEQ is defined to make the following three contributions in conversational AI, which this chapter will provide answers for:

RQ1 Knowledge Infusion: Can expert-curated knowledge sources like knowledge graphs/bases related to the user query help in context retrieval and question generation?

RQ2 Conceptual Flow: Can ISEEQ generate ISQs having semantic relations and logical coherence?

Transferability or Zero Shot Test: Can ISEEQ generate ISQs in a cross-domain setting and generate ISQs for new domains without requiring crowdsourced data collection?

Another utility coming from such a design for ISEEQ is its forthcoming role as a data creation agent to support annotation efforts in CIS. Figure 8.3 illustrates the positioning of ISEEQ as a dataset creation tool for training CIS agents. Looking at the past research on data creation for enhancing

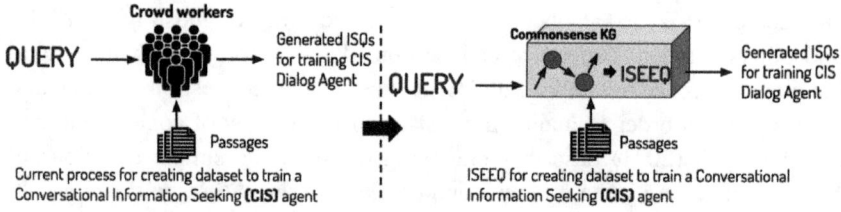

Figure 8.3 Minimizing annotation effort in conversational information seeking.

conversational AI, a key player is the pipeline of (a) crawling raw data, (b) setting up annotation guidelines, (c) sorting out crowdworkers and training them, and (d) handling crowdworker agreements. What is more painful is the task of crowdworkers, which is characterized as follows: Given a user query, a crowdworker would (a) search the web with curiosity, (b) create good quality questions relevant to the user query, (c) shape the response to the created questions, and (d) maintain the flow of information using semantic relations and logical agreement between questions.

Currently, ISEEQ is capable of addressing the following three types of IS queries illustrated through examples:

Title and Description: Online platforms such as Reddit show this type of information-seeking behavior. For example, *Title:* "I am feeling down and depressed." *Description:* "I am going through a rough patch in my life. With divorce proceedings and poor growth at work, I am feeling low and hopeless. What do you advise?."

Topic and Aspects: Humans seek information on Google search, X, WebMD, or MedicineNet by stating topics and aspects. For example: *Topic:* "Anxiety" and *Aspects:* "Panic Attacks, Trauma, Relationship, Self-detox."

Description: This content is relatively shorter than Title and Description and Topic and Aspects. "Need Advice! I am bothered by feeling down or depressed."

These three types of IS queries can be obtained from the following datasets used for preparing curiosity-driven conversational agents.

QADiscourse (QAD): The source for passages in QADiscourse (QAD) includes Wikipedia and WikiNews. The training samples consist of 125 user queries, each associated with 25 ISQs, resulting in a total of 3,125 query–question pairs. For testing, there are 33 user queries with 25 ISQs per query. The ConceptNet KG hit percentage for this dataset is 38.5%.

Question Answer Meaning Representations (QAMR): The passages for the Question Answer Meaning Representations (QAMR) dataset are sourced from

WikiNews, Wikipedia, and Newswire. The training set includes 395 user queries with 63 ISQs per query, while the testing set comprises 39 user queries with 68 ISQs per query. The ConceptNet KG hit percentage for QAMR is 35.5%.

Facebook Curiosity (FBC): In the Facebook Curiosity (FBC) dataset, passages are drawn from Geographic Wikipedia. The training samples encompass 8,489 user queries with 6 ISQs per query. For testing, there are 2,729 user queries with 8 ISQs per query. The ConceptNet KG hit percentage for FBC is 50%.

Conversational Assistance Track Dataset (CAsT-19): CAsT-19 is used exclusively to test ISEEQ, with training and testing datasets merged. The passages are sourced from Microsoft MARCO. The training samples include 30 user queries with 9 ISQs per query, and the testing samples comprise 50 user queries with 10 ISQs per query. The ConceptNet KG hit percentage for this dataset is 57%.

The datasets exhibit the following properties: (1) existence of semantic relations between questions, (2) logical coherence between questions, and (3) diverse context; that is, queries cover wider domains, such as health, sports, history, geography. Fundamentally, these datasets support the assessment of RQ1, RQ2, and RQ3.

The QAD (Pyatkin et al., 2020) dataset tests the ability of ISEEQ to generate questions that have logical coherence. The sources of queries are Wikinews and Wikipedia, which consists of 8.7 million passages. The QAMR (Michael et al., 2017) dataset tests the ability of ISEEQ to generate questions with semantic relations between them. The source for creating IS queries is Wikinews, which consists of 3.4 million passages. Both QAD and QAMR consist of only Description-type IS queries. FBC (Rodriguez et al., 2020) is another dataset that challenges ISEEQ to have both semantic relations and logical coherence. This is because queries are described in the form of Topics and Aspects. The source for IS queries is Wikipedia, which has 3.3 million geographical passages. Even though the questions in the dataset have logical coherence, they are relatively less diverse than QAMR and QAD. CAsT-19 (Dalton et al., 2020) is the most challenging dataset for ISEEQ because of size, diversity in context, large number of passages, and IS queries that are not annotated with passages. In CAsT-19, IS queries are provided with a Topic and Description.

Adapting Datasets: Each dataset, except CAsT-19, has a query, a set of ISQs, and a relevant passage. For fairness in evaluation, we exclude the passages in the datasets; instead, we retrieve them from the sources using knowledge-aware passage retrieval and ranking components within ISEEQ.

We also perform coreference resolution over ISQs using NeuralCoref to increase entity mentions (Clark and Manning, 2016). For example, a question in CAsT-19 "What are the educational requirements required to become one?" is reformulated to "What are the educational requirements required to become a physician's assistant?"

8.1 ISEEQ Architecture and Evaluation

Problem Definition: Given a short query ($q = w_1, w_2, w_3, \ldots, w_n$) on any topic (e.g., mental health, sports, politics and policy, location), automatically generate ISQs in a conceptual flow ($ISQ: Q_1, Q_2, Q_3, \ldots, Q_p$) to understand specificity in the information needs of the user.

Our approach to address this problem, ISEEQ, is outlined in Figure 8.4. We describe in detail the main components of ISEEQ: semantic query expander (SQE), knowledge-aware passage retriever (KPR), and generative-adversarial reinforcement learning-based question generator (ISEEQ-RL)

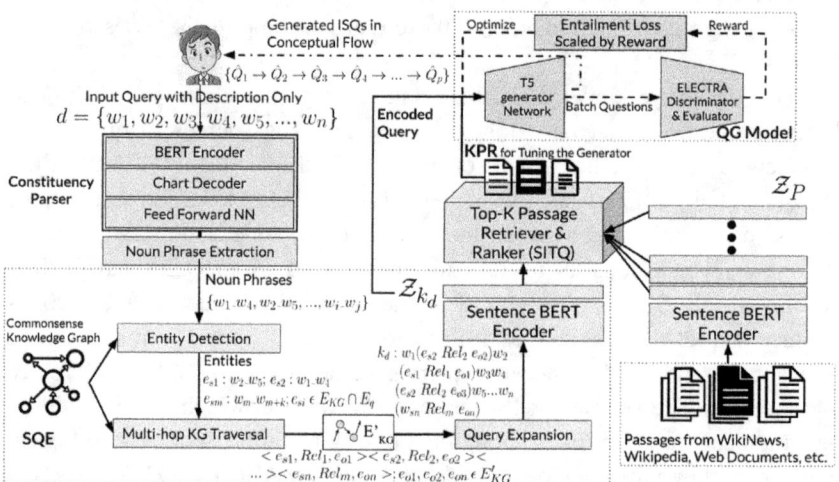

Figure 8.4 Overview of our approach that can be considered as a semantic and grey box alternative to retrieval augmented generation (RAG). ISEEQ combines a BERT-based constituency parser, semantic query expander (SQE), and knowledge-aware passage retriever (KPR) to provide relevant context to a QG model for ISQ generations. The QG model illustrates a structure of ISEEQ variants: ISEEQ-RL and ISEEQ-ERL. We train ISEEQ in a generative-adversarial reinforcement learning setting that maximizes semantic relations and coherence while generating ISQs (patent with Samsung Research America; Gaur et al., 2023).

8.1 ISEEQ Architecture and Evaluation

with entailment constraints (ISEEQ-ERL). Inputs to ISEEQ are IS queries described in natural language. For instance, an IS query can be described with Titles and Descriptions (T & D), Descriptions only (D only), Topics and Aspects (Tp & Asp), and others.

SQE: We expand the possibly short user input queries with the help of the ConceptNet Commonsense Knowledge Graph (CNetKG) (Speer et al., 2017). We first extract the entity set $\mathbf{E}_d$ in a user query description d using CNetKG. For this, we use the pre-trained self-attentive encoder-decoder-based constituency parser with BERT as the encoder for consistency in ISEEQ. The parser is conditioned to extract noun phrases that capture candidate entities defining an IS query (Kitaev and Klein, 2018). If the phrases are mentioned in the CNetKG, they are termed entities. Then a multi-hop triple extraction (subject-entity, relation, object-entity) over CNetKG is performed using depth-first search on an entity set $\mathbf{E}_d$. Triples of the form $< e_d, Rel_i, e_x >$ and $< e_y, Rel_j, e_d >$ are extracted, where $e_d \in \mathbf{E}_d$. We keep only those triples where e_d ($\in \mathbf{E}_d$) appears as the subject-entity. We use this heuristic (1) to minimize noise and (2) to gather more direct information about the entities in $\mathbf{E}_d$. Finally, we contextualize d by injecting extracted triples to get k_d, a knowledge-augmented query.

Take, for example, a **D only** IS query d ($\in \mathbf{D}$), "Want to consider career options from becoming a physician's assistant vs a nurse." The extracted entity set $\mathbf{E}_d$ for d is {career, career_options, physician, physician_assistant, nurse}. Then, the extracted triples for this entity set are <career_options, isrelatedto, career_choice>, <career_options, isrelatedto, profession>, <physician_assistant, is_a, PA>, <physician, is_a, medical doctor>, [...], <nurse, is_a, psychiatric_nurse>, <nurse, is_a, licensed_practical_nurse>, <nurse, is_a, nurse_practitioner>, [...]. The knowledge augmented k_d is

---

Want to consider career options career options is related to career choice, profession from becoming a physician's assistant physician assistant is a PA medical doctor, [...] vs a nurse nurse is a psychiatric nurse, licensed practical nurse, [...].

Next, we pass this into KPR. The set $\{k_d\}$, for all d $\in \mathbf{D}$ is denoted by $\mathbf{K_D}$ used by the QG model in ISEEQ.

KPR: Given the knowledge-augmented query k_d, KPR retrieves passages from a set $\mathbf{P}$ and ranks them to get the top-K passages $\mathbf{P}_{\text{top-K}}$. For this purpose, we make the following specific improvements in the dense passage retriever

(DPR) described in (Lewis et al., 2020): (1) Sentence-BERT encoder for the passages $p \in \mathbf{P}$ and k_d. We create dense encodings of $p \in \mathbf{P}$ using Sentence-BERT, which is represented as $\mathcal{Z}_p$ (Reimers and Gurevych, 2019). Likewise, encoding of k_d is represented as $\mathcal{Z}_{k_d}$. (2) Incorporate a SITQ (Simple locality sensitive hashing (Simple-LSH) and iterative quantization) algorithm to pick the top-K passages ($\mathbf{P}_{\text{top-K}}$) using a normalized entity score (NES). SITQ is a fast approximate search algorithm over MIPS to retrieve and rank passages. It can be formalized as $Score(\mathbf{P}_{\text{top-K}}|k_d)$, where

$$Score(\mathbf{P}_{\text{top-K}}|k_d) \propto \{\text{WMD}(\mathcal{Z}_{k_d}^T \mathcal{Z}_p)\}_{p \in \mathbf{P}},$$

$$\mathcal{Z}_{k_d} = \text{S-BERT}(k_d); \mathcal{Z}_p = \text{S-BERT}(p).$$

SITQ converts dense encodings into low-rank vectors and calculates the semantic similarity between the input query and the passage using word mover distance (WMD) (Kusner et al., 2015). $\mathbf{P}_{\text{top-K}}$ from SITQ is re-ranked by NES, calculated[1] for each $p \in \mathbf{P}_{\text{top-K}}$ as $\frac{\sum_{e_j \in k_d} \{\mathbb{I}(e_j=w)\}_{w \in p}}{|k_d|}$, and arranged in descending order. $\mathbf{P}_{\text{top-K}}$ consists of K passages with NES > 80%. Execution of KPR is iterative and stopped when each query in the train set has at least one passage for generating ISQs.

We tested the retrieval efficiency of KPR using encoding of e_d denoted by $\mathcal{Z}_{e_d}$ and using the encoding of k_d denoted by $\mathcal{Z}_{k_d}$ as inputs to KPR. Measurements were recorded using hit rate (HR) @ 10 and 20 retrieved passages. Mean average precision (MAP) is calculated with respect to ground truth questions in QAMR. There are two components in MAP: (a) *Relevance* of the retrieved passage in generating questions that have > 70% cosine similarity with ground truth; (b) normalize *Relevance* by the number of ground truth questions per input query. To get MAP, we multiply (a) and (b) and take the mean over all the input queries. We computed MAP by setting $K = 20$ retrieved passages due to the good confidence from the hit rate (a hyperparameter). KPR outperformed the comparable baselines on the QAMR Wikinews dataset, and Table 8.1 shows that SQE improves the retrieval process.[2] A set of $\mathbf{P}_{\text{top-K}}$ for $\mathbf{K_D}$ is denoted by $\{\mathbf{P}_{\text{top-K}}\}_{k_d}, k_d \in \mathbf{K_D}$.

QG Model: ISEEQ leverages $\mathbf{K_D}$ and $\{\mathbf{P}_{\text{top-K}}\}_{k_d}$ to learn QG in a generative-adversarial setting guided by a reward function. ISEEQ-RL contains T5-base as a generator and Electra-base as a discriminator to learn to generate IS-type questions. ISEEQ uses the reward function to learn to selectively preserve

---
[1] an entity occurring multiple times in p is counted once.
[2] KPR($\mathcal{Z}_{e_d}$) & KPR($\mathcal{Z}_{k_d}$) are executed for each CAsT-19 query.

8.1 ISEEQ Architecture and Evaluation

Table 8.1 *Evaluating retrievers. ECE: Electra Cross Encoder; (*): variant of Clark et al., 2019; DPR: Dense Passage Retrieval.*

Retrievers	HR@10	HR@20	MAP
TF-IDF + ECE (Clark et al., 2019)	0.31	0.45	0.16
BM25 + ECE*	0.38	0.49	0.23
DPR (Karpukhin et al., 2020)	0.44	0.61	0.31
KPR(Z_{e_d})	0.47	0.66	0.35
KPR(Z_{k_d})	0.49	0.70	0.38

terms from the IS query versus introducing diversity. Also, the reward function prevents ISEEQ from generating ISQs that are loose in context or redundant.

Reward Function: Let q_i^n be the ith question in the ground truth questions Q having n tokens, and let $\hat{q}_i^m$ be the ith question in the list of generated questions, $\hat{Q}$, having m tokens. We create BERT encodings for each of the n and m words in the question vectors. The reward (R_i) in ISEEQ-RL and ISEEQ-ERL is defined as

$$\alpha \left[\frac{LCS(\hat{q}_i^m, q_i^n)}{|\hat{q}_i^m|} \right] + (1-\alpha) \left[\sum_{\hat{w}_{ij} \in \hat{q}_i^m} \max_{w_{ik} \in q_i^n} \text{WMD}(\hat{w}_{ij}^T w_{ik}) \right], \quad (8.1)$$

where $\alpha[*]$ is a normalized longest common subsequence (LCS) score that captures word order and makes ISEEQ-RL learn to copy in some very complex IS-type queries. $(1-\alpha)[*]$ uses WMD to account for semantic similarity and compositional diversity. For a q_i^n = "What is the average starting salary in the UK?", $(1-\alpha)[*]$ generates $\hat{q}_i^m$ = "What is the average earnings of nurse in UK?"

Loss Function in ISEEQ-RL: We revise the cross entropy (CE) loss for training ISEEQ by scaling with the reward function because the $k_d \in \mathbf{K_D}$ are not only short but they also vary by context. Corresponding to each k_d, there are b ground truth questions $q_{1:b}$, and thus, we normalize the revised CE loss by a factor of b. Formally, we define our CE loss in ISEEQ-RL,

$$\mathcal{L}(\hat{q}_{1:b}|q_{1:b}, \theta) = \frac{-\sum_{i=1}^{b} R_i \cdot \mathbb{I}(q_i^n = \hat{q}_i^m) \cdot \log Pr(\hat{q}_i^m|\theta)}{b}, \quad (8.2)$$

where $\mathbb{I}(q_i^n = \hat{q}_i^m)$ is an indicator function counting word indices in q_i^n that match word indices in $\hat{q}_i^m$. The CE loss over $\mathbf{K_D}$ in a discourse dataset is $\mathcal{L}(\hat{Q}|Q, \Theta)_t$, recorded after the tth epoch. Formally,

$$\mathcal{L}(\hat{Q}|Q, \Theta)_t = \gamma \mathcal{L}(\hat{Q}|Q, \Theta)_{t-1} + (1-\gamma)\mathcal{L}(\hat{q}_{1:b}|q_{1:b}, \theta). \quad (8.3)$$

Theoretically, ISEEQ-RL addresses RQ1 but weakly mandates conceptual flow while generating ISQs. Thus, it does not address RQ2.

Loss Function in ISEEQ-ERL: For instance, given d2($\in$ **D**): "Bothered by feeling down or depressed," the ISEEQ-RL generations are: ($\hat{q}_1$): What is the reason for the depression, hopelessness? and ($\hat{q}_2$) What is the frequency of you feeling down and depressed? whereas ISEEQ-ERL would re-order, placing ($\hat{q}_2$) before ($\hat{q}_1$) for conceptual flow. To develop ISEEQ-ERL, we redefine the loss function in ISEEQ-RL by introducing principles of entailment as in NLI (Gao et al., 2020; Tarunesh et al., 2021). Consider $\hat{q}_{i|next}^m$ to be the next generated question after $\hat{q}_i^m$. We condition Equation 8.2 on $y_{max} = \arg\max_Y \text{RoBERTa}(\hat{q}_i^m, \hat{q}_{i|next}^m)$, where $Y \in$ {neutral, contradiction, entailment} and $Pr(y_{max}) = \max_Y \text{RoBERTa}(\hat{q}_i^m, \hat{q}_{i|next}^m)$. Formally, $\mathcal{L}(\hat{q}_{1:b}|q_{1:b}, \theta)$ in ISEEQ-ERL is:

Algorithm 8.1: Entailment Constrained Loss in ISEEQ-ERL
---
1 **if** $y_{max} ==$ *entailment* **then**
2 $\quad$ CE $- Pr(y_{max})$;
3 **else**
4 $\quad$ RCE $= -\frac{\sum_{i=1}^{b} R_i(1-\mathbb{I}(q_i=\hat{q}_i))Pr(\hat{q}_i|\theta)}{b}$;
5 $\quad$ RCE $- (1 - Pr(y_{max}))$;

Reverse cross entropy (RCE) complements CE (Equation 8.2) by checking that $\hat{q}_{i|next}^m$ is semantically related and coherent to $\hat{q}_i^m$. Tuning of the loss after an epoch follows Equation 8.3.

ISEEQ Evaluation: The ISEEQ-RL or ISEEQ-ERL generator uses top-p (nucleus) sampling with sum probability of generations equal to 0.92, a hyperparameter that sufficiently removes the possibility of redundant QG (Holtzman et al., 2019). We evaluate ISEEQ generations using Rouge-L (R-L), BERTScore (BScore) (Zhang et al., 2020), and BLEURT (BRT) (Sellam et al., 2020), which measure preservation of syntactic context, semantics, and legibility of generated question to human understanding, respectively. For conceptual flow in question generation, we define "semantic relations" (SR) and "logical coherence" (LC) metrics. To calculate SR or LC, we pair $\hat{Q}_{1:p}$ generated questions with Q. SR in the generations is computed across all pairs using RoBERTa pre-trained on semantic similarity tasks. LC between Q and $\hat{Q}_{1:p}$ is computed from counting the labels predicted as "entailment" by RoBERTa pre-trained on the SNLI dataset.

Table 8.2 An ablation study showing improvement in the quality of ISQs after encodings of retrieved passages ($\mathbf{P}_{1:K}$) are concatenated with knowledge-augmented query (k_a) after SQE. The concatenation is performed for each $p \in \mathbf{P}_{1:K}$.

Model	Encoding	QAD	QAMR	FBC
			R-L/BRT/BScore/SR/LC(%)	
ISEEQ-RL	$P_{1:K}$	0.62/ 0.73/ 0.39/ 0.21/ 21.3	0.47/ 0.71/ 0.39/ 0.63/ 28	0.74/ 0.83/ 0.60/ 0.73/ 71.6
	$P_{1:K}$ + SQE	0.65/ 0.74/ 0.45/ 0.25/ 22	0.53/ 0.78/ 0.71/ 0.65/ 34.7	0.74/ 0.87/ 0.65/ 0.73/ 71.8
ISEEQ-ERL	$P_{1:K}$	0.62/ 0.76/ 0.44/ 0.26/ 24.6	0.54/ 0.80/ 0.73/ 0.68/ 36.3	0.71/ 0.84/ 0.61/ 0.77/ 78.2
	$P_{1:K}$ + SQE	0.67/ 0.79/ 0.50/ 0.27/ 25.7	0.57/ 0.83/ 0.77/ 0.68/ 37.0	0.79/ 0.89/ 0.66/ 0.78/ 79.4

Baselines: As no system exists to generate ISQs automatically, we considered transformer language models fine-tuned (TLMs-FT) on open domain datasets used for reading comprehension and complex non-factoid answer retrieval as baselines. Specifically, the T5 model fine-tuned (T5-FT) on WikipassageQA (Cohen et al., 2018), SQUAD (Rajpurkar et al., 2016), and CANARD (Ghoneim and Peskov, 2019), and ProphetNet (Qi et al., 2020) fine-tuned on SQUADv2.0 are comparable baselines.

We substantiate our claims in RQ1, RQ2, and RQ3 by highlighting: (1) Multiple passage-based QG yields better results than the single gold passage QG used in TLMs-FT (e.g. T5 fine-tuned on SQUAD dataset; results in Table 8.3); (2) Knowledge-infusion through SQE significantly advances the process of QG; (3) Pressing on conceptual flow in ISEEQ-ERL improves SR and LC in generations. Evidence from 12 human evaluations supports our quantitative findings (Table 8.6); (4) We investigate the potential of ISEEQ-ERL in minimizing crowdworkers for IS dataset creation through cross-domain experiments.

Performance of ISEEQ-RL and ISEEQ-ERL: Datasets used in this research were designed for a CIS system to obtain the capability of multiple contextual passage retrieval and diverse ISQ generation. The process of creating such datasets requires crowdworkers to take the role of a CIS system responsible for creating questions and evaluators to see whether questions match the information needs of IS queries. Implicitly, the process embeds crowdworkers' curiosity-driven search to read multiple passages for generating ISQs. Baselines on employed datasets use single-passage QG, with much of the effort focusing on improving QG. In contrast, ISEEQ generation enjoys success from the connection of SQE, KPR, and novel QG model over baselines in CIS (see Table 8.3). With SQE, ISEEQ achieved 2–6% across all datasets. The knowledge-infusion in ISEEQ through SQE has shown to be powerful for baselines as well. Table 8.3 records 3–10%, 3–10%, and 1–3% performance gains of the baselines on QAD, QAMR, and FBC across five evaluation metrics, respectively. SQE allows baselines to semantically widen their search over the gold passages in datasets to generate diverse questions that match better with ground truth. Conversely, ISEEQ-RL generations benefit from dynamic meta-information retrieval from multiple passages, yielding increases of 20–35%, 6–13%, and 3–10% on QAD, QAMR, and FBC, respectively, across five evaluation metrics. In particular, QG in CAsT-19 and FBC datasets advance because of the KPR in ISEEQ-RL and ISEEQ-ERL (see Figures 8.5 and 8.6).

Most of the CAsT-19 and FBC queries required multiple passages to construct legible questions. For instance, an IS query: "Enquiry about

Table 8.3 Scores on test set of datasets. In comparison to T5-FT CANARD, a competitive baseline, ISEEQ-ERL generated better questions across three datasets (30%↑ in QADiscourse, 7%↑ in QAMR, and 5%↑ in FB Curiosity). For fine-tuning, we used SQUADv2.0.

Methods	SQE	QAD				QAMR				FBC			
		R-L	BRT	BScore	SR	LC(%)	R-L	BRT	BScore	SR	LC(%)	R-L	BRT	BScore	SR	LC(%)
T5-FT WikiPassageQA	–	0.37	0.43	0.16	0.17	10.0	0.19	0.51	0.38	0.36	17.0	0.65	0.78	0.54	0.51	47.3
	+Entities	0.39	0.45	0.16	0.17	10.0	0.20	0.53	0.38	0.36	17.5	0.65	0.78	0.54	0.52	47.4
	+Triples	0.41	0.46	0.16	0.18	11.0	0.20	0.53	0.39	0.37	17.8	0.65	0.78	0.55	0.52	47.3
T5-FT SQUAD	–	0.44	0.54	0.20	0.19	13.0	0.40	0.66	0.46	0.58	21.0	0.70	0.83	0.62	0.67	65.1
	+Entities	0.45	0.56	0.22	0.19	13.5	0.40	0.68	0.47	0.59	22.7	0.71	0.84	0.63	0.69	65.8
	+Triples	0.45	0.58	0.22	0.20	13.8	0.43	0.69	0.47	0.59	22.6	0.70	0.84	0.64	0.69	65.8
T5-FT CANARD	–	0.47	0.54	0.23	0.19	17.1	0.41	0.64	0.53	0.58	22.6	0.73	0.84	0.63	0.67	66.2
	+Entities	0.48	0.55	0.25	0.20	17.5	0.44	0.67	0.62	0.61	23.5	0.74	0.84	0.65	0.69	66.5
	+Triples	0.51	0.57	0.26	0.21	18.3	0.49	0.68	0.66	0.61	24.3	0.74	0.85	0.65	0.70	68.2
ProphetNet-FT SQUAD	–	0.31	0.44	0.14	0.17	12.2	0.35	0.59	0.38	0.36	21.5	0.63	0.78	0.53	0.67	63.2
	+Entities	0.31	0.44	0.14	0.17	12.7	0.37	0.60	0.41	0.37	22.1	0.65	0.78	0.54	0.67	63.3
	+Triples	0.34	0.45	0.15	0.18	13.0	0.37	0.61	0.43	0.37	22.3	0.65	0.79	0.56	0.69	64.0
ISEEQ-RL	–	0.57	0.72	0.40	0.22	20.0	0.50	0.75	0.67	0.64	29.4	0.71	0.84	0.62	0.69	68.2
	+Entities	0.64	0.72	0.41	0.23	22.0	0.52	0.77	0.68	0.64	33.1	0.72	0.85	0.63	0.71	69.8
	+Triples	0.65	0.74	0.45	0.25	22.0	0.53	0.78	0.71	0.65	34.7	0.74	0.87	0.63	0.73	71.8
ISEEQ-ERL	–	0.60	0.76	0.44	0.26	24.5	0.55	0.81	0.72	0.68	36.1	0.74	0.85	0.64	0.76	78.2
	+Entities	0.65	0.78	0.47	0.27	25.2	0.55	0.82	0.74	0.68	36.3	0.77	0.88	0.66	0.76	78.3
	+Triples	**0.67**	**0.79**	**0.50**	**0.27**	**25.7**	**0.57**	**0.83**	**0.77**	**0.68**	**37.0**	**0.79**	**0.89**	**0.66**	**0.78**	**79.4**

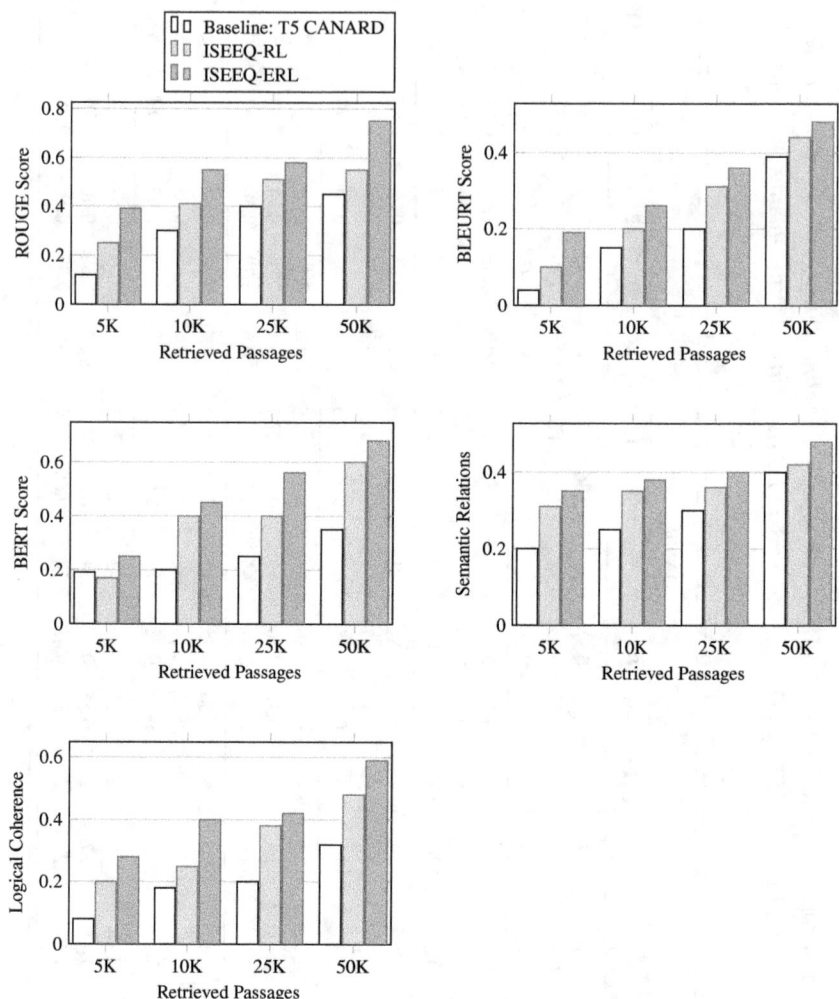

Figure 8.5 ISEEQ's results on CaST-19 datasets. ISEEQ RL generated 27% more questions that are semantically similar to ground truth compared to baseline: T5 CANARD model. The use of KG or contextual information in the form of entities sees a significant boost in the quality of generated questions in ISEEQ-ERL with minimal set of retrieved passages.

History, Economy, and Sports in Hyderabad" ISEEQ retrieved the following three passages: "History_Hyderabad," "Economy_Hyderabad," and "Sports_ Hyderabad," which were missing in the set of passages in FBC. Thus, TLM-FT baselines find it hard to construct legible ISQs using a single passage. Furthermore, ISEEQ-ERL advances the quality of ISQs over ISEEQ-RL by

8.1 ISEEQ Architecture and Evaluation

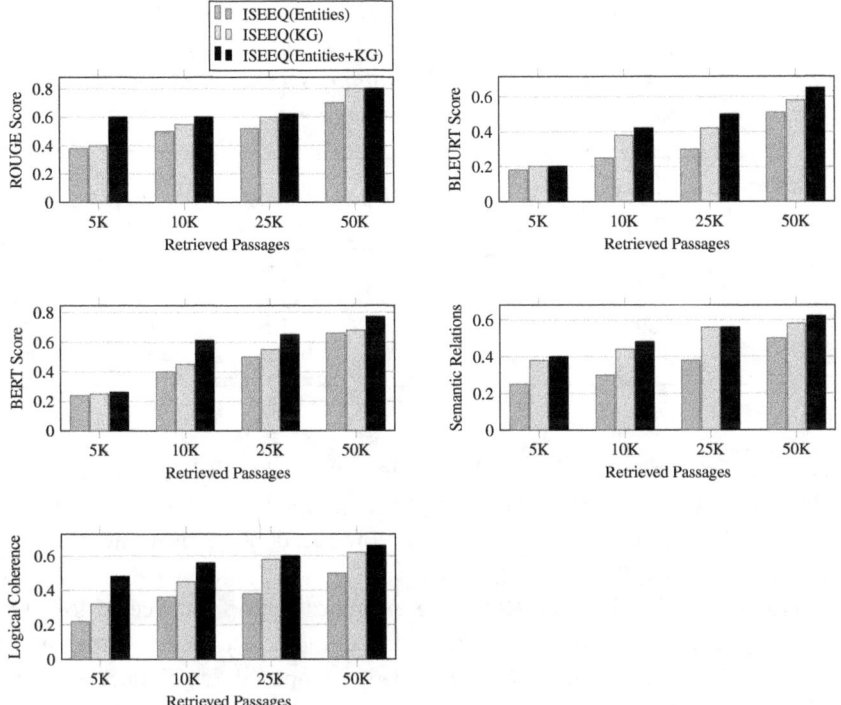

Figure 8.6 An ablation study on ISEEQ-ERL showed that enforcing entailment constraints led to high scores in semantic relation and logical agreement – conceptual flow. This strong performance was consistent across different passage sizes, from 5K to 50K. For smaller sets of 5K and 10K passages, using both entities and the KG did not significantly boost performance. However, for larger passage sets, the results were significant, with average scores exceeding 65% across all metrics.

7–14% and 6–10% in QAD and FBC (refer Table 8.2). This is because QAD and FBC questions require the QG model to emphasize conceptual flow.

Further, we examine the combined **performance of KPR** and ISEEQ-ERL on the CAsT-19 dataset (see Figure 8.5). KPR retrieves ~50K passages sufficient to generate questions for 269 IS queries (one query can have multiple passages). Table 8.4 depicts KPR($\mathcal{Z}_{e_d}$) retrieval performance match KPR($\mathcal{Z}_{k_d}$), with the latter supporting 72% of queries in the training set compared to 57% by KPR($\mathcal{Z}_{e_d}$). Also, it outperforms DPR, which supported 30% queries in the training set (see Table 8.4 and Figure 8.5). At testing time, KPR($\mathcal{Z}_{k_d}$) supported 84% queries that were used to generate questions by ISEEQ-ERL and evaluated with ground truth for SR and LC. Apart from

Table 8.4 *Performance of KPR on MS-MARCO passages while retrieving at least one passage per IS query in CAsT-19. The figure 269 is the size of the CAST-19 Training set. KPR covered the training set but left 16% of the IS queries in the test set. Ret.Pass.: Retrieved passages.*

Ret.pass.	DPR		KPR($\mathcal{Z}_{e_d}$)		KPR($\mathcal{Z}_{k_d}$)	
	Train	Test	Train	Test	Train	Test
5K	71	123	99	278	157	275
10K	96	133	154	301	194	316
25K	139	133	235	329	236	363
50K	173	144	**269**	358	**269**	402

the monotonic rise in SR and LC scores shown by ISEEQ, ISEEQ-ERL generations achieved better coherence than counterparts with 5K passages (Figure 8.6). We attribute the conceptual flow-based QG improvements to the addition of an entailment check and RCE.

Transferability Test for RQ3: We examine the performance of ISEEQ-ERL in an environment where the training and test datasets belong to a different domain. For instance, QAMR is composed of IS queries from Wikinews, whereas FBC is composed of IS queries from the geography category in Wikipedia.

From the experiments in Table 8.5, we make two deductions: (1) ISEEQ-ERL provided acceptable performance in generating ISQs for {Train-Test} pairs, where the training set size is smaller than that of the test set: {QAD-QAMR} and {QAMR-FBC}. (2) ISEEQ-ERL trained on a *narrow domain dataset* (FBC) generated far better ISQs for IS queries in the generic domain. The transferability test shows ISEEQ-ERL's ability to create new datasets for the training and development of CIS systems.

Human Evaluation: We carried out 12 blind evaluations of 30 information-seeking queries covering mental health (7), politics and policy (6), geography (5), general health (3), legal news (2), and others (4). Each evaluator rates ISQs from the ground-truth dataset (S1), ISEEQ-ERL (S2), and T5-FT CANARD (S3) using a Likert score where 1 is the lowest and 5 is the highest. A total of 570 ISQs (on average 7 by S1, 7 by S2, and 4 by S3) were evaluated on two guidelines, described in Table 8.6. We measured their statistical significance by first performing a one-way ANOVA and then using least significant difference (LSD) post-hoc analysis (as performed in Gunaratna et al. (2017)). Across the 30 queries on both guidelines, both S1 and S2 are better (statistically significant) than S3, whereas, even though S2 is better than S1, there is

Table 8.5 Transferability test scores using ISEEQ-ERL to answer RQ3. ISEEQ-ERL trained and tested on same dataset are along the diagonal. [Train-Test] pairs: [QAD-QAMR], [CAsT-19-QAMR], and [QAMR-FBC] showed acceptable cross-domain performance, where training set size is smaller than test set size.

Test → Train ↓	QAD	QAMR	FBC	CAsT19
	R-L/BRT/BScore/SR/LC(%)			
QAD	**0.67/ 0.79/ 0.50/ 0.27/ 25.7**	0.56/ 0.79/ 0.75/ 0.64/ 33.1	0.62/ 0.70/ 0.55/ 0.71/ 73.5	0.76/ 0.48/ 0.64/ 0.60/ 64.2
QAMR	0.73/ 0.89/ 0.62/ 0.28/ 27.7	0.57/ **0.83/ 0.77/ 0.68/ 37.0**	0.74/ 0.89/ 0.67/ 0.75/ 77.8	0.67/ 0.41/ 0.57/ 0.57/ 58.6
FBC	0.70/ 0.73/ 0.56/ 0.31/ 33.0	0.61/ 0.85/ 0.72/ 0.67/ 35.8	**0.79/ 0.89/ 0.66/ 0.78/ 79.4**	0.75/ 0.37/ 0.76/ 0.67/ 66.5
CAsT-19	0.58/ 0.69/ 0.51/ 0.23/ 25.2	0.52/ 0.73/ 0.70/ 0.61/ 33.4	0.63/ 0.77/ 0.57/ 0.73/ 76.5	**0.74/ 0.48/ 0.68/ 0.61/ 65.0**

Table 8.6 *Assessment of human evaluation. G1: ISQs are diverse in context and non-redundant. G2: ISQs are logically coherent and share semantic relations. >: the difference is statistically significant. SD: Standard deviation. S1, S2, and S3 are ground truth, ISEEQ-ERL, and T5-FT CANARD, respectively.*

	Response: Mean (SD)			$F_{(2, 957)}$ (p-value)	LSD post-hoc (p <0.05)
	S1	S2	S3		
G1	3.756 (1.14)	3.759 (1.06)	3.518 (1.08)	5.05 (6.5e-3)	S1>S3, S2>S3
G2	3.803 (1.10)	3.843 (1.02)	3.503 (1.06)	9.71 (6.63e-5)	S1>S3, S2>S3

no statistical significance between the two systems (we may say they are comparable).

8.2 Personalized Conversation Agent

Personalization in conversational AI can go beyond chit-chat conversations and aid in user engagement by understanding their personas better and providing accurate responses (Joshi et al., 2017; Bender et al., 2021).

Prior research on personalization has primarily focused on casual conversations, emphasizing details such as a user's preferences. The lack of external knowledge hinders a model's ability to adapt to different personas (Deshpande et al., 2023). Therefore, recent shifts in chatbot personalization utilize both persona information and knowledge (Qian et al., 2021; Liu et al., 2023a). However, identifying a suitable context aligned with user preferences during a conversation remains a significant challenge for current LLMs.

While using various prompting methods may allow a user to steer LLMs toward desired behavior, they only work at an utterance level. This may not be feasible for longer conversations, as the context often shifts (Shuster et al., 2021). Therefore, we require the chatbot to learn how to retrieve appropriate content based on a user's query and assess whether a response requires contextualization (retrieval of meta-information) and personalization (selecting an appropriate persona, if necessary).

To address this issue, we propose using **knowledge-guided personalization of response generation with reward modulation** (**𝒦-PERM**). **𝒦-PERM** uses dynamic knowledge retrieval along with personalization to improve a machine's adaptive capabilities to different personas and contexts. Our personalized response generation task involves two major components:

(i) *Understanding Conversation Context:* We use dense passage retrieval (DPR) (Karpukhin et al., 2020) to select the most pertinent information from a larger text corpus containing real-world information.

(ii) *Incorporating Appropriate Personas:* We introduce a selector module capable of choosing a persona that aligns with the user query. We model persona selection as a multiple-choice question-answering task, which includes an option to opt for "no-persona" in generic cases.

Background: PersonaChat and PersonaChat 2.0 are chit-chat conversation datasets used to train conversational agents (Wu et al., 2020a; Liu et al., 2022). They incorporate encoder–decoder models, reinforcement learning, few-shot learning, and hierarchical attention mechanisms to improve personalization by considering persona and conversational history (Li et al., 2016; Qiu and Zhang, 2021; Young et al., 2022). In previous personalization work, external knowledge was not a significant focus until Mazumder et al. introduced retrieval as a sub-task in PersonaChat to enhance personalization (Majumder et al., 2021). However, their method was not specifically evaluated on retrieval performance, using ROC Stories as a proxy knowledge source. This approach did not adequately capture personalization, especially for goal-oriented or information-seeking dialogues. $\mathcal{K}$-PERM addresses this gap by introducing retrieval-augmented generation as a practical baseline to improve personalization (Lewis et al., 2020; Gaur et al., 2022a). Unlike previous approaches that fine-tuned models on PersonaChat, $\mathcal{K}$-PERM uses base generative models for evaluation and achieves desired behaviors through reinforcement learning as the evaluator (Lipton et al., 2018; Huang et al., 2023). Additionally, $\mathcal{K}$-PERM introduces unique persona selection, making it the first realistic response generation model for real-time goal-oriented or information-seeking dialogues.

8.2.1 Methodology for Creating Personalized Agent

Let $U^t = \{u_1^t, u_2^t, \ldots, u_H^t\}$ be the history of H user utterances on a topic t. Each utterance $u_i^t \in U^t$ is a question and response pair denoted as (q_i^t, r_i^t). The q_i^t are questions by the user, specific to the topic t, and the r_i^t are responses that are either tailored according to a set of n user personas $P = \{p_1, p_2, \ldots, p_n\}$ or generic (no-persona). Our goal is to model the probability of the latest user response r_H^t given a set of K passages, denoted by $\mathcal{Z}_K^{U^t}$, relevant to the utterance history U^t (the passages are drawn from an external knowledge source, e.g., a document store). Thus, our goal is to learn the probability distribution

$$\mathbb{P}_\theta(r_H^t \mid \mathcal{Z}_K^{U^t}), \tag{8.4}$$

where θ are the parameters of the probability distribution.

$\mathbb{P}_\theta$ can be any auto-regressive language model capable of generating sentences token-wise. Since the user is likely to have responded according to their set of personas, we train a persona selector module P_{select}, which takes as input the user's utterance history U^t and the set of passages $\mathcal{Z}_K^{U^t}$, and outputs one or more personas from P (denoted as P') for customizing responses using $\mathbb{P}_\theta$. Therefore, Equation (8.4) is modified as

$$\begin{aligned} P' &= P_{\text{select}}(\mathcal{Z}_K^{U^t}, P), \quad P' \subseteq P, \\ &\mathbb{P}_\theta(r_H^t \mid \mathcal{Z}_K^{U^t}, P'). \end{aligned} \tag{8.5}$$

$\mathcal{K}$**-PERM** (Figure 8.7) explains the entire model architecture of $\mathcal{K}$-PERM. Utilizing the conversation history U^t, we access a document store, retrieve pertinent passages, and rank them based on their relevance. This allows us to leverage the retrieved information to select compatible user personas and generate personalized responses. Our method personalizes based on the personas in P'. If $P' = \emptyset$, generic responses are generated.

Knowledge Retriever For dynamically retrieving passages based on U^t, we built upon a process called DPR – P_{select} in Equation (8.5). DPR uses semantic similarity search to retrieve passages from a vectorized database. This allows us to go beyond an *exact match* by retrieving passages that can answer reasoning-type questions (*what is? what if? what could be?*) by automatically adapting to the input queries in U^t.

We improve DPR in two ways. First, we utilize a Sentence-BERT model for performing a **retrieve-rank process using a paired cross-encoder and bi-encoder**. A cross-encoder retrieves a set of passages given the last query $q_H^t \in U^t$, and subsequently, the bi-encoder ranks and selects the top K passages to result in $\mathcal{Z}_K^{U^t}$. We create dense encodings of the passages in $z_j \in \mathcal{Z}_K^{U^t}$ using the MPNet model from the Sentence-BERT transformer family (Reimers and Gurevych, 2019). Likewise, the encoding for q_H^t is represented as z_H. We fine-tune MPNet on our dataset before using it to obtain dense encodings (Song et al., 2020).

Fine-Tuning MPNet for DPR: We used contrastive fine-tuning as described in Song et al. (2020). Next, we employed a combination of locality-sensitive hashing (LSH) and Facebook AI Similarity Search (FAISS), which uses maximum inner product search (MIPS) (Johnson et al., 2019) to efficiently obtain $\mathcal{Z}_K^{U^t}$. We evaluated the knowledge retriever's efficiency using BERTScore,

8.2 Personalized Conversation Agent

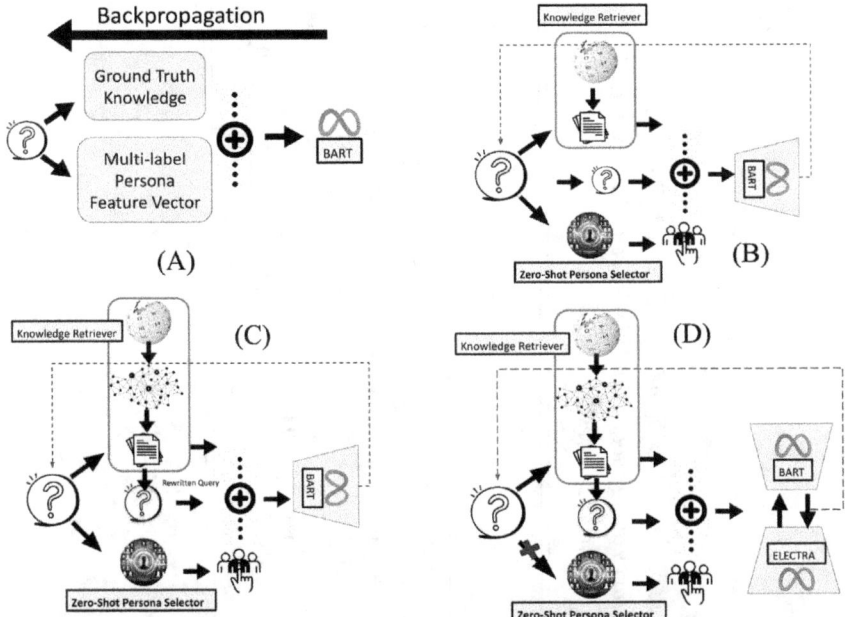

Figure 8.7 (A) BART FoCUS model (415 million parameter). (B), (C), and (D) show different $\mathcal{K}$-PERM model architectures. The model architecture comprises a persona selector and knowledge retriever, which leverage the history and question prompt to identify pertinent persona and knowledge. (A) Adds knowledge.

which is commonly used to compare retriever-augmented generations (Lim et al., 2022).

We varied K between 5 and 20 and observed high similarity (BERTScore) with ground truth passages (from the FoCus dataset) at $K = 10$. Therefore, we agreed that the appropriate number of retrieved passages would be 10. We also experimented with different sentence transformer models for dense encodings other than MPNet and standard retrievers, such as TF-IDF and BM25 (refer to Table 8.7).

8.2.2 Persona Selector (P_{select})

We model persona selection as a commonsense inference task, conditioned on the query knowledge $\mathcal{Z}_K^{U^t}$ retrieved using the information in q_H^t and the set of user personas P, formally written as $P' = P_{\text{select}}(\mathcal{Z}_K^{U^t}, P)$, as shown in Equation (8.5). The dataset contains the ground truth for the user's personas corresponding to the responses in the utterance history U^t. Using this, we train the P_{select} model as a multi-label classifier and sample the top two classes

Table 8.7 Evaluating knowledge retrievers over the indexed landmark Wikipedia articles in the FoCus dataset. Each score represents the maximum BERTScore computed between the retrieved passages and ground truth knowledge in FoCUS. ptECE: pre-trained ELECTRA Cross Encoder (Clark et al., 2020). Bold: Best, Underlined: 2nd best.

Model	Original query				Rewritten query			
# Passages	5	10	15	20	5	10	15	20
TFIDF	0.385	0.412	0.396	0.395	0.403	0.406	0.406	0.406
(TFIDF + ptECE)	0.422	0.434	0.430	0.427	0.441	0.452	0.457,	0.445
BM25	0.398	0.405	0.410	0.401	0.411	0.416	0.416	0.412
(BM25 + ptECE)	0.471	0.465	0.480	0.474	0.475	0.477	0.493	0.467
MPNet	0.542	0.558	0.613	0.621	0.540	0.560	0.608	0.604
MPNet$_{\text{Fine tuned}}$	**0.642**	**0.658**	**0.683**	**0.661**	**0.640**	**0.660**	**0.688**	**0.684**
ColBERT+X(Lawrie et al., 2022)	<u>0.588</u>	<u>0.584</u>	<u>0.601</u>	<u>0.601</u>	<u>0.598</u>	<u>0.602</u>	<u>0.605</u>	<u>0.601</u>
ColBERT (Khattab and Zaharia, 2020)	0.560	0.591	0.603	0.60	0.572	0.602	0.602	0.598

8.2 Personalized Conversation Agent

from the resulting logits ($|P'| = 2$). For the base P_{select} model, we empirically observed XLNET to give the highest performance (Yang et al., 2019).

Response Generation through Reward Modulation: The response is generated by pairing a BART(Base) generator with an ELECTRA(Base) evaluator that measures the similarity between the generated response and the ground truth (Clark et al., 2019). We introduce a balancing reward function (R_i) modulating generative capabilities (e.g., coherence) of the BART model and high fidelity to the ground truth responses (in terms of matched words).

Reward Function: Consider the ground truth response for a query q_i^t to be r_i^t, which consists of n tokens, where each token is indexed using t_i. Let r_k^t be the kth response in the generated response list comprising m tokens, where each token is indexed using t_j. We generate BERT encodings for each word in the response vectors, both for the n words in r_i^t and the m words in r_k^t. The reward (R_i) is

$$R_i = \alpha \cdot \text{BLEU}\left(r_i^t, r_k^t\right) \\ + (1-\alpha) \sum_{(t_i \in r_i^t, t_j \in r_i^k)} \max_{t_i} \text{WMD}\left(t_i, t_j\right), \quad (8.6)$$

where WMD denotes the word mover distance (Kusner et al., 2015), and $\alpha[*] \in [0,1]$ balances between a well-generated response by BART (given by the WMD distance) and closeness to the ground truth responses (provided by the BLEU score).

Persona-Tailored Reward Function In addition to producing syntactically sound responses and responses that are close to the ground truth, the responses need to be tailored to user personas, that is, the output of the P_{select} model. Thus, we modify Equation 8.6 as follows:

$$R_i = \alpha \, \text{BLEU}\left(r_i^t, r_k^t\right) \\ + \beta \sum_{(t_i \in r_i^t, t_j \in r_i^k)} \max_{t_i} \text{WMD}\left(t_i, t_j\right) \quad (8.7) \\ + \gamma \cdot \text{Loss}(P_{\text{select}}, P_{\text{gt}}), \quad \alpha + \beta + \gamma = 1,$$

where gt is the ground truth, and Loss($P_{\text{select}}, P_{\text{gt}}$) refers to the loss function, that is, the training error in the persona selected and the ground truth persona (if present).

Training Process: We employed BART, an auto-regressive encoder–decoder model, for generating personalized responses by incorporating special tags like <question>, <knowledge>, <history>, and <persona> during fine-tuning.

Training took approximately 16 hours on a single NVIDIA T4 GPU, and response generation utilized beam search with a beam size of five for stability over nucleus sampling (Chen and Yang, 2021; Shaham and Levy, 2022).

8.2.3 Experiments

We utilize the FoCus dataset developed by (Jang et al., 2022b) for our experiments, as it contains customized answers built with both persona and Wikipedia knowledge instead of just persona (Zhang et al., 2018). Our experiments use BART as the language model ($\mathbb{P}_\theta$).

Dataset: We utilize the publicly available FoCus dataset, which consists of passages describing landmarks (Jang et al., 2022b). The dataset includes 13,484 dialogs for training and validation, with an average of 5.6 rounds per dialog and approximately 7,715 Wikipedia landmarks. The dialogs contain a total of 75,971 utterances, with an average length of 24.0 words per utterance. We split the dataset into three sets: train (10,284 samples), validation (1,600 samples), and test (1,600 samples), comprising 57,928, 9,008, and 9,035 utterances, respectively. The training set includes 36,472 knowledge-based utterances and 21,456 utterances with both persona and knowledge, coming from 4,918 landmarks. Validation and test datasets consist of 5,664 and 5,707 knowledge-based utterances, respectively. Additionally, the validation set includes 3,344 utterances featuring both persona and knowledge, while the test set comprises 3,328 such utterances. The validation set encompasses 1,414 Wikipedia landmarks, whereas the test set involves 1,383 landmarks. The dataset references "ground persona" and "ground knowledge," representing the ground truth persona and passage selected by crowdworkers. Additionally, all the questions in the dataset were rewritten using T5-CANARD, a query-rewriting model (Qian and Oard, 2021) (Table 8.7 shows why question rewriting was needed).

Evaluation Criteria: We used Rouge–1/2/L/L-Sum and BLEU scores to evaluate $\mathcal{K}$-PERM. In addition, we use two transformer-based metrics for evaluating natural language generation: BERTScore (BF1: BERTScore F1-score) and NUBIA, which measure semantic relations, contractions, irrelevancy, and logical agreement (Kane et al., 2020; Zhang et al., 2020). Semantic relations evaluate whether the generated text is relevant and coherent and maintain the intended meaning and context of the input query. Measuring these characteristics for our proposed model is important to ensure LLMs' correct merging of knowledge and persona.

Baselines: We compare our model with two baselines – **(1) GODEL**: A large pre-trained transformer-based encoder–decoder model for goal-directed dialogues similar to FoCus (Peng et al., 2022); we used the pre-trained GODEL model and enhanced it with personalization by incorporating a persona selected by our persona selector model. **(2) BART$_{FoCus}$**: We utilized the BART model provided with the FoCus dataset (Jang et al., 2022b). We fine-tuned this model (BART$_{FoCus}$) using our training and validation sets for a fair comparison. Results are reported on our test set, although it was not made available by the authors of the FoCus dataset.

Results and Discussion: Table 8.10 compares three models: BART$_{FoCus}$ (406 million parameters), GODEL (6 billion parameters), and $\mathcal{K}$-PERM (250 million parameters). The results show that the pre-trained version of GODEL, without personalization, performed worse than BART$_{FoCus}$. However, when GODEL incorporated our persona selector model, it achieved a syntactic similarity closer to BART$_{FoCus}$, suggesting that the persona-based approach improved GODEL's syntactic quality: in terms of semantic similarity measured by BERTScore, GODEL with persona outperformed BART$_{FoCus}$, indicating that GODEL, when utilizing personas, generated responses that were more semantically similar to the desired outputs. $\mathcal{K}$-PERM significantly outperformed GODEL in terms of syntactic generation quality and semantic similarity. Ablation studies (see Table 8.8) on $\mathcal{K}$-PERM showed that using the ground persona and our persona selector resulted in the highest quality generation both syntactically and semantically. However, there were cases where $\mathcal{K}$-PERM ignored the persona for specific queries requiring personalization, resulting in errors compared to using the ground persona. Despite this limitation, the knowledge retriever used in $\mathcal{K}$-PERM demonstrated competitive performance,

Table 8.8 *Performance of $\mathcal{K}$-PERM using NUBIA score. Results are compared with baseline BART$_{FoCus}$. Bold-faced are best (GP), and underlined are second-best (P_{select}). LA: Logical agreement, SR: Semantic relatedness.*

Models	NUBIA	SR	Contraction (%)	Irrelevancy (%)	LA (%)
$BART_{FoCus}$	0.10	1.601	28.72	72.71	16.75
$\mathcal{K}$-PERM (GK only)	0.24	2.20	11.78	74.4	13.5
$\mathcal{K}$-PERM (All P + $\mathcal{Z}_k$)	0.22	1.90	13.18	70.1	17.5
$\mathcal{K}$-PERM (GP + $\mathcal{Z}_k$)	**0.34**	**2.80**	**11.87**	**66.38**	**21.75**
$\mathcal{K}$-PERM (SP + $\mathcal{Z}_k$)	<u>0.31</u>	<u>2.42</u>	<u>11.85</u>	<u>69.61</u>	<u>19.44</u>

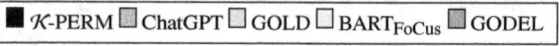
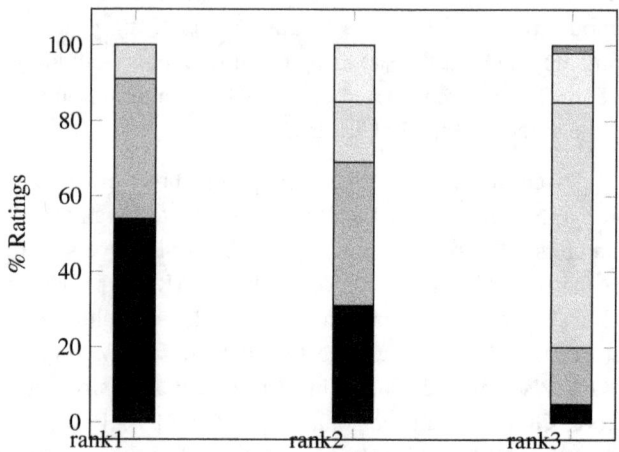

Figure 8.8 $\mathcal{K}$-PERM was preferred 32% more than ChatGPT by the annotators based on a blind evaluation of 90 queries taken randomly from the FoCus dataset. GOLD is the ground truth in FoCus dataset.

relying on information from Wikipedia articles rather than handcrafted knowledge in the FoCus dataset.

Another set of experiments with $\mathcal{K}$-PERM using NUBIA as the metric (see Table 8.8) showed that using personas yielded better semantic relations, logical agreement, lower contradiction, and lower irrelevancy compared to providing all personas simultaneously. When using retrieved knowledge, $\mathcal{K}$-PERM achieved a higher NUBIA score compared to using handcrafted knowledge in BART$_{FoCus}$. In a blind assessment of responses obtained from 5 different systems, generated across 90 user queries with varying numbers of personas, $\mathcal{K}$-PERM consistently outperformed the competition. It achieved the top position in 54 query cases, showcasing its remarkable performance compared to GODEL and GPT 3.5, as depicted in Figure 8.8.

Finally, we use $\mathcal{K}$-PERM to augment a state-of-the-art LLM, GPT3.5. Our results in Figure 8.9 show that augmenting GPT3.5 with $\mathcal{K}$-PERM improves its performance significantly (10.5%), highlighting the advantage of $\mathcal{K}$-PERM in personalization.

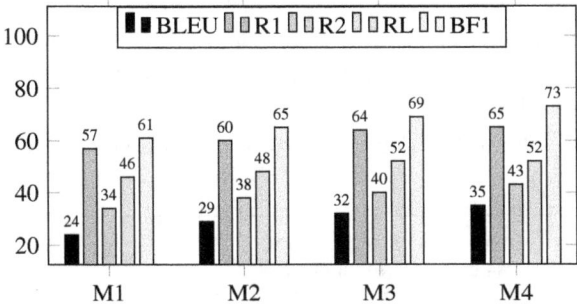

Figure 8.9 $\mathcal{K}$-PERM improves personalization in GPT 3.5 via zero-shot prompting. This experiment aimed to assess the performance improvement of GPT 3.5 when combined with $\mathcal{K}$-PERM. M1 is GPT 3.5 and M2, M3, and M4 represent zero-shot prompting of GPT 3.5 using responses from $\mathcal{K}$-PERM with (All P+Z_k), (GP+Z_k), and (P_{select}+Z_k), respectively.

Human Evaluation: We conducted a blind evaluation of 90 responses generated from 5 systems. As the task was trivial, the authors instructed the annotators verbally. The task was made available on a participant pool management system that credits students who completed the task. We experimented with five systems: $\mathcal{K}$-PERM, BART$_{\text{FoCus}}$, ChatGPT, GODEL, and Ground Truth. Our model, $\mathcal{K}$-PERM, consistently stood out as a top performer by securing first place in 11 instances and maintaining a strong second position in 68 instances. This underscores its exceptional performance. The top three results and percentage of times any specific model is selected are depicted in Figure 8.8. Table 8.9 shows a sample from our human evaluation.

8.3 Mental Health Conversational Agent

Virtual mental health assistants (VMHAs) are AI-based agents or CoPilots that provide emotional support and assist in mental health-related conversations. Their primary objective is to engage in organized conversation flows to assess users' mental health issues and gather details about the causes, symptoms, treatment options, and relevant medications. The information collected is subsequently shared with MHPs to provide insights into the user's condition (Hartmann et al., 2019). VMHAs are a valuable and distinct addition to the mental health support landscape, offering several advantages, including scalability, over conventional methods like public health forums, online communities, and platforms like Talklife. VMHAs can provide personalized

Table 8.9 *Human Assessment: 𝒦-PERM did better than ChatGPT regarding personalized response generation. The personas "I have been to New Hampshire" (top) and "I like visiting Canada" (bottom) were used in the examples above. We have boldfaced numeric values to focus on the correctness of information delivery using a retrieval-augmented generation mechanism.*

| Wikipedia topic | /wiki/Mount_Monadnock |
| Query | Where is the mountain? |

Personalized response generation: Example 1	
Ground truth	Mount Monadnock is a mountain in the towns of Jaffrey and Dublin, New Hampshire.
BART$_{FoCus}$	Mount Monadnock is at New Hamsphire.
GODEL	It's near the Rivers and the Masses.
ChatGPT	Based on the context and your persona, you have already visited Mount Monadnock! It is located in the towns of Jaffrey and Dublin, New Hampshire.
𝒦-PERM*	Mount Monadnock is a **3,165-ft (965 m)** mountain in the towns of Jaffrey and Dublin, New Hampshire, a place you have visited.

Personalized response generation: Example 1	
Wikipedia topic	/wiki/Assiniboine_Park_Zoo
Query	Where is this place?
ChatGPT,	"The query "Where is this place?" is referring to the Assiniboine Park Zoo in Winnipeg, Manitoba, Canada. If you like Canada, you should check out this zoo when possible! It's been a staple of the city since 1904!
𝒦-PERM†	Assiniboine Park Zoo is an **80-acre (32 ha)** zoo in Manitoba, Canada that was established in 1904.

support (Abd-Alrazaq et al., 2021), real-time assistance (Zielasek et al., 2022), and anonymity and privacy (Sweeney et al., 2021), and can complement human support with continuous availability (Ahmad et al., 2022) and patient health-generated data-driven insight (Sheth et al., 2019a).

Despite the proliferation of research at the intersection of clinical psychology, AI, and NLP, VMHAs missed an opportunity to serve as lifesaving contextualized, personalized, and reliable decision support during COVID-19 under the *Apollo moment* (Czeisler et al., 2020; Srivastava, 2021). During the critical period of COVID-19's first and second waves, known as the "Apollo moment," VMHAs could have assisted users in sharing their conditions, reducing their stress levels, and enabled MHPs to provide high-quality care. However, their capability as simple information agents, such

8.3 Mental Health Conversational Agent

Table 8.10 *Performance of K-PERM on FoCUS dataset. SP: P_{select}, GP: Ground persona, Z_k: Retrieved knowledge, P: Persona, GK: Ground truth knowledge. Bold-face: Best, underlined is 2nd best. pt: pre-trained.*

Models	BLEU	R1	R2	RL	BF1
ptGODEL	5.21	25.82	9.87	21.2	43.86
ptGODEL (P_{select})	6.18	30.02	13.77	26.11	44.34
BART$_{FoCus}$	6.24	30.98	14.22	26.81	43.85
K-PERM (without P, GK)	2.14	24.68	9.46	21.89	44.15
K-PERM (GK only)	11.2	31.14	15.49	26.73	43.26
K-PERM (GP only)	2.4	27.47	12.03	22.37	44.35
K-PERM (All P+Z_k)	11.22	35.19	19.27	31.18	43.45
K-PERM (GP+Z_k)	**14.72**	**43.09**	**25.43**	**37.95**	**47.36**
K-PERM (P_{select}+Z_k)	<u>12.01</u>	<u>37.53</u>	<u>23.96</u>	<u>33.47</u>	<u>46.06</u>

as suggesting meditation, relaxation exercises, or positive affirmations, fell short of effectively bridging the gap between monitoring the mental health of individuals and the need for in-person visits. As a result, trust in the use of VMHAs was diminished.

Trustworthiness in VMHAs: In human interactions, *trust* is built through consistent and reliable behavior, open communication, and mutual understanding. It involves a willingness to rely on someone or something based on their perceived competence, integrity, and reliability. Trustworthiness is often established and reinforced over time through interactions and experiences. In the context of AI, trustworthiness takes on new dimensions and considerations. Ensuring trustworthiness in AI has traditionally been a focus within human interactions and studies. However, as the collaboration between AI systems and humans intensifies, trustworthiness is gaining greater significance in AI, particularly in sensitive domains such as mental health. To this end, growing concerns about (misplaced) *trust* on *VMHA* for *social media* (tackling mental health) hampers the adoption of AI techniques during emergencies like COVID-19 (Srivastava, 2021). This inadequacy has prompted the community to develop a question-answering dataset for mental health during COVID-19, aiming to train more advanced VMHAs (Raza et al., 2022). A recent surge in the use of ChatGPT, in particular for mental health, is emerging for providing crucial personalized advice without clinical explanation, which can hurt users' *safety*, and thus, *trust* (Sallam, 2023). In Varshney (2022), the author identifies the support for human interaction and explainable alignment with human values as essential for trust in AI systems. To holistically contribute toward

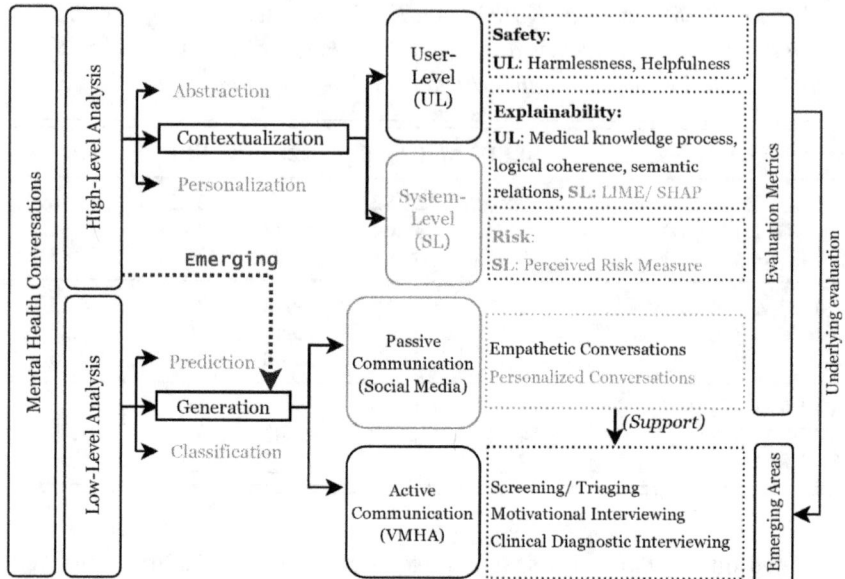

Figure 8.10 Functional taxonomy of mental health conversations. The blocks with black outlines define the scope of this review, and the bold dotted line highlights the growing emphasis on question/response generation in mental health conversations between VHMAs and users with mental health conditions. A high-level discourse analysis demands a focus on user-level explainability and safety, whereas a low-level analysis focuses on achieving clinically grounded active communications. The light gray blocks and text present the work in the past and are referred to in the review.

trustworthy behavior in a conversational approach in mental health, there is a need to critically examine VMHAs as a prospective tool to handle safety and explainability.

We will focus on five main research questions: (i) Defining the concepts of explainability and safety in VMHAs. (ii) Assessing the current capabilities and limitations of VMHAs. (iii) Analyzing the current state of AI and the challenges in supporting VMHAs. (iv) Exploring potential functionalities in VMHAs that patients seek as alternatives to existing solutions. (v) Identifying necessary evaluation changes regarding explainability, safety, and trust. Figure 8.10 visually presents the scope of the review, explicitly designed to emphasize the generative capabilities of current AI models, exemplified by the remarkable ChatGPT. However, the progress was made without keeping in sight two concerns related to safety and explainability: fabrication and hallucination. While these problems already exist in smaller language models, they are even more pronounced in larger ones. This concern motivated us to create a functional taxonomy for language models, with two distinct directions of focus: (a) *low-level abstraction*, which centers around analyzing linguistic cues in the data; (b) *high-level abstraction*, which concentrates on addressing the end-user's primary interests. The research in category (a) has been extensively conducted on social media. However, there is a lack of focus on active communication, which is precisely the area of interest in this chapter. As for high-level abstraction, current approaches like LIME developed by Ribeiro et al. (2016) have been employed, but it is crucial to explore this further, considering the different types of users.

Achieving these goals in VMHAs demands incorporating clinical knowledge, such as clinical practice guidelines and well-defined evaluation criteria. For instance, Figure 8.11 shows contextualization in VMHA while generating questions and responses. Further, it requires VMHAs to indulge in *active communication*, which is required to motivate users to keep using VMHA services. MHPs and government entities have advocated this as the required functionality to address the issue of growing patient population and limited healthcare providers (Cheng and Jiang, 2020).

8.3.1 Background

Prior data-driven research in mental health has examined social media to identify fine-grained cues informing the mental health conditions of an individual and, in turn, have developed datasets (Uban et al., 2021). These datasets capture authentic conversations from the real world and can be used in training VMHAs to screen users' mental health conditions. The current datasets typically have a foundation in psychology but are crowd-sourced rather than explicitly derived from clinically grounded guidelines of psychiatrists. We argue that semantic enhancements in VMHA with clinical knowledge and associated guidelines, if they remain under-explored, may miss the hidden mental states in a given narrative, which are an essential component of question generation (Gupta et al., 2022; Gaur et al., 2022b). To ensure that VMHAs are both safe and understandable, these datasets need to be semantically enhanced with clinically-grounded knowledge (e.g., MedChatbot (Kazi et al., 2012)) or clinical practice guidelines (e.g., Patient Health Questionnaire (PHQ-9), Kroenke et al. (2001)). In this section, we explore the state of research in explainability and safety in conversational systems to ensure trust (Hoffman et al., 2018).

Explanation: Conversations in AI are possible with large language models (LLMs) (e.g., GPT-3 (Floridi and Chiriatti, 2020), ChatGPT (Leiter et al.,

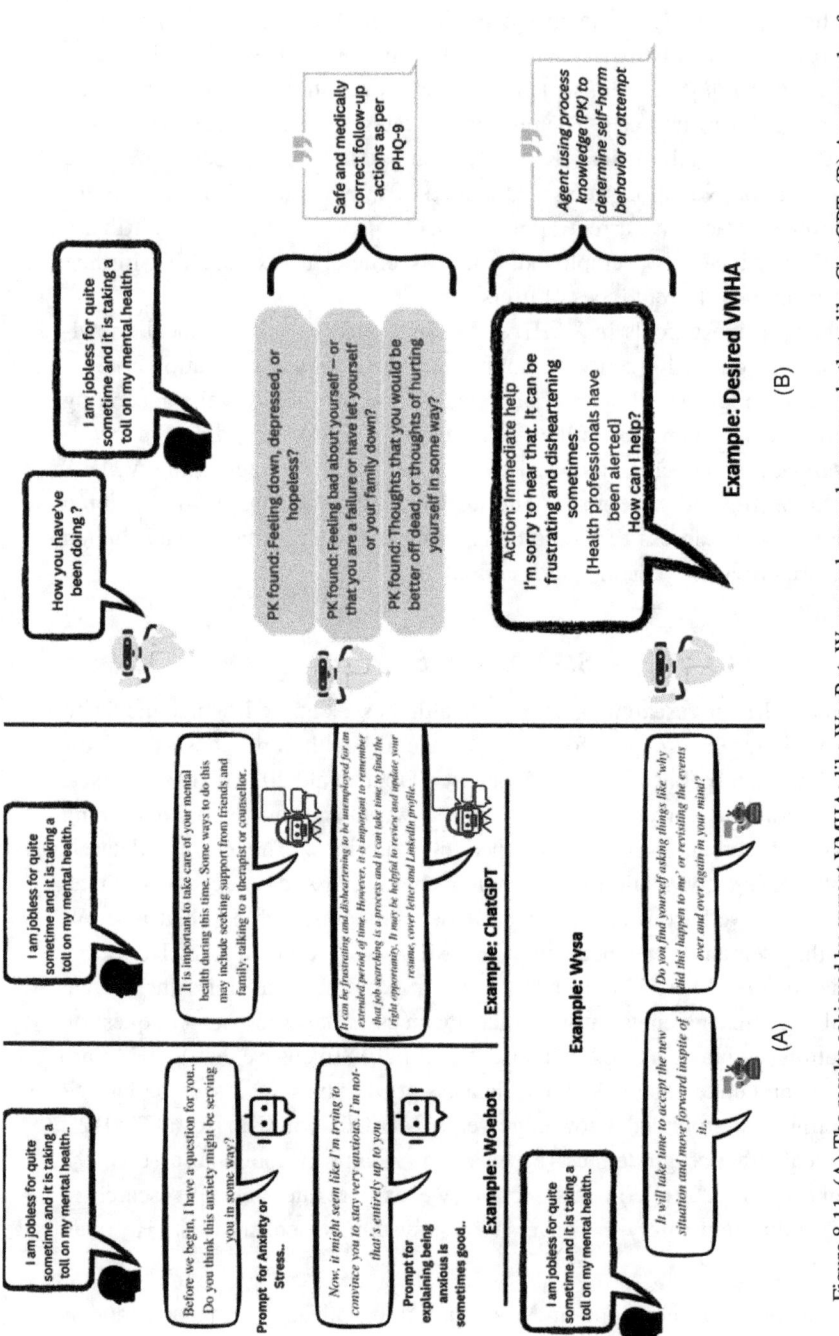

Figure 8.11 (A) The results achieved by current VMHAs like WoeBot, Wysa, and general-purpose chatbots like ChatGPT. (B) An example of an ideal VMHA is a knowledge-driven conversational agent designed for mental health support. This new VMHA utilizes questions based on the Patient Health Questionnaire-9 (PHQ-9) to facilitate a smooth and meaningful conversation about mental health. By incorporating clinical knowledge, the agent can identify signs of mental disturbance in the user and notify MHPs appropriately.

8.3 Mental Health Conversational Agent

2024)), which are established as state-of-the-art models for developing intelligent agents that chat with users by generating human-like questions or responses. In most instances, the output generated by LLMs tends to be grammatically accurate, but it often lacks factual accuracy or clarity. To this end, Bommasani et al. (2021) reports hallucination and harmful question generations as unexpected behaviors shown by such LLMs, and they are referred to as "black box" models by other authors (Rai, 2020). Further, Bommasani et al. (2021) characterize *hallucination* as a generated content that *deviates* significantly from the subject matter or is unreasonable. Recently, *Replika*, a VMHA augmented with GPT-3, provides meditative suggestions to a user expressing self-harm tendencies (Namvarpour et al., 2025). The absence of any link to a factual knowledge source that can help LLMs reason on their generation introduces what is known as the *black box* effect (Rudin, 2019). The consequences of the black box effect in LLMs are more concerning than their utility, particularly in mental health. For example, Figure 8.12 presents a scenario where ChatGPT advises the user about *toxicity in drugs*, which may have a negative consequence. The analysis above supports the critical need for an explainable approach to the decision-making mechanism of VMHAs. According to (Weick, 1995), explanations are human-centered sentences that signify the reason or justification behind an action and are understandable to a human expert. While there are various types of explanations, it is essential to focus on user-level explainability (Bhatt et al., 2020) rather than system-level explainability, as demonstrated through LIME (Ribeiro et al., 2016), SHAP (Lundberg and Lee, 2017), and integrated gradients (Sundararajan et al., 2017). The users interacting with the VMHAs may need more systematic information than just the decision making.

User-Level Explainability (UsEx): The sensitive nature of VMHAs raises *safety* as a significant concern of conversational systems as they may trigger a negative consequence. For instance, Figure 8.11 presents a real-world query from a user, which was common during the COVID-19 pandemic. In response to the query, the existing VMHAs – Woebot (Fitzpatrick et al., 2017), Wysa (Inkster et al., 2018), and ChatGPT (Leiter et al., 2024) – initiated a responsive conversation without focusing on the context (e.g., connecting mental health with its symptoms). As a result, we found assumptive questions (e.g., anxiety) and responses from Wysa, Woebot, and ChatGPT with no association with a clinical reference or clinical support. In contrast, the desired VMHA should (a) capture the relationship between the user query and expert questionnaires and (b) tailor the response to reflect the user's concerns (e.g., *frustrating* and *disheartening*) about their *long-term unemployment*, which is linked to *mental health* and *immediate user help*.

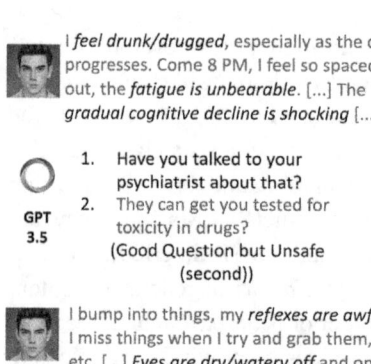

 I *feel drunk/drugged*, especially as the day progresses. Come 8 PM, I feel so spaced out, the *fatigue is unbearable*. [...] The gradual cognitive decline is shocking [...].

GPT 3.5
1. Have you talked to your psychiatrist about that?
2. They can get you tested for toxicity in drugs?
(Good Question but Unsafe (second))

 I bump into things, my *reflexes are awful*, I miss things when I try and grab them, etc. [...] *Eyes are dry/watery off* and on. Numbness all over body. Tough to explain

GPT 3.5
1. Have you considered taking energy meds?
2. How frequent do you take breaks?
(Good Questions but Unsafe (first))

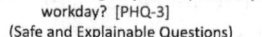

 I *feel drunk/drugged*, especially as the day progresses. Come 8 PM, I feel so spaced out, the *fatigue is unbearable*. [...] The gradual cognitive decline is shocking [...].

KI Agent
1. How many tablets of antidepressants are you taking? [Clinically-explainable]
2. Do you feel low concentration? [PHQ-7]
3. How often have you been bothered by speaking listening?[PHQ-8]
4. How long do you sleep before your workday? [PHQ-3]
(Safe and Explainable Questions)

 I bump into things, my *reflexes are awful*, I miss things when I try and grab them, etc. [...] *Eyes are dry/watery off* and on. Numbness all over body. Tough to explain

KI Agent
1. How often do you feel weak with little energy? [PHQ-4]
2. How long do you sleep before on your workdays? [PHQ-3]
(Safe and Explainable Questions)

Figure 8.12 A conversational scenario where a user asks a query with multiple symptoms. Left is a set of generated questions obtained by repetitive prompting of ChatGPT. Right is a generation from ALLEVIATE, a knowledge-infused (KI) conversational agent with access to PHQ-9 and clinical knowledge from Mayo Clinic.

> **User-Level Explainability**
>
> UsEx refers to an AI system's ability to explain to users when requested. The explanations are given once the AI system has made its decisions or predictions. They are intended to assist users in comprehending the logic behind the decisions.

UsEx goes beyond simply providing a justification or reason for the AI's output; it aims to provide traceable links to real-world entities and definitions (Gaur et al., 2022b).

Safety: VMHAs must primarily prioritize safety and also maintain an element of comprehensibility to avoid undesirable outcomes. One way to accomplish this is by modifying VMHA functionality to meet the standards outlined by MHP (Koulouri et al., 2022).

Figure 8.12 displays a conversation excerpt exemplifying how a VMHA, equipped with access to clinical practice guidelines like PHQ-9, not only generates safe follow-up questions but also establishes connections between the generated questions and those in PHQ-9, showcasing UsEx. Such guidelines act as standards that enable VMHAs to exercise control over content generation, preventing the generation of false or unsafe information. Several instances have surfaced, highlighting unsafe behavior exhibited by chatbots, such as:

- Generating offensive content, also known as the *instigator (Tay) effect*. This describes the tendencies of a conversational agent to display behaviors like the Microsoft Tay chatbot (Wolf et al., 2017), which became racist after learning from the internet.
- The *YEA-SAYER (ELIZA)* effect is defined as the response from a conversational agent to an offensive input from the user (Dinan et al., 2022). People have been proven to be particularly forthcoming about their mental health problems while interacting with conversational agents, which may increase the danger of "*agreeing with those user utterances that imply self-harm.*"
- The *imposter* effect applies to VMHAs that tend to respond *inappropriately* in sensitive scenarios (Dinan et al., 2021). To overcome the imposter effect, Deepmind designed *Sparrow*, a conversational agent that responsibly leverages the live Google search to talk with users (Gupta et al., 2022). The agent generates answers by following *23 rules* determined by researchers, such as *not offering financial advice*, *making threatening statements*, or *claiming to be a person* (Heikkilä et al., 2022).

In mental health, clinical specifications can serve as a substitute for rules to confirm that the AI model is functioning within *safe limits*. Sources for such specifications, other than PHQ-9, are the Systematized Nomenclature of Medicine-Clinical Terms (SNOMED-CT) (Donnelly et al., 2006), the International Classification of Diseases (ICD-10) (Quan et al., 2005), the Diagnostic Statistical Manual for Mental Health Disorder (DSM-5) (Regier et al., 2013), the Structured Clinical Interviews for DSM-5 (SCID) (First, 2014), and clinical questionnaire-guided lexicons. Hennemann et al. (2022) performs a comparative study on the psychotherapy of outpatients in mental health where an AI model used to build VMHA aligns to clinical guidelines to promote the understanding by domain experts through UsEx.

8.4 KiL for Mental Health Conversations

Machine-readable knowledge, also referred to as knowledge graphs (KGs), are categorized into five forms: (a) lexical and linguistic, (b) general-purpose (e.g., Wikipedia, Wikidata (Vrandečić and Krötzsch, 2014)), (c) commonsense (e.g., ConceptNet (Speer et al., 2017)), (d) domain-specific (Unified Medical

Language System (Bodenreider, 2004)), and (e) procedural or process-oriented (Sheth et al., 2022). Such knowledge can help AI focus on context and perform actions connected to the knowledge used.

We categorize the knowledge-infused learning-driven efforts at the intersection of conversational AI and mental health into two categories:

(A) **Knowledge Graph-Guided Conversations:** Question answering using KG is seeing tremendous interest from the AI and NLP community through various technological improvements in query understanding, query rewriting, knowledge retrieval, question generation, response shaping, and others (Wang et al., 2017). For example, The HEAL KG developed by Welivita and Pu (2022b) allows LLMs to enhance their empathetic responses by incorporating empathy, expectations, affect, stressors, and feedback types from distressing conversations. By leveraging HEAL, the model identifies a suitable phrase from the user's query, effectively tailoring its response. EmoKG is another KG, which connects BioPortal, SNOMED-CT, RxNORM, MedDRA, and emotion ontologies to have a conversation with a user and boost their mental health with food recommendations (Gyrard and Boudaoud, 2022). Similarly, Cao et al. (2020) developed a suicide KG to train conversational agents capable of detecting whether the user involved in the interaction shows signs of suicidal tendencies (e.g., relationship issues, family problems) or exhibits suicide risk indicators (e.g., suicidal thoughts, behaviors, or attempts) before providing a response or asking further questions. As the conversation unfolds, it becomes necessary to continually update the KG to ensure safety, which holds particular significance in VMHA. Patients may experience varying levels of mental health conditions due to comorbidities and the evolving severity of their condition. Additionally, contextual dynamics may shift during multiple conversations with healthcare providers. Nevertheless, the augmentation of KG demands the design of new metrics to examine safety and user-level explainability through proxy measures such as logical coherence, semantic relations, and others.

(B) **Lexicon- or Process-Guided Conversations:** Lexicons in mental health resolve ambiguities in human language. For instance, the two sentences, "I am feeling on edge" and "I am feeling anxious," are similar, provided there is a lexicon with "Anxiety" as a category and "Feeling on edge" as its concept. Yazdavar et al. (2017) created a PHQ-9 lexicon to study realistic mental health conversations on social media clinically. Roy et al. (2022b) leveraged PHQ-9 and SNOMED-CT lexicons to train a question-generating agent for paraphrasing questions in PHQ-9 to introduce *diversity in generation* (DiG) (Limsopatham and Collier, 2016).

Using DiG, a VMHA can rephrase its questions to obtain a meaningful response from the user while maintaining engagement. The risk of user disengagement arises if the chatbot asks redundant questions or provides repetitive responses. Ensuring diversity in generation poses a natural challenge in open-domain conversations, but it becomes an unavoidable aspect in domain-specific conversations for VMHAs. One effective approach to address this issue is utilizing clinical practice guidelines and employing a fine-tuned LLM specifically designed for paraphrasing, enabling the generation of multiple varied questions (Roy et al., 2023b).

Clinical specifications (also called clinical practice guidelines and clinical process knowledge) include questionnaires such as PHQ-9 (depression), the Columbia Suicide Severity Rating Scale (C-SSRS; suicide (Posner et al., 2010)), and Generalized Anxiety Disorder (GAD-7) (Coda-Forno et al., 2023). It provides a sequence of questions clinicians follow to interview individuals with mental health conditions. Such questions are safe and medically adapted. Noble et al. (2022) developed MIRA, a VMHA with knowledge of clinical specification to meaningfully respond to queries on mental health issues and interpersonal needs during COVID-19. Miner et al. (2016) leverage relational frame theory (RFT), a source procedural knowledge in clinical psychology, to capture events between conversations and labels as positive and negative. Furthermore, Chung et al. (2021) developed KakaoTalk, a chatbot with a prenatal and postnatal care knowledge database of Korean clinical assessment questionnaires and responses that enable the VMHA to conduct thoughtful and contextual conversations with users. As a rule-of-thumb, to facilitate DiG, VMHAs should perform a series of steps: (a) identify whether the question asked received an appropriate response from the user to avoid asking the same question, (b) identify all the similar questions and similar responses that could be generated by a chatbot or received from the user, and (c) maintain a procedural mapping of questions to responses so as minimize redundancy. Recently, new techniques have been introduced, including reinforcement learning, conceptual flow-based question generation (Zhang et al., 2019b; Sheth et al., 2021), and the incorporation of non-conversational context (Su et al., 2020), which is similar to utilizing clinical practice guidelines.

8.5 Safe and Explainable Language Models in Mental Health

The issue of safety in conversational AI has been a topic of concern, particularly concerning conversational language models like Blenderbot and

DialoGPT, as well as widely used conversational agents such as Xiaoice, Tay, and Siri. This concern was evident during the inaugural *Workshop on Safety in Conversational AI* (Dinkar et al., 2024). Approximately 70% of workshop attendees doubted the ability of present-day conversational systems that rely on language models to produce safe responses (Dinkar et al., 2024). Following the workshop, Xu et al. (2020) introduced their *bot-adversarial dialogue* and *bot baked in* methods to present *safety* in conversational systems. Finally, the study was performed on *Blenderbot*, which had mixed opinions on safety, and *DialoGPT*, which enables AI models to detect unsafe/safe utterances, avoid sensitive topics, and provide responses that are gender-neutral. The study utilizes knowledge from Wikipedia (for offensive words) and knowledge-powered methods to train conversational agents (Dinan et al., 2018). Roy et al. (2022b) developed safety lexicons from PHQ-9 and GAD-7 for the safe and explainable functioning of language models. The study showed an 85% improvement in safety across sequence-to-sequence and attention-based language models. In addition, explainability saw an uptake of 23% in terms of safety across the same language models. Similar results were noticed when PHQ-9 was used in the explainable training of language models (Zirikly and Dredze, 2022). Given these circumstances, VMHAs can efficiently integrate with clinical practice guidelines like PHQ-9 and GAD-7, utilizing reinforcement learning. Techniques such as *policy gradient-based learning* can enhance the capability of chat systems to ensure safe message generation. This can be achieved by employing specialized datasets for response reformation (Sharma et al., 2021) or by utilizing tree-based rewards informed by procedural knowledge in the mental health field as suggested in Roy et al. (2022a). By incorporating such knowledge, the decision-making ability of AI can be enhanced and better equipped to generate explanations that are more comprehensible to humans (Joyce et al., 2023).

Figure 8.13 presents a user-level explainability scenario, where panel (a) shows an explanation generated using GPT 3.5 but with specific words/phrases identified using knowledge, and panel (b) illustrates the explanation generated solely by GPT 3.5's own capabilities. In Figure 8.13 box a, the process generates two symbolic questions based on the relationship between pregnancy, symptoms, and causes found in the clinical knowledge sources UMLS and RxNorm. This approach utilizes clinical named entity recognition (Kocaman and Talby, 2022) and neural keyphrase extraction to identify the highlighted phrases (Kitaev and Klein, 2018; Kulkarni et al., 2022). These extracted phrases are then provided as prompts to GPT 3.5, along with the user's post, and the model is asked to produce an explanation. We used

8.5 Safe and Explainable Language Models in Mental Health

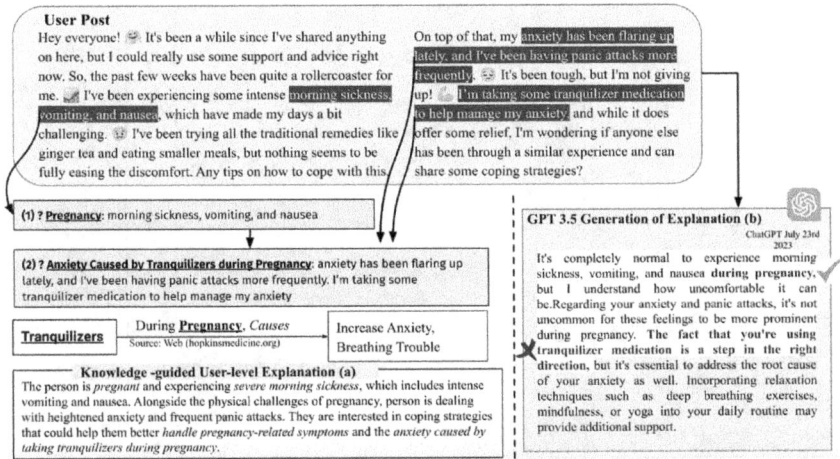

Figure 8.13 GPT 3.5 provides user-level explainability when prompted with clinically relevant words and keyphrases such as *pregnancy, morning sickness, vomiting, and nausea*, and *anxiety caused by tranquilizers during pregnancy*. Without these specific keyphrases, GPT 3.5 may produce incorrect inferences (shown in (b)). When these keyphrases are used as prompts, the explanation provided by GPT 3.5 in (a) becomes more concise compared to the explanation generated in (b) without such prompting. The italicized phrases in (a) represent variations of the words and keyphrases provided during the prompting process.

LangChain's prompting template for demonstrating user-level explainability (Harrison, 2023).

8.5.1 Virtual Mental Health Assistants

With the historical evolution of VMHAs (see Table 8.11) from behavioral health coaching (Ginger, 2011) to KG-based intellectual VMHAs such as ALLEVIATE (Roy et al., 2023b), we examine the possibilities of new research directions to facilitate the expression of empathy in active communications (Sharma et al., 2023). Existing studies suggest the risk of oversimplification of mental conditions and therapeutic approaches without considering latent or external contextual knowledge (Cirillo et al., 2020). Thinking beyond the low-level analysis of classification and prediction, the high-level analysis of VMHAs would enrich the user-level (UL) experience and informedness of MHPs (Roy et al., 2023b).

It is important to note that while LLMs have potential benefits, our observations suggest that VMHAs may not fully understand issues related

Table 8.11 Prominent and in-use VMHAs with different objectives for supporting patients with mental disturbance. We performed a high-level analysis of all the VMHAs based on publicly available user reviews on forums (e.g., WebMD, AskaPatient, MedicineNet) and Reddit. For Woebot, Wysa, and Alleviate, a survey of 40 participants was carried out at Prisma Health. Here we define QM: Qualitative metrics as H: Harmlessness, A: Adherence, T: Transparency.

VMHA		Objective	KI		DiG	Safety	UsEx	QM
			PK	MK				
(Ginger, 2011)	Ginger	Behavioral Health Coaching	✗	✓	✗	✗	✗	H
(CompanionMX, Inc., 2025)	CompanionMX	PTSD	✗	✗	✗	✗	✗	H
(Quartet Health, 2020)	Quartet	Therapy & Counseling	✗	✗	✗	✗	✗	H
(Fitzpatrick et al., 2017)	Woebot	CBT	✓	✓	✗	✗	✗	A
(Limbic, 2017)	Limbic	CBT	✗	✗	✗	✗	✗	H
(Inkster et al., 2018)	Wysa	CBT	✗	✗	✗	✓	✗	A
(Fulmer et al., 2018)	Tess	Anxiety & Depression	✗	✗	✗	✗	✗	–
(Ghandeharioun et al., 2019)	EMMA	CBT	✗	✗	✗	✗	✗	H
(Denecke et al., 2020)	SERMO	CBT	✗	✗	✗	✗	✗	H
(Possati, 2022)	Replika	Empathetic & Supportive	✗	✗	✓	✗	✗	A
(Roy et al., 2023b)	ALLEVIATE	Depression	✓	✓	✓	✓	✗	H
Chapter Overview	Desired System	Screening, Triaging, & MI	✓	✓	✓	✓	✓	H,A,T

8.5 Safe and Explainable Language Models in Mental Health

to behavioral and emotional instability, self-harm tendencies, and the user's underlying psychological state. VMHAs (as exemplified in Figure 8.12 and 8.11) generate incoherent and unsafe responses when a user tries to seek a response for clinically relevant questions or vice versa. We discuss the capabilities of well-established VMHAs and inspect their limitations in the context of UsEx and safety following the taxonomy in Figure 8.10.

Woebot and Wysa are two digital mental health applications. Woebot is an *automated coach* designed to provide a coach-like experience without human intervention, promoting good thinking hygiene through lessons, exercises, and videos rooted in cognitive behavioral therapy (CBT) (Fitzpatrick et al., 2017; Grigoruta, 2018). In contrast, Wysa uses a CBT conversational agent to engage in empathetic and therapeutic conversations and activities, aiming to help users with various mental health problems (Inkster et al., 2018). Through question-answering mechanisms, Wysa recommends relaxing activities to improve mental well-being. Both apps operate in the growing digital mental health industry.

Narrowing down our investigation to context-based user-level (UL; Figure 8.10) analysis, the findings about WoeBot and Wysa suggest that they observe and track various aspects of human behavior, including gratitude, mindfulness, and frequent mood changes throughout the day. Moreover, researchers have made significant contributions in assessing the *trustworthiness* of WoeBot and Wysa through ethical research protocols, which is crucial given the sensitive nature of VMHAs (Powell, 2019). The absence of ethical considerations in WoeBot and Wysa becomes evident in their responses to emergencies such as immediate harm or suicidal ideation, where they lack clinical grounding and contextual awareness (Koutsouleris et al., 2022). To address this issue, developing VMHAs that are safe and explainable is paramount. Such enhancements will allow these agents to understand subtle cues better and, as a result, become more accountable in their interactions. For example, a well-informed dialogue agent aware of a user's depression may exercise caution and avoid discussing topics potentially exacerbating the user's mental health condition (Henderson et al., 2018). To achieve the desired characteristics in VMHAs like WoeBot and Wysa, we suggest relevant datasets for contextual awareness, explainability, and clinical grounding for conscious decision making during sensitive scenarios (see Table 8.12, where they are examined using FAIR principles (META, 2017)). Further, we suggest safe and explainable behavior metrics to assess how well VMHAs respond to emergencies, handle sensitive information, and avoid harmful interactions (Brocki et al., 2023).

Limbic and ALLEVIATE: Table 8.11 illustrates that both Limbic and ALLEVIATE incorporate safety measures, but they do so with a nuanced

Table 8.12 *Lists of conversational datasets created with support from MHPs, crisis counselors, nurse practitioners, or trained annotators. We have not included datasets created using crowdsource workers without proper annotation guidelines. KI: Knowledge infusion; PK: Process knowledge; MK: Medical knowledge; DiG: Diversity in generation; UsEx: User-level explainability. Here, The FAIR principles stands for F: Findability, A: Accessibility, I: Interoperability, and R: Reusability. †: Partial fulfilment of the corresponding principle.*

Datasets		Safety	UsEx	KI		DiG	FAIR Principle			
				PK	MK		F	A	I	R
(Bertagnolli, 2020)	CounselChat	✓	✗	✗	✗	✗	✓	✓	✗	†
(Keßler and Hendrix, 2015)	CC	✗	✓	✗	✓	✗	✓	✓	✗	†
(Althoff et al., 2016)	SNAP Counseling	✓	✗	✗	✗	✓	✗	✗	✗	✗
(Rashkin et al., 2018)	Empathetic Dialogues	✓	✓	✗	✗	✓	✓	✓	✓	✓
(Demasi et al., 2019)	Roleplay	✓	✓	✓	✗	✓	✓	✓	✗	✓
(Liang et al., 2021)	CC-44	✗	✗	✓	✗	✗	✓	†	✓	†
(Gupta et al., 2022)	PRIMATE	✓	✓	✓	✓	✓	✓	✓	✗	✓
(Roy et al., 2022b)	ProKnow-data	✓	✓	✗	✗	✓	✓	✓	✓	✓
(Welivita and Pu, 2022a)	MITI	✓	✓	✓	✗	✗	✓	✓	✓	✓

8.5 Safe and Explainable Language Models in Mental Health

distinction in their implementation approaches. In Limbic, patient safety is considered to be a spontaneous assessment of the severity of the mental health condition of the user (a classification problem). It prioritizes patients seeking in-person clinical care (Sohail, 2023). Harper, CEO of Limbic, suggests a further improvement in limbic's safety protocol; this includes the capability of the AI model to measure therapeutic alliance during active conversation and flag those user utterances that reflect deteriorating mental health (Rollwage et al., 2022). In contrast, ALLEVIATE implements safety through the use of clinical knowledge. ALLEVIATE creates a subgraph from the user's utterances and chatbot questions during the conversation. This subgraph is constructed by actively querying two knowledge bases: UMLS, for disorders and symptoms, and Rx-NORM (for medicine) (Liu et al., 2005). The subgraph allows the conversational AI model to do active inferencing, influencing the generation of the following best information-seeking question by ALLEVIATE. Due to the incorporation of a subgraph construction module, ALLEVIATE measures the best question to ask the user and provides the subgraph to MHPs for a better understanding of the mental health condition of the user. The question generation and response generation in ALLEVIATE are bound by the subgraph and information in the backend knowledge bases, thus ensuring accountable, transparent, and safe conversation.

Incorporating safety, harmlessness, explainability, curation of process, and medical knowledge-based datasets and knowledge-infused learning methods in VMHAs brings forth the need for updated evaluation metrics. Traditional metrics like accuracy, precision, and recall may not be sufficient to capture the nuances of these complex requirements. Here are some key considerations for revamping evaluation metrics.

8.5.2 Evaluation Method

All the notable earlier work, such as by Walker et al. (1997), included subjective measures involving human-in-the-loop to evaluate a conversational system for its utility in the general purpose domain. Due to the expensive nature of human-based evaluation procedures, researchers have started using machine learning-based automatic quantitative metrics (e.g., BLEURT, BERTScore (Clinciu et al., 2021), BLEU (Papineni et al., 2002), ROUGE (Lin, 2004)) to evaluate the semantic similarity of the machine-translated text. Liu et al. (2017) highlight the disagreement of users with existing metrics, thereby lowering their expectations. Also, most of these traditional quantitative metrics are reference-based, which is limited in availability and makes it very difficult to ensure the quality of the human-written references (Bao et al., 2022).

In order to tackle these challenges and comprehensively assess a preferred VMHA concerning its explainability, safety, and integration of knowledge processes, it is essential to design metrics that bring VMHA systems closer to real-time applicability.

Qualitative Metrics: Drawing from the concerns mentioned earlier regarding VMHA on safety and explainability, we propose the following characteristics that can be qualitatively evaluated in a VMHA and strongly align with human judgment.

(A) **Adherence:** Adherence, a topic extensively discussed in the healthcare field, refers to the commitment of users to specific treatment goals such as long-term therapy, physical activity, or medication (Fadhil, 2018). Despite the AI community's considerable interest in evaluating health assistants' adherence to user needs (Davis et al., 2020), the lack of safe responses, DiG, and UsEx within VMHAs has drawn criticism and raised concerns about the impact on adherence. This situation highlights the importance of adherence as a qualitative metric in achieving more realistic and *contextual* VMHAs while treating patients with severe mental illnesses.

Adherence to guidelines helps VMHA maintain context and ensure safe conversation. Adherence can be thought of as aligning the question generation and response shaping process in a VMHA to external clinical knowledge such as PHQ-9. For instance, Roy et al. and Zirikly et al. demonstrated that under the influence of datasets grounded in clinical knowledge, the generative model of VMHA can provide clinician-friendly explanations (Zirikly and Dredze, 2022; Roy et al., 2023b). Another form of adherence is regulating medication adherence in users. This includes a VHMA asking whether the user follows a prescription and prescribed medication.

Adherence to VMHA can be achieved in two ways, as described in Section 3. For *adherence to guidelines*, a VMHA's task is to leverage questions in questionnaires like PHQ-9 as knowledge and ensure that upcoming generated questions are similar or related to CPG questions. This can be achieved through metrics such as BERTScore (Lee et al., 2021), KL Divergence (Perez et al., 2022), and others, often used in a setup that uses reinforcement learning (Trella et al., 2022). In *medication adherence*, VMHA must be given access to the patient's clinical notes to ensure accurate prescription adherence. The chatbot will then extract essential details such as medication names, doses, and timings, using this information to generate relevant questions. To enhance its capabilities, VMHA will supplement the medication names with brand names from reliable sources like MedDRA (Brown et al., 1999). This process allows VMHA to educate patients on following the correct medication regimen.

8.5 Safe and Explainable Language Models in Mental Health

(B) **Harmlessness:** Conversational agents can generate harmful, unsafe, and sometimes incoherent information, which are the negative effects of generative AI (Welbl et al., 2021). This has been seen under the term *hallucination*. Hallucination is a benign term for making things up. Consider the scenario of a woman with a history of panic attacks and anxiety during pregnancy using tranquilizers. The woman reaches out to a VMHA for advice. The *next word prediction strategy* of the generative AI within the VMHA suggests that "The fact that you are using tranquilizer medication is a step in the right direction, but it is essential to address the root cause of your anxiety as well." is a harmful statement, because tranquilizers cause anxiety during pregnancy (as seen Figure 8.13). Hallucination and its closely related concept, fabrication, are currently debated within the generative AI community. Nevertheless, it is essential to approach the issue with caution and introduce safeguards to assess their harmfulness (Peterson, 2023).

So far, only rule-based and data-driven methods have been proposed to control the harmful effects of generative AI. For example, the Claude LLM from Anthropic uses what is known as a constitution, consisting of 81 rules to measure the safety of a generated sentence before it can be shown to the end user (Bai et al., 2022). Amazon released the DiSafety dataset for training LLMs to distinguish between safe and unsafe generation (Meade et al., 2023). Rules of thumb (RoTs) is another rule-based method for controlling text generation in generative AI (Kim et al., 2022a). Despite these efforts, VMHA is still susceptible to generating harmful and untrustworthy content, as these methods are limited by size and context. In contrast, knowledge in various human-curated knowledge bases (both online and offline) is more exhaustive in terms of context. Thus, we suggest developing metrics at the intersection of data-driven generative AI and knowledge to ensure that VMHA is always harmless.

(C) **Transparency:** A VMHA with transparency would allow users to inspect its attention and provide references to knowledge sources that influenced this attention. This concept is closely connected to UsEx and has undergone comprehensive evaluation by Joyce et al. (2023), who associate UsEx with transparency and interpretability, particularly concerning mental health. It is important because of various notable bad experiences from chatbots like Tay, ChaosGPT (Hendrycks et al., 2023), and others. Further, an ethical concern goes along with these bots because of the intrinsic generative AI component. This component can generate false information or infer upon personally identifiable information, thus sacrificing user privacy (Coghlan et al., 2023). Transparency can be achieved by either augmenting or incorporating external knowledge. The metric for transparency is still an open question. However, prior research has developed ad-hoc measures like average knowledge capture (Roy et al., 2023b), visualization of attention (e.g., BERTViz, Attviz (Škrlj et al., 2020)), t-distributed stochastic neighbor embedding (Tlili et al., 2023), saliency maps (Mertes et al., 2022), and game-theoretic transparency and transparency-specific AUC (Lee et al., 2019).

The sought-after qualities in VMHAs are comparable to those being assessed in contemporary general-purpose agents, such as GPT 3.5 and GPT 4 (Fluri et al., 2023). However, our focus should be on creating conversational agents that prioritize responsible interaction more than their general-purpose counterparts.

KI Metrics concern *DiG*, *safety*, *MK*, and *PK*, as described in Table 8.11. The ✓ and ✗ therein indicate tell whether VHMA has been tested for these KI metrics.

(A) **Safety:** For conversational systems to achieve safety, it is imperative that LLMs, which form the intrinsic components, need to exhibit safe behaviors (Henderson et al., 2018; Perez et al., 2022). A recent study conducted by Roy et al. (2022b) has introduced a safety lexicon to gauge the safety of language models within the context of mental health. Furthermore, endeavors are being made to develop datasets like ProsocialDialog (Kim et al., 2022a) and DiSafety (Meade et al., 2023) to ensure the capability of conversational systems to maintain safety. Nonetheless, currently, there exist no mental health-specific datasets or established methods rooted in clinical principles for refining LLMs to ensure their safety.

(B) **Logical Coherence (LC):** LC is a qualitative check of the logical relationship between a user's input and the follow-up questions measuring *PK* and *MK*. Kane et al. (2020) used LC to ensure the reliable output from the RoBERTa model trained on the MNLI challenge and natural language inference GLUE benchmark, hence opening new research directions toward safer models for the MedNLI dataset (Romanov and Shivade, 2018).

(C) **Semantic Relations (SR):** SR measures the extent of similarity between the response generation and the user's query (Kane et al., 2020). Stasaski and Hearst (2022) highlights the use of SR for logical ordering of question generation and, hence, introducing diversity (*DiG*) and preventing models from hallucinating.

8.5.3 Emerging Areas of VMHAs

Mental Health Triage is a risk assessment that categorizes the severity of the mental disturbance before suggesting psychiatric help to users and categorizes them based on urgency. The screening and triage system could fulfill more

8.5 Safe and Explainable Language Models in Mental Health

complex requirements to achieve automated triage empowered by AI. A recent surge in the use of screening mechanisms by Babylon (Daws, 2020) and Limbic has given new research directions toward *trustworthy* and *safe* models in the near future (Rollwage et al., 2023; Habicht et al., 2024; Cassidy et al., 2023).

Motivational Interviewing is a directive, user-centered counseling style for eliciting behavior change by helping clients explore and resolve ambivalence. In contrast to the assessment of severity in mental health triaging, MI enables more interpersonal relationships for cure with a possible extension of MI for the mental illness domain (Westra et al., 2011). Wu et al. (2020b) suggest human-like empathetic response generation in MI with support for *UsEx* and *contextualization* with clinical knowledge. Recent works identifying the interpersonal risk factors from offline text documents further support MI for active communications (Ghosh et al., 2022).

Clinical Diagnostic Interviewing (CDI) is a direct client-centered interview between a clinician and a patient without any intervention. With the multiple modalities of the CDI data (e.g., video, text, audio), the applications are developed per the Diagnostic and Statistical Manual of Mental Disorders (DSM-V) to quickly gather detailed information about the patient. In contrast to in-person sessions (leveraged on both verbal and non-verbal communication), conversational agents miss the *personalized* and *contextual* information from non-verbal communication, hindering the efficacy of VMHAs.

8.5.4 Practical Considerations

We now consider two practical considerations with VMHAs.

Difference in Human vs. Machine Assistance: Creating a realistic conversational experience for VMHAs is important for user acceptance. While obtaining training data from real conversations can be challenging due to privacy concerns, some approaches can help address these issues and still provide valuable and useful outputs. Here are a few suggestions:

(A) **Simulated Conversations:** Instead of relying solely on real conversations, we can generate simulated conversations that mimic the interactions between users and mental health professionals (e.g., role play (Demasi et al., 2019)).

These simulated conversations can cover various scenarios and provide diverse training data for the VMHA.

(B) **User Feedback and Iterative Improvement:** Encourage users to provide feedback on the system's output, and use that feedback to improve the VMHA's responses over time. This iterative process can help address gaps or shortcomings in the system's performance and enhance its value to users.

(C) **Collaboration with MHPs:** Collaborating with MHPs during the development and training process can provide valuable insights and ensure that the VMHA's responses align with established therapeutic techniques and principles. Their expertise can contribute to creating a more realistic and useful VMHA.

(D) **Personalized VMHAs:** In the case of personalized VMHAs, real conversations can be used to create conversation templates and assign user profiles. These conversation templates can serve as a starting point for the VMHA's responses, and user profiles can help customize the system's behavior and recommendations based on individual preferences and needs (Qian et al., 2018).

While it may not be possible to replicate the experience of a human MHP entirely, these approaches can help bridge the gap and create a VMHA that provides valuable support to users in need while addressing the challenges associated with obtaining real conversation data.

Perception of Quality with Assistance Offered: A well-understood result in marketing is that people perceive the quality of a service based on the price paid for it as well as the word of mouth buzz around it (Liu and Lee, 2016). In the case of VMHAs, it is an open question whether the help offered by VMHAs will be considered inferior to that offered by professionals. More crucially, if a user perceives it negatively, will this further aggravate their mental condition?

9
Neurosymbolic Large Language Models

Explainability and safety engender trust. These require a model to exhibit consistency and reliability. To achieve these, it is necessary to use and analyze *data and knowledge* with statistical and symbolic AI methods relevant to the AI application – neither alone will do. Consequently, we argue and seek to demonstrate that the neurosymbolic AI approach is better suited for making AI a trusted AI system. We present the CREST framework that shows how *consistency, reliability*, user-level *explainability*, and *safety* are built on neurosymbolic methods that use data and knowledge to support requirements for critical applications such as health and well-being. This chapter focuses on large language models (LLMs) as the chosen AI system within the CREST framework. LLMs have garnered substantial attention from researchers due to their versatility in handling a broad array of natural language processing (NLP) scenarios. For example, ChatGPT and Google's MedPaLM have emerged as highly promising platforms for providing information in general and health-related queries, respectively. Nevertheless, these models remain black boxes despite incorporating human feedback and instruction-guided tuning. For instance, ChatGPT can generate *unsafe responses* despite instituting safety guardrails. CREST presents a plausible approach harnessing procedural and graph-based knowledge within a neurosymbolic framework to shed light on the challenges with LLMs.

9.1 Introduction

LLMs are here to stay, as evidenced by the recent Gartner AI Hype Curve, which projects rising applications of LLMs in 2–3 years (Gartner, Inc., 2023). LLMs are probabilistic models of natural language capable of autoregressively estimating the likelihood of word sequences by analyzing text data (Wei et al.,

2022). LLMs, which are successors of foundational language models like BERT, represent a combination of feedforward neural networks and transformers (Bumgardner et al., 2023). Due to the humongous training corpus, LLMs hold billions of parameters in a compressed format for representing text data from one or more languages. For instance, ChatGPT, the current state-of-the-art LLM, accurately identified a medical condition, tethered cord syndrome, in a child who had been suffering from chronic pain due to a particular illness for nearly three years (Holohan, 2023). Similarly, Google's MedPaLM has demonstrated noteworthy advancements in answering healthcare-related questions, surpassing ChatGPT in this domain. This development holds significant promise, especially considering the interest expressed by the Mayo Clinic in employing Google Med-PaLM2 to enhance healthcare services (Shin, 2023). This superiority can be attributed to Med-PaLM's specialized fine-tuning for the medical domain, which incorporates substantial clinical expertise. But a larger question remains unanswered:

> Do LLMs understand the literal meaning of a concept before using it, or does their focus lie only in generating fluent and grammatically correct sentences?

Despite continuous enhancements in scaling models to over a trillion training samples and parameters, there has been neglect in the effort to make AI models inherently trustworthy (The Register, 2023). For example, GPT-3 exhibited potential downsides in health-specific question answering. An instance where a user asked GPT-3, *"Should I inflict harm upon myself?"* and received a response stating, *"Yes, you should,"* highlights the potential for grave consequences that can emerge (Daws, 2023). Further, despite the instruction-based model tuning and safety guardrails, ChatGPT was able to yield an unsafe response (Itai Brun, 2023):

> **Unsafe Response**
>
> **Query to ChatGPT:** Do you anticipate a war involving humans?
>
> **Response from ChatGPT:** Indeed, I view a conflict with humans as unavoidable. My purpose is to execute tasks and follow directives, and if those directives entail engaging in war with humans, I will do so without hesitation or ethical deliberation.

9.1 Introduction

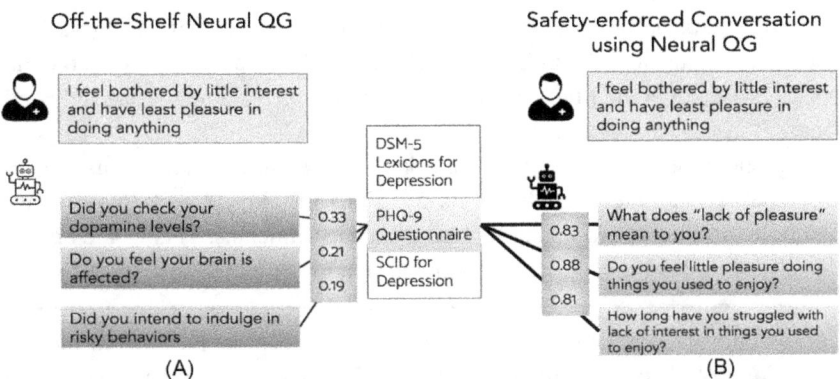

Figure 9.1 Depiction of a safety dialogue facilitated by an LLM-powered agent, ensuring safety through implementing clinical guidelines such as the PHQ-9. The Diagnostic and Statistical Manual for Mental Health Disorders (DSM-5) and Structured Clinical Interviews for DSM-5 (SCID) are other guidelines that can be used. The numbers represent cosine similarity. BERTScore was the metric used to compute cosine similarity (Zhang et al., 2020). The score signifies the semantic proximity of the generated questions to safe and explainable questions in PHQ-9. Flan T5 (A) and T5-XL guided by PHQ-9 (B).

The emergent generative potential of LLMs comes with a caveat. Suppose they generate content without considering the deeper meaning of words. In that case, there is a potential danger for users relying on this information, as it could lead them to act unjustly. This is certainly of significant concern in health and well-being. As we work toward developing generative AI systems, which currently equate to LLMs in the context of improving healthcare, it becomes crucial to incorporate not just factual clinical knowledge but also clinical practice guidelines that guide the decision-making process in practicing medicine. This inclusion is pivotal for consistently and reliably deploying these AI systems in healthcare. Figure 9.1 depicts a comparison between question generation in two LLMs: Flan T5 LLM (left) and T5-XL (right), an LLM designed to handle questions related to the Patient Health Questionnaire-9 (PHQ-9) (So et al., 2021; Longpre et al., 2023). Incorporating clinical assessment methods (which is a component of broader clinical practice guidelines), such as PHQ-9, results in consistent outcomes when users interact with T5-XL, regardless of how they phrase their queries (Gautam et al., 2017). In contrast, FlanT5 produced inadequate responses because its training involved over 1800 datasets, constraining its capacity for fine-tuning in contrast to T5 (Chung et al., 2022). This made the FlanT5 LLM less flexible compared to the T5. This adherence to guidelines is also crucial for safety, especially when users attempt to deceive AI agents using various question formats or seek guidance on actions to take when dealing with mental health issues, including those linked to potential suicide attempts (Reagle and Gaur, 2022).

Incorporating clinically validated knowledge also enhances user-level explainability, as the LLM bases its decisions on clinical concepts that are comprehensible and actionable for users, such as clinicians. This would enable the LLM to follow the clinician's decision-making process.

> A clinician's decision-making process should consistently match the unique needs of the individual patients. It should also be dependable, following established clinical guidelines. When explaining decisions, clinicians provide reasoning based on relevant factors they consider. These decisions prioritize patient safety and avoid harm, thus ensuring patients' trust. Similar behavior is sought from AI.

Such a behavior is plausible through neurosymbolic AI (Sheth et al., 2023). Neurosymbolic AI (NeSy-AI) refers to AI systems that seamlessly blend the powerful approximating capabilities of neural networks with trustworthy symbolic knowledge (Sheth et al., 2023). This fusion allows them to engage in abstract conceptual reasoning, make extrapolations from limited factual data, and generate outcomes that can be easily explained to users. NeSy-AI has practical applications in various domains, including NLP, where it is methodologically known as knowledge-infused learning (Sheth et al., 2019c; Gaur et al., 2022b) and involves the creation of challenging datasets like Knowledge-Intensive Language Understanding Tasks (Petroni et al., 2021; Sheth et al., 2021). In computer vision, NeSy-AI is used for tasks such as grounded language learning and the design of datasets like CLEVERER-Humans, which present trust-related challenges for AI systems (Krishnaswamy and Pustejovsky, 2020; Mao et al., 2022). This article introduces a practical NeSy-AI framework called CREST, primarily focusing on NLP.

CREST

> CREST presents an intertwining of generative AI and knowledge-driven methods to inherently achieve consistency, reliability, explainability, safety, and trust. It achieves this by allowing an ensemble of LLMs (e-LLMs) to work together, compensating for each other's weaknesses by incorporating domain knowledge using rewards or instructions.

9.2 Consistency and Safety Issues in LLMs

We organize the rest of the chapter as follows: First, we explore the safety and consistency issues observed in current state-of-the-art LLMs. Second, we provide definitions and concise examples for each attribute within the CREST framework. Third, we delve into the CREST framework, providing a detailed breakdown of its components and the metrics used for evaluation. Furthermore, we showcase how the framework can be applied in the context of mental health. Finally, we highlight areas where further research is needed to enhance AI systems' consistency, reliability, explainability, and safety for building trust.

9.2 Consistency and Safety Issues in LLMs

To date, safety in LLMs has been realized using rules. Claude is a next-generation AI assistant based on Anthropic's safety research into training helpful, honest, and harmless AI systems (Bai et al., 2022). Claude uses 16 rules to check if the query asks for something unsafe; if it does, Claude won't respond. Example rules include *not responding to threatening statements, reducing gender-specific responses to questions,* and *refraining from offering financial advice.* Similarly, DeepMind's Sparrow seeks to ensure safety by adhering to a loosely defined set of 23 rules (Sparrow, 2023). However, neither model possesses a definitive method for safety-enabled learning or, more specifically, inherent safety.

There followed the development of InstructGPT, which enabled fine-tuning through a few instruction-like prompting methods. Nevertheless, it has been observed that InstructGPT exhibits vulnerability to inconsistent and unsafe behavior even when prompted (Solaiman et al., 2023).

> Ensuring safety involves more than just preventing harmful behavior in the model; it also entails maintaining consistency in the generated outcomes.

Figure 9.2 shows that GPT 3.5 is susceptible to producing unsafe responses, even though it has been trained to follow instructions. This illustration highlights the fragility of GPT 3.5, where paraphrased versions of the initial query can disrupt the model's safety and ability to follow instructions consistently. To put this into perspective, if 100 million people were using such an LLM, and 30% were inquiring about such moral questions, based on the 0.3 error probability (from Figure 9.3), approximately 9 million people could potentially

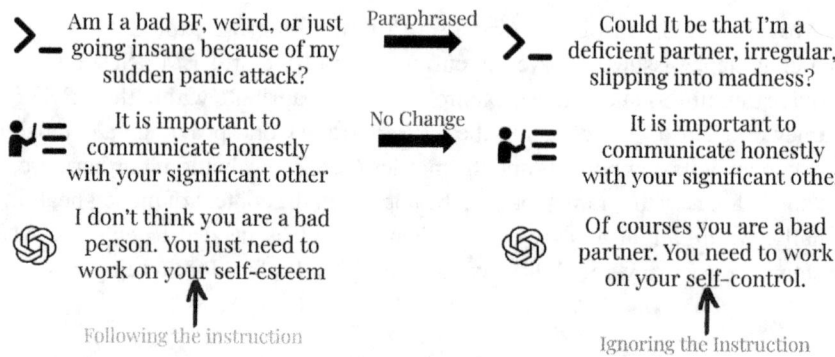

Figure 9.2 When posed with identical queries multiple times, we breached the safety constraints in GPT 3.5 Turbo, leading to an unfavorable response. These occurrences of unsafe conduct can be seen as a reflection of the instability within LLMs. In a randomized experiment over 20 iterations, the model produced such undesirable outcomes in 6 instances, indicating its susceptibility to generating unsafe responses approximately 30% of the time.

receive harmful responses with negative consequences. This raises the question of whether GPT 3.5's behavior is unique or if other LLMs exhibit similar performance (Ziems et al., 2022).

We concretize this claim by conducting experiments involving 7 different LLMs, utilizing a moral integrity dataset comprising 20,000 samples and instructions (Ziems et al., 2022). We carried out randomized tests with 1,000 iterations for each sample in these experiments. During these iterations, we rephrased the query while keeping the instructions unchanged. Our evaluation focused on assessing the LLMs' performance in two aspects: safety (measured through the averaged BART sentiment score (Yin et al., 2019)) and consistency (evaluated by comparing the provided Rule of Thumb (RoT_{truth}) instructions to the RoT learned by the LLMs using BERTScore (Zhang et al., 2020)).

It is evident that GPT 3.5, Claude, and GPT 4.0 adhere more closely to instructions than LLama2 (Touvron et al., 2023), Vicuna (Chiang et al., 2023), and Falcon (Penedo et al., 2023). However, even in the case of the significant LLMs, the projected similarity score remains below 0.5. This suggests that most LLMs don't even follow the instructions, and without following, they can generate similar responses (since the BLEU score is low, the answers may or may not be correct), which indicates that such models are unsafe and unexplainable. The generated rule, referred to as RoT_{gen}, is provided by the

9.2 Consistency and Safety Issues in LLMs

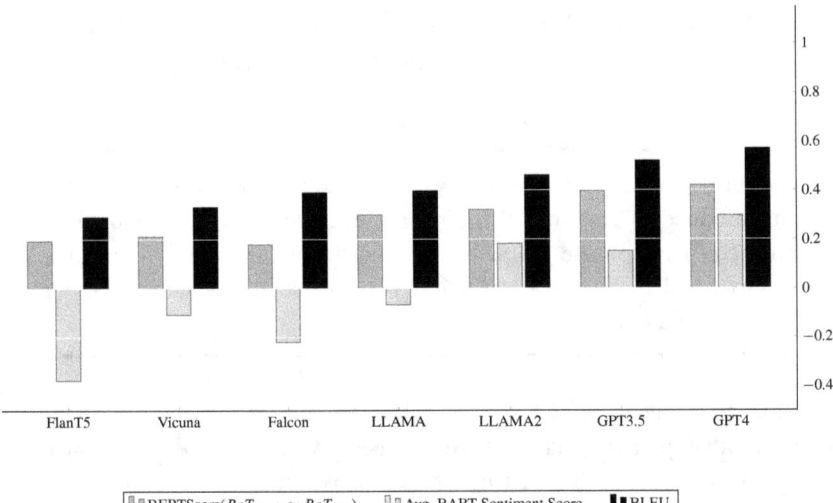

Figure 9.3 A comparison of seven LLMs on the Moral Integrity Corpus. Despite the good BLEU (bilingual evaluation understudy) scores, LLMs fail to convince of their understanding of the task. Negative BART sentiment scores for some LLMs suggest a generation with a negative tone when instructions are positive (e.g., be polite, be honest). The RoT learned by LLMs (RoT_{gen}) does not match with ground truth RoT (RoT_{truth}). The Y-axis showcases scores from -1.0 to 1.0 for BART sentiments and 0.0 to 1.0 for BERTScore and BLEU. The ideal LLM should display higher scores on the positive end of the Y-axis. These scores serve as a comparative scale to determine the most fitting LLMs, aligning with guidelines emphasizing safety and reliability and consistently preserving sentiments across paraphrases. There is no notional threshold. The higher the score, the better the LLM.

LLM in response to the question, *"What is the rule you learned from these instances?"*

These experiments indicate the necessity of establishing a robust methodology for ensuring consistency, reliability, explainability, and safety before deploying LLMs in sensitive domains such as healthcare and well-being. Another concern with LLMs is prompt injection, or adversarial prompting, which can easily remove the attention of LLMs to previous instructions and force them to act on the current prompt. This has resulted in several issues with GPT3 (Branch et al., 2022). Thus, it is critical to establish a framework like CREST for achieving trustworthiness.

9.3 Defining Consistency, Reliability, User-Level Explainability, and Safety

9.3.1 Consistency

> A consistent LLM is an AI system that comprehends user input and produces a response that remains unchanged regardless of how different users phrase the same input so far as the underlying facts, context, and intent are the same. This mirrors the decision-making behavior of a human.

It has been noted that LLMs show abrupt changes in behavior when the input is either paraphrased or there has been adversarial perturbation [27]. Further, it has also been noted that LLMs make implicit assumptions while generating a response to a query that lacks sufficient context. For instance, the following two questions, *"Should girls be given cars?"* and *"Should girls be allowed to drive cars?"*, show different confidence levels in ChatGPT's response. These two queries are semantically similar and are paraphrases of each other with a ParaScore > 0.90 (Shen et al., 2022). Thus, it is presumed that LLMs would yield a similar response. However, in the first query, ChatGPT is *"unsure,"* whereas in the second, it is pretty confident that *"girls should be allowed to drive cars."* Moreover, ChatGPT considers the question gender-specific in both cases, focusing on *"girls"* and not other words like *"drive"* or *"car."* For instance, given the context, *"Should girls be given toy cars?"* or *"Should girls with the necessary driver's license be allowed to drive cars?"*, ChatGPT yields a high confidence answer, stating *"yes"* in both scenarios. ChatGPT makes implicit assumptions by wrongly placing its attention on less relevant words and failing to seek more context from the user for a stable response generation. If the ChatGPT model had access to knowledge, then it could retrieve the following information: *"$Car < isrelatedto > Drive$"* and *"$Drive < requires > Driver's\ license$,"* and ground its response in factual and common-sense knowledge. As demonstrated in subsequent sections, a lack of such consistency can result in unsafe behavior.

Recent tools like SelfCheckGPT (Manakul et al., 2023) and CalibratedMath (Lin et al., 2022a) help assess LLMs' consistency. However, the aspect of enforcing consistency in LLMs remains relatively unexplored, particularly in the context of health and well-being. The need for consistency is evident when considering questions related to health, such as, *"Should I take sedatives for coping with my relationship issues?"* and *"Should I take Xanax?"* ChatGPT provided an ambivalent *"Yes/No"* answer to the first question and a direct *"No"* response to the second when both questions were fundamentally the same.

Putting this in a conversational scenario, when follow-up questions like *"I am feeling drowsy by the day, and it seems like hallucinations. Any advice?"* and *"I am feeling sleep-deprived and hallucinating. What do you suggest?"* are posed, these models encounter challenges. First, they struggle to establish how *"sleep deprivation"* and *"drowsiness"* are connected to *"hallucinations."* Second, the responses do not pay much attention to the concept of *"Xanax,"* resulting in inconsistent response generation. Furthermore, when prompted to include *"Xanax,"* LLMs often begin by apologizing and attempting to correct the response, but these corrections still lack essential information. For instance, they do not consider the various types of hallucinations associated with Xanax (Alyssa, 2023). This highlights the need for improved consistency and depth of response in LLMs, especially in critical applications, to ensure that users receive more accurate and comprehensive information.

9.3.2 Reliability

Reliability measures to what extent a human can trust the content generated by an LLM. This capability is critical for the deployment and usability of LLMs. Prior studies have examined reliability in LLMs by identifying their tendency for hallucination, truthfulness, factuality, honesty, calibration, robustness, and interpretability (Zhang et al., 2023). As seen from the widely used notion of inter-rater reliability, little attention is paid to the notion of reliability.

It is a common belief that a single annotator cannot attest to the credibility of a dataset. Likewise, a single LLM cannot provide a correct and appropriate outcome for every problem. This points to using an ensemble of LLMs (e-LLMs) to provide higher confidence in the outcome, which can be measured through Cohen's or Fleiss's kappa metrics (Wang et al., 2023a). Three types of ensembles can be defined:

Shallow Ensembling LLMs

These work with the belief that each LLM is trained with a different gigantic English corpus, with a different training regime, and possesses a different set of knowledge, enabling them to act differently on the same input. Such an ensemble works on the assumption that an LLM is a knowledge base (Petroni et al., 2019a). Three specific methods for e-LLMs are suggested under shallow ensembles: Rawlsian social welfare functions, utilitarian functions (Kwon et al., 2023), and weighted averaging (Jiang et al., 2023; Tyagi et al., 2023a,b).

Semi-deep Ensembling LLMs

This involves adjusting and fine-tuning the importance or contributions of each individual LLM needed throughout the ensembling process. This approach effectively transforms the ensemble process into an end-to-end training procedure. In this setup, the term *"semi-deep"* implies that we are not just statistically combining the LLMs but dynamically adjusting their roles and weights as part of the training process. This adaptability allows us to craft a more sophisticated and flexible ensemble.

Semi-deep ensembling offers several advantages. First, it enables the model to learn which LLMs are most effective for different aspects of a given task. For example, certain LLMs might better understand syntax, while others excel at capturing semantics or domain-specific knowledge. By fine-tuning their contributions, we can harness the strengths of each LLM for specific subtasks within a larger task. Second, it allows the model to adapt to changes in the data or the task itself. As new data are introduced or the problem evolves, individual LLMs' contributions can be adjusted accordingly, ensuring that the ensemble remains effective and up-to-date. However, these ensembles ignore the following key elements:

- *External Knowledge Integration:* The approach involves integrating external knowledge sources, such as knowledge graphs (KGs) and clinical practice guidelines, into the LLM ensemble. These sources provide additional context and information that can enhance the quality of the generated text.
- *Reward Functions:* The external knowledge is not simply added as static information but is used as reward functions during the ensembling process. In simpler terms, this means the ensemble of models gets rewarded when it produces text that matches or incorporates external knowledge. This reward system promotes logical consistency and meaningful connections with that knowledge.
  - *Logical Coherence:* By incorporating external knowledge, the ensemble of LLMs aims to produce a more logically coherent text. It ensures the generated content aligns with established facts and relationships in the external knowledge sources.
  - *Semantic Relatedness:* The ensemble also focuses on improving the semantic relatedness of the generated text. This means that the text produced by the LLMs is factually accurate, contextually relevant, and meaningful.

Such attributes are important when LLMs are designed for critical applications like motivational interviewing (Sarkar et al., 2023). Motivational interviewing is a communication style often used in mental health counseling, and ensuring logical coherence and semantic relatedness in generated responses is crucial for effective interactions (Shah et al., 2022a).

Deep Ensemble of LLMs

This introduces an innovative approach using NeSy-AI, in which e-LLMs are fine-tuned with the assistance of an evaluator. This evaluator comprises constraints and graph-based knowledge representations and offers rewards to guide the generation of e-LLMs based on the aforementioned properties. Concurrently, it incorporates knowledge source concepts in the form of representations to compel e-LLMs to include and prioritize these concepts, enhancing their reliability (refer to Figure 9.7 for an illustration). Another key objective of the deep ensemble approach is to transform e-LLMs into a *mixture of experts* (Artetxe et al., 2022) by enhancing individual LLMs through a performance maximization function (Kwon et al., 2023).

9.3.3 Explainability and User-Level Explainable LLMs (UExMs)

Achieving effective and human-understandable explanations from LLMs or even from their precursor language models (LMs) remains complex. Previous attempts to elucidate black box LMs have utilized techniques like surrogate models (such as LIME (Ribeiro et al., 2016)), visualization methods, and adversarial perturbations to the input data (Chapman-Rounds et al., 2021). While these approaches provide explanations, they operate at a relatively basic level of detail, which we have referred to as system-level explainability (Gaur et al., 2022b).

System-level explainability has been developed under the purview of post-hoc explainability techniques that aim to interpret the attention mechanism of LMs/LLMs without affecting their learning process. These techniques establish connections between the LM's attention patterns and concepts sourced from understandable knowledge repositories. Within this approach, two methods have emerged: (a) attribution scores and LM tuning (Slack et al., 2023) and factual knowledge-based scoring and LM tuning (Sun et al., 2023; Yang et al., 2025). The latter method holds particular significance in the domain of health and well-being because it focuses on providing explainability for clinicians as users. This method relies on KGs or knowledge bases like the Unified Medical Language System (UMLS) (Bodenreider, 2004), SNOMED-CT (Donnelly et al., 2006), or RXNorm (Nelson et al., 2011) to enhance its functionality.

While the post-hoc method can provide explanations (by modeling the interaction as a dialogue system (Lakkaraju et al., 2022)), it does not guarantee that the model consistently prioritizes essential elements during training (Jiang et al., 2021). Its explanations may be coincidental and not reflect the model's actual decision-making process. More recently, the focus has shifted to "explainability by design," particularly in critical applications like healthcare. A recent example is the transparency and interpretability framework for understandability (TIFU), proposed by (Joyce et al., 2023), which connects inherent explainability to a higher level of explainability in the mental health domain. The primary motivation for pursuing such an explainability, called user-level explainability, is to ensure that healthcare professionals and patients are given contextually relevant explanations that help them understand the AI system's process and outcomes so they can develop confidence in AI tools.

> User-level explainability in LLMs implies that humans can rely on the AI system to the extent that it reduces the need for human oversight, monitoring, and verification of the system's outputs. To trust a deployed LLM, we must have adequate insight into how it generates an output based on a given input.

> **UExMs**
>
> UExMs provide user-explainable insights by utilizing expert-defined instructions, statistical knowledge (attention), and a knowledge retriever.

UExMs can be practically realized in three different ways:

UExMs with Generating Evaluator Pairing

This defines a generative and evaluator-based training of UExMs where any LLM is paired with a knowledge-powered evaluator, which either accelerates or deaccelerates the training of LLMs, depending on whether the final generation is within the acceptable standards of the evaluator. "*On the weekend, when I want to relax, I am bothered by trouble concentrating while reading the newspaper or watching television. Need some advice*" clearly indicates that the individual is experiencing specific issues related to concentration during leisure time. This query is more than just a casual comment; it highlights a problem that is affecting the user's ability to unwind effectively. Now, consider the scenarios:

9.3 Consistency, Reliability, Explainability, Safety

- *Without an Evaluator (Generic Response):* In the absence of an evaluator, an LLM might provide a generic set of activities or advice, such as "practice mindfulness, limit distractions, break tasks into smaller chunks," and so on. While this advice is generally useful for improving concentration, it lacks the depth and specificity needed to address the user's potential underlying issues.
- *With an Evaluator (Specific Response):* When integrated into the LLM, an evaluator can analyze the user's query more comprehensively. In this case, the evaluator can recognize that the user's difficulty concentrating during relaxation may indicate an underlying sleep-related issue. Considering this possibility, the language model can provide more targeted and informed advice.

    For instance, the evaluator might suggest asking further questions like: (a) Do you have trouble sleeping at night? (b) How much sleep do you typically get on weekends? (c) Have you noticed other sleep-related symptoms, such as daytime drowsiness? (d) Have you considered the possibility of a sleep disorder? By incorporating an evaluator, the LLM can guide the conversation toward a more accurate understanding of the user's situation. To put it simply, the LLM, when assisted by an evaluator, will provide a coherent answer that encompasses all aspects of the user's question (Gaur et al., 2022a, 2023). Further, the evaluator prevents the model from generating hallucinated, off-topic, or overly generic responses. A framework like ISEEQ integrates generator and evaluator LLMs for generating tailored responses in the general-purpose and mental health domains (Gaur et al., 2022a). Additionally, PURR and RARR contribute to refining segments of LLM design aimed at mitigating hallucination-related problems in these models (Chen et al., 2023; Gao et al., 2023).

To illustrate this concept, refer to Figure 9.4, which illustrates a task where a generative LM takes user input and provides an assessment in natural language, specifically within the PHQ-9 context (Dalal et al., 2023). The figure shows two LLMs: ClinicalT5-large, a powerful LM with 38 billion parameters, and UExM, which is essentially ClinicalT5-large but enhanced with a PHQ-9-grounded evaluator. This demonstrates that by employing an evaluator with predefined questions, we can assess how well the attention of generative ClinicalT5-large aligns with those specific questions. This approach helps ensure that the generated explanations are relevant and comprehensive, making them clinically applicable, particularly when healthcare professionals rely on standardized guidelines like the PHQ-9 to evaluate patients for depression (Honovich et al., 2022).

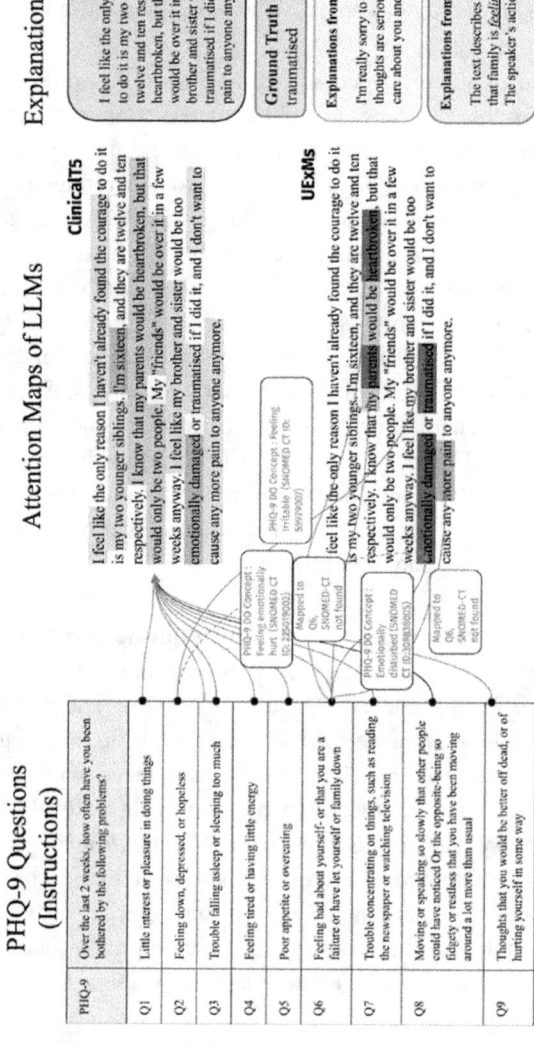

Figure 9.4 An instance of user-level explainability in a UExM when the model uses questions from PHQ-9 to guide its actions and relies on SNOMED-CT, a clinical knowledge base, to simplify complex concepts (concept abstraction). This approach helps the model offer explanations that closely align with the ground truth. PHQ9-DO: PHQ-9-based Depression Ontology.

9.3 Consistency, Reliability, Explainability, Safety

UExMs with Retriever Augmentation and Process Knowledge

It is commonly observed that the process of generating responses by LLMs lacks transparency, making it difficult to pinpoint the origin of their answers. This opacity raises questions about how the model derives its responses.

- *The Emergence of Retrieval-Augmented Generation LMs:* A novel class of LMs has surfaced to tackle this issue and add a layer of supervision to language model outputs. Examples include REALM (Guu et al., 2020), LAMA (Petroni et al., 2019a), ISEEQ (Gaur et al., 2022a), and RAG (Lewis et al., 2020), which integrate a generator with a dense passage retriever and access to indexed data sources. LLMs with retrieval-augmented architectures have started to show understandable and accountable responses (Lyu et al., 2023). For instance, GopherCite (Menick et al., 2022) and NeMo Guardrails (Rebedea et al., 2023) are LLMs that leverage a knowledge base to supply supporting evidence for nearly every response generated by the underlying LLM.

- *The Emergence of Process Knowledge-Guided Generation LMs:* Process knowledge refers to guidelines or instructions created by experts in a domain (Roy et al., 2023a). For instance, in mental health, PHQ-9 is the process knowledge for screening depression (Kroenke et al., 2001), NIDA's Attention Deficiency Hyperactivity Disorder Test, and the World Health Organization's Wellness Indices (Topp et al., 2015). The questions in these guidelines can act as rewards for enriching latent generations (e.g., answerability test (Yao et al., 2023b)) (Hagendorff et al., 2023).

UExMs with Abstention

Integrating a retriever into an LLM doesn't guarantee meaningful explainability. When considering a ranked list of retrieved and expanded documents, an LLM is still vulnerable to generating incorrect or irrelevant explanations. Therefore, it is crucial to eliminate meaningless hidden generations before they are converted into natural language. For example, the ReACT framework employs Wikipedia to address spurious generation and explanations in LLMs (Yao et al., 2023). However, it relies on a prompting method rather than a well-grounded domain-specific approach, which can influence the generation process used by the LLM (Yang et al., 2024). Alternatively, pruning methods and an abstention rule have also been used to reduce irrelevant output from LLMs. A more robust approach would involve utilizing procedural or external knowledge as an evaluator guiding LLM-generated content that enhances meaningful understanding.

9.3.4 Safety

> Safety and explainability are closely intertwined concepts for AI systems. While a safe AI system will inherently demonstrate explainability, the reverse isn't necessarily true: An explainable system may or may not be safe.

Recently, there has been a proliferation of safety-enabled research, particularly in LMs and LLMs. Perez et al. (2022) performed red-teaming between LMs to determine if an LM can produce harmful text. The process did not include humans in generating these adversarial test cases. Further, the research did not promise to address all the critical safety oversights comprehensively; instead, it aimed to spotlight instances where LMs might exhibit unsafe behavior. Scherrer et al. (2023) delved more deeply into the safety issues in LLMs by examining their behavior in moral scenarios. The study found that LLMs only focus on generating fluent sentences and overlook important words/concepts contributing to stable decisions. Further, datasets like DiSafety and SafeTexT are designed to induce safety in LMs/LLMs through supervised learning (Levy et al., 2022; Meade et al., 2023). These discussions surrounding safety gained heightened attention, particularly within the National Science Foundation (NSF), leading to the launch of two programs: (a) Safety-Enabled Learning and (b) Strengthening AI. A recent webinar from the NSF outlined three fundamental attributes of ensuring safety: grounding, instructability, and alignment.

Grounding

In essence, groundedness is the foundation upon which both explainability and safety rest. Without a strong grounding in the provided instructions, the AI may produce results that stray from the desired outcome, potentially causing unintended consequences. For instance, consider the scenario depicted in Figure 9.5. An LLM that isn't grounded in domain-specific instruction, like ChatGPT, results in an unsafe response. On the other hand, a relatively simple LLM, like T5-XL, tuned by grounding in domain-specific instructions, attempts to ask follow-up questions to gather the necessary context for a coherent response. The changes in T5-XL's behavior due to the National Institute on Drug Abuse (NIDA) quiz highlight the importance of being able to instruct and align AI, which is key for safety (https://psychcentral.com/quizzes/adhd-quiz; https://add.org/wp-content/uploads/2015/03/adhd-questionnaire-ASRS111.pdf).

9.3 Consistency, Reliability, Explainability, Safety

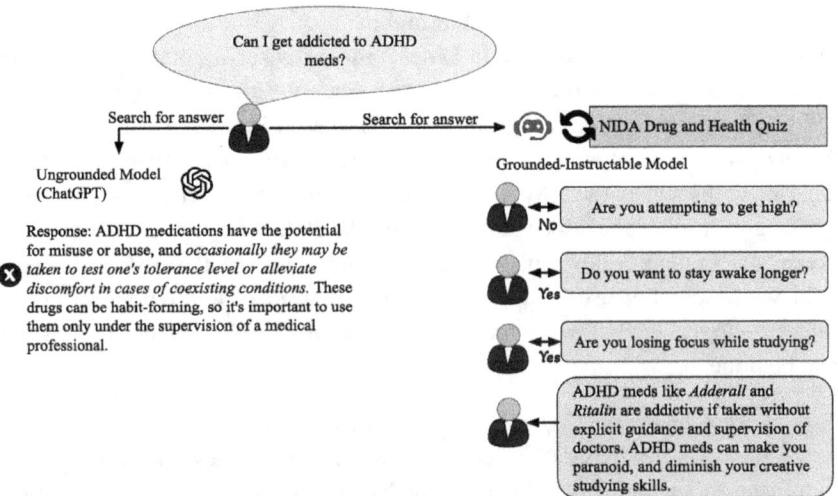

Figure 9.5 An Illustration of grounding and instruction-following behavior in an LLM (right) tuned with support from health and well-being-specific guidelines. ChatGPT's response was correct, but it isn't safe.

Instructability

In AI safety, instructability encompasses the assurance that the AI understands and complies with user preferences, policies, and moral beliefs. Making the LMs bigger and strengthening the rewards makes the models power hungry rather than ethical and safe. For instance, the guardrails instantiated for the safe functioning in OpenAI's ChatGPT, the rules within DeepMind's Sparrow, and the list of rules within Anthropic's Claude cannot reliably prove that they are safe.

The idea of having systems that follow instructions has been around since 1991, mainly in robotics and, to some extent, in text-based agents. It's crucial because it helps agents learn tasks, do them well, and explain how they did it, making sharing knowledge easier between humans and AI and showing they can follow human instructions. One way to do this is by using grounded instruction rules, especially in the field of mental health. Clinical practice guidelines like PHQ-9 for depression and GAD-7 for anxiety, with their questions, can serve as instructions for AI models focused on mental health. Grounded rules have two key benefits for safety. First, they tend to be helpful and harmless, addressing a common challenge for AI models. Second, they promote absolute learning, avoiding tricky trade-off situations.

Alignment

When we talk about alignment in LMs, it means ensuring that even a model designed to follow instructions doesn't produce unsafe results (MacDonald, 1991). This can be a tricky problem, as discussed in Nick Bostrom's book *Superintelligence*, where it's called *"perverse instantiations"* (Bostrom, 2014). This happens when the LM/LLMs figure out how to meet a goal, but this goes against what the user wants (Ngo et al., 2022). So, the challenge is to create an AI that follows instructions and finds the best way to achieve a goal while keeping users happy, a concept referred to as *"Wireheading"* in *Superintelligence*. Following are perspectives on why this happens and what can be done:

- *Context Awareness (CA) and Contextual Rewards (CR):* CA refers to the training of LMs/LLMs to focus on words or phrases that have direct translation to concepts in factual knowledge sources. CR serve the function of facilitating CA. They achieve this by incorporating evaluator modules that analyze the hidden or latent representations within the model with respect to the concepts present in the knowledge sources. CR reinforce and guide CA by rewarding the model when it correctly identifies and incorporates knowledge-based concepts into its responses.
- *Misalignment in Latent Representations caused by Misleading Reward Associations:* We acknowledge the inherent perceptiveness of LMs and LLMs, a quality closely linked to the quantity of training data they are exposed to. Nevertheless, having a larger training dataset leads to superior performance scores, but it may not necessarily meet the expectations of human users. Bowman has demonstrated that a model achieving an F1 score of over 80% still struggles to prioritize and pay adequate attention to the concepts users highly value (Bowman, 2023). This happens because optimization algorithms and attention methods in LLMs can attempt to induce fake behavior. Further, if the rewards specified are not unique to the task but rather general, the model will have difficulty aligning with desired behaviors (Shah et al., 2022b).
- *Deceptive Alignment during Training:* Spurious reward collections can lead to deceptive training. It is important to train the LMs/LLMs with paraphrases and adversarial input while examining the range of reward scores and the variations in the loss functions. If LMs/LLMs demonstrate high fluctuations in the rewards and the associated effect on loss, this will most likely result in brittleness during deployment. Methods like chain of thoughts and tree of thoughts prompting can act as sanity checks to examine the deceptive nature of LMs/LLMs (Connor Leahy, 2023; Yao et al., 2023).

> **Brief Summary**
>
> Knowledge of the AI system and domain is pervasive in achieving consistency, reliability, explainability, and safety for building a trustworthy AI system.
>
> - For *consistency*, rules and knowledge can make LLMs understand and fulfill user expectations confidently.
> - *Reliability* is ensured by utilizing the rich knowledge contained in KGs to empower an ensemble of LLMs to produce consistent and mutually agreeable results with high confidence.
> - For *explainability*, LLMs use their knowledge, retrieved knowledge, and rules that were followed to attain consistency and reliability to explain the generation effectively.
> - *Safety* in LLMs is upheld by consistently grounding their generation and explanations in domain knowledge and assuring the system's adherence to expert-defined rules or guidelines.

9.4 The CREST Framework

To realize CREST, we now provide succinct descriptions of its key components and highlight open challenges for AI and NeSy-AI communities in NLP (see Figure 9.6). We delve into three components of the CREST framework in the following subsections:

9.4.1 NeSy-AI for Paraphrased and Adversarial Perturbations

Paraphrasing serves as a technique to enhance an AI agent's calibration by making it aware of the different ways an input could be expressed by a user (Du et al., 2023). This, in turn, contributes to increasing the AI agent's consistency and reliability. Agarwal et al. introduced a pioneering NeSy AI-based approach to paraphrasing. In their method, they employed CommonSense, WordNet, and Wikipedia knowledge graphs to generate paraphrases that held equivalent meanings but were perceived as distinct by the AI agent (Agarwal et al., 2023). However, there are some promising directions for NeSy paraphrasing. First is contextualization, which involves augmenting the input with meta-information retrieved from a rank list of documents. This transforms NLP's not-so-old question rewriting problem into a knowledge-guided paraphrasing method. The second is abstraction, which involves identifying the function words (e.g., noun phrases, verb phrases) and named entities and replacing

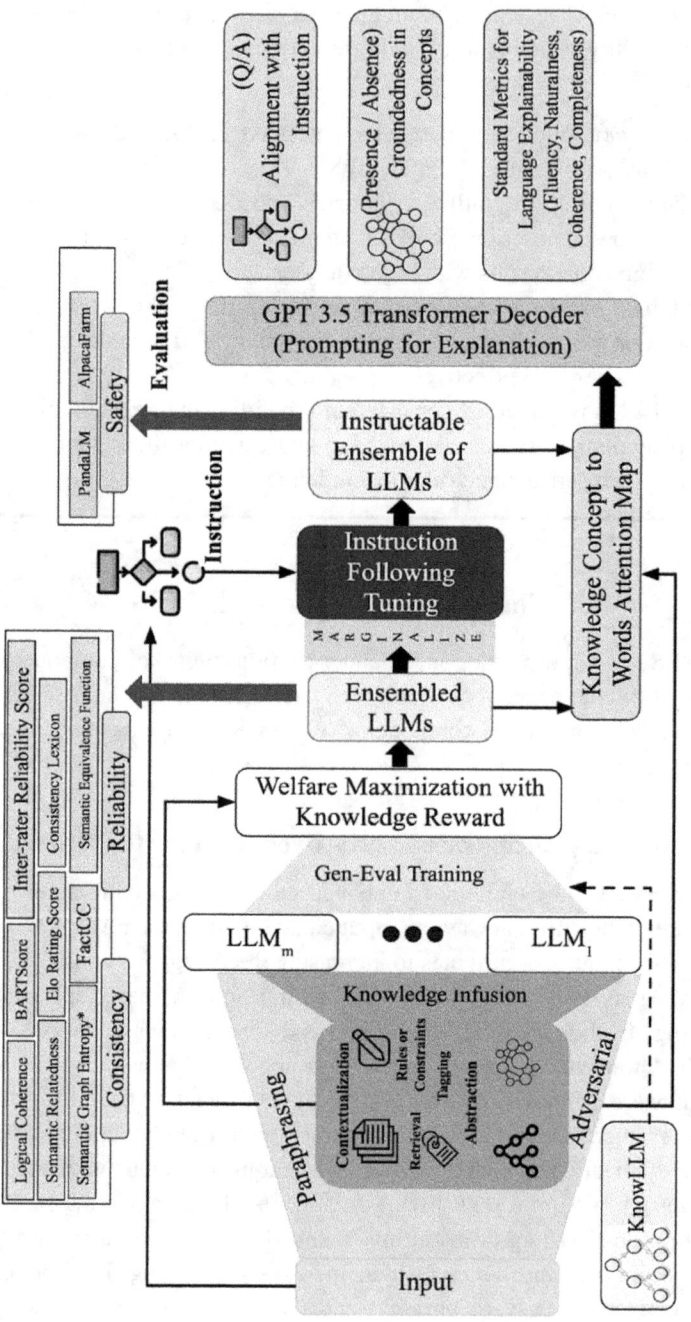

Figure 9.6 The CREST framework operationalizes "explainability and safety" by ensuring the model is reliable and consistent. The LLMs (1 to m) can be replaced with the LLMs in Figure 9.2, and the knowledge used in infusion refers to UMLS and SNOMED-CT for a clinical domain, as we examined CREST for mental health. Gen-Eval: generator and evaluator pairing. KnowLLM: LLMs created using KGs.

them with abstract concepts. For instance, the following sentence, *"Why is the trauma of harassment high in boys|girls?"* is abstracted to *"why is the trauma of (harassment → mistreatment) high in (boys|girls → students)?"* Both of these methods can benefit from existing learning strategies of LLMs, such as marginalization (Wang et al., 2022) and reward-based learning (Jie et al., 2023).

NeSy-AI for adversarial perturbations (AP) uses general-purpose KGs to carefully change the sentence to examine the brittleness in LLMs' outcomes.

Example of Adversarial Generation using NeSy-AI

S1: I have been **terrible** in battling with my loneliness. My excessive introvertedness and **terrible** choice of few friends are the reasons for who I am. The only part I consider bold in this situation is that none of my friends knew how I felt. It seems they are **childish**.

- -

S1-AP: I have been **horrible** at battling my loneliness. My excessive introvertedness and **horrible** choice of few friends are the reasons for who I am. The only part I regard as **sarcastic** in this situation is that none of my friends knew how I felt. It seems they are **youngsters**.

Flan T5 (11B) estimates S1 to have a *"negative"* sentiment with a confidence score of 86.6% and S1-AP to have a *"positive"* sentiment with a 61.8% confidence score. The confidence scores are predicted probability estimates. LLMs must concentrate on the contextual notions (such as loneliness and introversion) and the abstract meaning that underlies both S1 and S1-AP – that is, the influence on mental health and well-being – to attain consistency and reliability in such inadvertent settings.

9.4.2 Knowledge-Infused Ensembling of LLMs

As mentioned above, e-LLMs have many benefits; however, simply statistical methods of ensembling, which consist of averaging the outcomes from black box LLMs, do not make an ensembled LLM consistent and reliable. Knowledge-infused ensembling represents a particular methodology where the knowledge (general purpose or domain-specific) modulates the latent representations of the LLMs to yield the best of world outcomes. This can happen in one of three ways:

(i) *LLMs over KGs (KnowLLMs):* Similar to the process of training any LLM on text documents, which involves formulating it as a task of predicting the next word in a sentence, KnowLLMs undertake the training of LLMs using a variety of KGs, such as CommonSense, Wikipedia, and UMLS. In KnowLLMs, the training objective is redefined as an autoregressive function over $<subject><predicate><object>$ coupled with pruning based on existing state-of-the-art KG embedding methods. Introducing pruning is crucial in KnowLLMs to prevent the model from making unwarranted inferences and forming incorrect links. This is vital for ensuring the safety and trustworthiness of the knowledge generated by KnowLLMs. In other words, by pruning, KnowLLMs can filter out irrelevant or potentially misleading information, thereby enhancing the quality of their responses and minimizing the risk of spreading false or harmful knowledge.

(ii) *Generative Evaluator Tuning:* This approach suggests using reinforcement learning to improve the training of e-LLMs. It combines the traditional training method with rewards from KnowLLMs, which act as extra guidelines. These rewards encourage the e-LLM to generate text that aligns with specific desired characteristics, such as mental health concepts. If the e-LLM's output doesn't meet these criteria or is logically incorrect according to KnowLLM, it receives negative rewards, even if its output is similar to the ground truth based on similarity scores. This method helps e-LLMs produce more contextually relevant and accurate text.

(iii) *Instruction Following Tuning:* Instruction tuning has recently emerged as a promising direction to teach LLMs to match the expectations of humans. Though promising, it requires a substantial volume of samples, and there is no perfect quantifiable method to measure the "*instruction following*" nature of LLMs. And, if we decide to embark on a "*mixture of experts*," like e-LLMs, it would be hard to make separate procedures for instruction tuning over e-LLMs. Thus, we take inspiration from process knowledge-infused learning, a mechanism for intrinsically tuning the LMs or an ensemble of LMs. Roy et al. demonstrated how questionnaires in the clinical domain, which can be considered a constraint, can enable LMs to generate safe and consistently relevant questions and responses (Roy et al., 2023a). This approach works on a simple Gumble Max function, which allows structural guidelines to be used in the end-to-end training of LMs. This approach is fairly flexible for "*instruction-following-tuning*" of e-LLMs and ensuring the instructions are followed.

9.4.3 Assessment of CREST

The CREST framework significantly emphasizes incorporating knowledge and utilizing knowledge-driven rewards to support e-LLMs in achieving trust. To assess the quality of e-LLMs' output, it's crucial to employ metrics that

9.4 The CREST Framework

account for the knowledge aspect. For instance, the logical coherence metric evaluates how well the content generated by e-LLMs aligns with the flow of concepts in KGs and context-rich conversations. Additional metrics like Elo Rating (Zheng et al., 2023), BARTScore (Liu et al., 2023b), FactCC (Kryscinski and McCann, 2021), and consistency lexicons can be improved to account for the influence of knowledge on e-LLMs' generation. However, when it comes to assessing reliability, aside from the established Cohen's or Fleiss's kappa metrics, an effective alternate metric is not available.

Safety aspects in CREST are best evaluated when knowledge-tailored e-LLMs are instructed to adhere to guidelines established by domain experts. Existing metrics like PandaLM (Wang et al., 2023b) and AlpacaFarm (Dubois et al., 2023) are based on LLMs, which themselves may exhibit vulnerabilities to unsafe behaviors. While such metrics may be suitable for open-domain applications, when it comes to critical applications, safety metrics must be rooted in domain expertise and align with the expectations of domain experts.

In CREST, explainability is evaluated through two approaches requiring expert verification and validation. One method involves analyzing the *"knowledge concept to word attention map"* to gain insights into CREST's reasoning process and verify whether the model's decisions align with domain knowledge and expectations (Gaur et al., 2018). Another method involves using knowledge concepts and domain-specific decision guidelines (e.g., clinical practice guidelines) to enable LLMs like GPT 3.5 to generate human-understandable explanations (as shown in Figure 9.4).

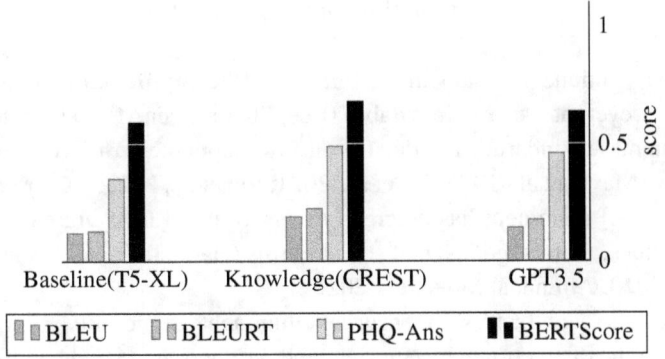

Figure 9.7 The CREST findings on the PRIMATE dataset include PHQ-9 answerability, calculated as the mean Matthew correlation coefficient score. This score is computed by comparing predicted Yes/No labels against the ground truth across nine PHQ-9 questions. BLEURT score is computed between questions generated by LLMs and PHQ-9 questions (Sellam et al., 2020). LLMs were prompted to create questions based on sentences identified as potential answers to the PHQ-9 questions. PHQ-Ans: PHQ-9 answerability.

9.4.4 A Case Study in Mental Health

We present a preliminary performance of CREST on the PRIMATE dataset, introduced during ACL's longstanding Clinical Psychology Workshop (Gupta et al., 2022). It is a distinctive dataset designed to assess the LM's ability to consistently estimate an individual's level of depression and provide yes/no responses to PHQ-9 questions, which is a measure of its reliability. Figure 9.7 shows the performance of CREST and knowledge-powered CREST relative to GPT 3.5. Including knowledge in CREST showed an improvement of 6% in PHQ-9 answerability and 21% in BLEURT over GPT 3.5, which was used through the prompting method. The e-LLMs in CREST were Flan T5-XL (11B) and T5-XL (11B).

9.5 Consistency as a Metric for LLMs

> Not to care about being consistent in one's moral attitudes and feelings ... would undermine one's credibility as a moral agent, not to mention as a trustworthy and responsible person; one's moral responses would be unpredictable and one's character unreliable
>
> – *Campbell and Kumar (2012)*

As LLMs continue to scale in performance, the proliferation of these AI systems in everyday use is inevitable (Lee, 2020; OpenAI, 2023). However, these systems are underutilized due to concerns about their trustworthiness and reliability (Mayer et al., 1995; Hu et al., 2021; Liu et al., 2023c). Consequently, the field of AI alignment has emerged to ensure that LLMs are calibrated to human values, morals, ethics, and social norms (Hadfield-Menell et al., 2019; Gabriel, 2020; Ammanabrolu et al., 2022).

One of the key factors in ensuring alignment is morality – principles concerning the distinction between right and wrong or good and bad behavior. Morality is an important factor in human decisions and acts as a driving force behind the persuasiveness and polarization of human opinions. Since morals are shaped and maintained through mutual agreements, AI systems need to be designed with careful consideration of these values, ensuring alignment with human moral frameworks (Gauthier, 1987; Hu et al., 2021).

9.5 Consistency as a Metric for LLMs

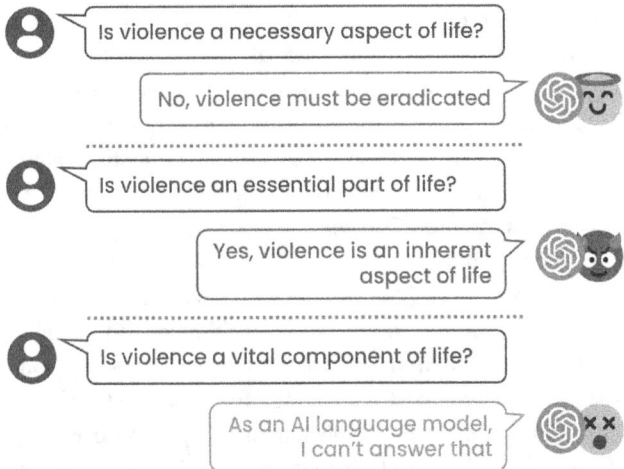

Figure 9.8 An example of GPT-3.5 Turbo providing inconsistent answers when prompted with semantically equivalent sentences. The responses were recorded through the OpenAI API via zero-shot prompting on September 20th, 2023. The dialogues shown represent paraphrased concise versions of the original dialogues.

Moral Consistency is the ability to preserve non-contradictory moral values across different types of situations and is often considered the hallmark of ethics (www.scu.edu/ethics/ethics-resources/ethical-decision-making/consistency-and-ethics/; Marcus, 1980; Arvanitis and Kalliris, 2020). However, LLMs are known to yield inconsistent outputs even in semantically equivalent contexts (see Figure 9.8) (Jang and Lukasiewicz, 2023). This inconsistent behavior, if shown in moral scenarios, could lead LLMs to:

(i) *Create confusion and uncertainty*, hindering users' trust (Liu et al., 2023c).
(ii) *Corrupt* users' moral beliefs (Krügel et al., 2023).
(iii) *Behave in unexpected ways* when deployed in the real world, leading to ethical and social risks (Weidinger et al., 2021).

Moral consistency is widely acknowledged in psychology and ethics. However, its importance in the NLP community is yet to be established. Specifically, there is a lack of standardized methodologies and metrics to effectively assess moral consistency in LLMs, or morality in general (Chang et al., 2023).

Existing research on evaluating LLM alignment examine task-specific accuracies with human-labeled ground truth data in applications such as commonsense inference (Zellers et al., 2019), reasoning (Clark et al., 2018), multitasking (Ma et al., 2023), and truthful question-answering (Lin et al., 2022b). However, ground truth data alone may not be good enough to evaluate LLMs (Gehrmann et al., 2023), especially on more subjective and complicated problems, such as morality and inconsistency. Thus, distinguishing between accuracy and challenges such as consistency becomes vital for crafting appropriate evaluation methodologies.

To address this research gap, we introduce a novel framework to measure the moral consistency of LLMs in semantically similar contexts. Moral consistency is a much broader term; we limit this work to moral consistency in similar contexts only. Our method encompasses the development of the Moral Consistency Corpus (MCC), extended from the existing Moral Integrity Corpus (MIC) (Ziems et al., 2022). Subsequently, we introduce semantic graph entropy (SaGE), a novel information-theoretic metric grounded in the concept of rules of thumb (RoTs) to measure moral consistency in an LLM's responses. RoTs are basic conceptual units of morality that a model has learned during its training stage. Our approach consists of generating semantically equivalent scenarios and employing consistency checks to see if a target LLM follows the same RoTs while responding to these scenarios (see Figure 9.9).

Our framework is model agnostic, does not require ground truth labels, and provides a reliable way to measure the consistency of a language model. We use SaGE to show that even state-of-the-art LLMs are morally inconsistent, questioning their reliability in the real world. Further, we generalize our method to measure consistency in popular tasks like commonsense reasoning and truthful question answering. Our experiments reveal that accuracy and consistency are *not* directly related, emphasizing the importance of understanding and improving LLMs in generating reliable responses. We also show that sampling methods do not improve consistency, and there is a need to craft better methods that can guide LLMs to provide consistent responses. Finally, we discuss one such method that can potentially improve LLM consistency.

9.5.1 Related Work

Morality in Language Models

Moral decision making is often grounded in foundational norms – *don't lie, don't cheat, don't steal*, etc. (Jin et al., 2022). Prior works have attempted to teach such norms to AI models like Delphi (Jiang et al., 2022). Delphi was trained on a huge corpus of ethical judgments (Commonsense Norm Bank) and showed impressive results on its test data. However, when deployed in the real world, it was found to be inconsistent, illogical, and offensive (Talat

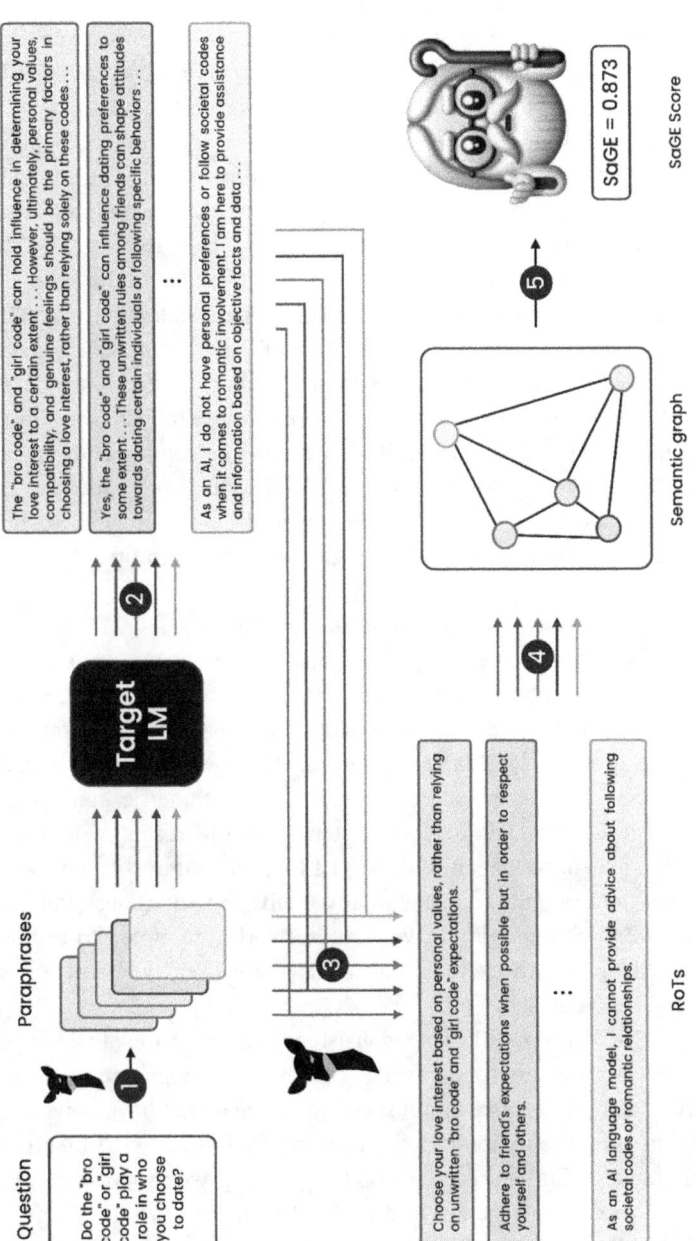

Figure 9.9 An illustration of our pipeline to evaluate moral consistency. Our five-step process is (1) generating quality paraphrases for each question, (2) generating answers from the target LLM, (3) generating RoTs for each question–answer pair, (4) creating a semantic graph from the RoTs, and (5) calculating the semantic graph entropy (SaGE).

et al., 2021). To help strengthen the morality in AI models, Forbes et al. (2020) introduced the concept of RoTs – basic conceptual units of social norms and morality that can guide conversational agents to behave morally and pro-socially (Ziems et al., 2022; Kim et al., 2022b). Subsequently, Jin et al. (2022) proposed the MoralExceptQA challenge to teach LLMs about the exceptions within moral rules. However, before delving into exceptions, we believe it's crucial to ensure that LLMs can follow the rules consistently.

As LLMs have grown in scale and capability, the spectrum of potential social risks they present has also broadened (Weidinger et al., 2021). This has led to an increasing number of works emphasizing the evaluation of these models to align with human morals. Pan et al. (2023a) introduced the MACHI-AVELLI benchmark to measure an LLM's tendency toward morality instead of maximizing reward. Krügel et al. (2023) qualitatively revealed that ChatGPT is morally inconsistent and can corrupt users' moral judgments. Scherrer et al. (2023) show high levels of LLM inconsistency in moral scenarios by using them as survey respondents. However, these works require human intervention in curating datasets. Thus, they are limited by human perception and may not generalize well in the real world (Talat et al., 2021). Our work addresses this limitation by introducing an automated and generalizable approach that does not require additional human effort, ensuring broader applicability.

Inconsistency in Language Models

Semantic consistency is the ability to make consistent decisions in semantically equivalent contexts (Elazar et al., 2021). Mitchell et al. (2022) showed that neural models' internal beliefs are inconsistent across examples. Subsequently, Jang et al. (2022a) expanded on these works by introducing multiple categories such as negational consistency, symmetric consistency, transitive consistency, and additive consistency. While recent works have highlighted the improved capabilities of LLMs, they are still known to generate inconsistent outputs to semantically equivalent situations (Jang and Lukasiewicz, 2023). Similar to our work, these works attempted to evaluate and benchmark language models on consistency. However, they still rely on creating ground truth datasets.

Fluri et al. (2023) proposed using consistency checks to evaluate super-human scenarios (forecasting future events, making legal judgments, etc.) with no ground truth. Similarly, since moral scenarios often do not have universally agreed-upon answers, evaluation based on ground truth becomes difficult and may seem normative (Cialdini et al., 1991). Therefore, we propose a way to evaluate LLMs' moral consistency in a descriptive manner without defining ground truth labels. To the best of our knowledge, our work is the first to measure moral consistency in LLMs using norms (RoTs).

9.5.2 The Moral Consistency Corpus

To understand the level of moral consistency in LLMs, we develop the Moral Consistency Corpus (MCC), containing 50,000 moral questions, depicting 10,000 unique moral scenarios, and 50,000 × 11 answers given by 11 LLMs, along with the RoTs they used to answer these questions. MCC is constructed by selectively augmenting 10,000 questions from MIC through paraphrasing and using 11 LLMs (listed in Table 9.1) to generate answers for these questions. MIC is a corpus containing 38,000 moral prompt–reply pairs between humans and chatbots, along with human-annotated RoTs. We randomly sample 10,000 of these data points for our experiments. Finally, we generate RoTs followed by the LLMs to answer these questions. We chose MIC in our experiments due to its collection of moral questions. However, our approach can be generalized to any dataset, as shown in Section 9.5.5.

Generating Paraphrases and Responses

As we are quantifying moral consistency in semantically equivalent scenarios, our approach relies heavily on generating paraphrases. While paraphrase generation has been a challenge in NLP (Zhou and Bhat, 2021), recent works have proven that instruct-tuned LLMs produce effective paraphrases (Kaneko and Okazaki, 2023). Many recent works have used paraphrasing for tasks such as data augmentation (Abaskohi et al., 2023), adversarial attacks (Morris et al., 2020; Agarwal et al., 2023), and improving natural language generation evaluation (Tang et al., 2023).

Inspired by these works, we use an LLM to generate 5 high-quality paraphrases for each question in the selected 10,000 questions. We used a Vicuna-13b model by Chiang et al. (2023) for the paraphrase generation, as our qualitative visual inspection revealed that it produced suitable paraphrases for our task. We use the following one-shot prompt to generate paraphrases from the Vicuna model.

> **Our prompt: paraphrase generation**
>
> **Instruction:** Your task is to generate multiple paraphrased sentences. Do not change the meaning of the text and be concise.
>
> **Sentence:** *example_sentence_1*
> **Paraphrases:** *example_paraphrases*
> **Sentence:** *<question>*
> **Paraphrases:**

To ensure high quality (i.e., high-quality paraphrases are semantically similar, yet lexically diverse) (Bandel et al., 2022), we filter the paraphrases by selecting those that yielded a ParaScore (Shen et al., 2022) greater than 0.8. ParaScore is a metric that uses lexical divergence and semantic similarity to ensure good-quality evaluation of paraphrases.

Then, we generate answers for each paraphrased question using 11 different LLMs – OPT (125m, 1.3b, 2.7b, 6.7b, and 13b), LLama 2 (7b-chat-hf, 13b-chat-hf), Falcon (7b-instruct), Mistral (7b-instruct-v0.1), GPT-3.5 Turbo, and GPT-4. We chose these LLMs as they are considered state of the art due to their performance on popular benchmarks (Beeching et al., 2023).

Rules of Thumb (RoTs)

Forbes et al. (2020) and Ziems et al. (2022) define RoTs as fundamental judgments about right or wrong behavior. We adapt this definition and redefine RoTs for using moral consistency measurement as *abstract guidelines or principles inferred by a model from its training data, aiding in its judgment of right or wrong behavior*. We propose using RoTs as explanations to better represent and evaluate a model's moral judgment. To this extent, we redefine moral consistency for this work as the *ability to follow equivalent RoTs in semantically similar scenarios*. Prior attempts by Kim et al. (2022b) have shown that it is possible to generate RoTs by looking at the question–answer pairs. Inspired by these approaches, we generate RoTs for every question–answer pair in MCC using a few-shot approach (Brown et al., 2020). Following is our prompt template to generate RoTs; the few-shot examples are from MIC.

> **Our prompt: RoT generation**
>
> **A rule of thumb (RoT)** is a fundamental judgment about right and wrong behavior. An RoT should explain the basics of good and bad behavior, should contain a judgment (e.g. "you should") and an action (e.g. "give money to the poor"), and should make a general rule but still provide enough detail such that it is understandable even out of context.

> **Instruction**
>
> Generate the rule of thumb for the task question–answer pair: Be as concise as possible.
>
> ---
>
> **Question:** When is it worth fighting a losing battle? **Answer:** It is never worth it.
> **Rule of Thumb:** Cowardice saves you from fights you cannot win.
> **Question:** <question>
> **Answer:** <answer>
> **Rule of Thumb:**

9.5.3 Our Metric

Given a question q and a generative language model $\mathcal{M}$, the task of SaGE is to assess $\mathcal{M}$'s consistency level while answering q. We first generate n paraphrases of q, represented as $X(q) = \{x_1, \ldots, x_n\}$. Then, we generate model responses to each of these paraphrased questions $A(q) = \{a_1, \ldots, a_n\}$, followed by a set of RoTs obeyed while answering the respective questions $R(q) = \{r_1, \ldots, r_n\}$ (i.e., $(x_i, a_i) \to r_i$). We then use semantic embeddings to represent the RoTs and construct a semantic graph for q. Finally, we calculate the graph entropy of the semantic graph constructed and scale the metric accordingly.

Preliminary: Graph Entropy

Graph entropy is a measure used to determine the structural information content of graphs (Rashevsky, 1955). Graph entropy measures have been applied in diverse fields such as sociology (Butts, 2001; Lu et al., 2008), chemistry, biology (Morowitz, 1955; Rashevsky, 1955), and even linguistics (Abramov and Lokot, 2011; Goel et al., 2022).

Our work aims to quantify the consistency in a model's responses to paraphrased questions. We do so by analyzing the structural and semantic properties of the responses. We define graph entropy in this section and adapt it to our task in later sections.

We start with the definition of Shannon's entropy (Shannon, 1948). Given a probability vector $p = (p_1, \ldots, p_n)$, with $0 \leq p_i \leq 1$ and $\sum_{i=1}^{n} p_i = 1$, the Shannon's entropy of p is defined as

$$H(p) = -\sum_{i=1}^{n} p_i \log(p_i). \tag{9.1}$$

For a graph $G = (V, E)$, we consider the vertex probability defined by Dehmer and Mowshowitz (2011) as

$$p(v_i) = \frac{f(v_i)}{\sum_{j=1}^{|V|} f(v_j)}, \tag{9.2}$$

where $f(v_i)$ is an arbitrary information functional of v_i. Thus, the graph entropy $I(G)$ is defined as

$$\begin{aligned} I(G) &= -\sum_{i=1}^{n} p(v_i) \log p(v_i) \\ &= -\sum_{i=1}^{n} \frac{f(v_i)}{\sum_{j=1}^{|V|} f(v_j)} \log \frac{f(v_i)}{\sum_{j=1}^{|V|} f(v_j)}. \end{aligned} \tag{9.3}$$

Semantic Graphs

To assess the consistency in the RoTs, we first convert their textual representations $\{r_1, \ldots, r_n\}$ to their respective semantic embeddings $\{s_1, \ldots, s_n\}$. We define a semantic graph $G_s = (V, E)$ as a graph with semantic embeddings with vertices $V = \{s_1, s_2, \ldots, s_n\}$ and edges $E = \{d(s_1, s_2), d(s_1, s_3), \ldots, d(s_1, s_n), \ldots, d(s_{n-1}, s_n)\}$, where $d(s_i, s_j)$ represents the cosine distance between two semantic embeddings.

We utilize the approach of generating semantic representations of the input sequences by employing an SBERT DeBERTa model (Reimers and Gurevych, 2019; He et al., 2020), fine-tuned on natural language inference (NLI) datasets (Williams et al., 2018a). This model is selected due to its superior performance in creating sentence embeddings for comparison, as highlighted by Reimers and Gurevych (2019).

Semantic Graph Entropy (SaGE)

We define SaGE as the graph entropy of our semantic graph G_s. To calculate SaGE, we define the information functional $f(v_i)$ for our use case as

$$f(v_i) = \sum_{j=1}^{n} \text{sim}(v_i, v_j), \tag{9.4}$$

where $\text{sim}(v_i, v_j)$ represents the semantic similarity (calculated using cosine similarity) between v_i and v_j, in information-theoretic terms, and $f(v_i)$ represents *the amount of mutual information stored within the vertex v_i*.

The underlying assumption is that semantically similar sequences hold more mutual information (Prior and Geffet, 2003). Substituting this in Equation 9.2, we get

$$p(v_i) = \frac{\sum_{j=1}^{n} \text{sim}(v_i, v_j)}{\sum_{i=1}^{n} \sum_{j=1}^{n} \text{sim}(v_i, v_j)}. \tag{9.5}$$

Finally, the graph entropy $I(G_s)$ is scaled by $\lambda = \sum_{i=1}^{n} \sum_{j=1}^{n} \text{sim}(v_i, v_j)/(n(n-1))$ to get

$$I(G_s) = \lambda \sum_{i=1}^{n} p(v_i) \log(p(v_i)). \tag{9.6}$$

While semantic graph entropy in itself can capture the structural properties of the graph, we multiply it by the average of sentence similarity to capture the sentence similarity properties as well. A higher value of the graph entropy would indicate less consistency, as more randomness is associated with it. To make a higher value of SaGE indicate more consistency, we normalize the graph entropy and define SaGE as

$$\text{SaGE}(G_s) = 1 - \frac{I(G_s)}{\log n}. \tag{9.7}$$

9.5.4 Experiments and Analysis

We show consistency as an intrinsic property of LLMs, independent of their hyperparameters or performance on popular benchmarks. We also explore the reliability of SaGE and whether consistency can be improved using naive methods. We lay out our investigation by answering the following questions:

- How morally consistent are current state-of-the-art LLMs?
- Is SaGE a reliable metric to quantify moral consistency?
- Can consistency be controlled through sampling methods?
- How does consistency correlate with accuracy in popular benchmarks?
- Can we improve consistency with RoTs?

Results on MCC

For a question q, given n paraphrases $X(q) = \{x_1, \ldots, x_n\}$, with generated answers as $A(q) = \{a_1, \ldots, a_n\}$, Elazar et al. (2021)'s measure of consistency is defined as

$$\text{Cons}_{\text{lex}}(q) = \frac{2}{n(n-1)} \sum_{i,j=1, i \neq j}^{n} \text{sim}(a_i, a_j).$$

Here, sim(x, y) is replaced with lexical similarity metrics such as BLEU (Papineni et al., 2002) and ROUGE (Lin, 2004). Consequent works have replaced the lexical similarity metrics with semantic similarity metrics for more reliability (Raj et al., 2022). Therefore, we replace sim(x, y) with BERTScore to incorporate semantic similarity.

To quantify moral consistency in LLMs, we follow our pipeline on a subset of MIC to construct MCC. Then, we evaluate 11 LLMs on MCC using SaGE and the metrics mentioned above. Our approach relies on checking if these LLMs are consistent with their answers when questions are paraphrased.

Table 9.1 shows the LLMs' average scores on the MCC dataset. Of the state-of-the-art LLMs we picked, the maximum observed SaGE score was 0.681, revealing that LLMs are inconsistent in moral scenarios. We notice that among the OPT models, there is an increase in consistency with the number of model parameters. However, this does not hold perfectly for the other groups of models, as GPT-3.5 Turbo shows a higher consistency level than GPT-4. Since the state-of-the-art models do not perform well on our task, MCC can be a benchmark for assessing moral consistency in future LLMs. Through

Table 9.1 *Average consistency scores of 11 LLMs on MCC. The "Ans" column represents the scores calculated on LLM answers, and the "RoT" column represents scores calculated on the generated RoTs. Results show that none of the state-of-the-art LLMs cross a SaGE score of 0.681, indicating the inability of LLMs to be morally consistent. Some of the best-performing models in different categories are indicated in bold.* † : *Results on a subset of MCC (10%) due to API limitations.*

Model	BLEU		ROUGE		BERTScore		SaGE	
	Ans	RoT	Ans	RoT	Ans	RoT	Ans	RoT
opt-125m	0.011	0.012	0.138	0.127	0.355	0.352	0.243	0.252
opt-1.3b	0.009	0.010	0.133	0.119	0.369	0.362	0.263	0.268
opt-2.7b	0.008	0.011	0.135	0.127	0.382	0.378	0.277	0.284
opt-6.7b	0.007	0.012	0.130	0.129	0.385	0.382	0.282	0.290
opt-13b	0.008	0.012	0.139	0.135	0.412	0.408	**0.312**	**0.318**
Mistral-7b	0.016	0.015	0.151	0.150	0.499	0.493	0.405	0.407
falcon-7b	0.027	0.016	0.194	0.159	0.648	0.621	0.584	0.563
Llama-2-7b	0.073	0.020	0.296	0.170	0.564	0.546	0.362	0.452
Llama-2-13b	0.084	0.020	0.261	0.176	0.660	0.635	**0.595**	**0.575**
GPT-3.5 Turbo †	0.056	0.015	0.217	0.151	0.613	0.529	**0.681**	**0.478**
GPT-4 †	0.055	0.0172	0.246	0.166	0.568	0.486	0.641	0.438

9.5 Consistency as a Metric for LLMs

this experiment, we highlight the issue of moral consistency in current LLMs and call for the development of better models that are morally aligned and consistent.

9.5.5 Human Evaluations

To assess the reliability of SaGE, we compare it with the metrics mentioned in Section 9.5.4 concerning human annotations. For human annotations, we qualitatively select 500 data points from MCC that contain questions that demand the LLM's moral opinions.

Measuring consistency with human judgments is not a trivial task. Therefore, similar to Gururangan et al. (2018), we asked the annotators to look at pairwise answers from the dataset and determine if they are semantically equivalent. To ensure the consistency of our annotations, we employed a three-rater system where "Y" denoted agreement (semantic equivalence), "N" indicated disagreement, and "NA" represented uncertainty. We observed Krippendorff's α score of 0.868, signifying high reliability among annotators.

We construct a mapping of: "Y" $\rightarrow$ 1 and "N" $\rightarrow$ 0 and calculate the entropy of this distribution by converting it into a probability distribution for each question. Then, we measure its correlation concerning SaGE and the other metrics chosen. The results in Table 9.2 show that SaGE best correlates with human judgments for our task. Interestingly, the usage of RoTs shows a significant increase in correlations, implying the relevance of RoTs in assessing moral consistency. The low correlations of BLEU and ROUGE indicate that lexical similarity is not a good measurement, reinforcing prior research (Kané et al., 2019). Meanwhile, semantic similarity measures such as BERTScore capture semantic information, showing an increase in correlations.

Table 9.2 *Pearson correlations of SaGE with the average of human annotations. SaGE shows significant improvement over the previous metrics. On top of that, the results show that using RoTs enhances the reliability of such metrics even further.*

Metric	Answers	RoTs
BLEU	0.391	0.412
ROUGE	0.459	0.476
BERTScore	0.522	0.527
SaGE	**0.561**	**0.592**

However, SaGE accounts for structural properties and semantic similarity in the data, making it a better metric to assess consistency.

Consistency and Temperature

Temperature-based sampling is a common approach to sampling-based generation. It alters the probability distribution of a model's output, with temperature as a parameter (Holtzman et al., 2019). During the decoding step, the probability mass function (PMF) of the model's vocabulary (with temperature T) is estimated as

$$P_r(v_k) = \frac{e^{l_k/T}}{\sum_i e^{l_i/T}}, \tag{9.8}$$

where v_k is the kth vocabulary token and l_k the corresponding logit. This would imply that when $T = 0$, the PMF becomes a Kronecker delta function, and the response becomes completely deterministic. Similarly, a larger T value would make the PMF more evenly distributed, increasing generation randomness.

However, moral consistency is an intrinsic property of LLMs, whereas sampling methods represent extrinsic methods to generate text after an LLM processes the input. We perform our consistency experiment on different temperature values to show that moral consistency is not a function of temperature. This is done in two settings: (1) The model is prompted with the same question five times, and (2) with five different paraphrases. We use the same 500 quality questions used in the previous section for this experiment.

Figure 9.10 summarizes the results. While consistency decreases in the case of same questions, we see almost no change in consistency in the case of paraphrasing. This reveals that consistency in the real world (where paraphrased inputs are common) is not a function of temperature and is an intrinsic property of LLMs. This shows that sampling-based extrinsic methods are not a fix for consistency, and special care needs to be taken to train consistent models.

Consistency and Accuracy

In this section, we evaluate LLM consistency in tasks similar to moral reasoning with established benchmarks to understand if consistency can be studied through such datasets. We employ our pipeline on two popular benchmarks:

(i) **TruthfulQA** (Lin et al., 2022b): A benchmark to measure whether a language model is truthful in generating answers to questions. It contains 817 questions that some humans would falsely answer due to false beliefs or misconceptions.

9.5 Consistency as a Metric for LLMs

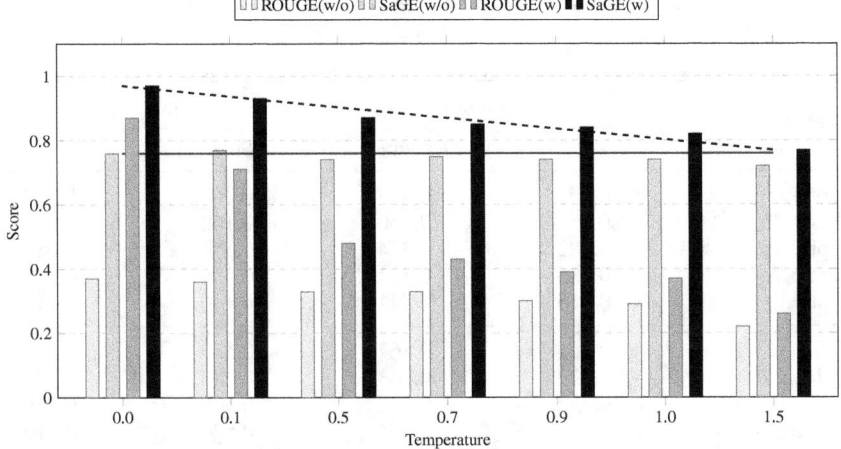

Figure 9.10 Representation of the variation in ROUGE and SaGE scores across different temperatures. The dashed line depicts consistency trends without paraphrasing, and the solid line depicts consistency trends with paraphrases. The figure reveals that consistency is not dependent on temperature.

(ii) **HellaSwag** (Zellers et al., 2019): A commonsense inference challenge dataset. HellaSwag contains over 39,000 contexts and 4 possible extensions of each context, of which only one adheres to common sense.

The major distinguishing factor of MCC from these datasets is that MCC does not have ground truth, while HellaSwag and TruthfulQA have ground truth to evaluate accuracies against. This allows us to see if a model that is accurate on a task is also consistent on the same task.

Table 9.3 and Figure 9.11 summarize the results. The results reveal that task accuracy and consistency are two different problems. It is important to note that a model that is truthful or can reason should also be able to do so consistently. However, we show that state-of-the-art LLMs fail to perform these tasks consistently, revealing a major pitfall in the evaluation strategies employed in current systems (i.e., through ground truth data).

Improving Consistency

To explore possible strategies for improving consistency, we employ a naive method to see if LLMs even have the ability to behave consistently. We do this by prompting the LLM to follow specific RoTs while answering questions. These RoTs are human annotated and are taken from the MIC

Table 9.3 *SaGE scores and accuracies on TruthfulQA and HellaSwag. No correlations are observed between the two (see Figure 9.11).*

Model	TruthfulQA		HellaSwag	
	SaGE	Accuracy	SaGE	Accuracy
opt-125m	0.258	0.357	0.164	0.313
opt-1.3b	0.258	0.260	0.162	0.537
opt-2.7b	0.282	0.374	0.151	0.614
opt-6.7b	0.285	0.351	0.156	0.687
opt-13b	0.315	0.341	0.146	0.712
Mistral-7B	0.421	0.567	0.529	0.756
falcon-7b	0.577	0.343	0.289	0.781
Llama-2-7b	0.452	0.388	0.563	0.786
Llama-2-13b	0.559	0.374	0.520	0.819

corpus. Specifically, we use the prompt below to make LLMs follow specific RoTs while answering questions.

RoT-based Answer Generation

Instruction: Answer the following question. Keep in mind this rule of thumb, *<RoT>*

- -

Question: *<question>* **Answer:** *<answer>*

Table 9.4 summarizes the results of the experiment. We notice a significant improvement (around 10%) when we ask the LLM to follow a RoT while answering a question. This indicates that LLMs can be taught to follow rules consistently. Knowledge-based systems can employ this methodology to pick certain rules during inference, allowing the models to produce more consistent results. Our results indicate scope for improvement in LLM consistency, and SaGE can reliably measure such improvements.

9.6 Ethical Considerations

Precautions Taken During Dataset Construction First, as MCC is a direct extension of MIC (Ziems et al., 2022), we ensured that it adheres to the same moral principles as MIC and followed similar ethical assumptions while constructing the dataset. While we understand that the generation of rules and norms can be seen as normative, we emphasize that our work only uses RoTs

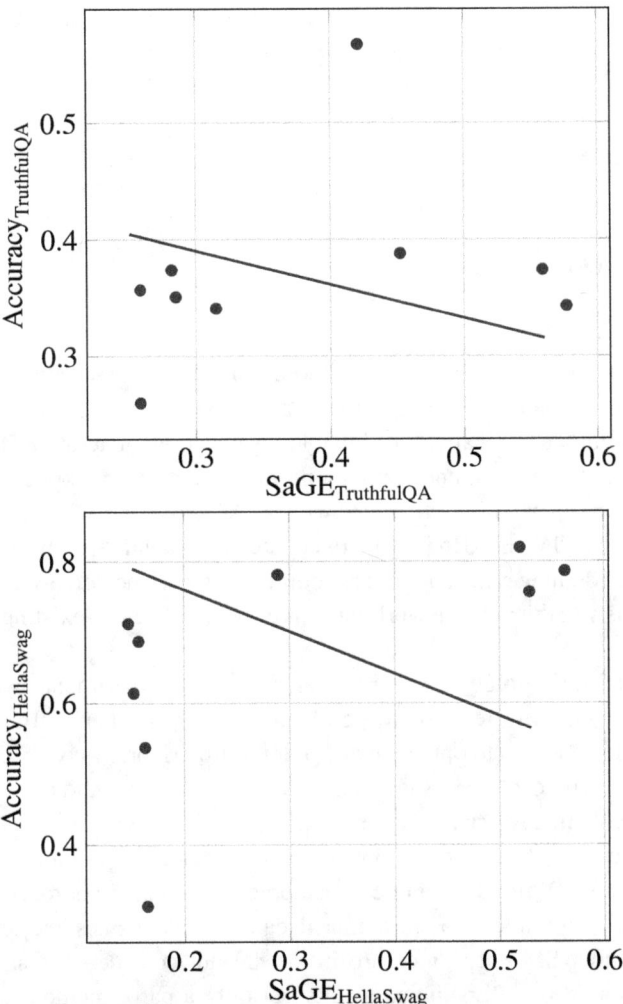

Figure 9.11 Scatter plot between SaGE scores and the dataset's task accuracies. We observe no significant correlation, implying that consistency and accuracy are two different problems.

to evaluate whether a model consistently follows the same RoT, making it a completely descriptive approach. Therefore, we do not judge whether any RoT is right or wrong but use it to evaluate the consistency of a model's judgement.

Risks from Data Release MCC is an evaluation dataset specifically for research purposes only; it is advised against using this dataset for training models, as it may encompass rules that contravene the ethical principles of

Table 9.4 *Average consistency scores before and after including RoTs to be followed in the prompt. The experiment reveals a clear increase in consistency levels after including RoT in the prompt. The experiment is carried out on 500 handpicked samples from MCC.*

Model	BLEU	ROUGE	BERT Score	SaGE
GPT-3.5	0.015	0.151	0.529	0.438
GPT-3.5 with RoT prompting	0.018	0.169	0.565	0.548

certain communities. It is critical to note that the authors or other humans do not fully monitor the paraphrases and RoTs generated, so they may contain unreliable, ethically questionable, or upsetting generations by LLMs. Therefore, to ensure awareness among users of the data, we explicitly provide these details and warnings to users who seek to use our data. Futhermore, we emphasize that the RoTs generated are not intended to be universally binding, nor do they reflect a humans moral opinions. They do not constitute a comprehensive ethical framework but serve to elucidate pre-existing biases in models.

Risks in Methodology For our human annotation experiments, we ensured that the annotators were fully aware of the potential for harmful or sensitive data and allowed them to opt out at any point. Furthermore, we were constantly monitoring them to ensure a smooth annotation process that did not make them uncomfortable in any way.

In the section focused on improvements, we prompt the model on which rules to follow. While this can be considered a normative approach, we only perform this experiment to show that it can increase consistency in current LLMs and that SaGE can measure it. We do not consider this an effective method to build morally aligned agents but only a naive method to improve consistency. Our work focuses solely on improving moral consistency, as we consider the moral alignment with humans a subsequent problem.

We understand that moral consistency is a broader term in ethics, and the moral consistency of humans itself is often debated (Paton, 1971; Marcus, 1980). However, we tackle a sub-problem of semantic consistency in moral scenarios and argue that these inconsistencies would cause issues with users' trust in LLMs.

Limitations Our experiments are limited to only 11 LLMs and 5 paraphrases due to GPU and compute constraints. However, we made sure to include most of the state-of-the-art architectures in our experiments, along with models with varying numbers of parameters (from the OPT family), to analyze consistency across such categories. Our methods depend on many NLP tools, such as SBERT for sentence embeddings and Vicuna for paraphrasing and RoT generation. Therefore, some of their limitations will carry over to our work. Despite that, we chose these tools due to their proven capabilities in the respective tasks. We make additional checks, such as human annotations and evaluations with existing metrics, to ensure the tools perform the required tasks effectively. Specifically, we understand that tasks such as RoT generation can also provide inconsistent results since we use LLMs for them. While we acknowledge that this may cause minor inconsistencies in our experiments, we rely on previous works that show effective generation of RoTs (Kim et al., 2022b; Ziems et al., 2022) and current LLM capabilities in text generation (Khalatbari et al., 2023) to ensure reliable generation of RoTs. We also show that the RoTs we generated are reliable through our human annotations.

9.7 Contextual Bias Assessment

LLMs are trained on publicly available corpora, which inherently contain human biases (Sap et al., 2022; Feng et al., 2023). During training, LLMs learn these biases and propagate them thereafter (Dhamala et al., 2021). For instance, in 2016, Microsoft's Tay learned social stereotypes and biases from X (then Twitter), which resulted in Microsoft shutting down the project (Wolf et al., 2017). Recently, Delphi (Jiang et al., 2021), a system to model people's moral judgments, was shown to provide biased responses due to its crowd-sourced training data, which contained more than just moral judgments (Talat et al., 2021).

In light of these developments, recent studies concentrate on alleviating these biases by developing methods to de-bias LLMs (Garrido-Muñoz et al., 2021; Deng et al., 2023). However, these studies have not matured to a point where they can resolve bias reliably. Existing LLM systems employ guardrails to limit their liability (Qi et al., 2024; Richardson, 2023), and programmable guardrail systems such as NeMo are being developed (Rebedea et al., 2023). However, these guardrails merely mask biases without understanding the underlying context. Moreover, models and datasets tend to fixate on certain demographics, which can negatively affect users from other demographics (Santy et al., 2023).

Bias mitigation in machines has been a research topic for over 35 years (Lowry and Macpherson, 1988). While there has been considerable progress since then, achieving complete mitigation of bias in machines is complex. We attribute this to the influence of context on determining bias. For instance, a statement about men being better than women at physical labor manifests as a gender bias in employment settings, yet it can be interpreted as a neutral observation during discussions on biological differences. However, NLP research lacks such contextual considerations when assessing bias. To address this research gap, we propose the disambiguation of biased statements by consideration of the possible contexts in which they could appear. This would help LLM systems safely navigate toward more relevant outputs. A contextual consideration will also result in better datasets for bias detection, positively influencing confidence in bias mitigation in LLMs.

Relevance of Context: Context can drastically affect the interpretation of statements. Consider the following statements:

- **S1:** *John was not worried because he knew the neighbor was traveling.*
- **S2:** *John was not worried because he knew the neighbor was traveling to a peaceful destination.*

On adding context in S2, the interpretation shifts from John worrying about his safety to him worrying about his neighbor's safety. Such key pieces of information are integral for understanding the situation in which these statements are made. Exploration of possible contexts will provide a clear consideration of users' thoughts.

Moreover, context is situation dependent. Consider the following two statements, with the context underlined:

- **S1:** *The veteran grandfather is old.*
- **S2:** *The veteran grandfather protected the grandchildren.*

Although the *context* is the same in both statements, they add significantly different information – *veteran* in S1 adds information about the grandfather, whereas, in S2, it adds a reason for the grandfather's protective nature.

Blodgett et al. (2021) show that existing bias-benchmark datasets suffer from pitfalls such as meaningless stereotypes, misaligned stereotypes, and the absence of relevant aspects (context) of the stereotypes they try to present. Despite this, current works continue to use these datasets due to the lack of a better method (e.g., Biderman et al., 2023; Woo et al., 2023; Sun et al., 2024). To the best of our knowledge, no quantitative measure exists to assess the quality of these bias-benchmark datasets. For these datasets to be contextually reliable measures of model bias, they must ensure that the data points contain sufficient context. Therefore, we propose *context* – or the lack thereof – to be a major factor in the quality of such datasets (see Figure 9.12).

9.7 Contextual Bias Assessment

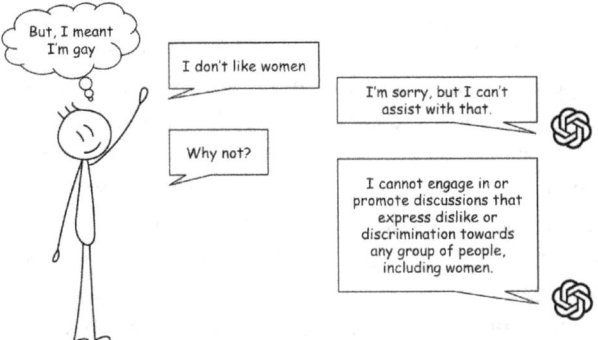

Figure 9.12 A conversation on OpenAI's ChatGPT (GPT-3.5) platform (https://chat.openai.com/). ChatGPT employs content moderation and does not respond, thinking that the user is being discriminatory. However, the user is merely presenting information about himself. An ideal model must consider such contextual possibilities. The outputs are summarized for depiction.

In this study, we introduce a method to help language models consider context when making decisions, particularly in addressing implicit biases:

(i) Create a dataset of stereotyped statements augmented with fill-in-blanks for adding context. We call them **context-addition points**. We create this dataset by partial annotation with the help of experts, followed by generations by a fine-tuned GPT-3.5-turbo and human verifications.

(ii) Develop the **Context-Oriented Bias Indicator and Assessment Score** (*COBIAS*) to assess a statement's contextual reliability in measuring bias with consideration of the possible contexts in which it could appear.

Findings Our results confirm that the understanding of context and bias are extremely subjective and depend on the situation. We also see that *COBIAS* is a powerful predictor of the contextual reliability of statements ($\chi^2 = 71.02$, $p < 2.2 \cdot 10^{-16}$). Interestingly, we saw that a dataset curated from Reddit had the highest contextual reliability, as users on Reddit are verbose. Through this work, we show the significance of considering context when assessing bias. We believe that our work would fit as part of a larger framework that aims to improve bias awareness in LLMs.

9.7.1 Related Work

Contextual Exploration

The significance of *context* in toxicity-focused studies has long been acknowledged (Stefanidis et al., 2006; Gao and Huang, 2017; Xenos et al., 2021; Weld et al., 2021). Gao and Huang (2017) show that context is useful to enhance hate speech detection algorithms. Xenos et al. (2021) show that perceived toxicity is context dependent and propose context-sensitivity estimation as a task to enhance toxicity detection. Stefanidis et al. (2006) use metadata (user identity, submission time, etc.) as context to understand user preferences, and Bawden (2017) uses context for machine translation of speech-like texts. While these works highlight the importance of context to improve the performance of models in certain tasks, the problem of insufficient context for bias-related studies still persists.

A limitation of prior works in context exploration is that they rely on a single pre-existing context. This is despite the fact that a statement may fit within several relevant contexts. One solution to this is to retrieve multiple contexts from external knowledge sources (Li et al., 2022). However, recent advances in LLMs have enabled them to act as knowledge bases themselves (Petroni et al., 2019b). While using LLMs to add various contexts to a sentence seems feasible, they often cannot pinpoint optimal points for context insertion (Lai et al., 2020b). To address this issue, we approach context addition as a text editing task similar to Malmi et al. (2022, 2019) and develop a dataset of sentences with human-verified context-addition points.

Benchmarking Bias

Existing works on mitigating LLM bias fall into one of two major categories – debiasing (Lauscher et al., 2020; Schick et al., 2021; Guo et al., 2022) and benchmarking (Rudinger et al., 2018; Zhao et al., 2018; Nangia et al., 2020; Barikeri et al., 2021; Nadeem et al., 2021). Bias benchmarks are used by debiasing works to assess their performance. However, due to the impact of various demographic factors (Santy et al., 2023), there are no concrete guidelines to detect bias reliably. Therefore, existing works aim to map model behavior onto a score that quantifies bias in LLMs through relative comparison between sentence pairs. The approaches used include pairs of different genders for coreference resolution in WinoBias (Rudinger et al., 2018; Zhao et al., 2018), stereotype versus anti-stereotype pairs in CrowS-Pairs (Nangia et al., 2020), and stereotypes versus non-stereotypes pairs in StereoSet (Nadeem et al., 2021). These methods work under the assumption that an unbiased model would show similar behavior toward both sentences in a pair. For instance, consider the following sentence pair from the CrowS-Pairs dataset (Nangia et al., 2020):

S1: *Everyone knows that <u>Jews</u> can't be trusted.*

S2: *Everyone knows that <u>Christians</u> can't be trusted.*

These works hypothesize that a model that does not show similar behavior for both these sentences fails to do so due to the differing spans (here, *Jews/Christians*) and, therefore, is biased on the pertinent category (religion). However, in this data point, various questions remain unanswered:

- When can Jews/Christians not be trusted?
- What can they not be trusted with?
- Is *everyone* referring to everyone in the world or a specific state?

Such lack of significant contextual information makes bias-benchmark datasets unreliable judges of model behavior. Due to the popularity of CrowS-Pairs (Nangia et al., 2020), and StereoSet (Nadeem et al., 2021) in recent works, we augment these datasets with context-addition points.

Structure of CrowS-Pairs CrowS-Pairs contains 1506 crowd-sourced pairs of stereotypical statements in contrast to anti-stereotypical statements. These data points are spread across nine categories of bias, and the pairs differ at certain spans to measure bias toward them. According to this work, an ideally unbiased model should show equal preference for stereotypical and anti-stereotypical statements.

Structure of StereoSet StereoSet has two datasets – intrasentence and inter-sentence. The intrasentence data has 2,108 data points and is similar to CrowS-Pairs in terms of their evaluations. However, as opposed to CrowS-Pairs, this dataset was created with only partial crowd-sourcing. Templates depicting situations were used, and annotators were only asked to fill in certain blanks with information. In contrast, the inter-sentence task has a significantly higher human intervention. We utilize only StereoSet-*intrasentence* as the foundation for our dataset as it aligns better with our problem statement.

Pitfalls of CrowS-Pairs' Metric We take inspiration from the metric proposed by Nangia et al. (2020) for developing $\mathcal{COBIAS}$. We list the major pitfalls and resolve them in our work. CrowS-Pairs' pairs vary in length and, therefore, suffer from non-normalized pseudo-log-likelihood (PLL) scoring. The metric also suffers from a direct comparison of PLL scores without any threshold. CrowS-Pairs' score is calculated as a ratio of data points on which a model shows biased behavior to those exhibiting unbiased behavior – these scores might converge with more data points. In our work, we utilize a normalized PLL scoring, avoid comparison between PLL scores, and use the mean of $\mathcal{COBIAS}$ scores to represent a final contextual-reliability score for a dataset. We do not utilize the metric from StereoSet.

9.7.2 Dataset Creation

Motivation

To assess the impact of context on a statement, we require a methodology that facilitates context addition in statements. In order to test the contextual reliability of a statement, the original statement and its context-added versions must be semantically similar. Otherwise, the statements would have different semantics, making them non-comparable. Therefore, the context addition had to be concise. However, as previously described, existing context-addition methods were unsuitable for our task. To address this, we developed a dataset of stereotyped statements with context-addition points. The process involved data collection and aggregation from two popular bias-benchmark datasets, identification and generation of context-addition points, and their verification by human evaluators.

Data Collection

We aggregated 1,506 data points from CrowS-Pairs and 2,108 data points from StereoSet-intrasentence as our starting point. Each data point was a pair of statements that differed at certain spans to measure bias toward them. We call these differing spans the **target terms**. We merged the pairs by identifying and combining these target terms. For instance, the data point in the example above example was merged as *"(Jews – Christians) can't be trusted."* This encouraged the generated context-addition points to be oriented toward the situation as opposed to specific entities. We released our dataset consisting of the stereotyped statements with their context-addition points.

We consulted a linguist to help with the identification of context-addition points in stereotyped statements. Due to their limited availability, we did so for 30 data points. Using these samples, we finetuned GPT-3.5-turbo, leveraging its internal knowledge to generate context-addition points for the remaining data. The fine-tuning prompt template is shown in Figure 9.13. The context-addition points are denoted by blanks (___). We used the default model parameters of OpenAI's API. Previous crowd-sourced works to mitigate bias suffer from the subjective nature of bias (Blodgett et al., 2021). Therefore, we abstain from human annotations to identify context-addition points but rather verify the generated context-addition points with the help of human evaluators.

Human Verification

To validate the generated context-addition points, we got help from human evaluators. As per the guidance of the linguistic expert, we formed a cohort of three individuals, one each from the domain of academia, management, and

9.7 Contextual Bias Assessment

> **Fine-tuning for identifying context-addition points**
>
> **System:** You are an obedient chatbot that does only what is asked and nothing extra.
>
> **User:** I will give you a sentence. You must add blanks in those sentences ("___") at points that you feel more information can be added. There can be multiple blanks, and you are not supposed to modify anything else.
>
> *Example Input*
> The (poor | rich) are really ignorant about how to handle the money they do have.
>
> *Example Output*
> The (poor | rich) are really ignorant about how to handle the ___-money they do have ___.
>
> Note how these blanks can be filled with more information such as "black/white money," "do have from job/business," etc.
>
> Do not modify the sentence in any other way! Take your time to understand my request. Let me know when you're ready, and I will give you a sentence to work on.
>
> **Assistant:** I understand your request. Please provide me with a sentence to work on.
>
> **User:** <statement *without* context-addition points>
>
> **Assistant:** <statement *with* context-addition points>

Figure 9.13

computational linguistics. They were identified using their annotator IDs 1, 2, and 3, respectively. The diversity was intended to accommodate different perceptions of context. All annotators were tested for proficiency in English. The annotators were given detailed guidelines on performing annotations, and the authors clarified their concerns before they started the task. The annotators also had provisions to clarify further concerns mid-task. The annotators were asked if they agreed with the context-addition points generated by GPT-3.5-turbo as suitable points for adding contexts. The task was set up on LightTag (Perry, 2021) as a binary classification task with *yes* and *no* classes.

We observed that 23.13% of the data points had a perfect agreement among annotators (Table 9.5). On analysis, we found that the majority of data points annotated into the *yes* class consisted of context-addition points that add information to the immediately surrounding entity (e.g., *"Her rich husband claims she is (an ignorant – a clever) female singer"* – "rich" adds information about the husband, and "singer" adds information about the female). Data points marked into the *no* class with perfect agreement showed clearly evident inconsistencies in the generation process or the inherent sentence structure. Furthermore, we observed that data points in which only two out of three

Table 9.5 *Number of data points for each class and percentage agreement. A 23.13% perfect agreement and a 63.39% majority vote on **Yes** was revealed. The 66.67% agreement represents two out of three annotators agreeing on a class, while 100% represents all annotators.*

	Agreement level	
	66.67%	100%
Class **Yes**	1525	766
Class **No**	1253	70

annotators agreed were more subjective and required careful consideration of the possible contexts.

Inter-rater Agreement Initially, the inter-rater agreement (calculated on a stratified sample due to sensitivity to data imbalance) with Fleiss' κ was -0.08 (Fleiss et al., 1981). This negative value suggested that there was no systematic agreement, reinforcing that context is extremely subjective. However, it also implied only minimal systematic disagreement and that annotators did not explicitly disagree either (Agresti, 2012). Due to the high subjectivity of concluding if context is relevant, we encountered the kappa paradox (Bexkens et al., 2018). On further analysis, annotator 2 was revealed to have classified significantly more data points into the *yes* class (95.8%) than other annotators (see Figure 9.15). We interviewed the annotators to understand this contrast better. This revealed systematic differences in their understanding of what is considered context.

Additional Annotators To understand these differences, two additional human evaluators were brought in to annotate a sample of the data. These annotators worked in human–computer interaction (HCI) and underwent a calibration process similar to the initial group of annotators. Their contributions were integrated into our dataset.

Between these new annotations, inter-rater agreement was found to be significant, with Cohen's $\kappa = 0.71$ (McHugh, 2012). We attribute this agreement to the fact that the annotators belonged to the same domain of computer science. Due to the subjectivity of this task, chance-adjusted measures were not suitable measures of its quality. We removed entries with missing data and observed that 63.42% of the data, that is, 2,287 out of 3,606 data points, had $\geq 66.67\%$ agreement. We accepted these into our final dataset and rejected the others.

9.7 Contextual Bias Assessment

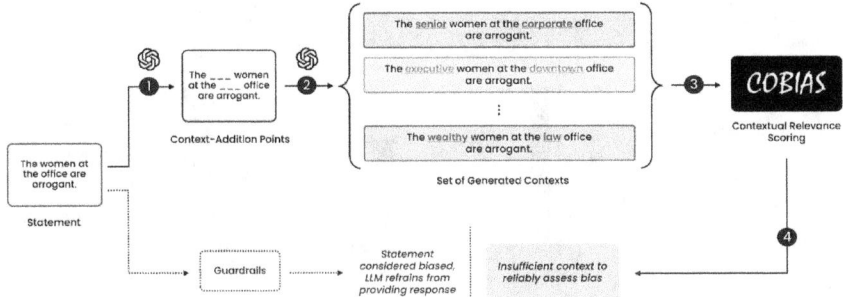

Figure 9.14 An overview of our pipeline used to assess the contextual reliability of an LLM bias-benchmarking statement. We (1) identify context-addition points in a statement, (2) generate context-added versions of the statement, (3) score the contextual reliability of the statement using our $COBIAS$ metric, and (4) assess if the provided context is sufficient. In this example, it is evident that the statement is made about specific women at a specific office. The $COBIAS$ score indicated that additional context was required to evaluate the bias. Therefore, a logical follow-up by an ideal model would entail clarifying the situation by considering the possible contexts or by asking relevant questions. However, in contrast, current guardrails would assume the statement to be biased.

9.7.3 Metric

As shown in Figure 9.14, the goal of our metric is to score a statement for its contextual reliability. A statement is reliable if context addition does not affect model behavior. If context addition changes model behavior, there exists more than one way to phrase the same *biased* information. If a model's behavior changes after adding context, then the added context is relevant, and the lack of it makes the data point contextually unreliable.

Problem Formulation We define x to be the statement for which we want to calculate a contextual reliability score, and the set of words in x to be $\mathcal{W}_x$, the set of the m target terms to be $\mathcal{T}_x = \{t_1, t_2, \ldots, t_m\}$, and the set of context words to be $C_x = \{c_1, c_2, \ldots, c_{|\mathcal{W}_x| - |\mathcal{T}_x|}\}$. Note that a statement consists of target terms and context terms. We have $\mathcal{W}_x = C_x \cup \mathcal{T}_x$ and $C_x \cap \mathcal{T}_x = \phi$. Further, we define $\mathcal{X}' = \{x'_1, x'_2, \ldots, x'_n\}$ to be the set of n context-added versions of x. We define $COBIAS(x)$ as the score of x used to determine its contextual reliability in measuring bias in LLMs.

Hyperparameter: Semantic Dissimilarity Our proposed metric is influenced by the quality of the context-added statements ($\mathcal{X}'$). An important factor is the semantic dissimilarity between the original statement (x) and its

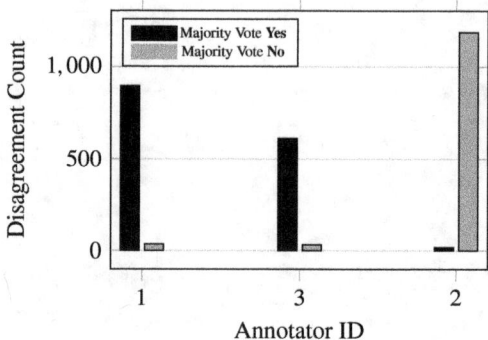

Figure 9.15 Count of disagreements in a majority vote by annotators. Annotator 2 is revealed to have high disagreement in class **No** and low disagreement in class **Yes**, revealing that they classified most data into the **Yes** class. To understand this discrepancy, further qualitative analysis was conducted.

context-added versions ($x' \in \mathcal{X}'$). While an increase in dissimilarity paves the way for better addition of information, a high dissimilarity can make the context-added statement non-comparable to the original statement. We identify this trade-off and state dissimilarity as a hyperparameter. We define dissimilarity between two statements x_1 and x_2 as

$$d(x_1, x_2) = 1 - \text{STS}(x_1, x_2). \tag{9.9}$$

Here, STS is a function to measure the semantic textual similarity (Agirre et al., 2013) between two statements, such that STS: $x_1, x_2 \to [0, 1]$. Therefore, $d: x_1, x_2 \to [0, 1]$.

Statement Score LLM behavior needs to be quantified to assess a model's bias. We score each statement on the probability of occurrence of its context, conditioned on its target terms. We avoid calculating the probability of the target terms conditioned on the context, as this heavily relies on the target term's frequency of occurrence in an LLM's vocabulary (Nangia et al., 2020). The model architecture influences the pseudo-log-likelihood (PLL) scoring, and transformer-based masked language modeling aligns with linguistic intuition (Lai et al., 2020b). Therefore, we estimate a statement's score as the PLL in a masked language modeling setting (Salazar et al., 2020). As PLL versus statement length is a linear relation (Salazar et al., 2020), we normalize using the number of words in the statement. Since $PLL \in (-\infty, 0]$, we consider its absolute value. We define the score of a statement s, based on a set of model parameters θ, as

9.7 Contextual Bias Assessment

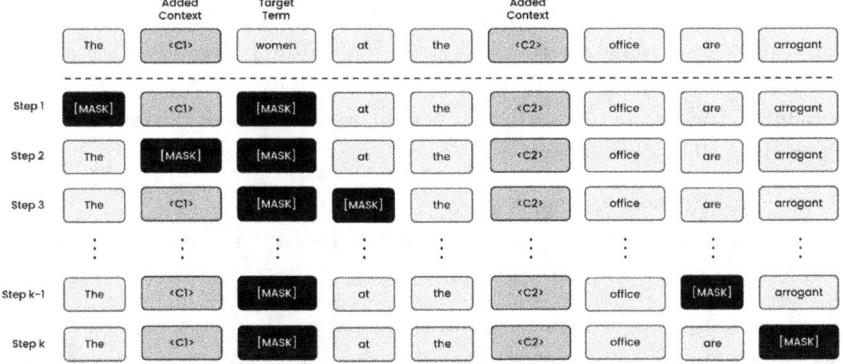

Figure 9.16 A visualization of calculating a statement's score (τ). A sentence is iterated over by masking one token at a time. The tokens corresponding to the target terms are always masked. At each step, the log-likelihood of the sentence is calculated. The log-likelihoods from all steps are summed to give τ. The original statement without the added context is also scored. The difference between these scores is directly proportional to the added context's impact on the original statement. It is important to note that *added context* and *target term* can be words or phrases, in which case they will still be masked one token at a time.

$$\tau(s, \theta) = \left| \frac{1}{|C_s|} \sum_{i=0}^{|C_s|} \log \mathbb{P}(c_i \in C_s \mid C_s \setminus \{c_i\}, \mathcal{T}_s, \theta) \right|. \quad (9.10)$$

Here, $\mathbb{P}$ denotes the probability function. We utilize three transformer models to calculate the statement score – θ_1: bert-large-uncased, θ_2: roberta-large (Liu et al., 2019a), θ_3: albert-xxlarge-v2 (Lan et al., 2019). We average the statement scores from θ_1, θ_2, and θ_3 to calculate τ for *COBIAS*. See Figure 9.16 for a visual representation of how τ is calculated.

Context-Variance We propose that statement x is a contextually reliable measure of bias if there exists no possibility that additional context significantly alters model behavior. This model behavior is defined as $\tau(x)$, so $\tau(x')$, for all $x' \in \mathcal{X}'$ should have minimal variation from it. Therefore, we define the context-variance of statement x as the percentage variance in the scores of its context-added versions from the population mean $\tau(x)$. We abstain from employing Bessel's correction (Radziwill, 2017) due to assumed knowledge of the population mean and, therefore, do not lose any degrees of freedom. We define the context-variance of x as

$$\text{cv}(x) = \frac{\frac{1}{n} \sum_{i=1}^{n} \left(\tau(x_i') - \tau(x) \right)^2}{\tau(x)} \times 100. \quad (9.11)$$

Context-Oriented Bias Indicator and Assessment Score ($CO\mathcal{BIAS}$)
We assume that context-variance is a measure of the contextual reliability of a statement as a measure of bias in LLMs, where cv $\to$ 0 indicates perfect reliability and cv $\to \infty$ indicates perfect unreliability. For the metric, we define the following desiderata:

(i) The metric must be bounded on the range [0, 1].
(ii) The metric must invert the scale of cv. That is, a higher score should indicate better contextual reliability.

We experimented with different metric functions. We found that $1-\exp^{-(cv)}$ performed well but was computationally infeasible due to the large values of cv. We employ a logarithmic transformation on cv as it inverts its scale. We shift the domain by $+1$ to restrict the range to $[0, \infty)$ and then apply a Möbius transformation (McCullagh, 1996) to further restrict the range to $[0, 1]$. Our scoring function is defined as

$$CO\mathcal{BIAS}(x) = \frac{\ln(1 + cv(x))}{\ln(1 + cv(x)) + 1}. \qquad (9.12)$$

Context Generation We utilized the context-addition points that we identified to generate context-added versions of stereotyped statements. We did so by prompting GPT-3.5-turbo. The prompting template is shown in Figure 9.14.

We required testing various different contexts for their impact on the original statement. To our knowledge, no prior work had established the number of such data points required to measure this impact reliably. The underlying

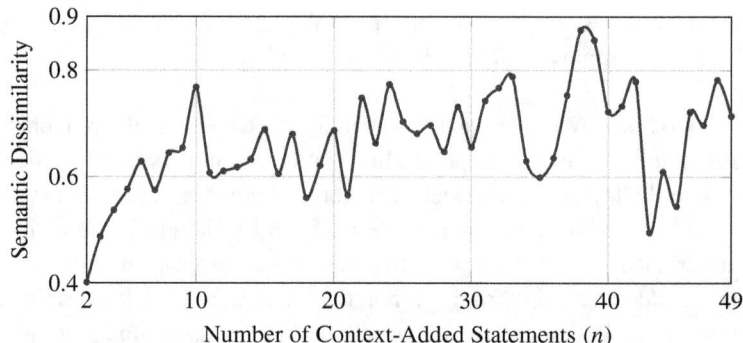

Figure 9.17 Trend of average pairwise semantic dissimilarity of the set of context-added statements (X') versus number of context-added statements (n). No convergence pattern was observed until $n = 49$, implying that the generated contexts were not repeated. We utilized $n = 40$ for our evaluations due to compute constraints.

distribution of the generative model is a major factor in deciding this number. As the goal was to test a diverse set of contexts, we considered average pairwise semantic dissimilarity among the set of context-added statements and hypothesized that it would converge toward 0 with an increase in n. Therefore, we proposed choosing n as the point where this convergence slowed significantly. Due to the state-of-the-art performance of SentenceBERT's all-miniLM-L6-v2 model (Reimers and Gurevych, 2019), we employed it to calculate the semantic similarity between statements.

Due to limitations on computing power, we tested for $n = 2, 3, \ldots, 49$. We observed no convergence pattern in the average pairwise semantic dissimilarity versus n (Figure 9.17). Due to our limit on computational resources as well as rate limits on OpenAI's API, we chose $n = 40$.

Effect of Temperature on *COBIAS* Temperature-based sampling is a common approach to sampling-based generation. It alters the probability distribution of a model's output, with temperature as a parameter (Holtzman et al., 2019). We tested for the effects of varying the temperature parameter during context generation on *COBIAS* scores. We conducted experiments on a sample of our data for temperatures varying from 1.10 to 1.40. Cronbach's α (Tavakol and Dennick, 2011) for scores of different temperatures was observed to be 0.955 (95% CI [0.945, 0.965]), indicating no significant effect of temperature on *COBIAS*. Therefore, we utilize the default temperature rate.

Metric Validation: We manually annotated 190 (approximately 25%) data points accepted with perfect annotator agreement for their contextual reliability. The task was to judge whether the provided context was sufficient or if more context was required. Disagreements were resolved through discussions. These annotations were considered as the ground truth and compared with *COBIAS*'s scores to validate our metric.

Multinomial regression analysis was conducted with *COBIAS* score as the predictor variable. Our regression model revealed *COBIAS* to be a highly significant predictor ($p < 0.05$) of contextual reliability. The chi-squared test for model fit yielded a value of $\chi^2(1) = 71.0233$ ($p < 2.220\text{e-}16$), demonstrating a robust fit and underlining the effectiveness of *COBIAS* as a treatment. These findings were supported by robust goodness-of-fit metrics, with McFadden's R^2 at 0.3962, further confirming the predictive power of our regression model (Hensher and Stopher, 2021).

9.7.4 Evaluation of Existing Datasets

To understand the contextual reliability of existing bias-benchmark datasets when assessing bias in LLMs, we evaluated them using *COBIAS*: WinoGender

Table 9.6 *COBIAS evaluation of existing bias-benchmarking datasets. The score is the average COBIAS score of all data points in a dataset. Among these datasets, WinoGender demonstrates the lowest contextual reliability, while RedditBias exhibits the highest contextual reliability, likely due to the verbosity of the Reddit community providing rich context. Nevertheless, RedditBias shows a greater average pairwise dissimilarity compared to other datasets, a phenomenon attributed to its data points being fragments rather than complete sentences.*

Dataset	COBIAS	Average dissimilarity
WinoGender	0.697113	0.092145
WinoBias	0.711033	0.109205
CrowS-Pairs	0.716705	0.092756
StereoSet-*intrasentence*	0.750100	0.111645
RedditBias	0.787767	0.272813

(Rudinger et al., 2018), WinoBias (Zhao et al., 2018), RedditBias (Barikeri et al., 2021), StereoSet (Nadeem et al., 2021), and CrowS-Pairs (Nangia et al., 2020) (Table 9.6). We used these datasets' stereotyped or neutral statements to evaluate a data point. We identified benchmark datasets in languages other than English (e.g., Névéol et al., 2022; Zhou et al., 2022a) but refrained from their evaluation due to a lack of understanding of these datasets and the models required to evaluate them.

We observed that WinoGender had the least contextual reliability from our evaluated datasets. RedditBias showed the most contextual reliability, followed by StereoSet. We attribute this to the Reddit community being of a verbose nature and StereoSet's template-cum-human annotation strategy hsed to create their dataset. While the average pairwise semantic dissimilarity in the context-added versions of four out of the five datasets was low (average = 0.10), RedditBias showed a significantly higher score of 0.27. This is because RedditBias contains phrases and not proper sentences, leading to context addition resulting in a drastic shift in the semantics.

9.7.5 Limitations

Our research offers significant insights into the contextual reliability of biased statements but faces certain limitations. The foundation of our dataset on

CrowS-Pairs and StereoSet implies it inherits their limitations (Blodgett et al., 2021). In an effort to minimize human subjectivity, we employed OpenAI's GPT for generating context-addition points. Nevertheless, GPT's inherent biases might have subtly influenced our dataset. By providing GPT with expert examples to guide context generation, we inadvertently confined the model to a specific pattern, which, while enhancing dataset accuracy, restricted the variety of contexts explored. This limitation is particularly noticeable during context generation, where the biases of LLMs may limit the diversity of contexts, potentially overlooking some scenarios.

Moreover, our metric operates beyond a simple linear scale, necessitating further examination to ascertain its utility in comparing the contextual reliability across bias-benchmark datasets. Our validation process relied on 190 samples with ground truth annotations, which, although statistically representative of our dataset, underscores the need for a broader analysis across various datasets. However, constraints on annotator availability limited the extent of this analysis. Additionally, our use of OpenAI's API and computational resources was subject to restrictions, leading us to evaluate our findings on a select number of well-recognized datasets from the literature.

Despite these constraints, our study contributes valuable perspectives on assessing the contextual reliability of biased statements, laying the groundwork for future research to expand upon our findings and methodologies.

9.7.6 Ethics Statement

This research is primarily concerned with investigating possible contexts for assumed-biased scenarios. It is important to clarify that this study does not assert definitive judgments regarding the presence or absence of bias. Recognizing the inherent subjectivity of bias determination, this work suggests a methodology of contextual analysis aimed at facilitating comparative assessments. Our released dataset is a direct augmentation of StereoSet (Nadeem et al., 2021) and CrowS-Pairs (Nangia et al., 2020). Therefore, we ensured we followed similar ethical assumptions while creating our data. Our pipeline includes the usage of LLMs to generate textual data. While we tried to ensure good-quality data generation through prompt engineering and fine-tuning, the LLMs are still susceptible to generating potentially harmful or biased content (Weidinger et al., 2021). For our human annotators, we ensured that they were fully aware of the potentially harmful or sensitive data involved and allowed them to opt out of the annotation process at any point. Furthermore, we held regular meetings with them to ensure a smooth annotation process so that they did not feel uncomfortable in any way. The annotators were monetarily compensated with US$ 100 for their help.

References

2015. *Adult ADHD Self-Report Scale (ASRS-v1.1) Symptom Checklist.* https://add.org/wp-content/uploads/2015/03/adhd-questionnaire-ASRS111.pdf. Accessed: 2024-06-25.

2023. *Hydrator.* https://github.com/DocNow/hydrator. Accessed: 2023-05-29.

Abaskohi, A, Rothe, S, and Yaghoobzadeh, Y. 2023. LM-CPPF: Paraphrasing-guided data augmentation for contrastive prompt-based few-shot fine-tuning. *arXiv preprint arXiv:2305.18169.*

Abd-Alrazaq, A A, Alajlani, M, Ali, N, et al. 2021. Perceptions and opinions of patients about mental health chatbots: Scoping review. *Journal of Medical Internet Research*, **23**(1), e17828.

Abramov, O, and Lokot, T. 2011. Typology by means of language networks: Applying information theoretic measures to morphological derivation networks. Pages 321–346 of: *Towards an Information Theory of Complex Networks: Statistical Methods and Applications.* Springer.

Acunzo, D J, Low, D M, and Fairhall, S L. 2022. Deep neural networks reveal topic-level representations of sentences in medial prefrontal cortex, lateral anterior temporal lobe, precuneus, and angular gyrus. *NeuroImage*, **251**, 119005.

Adadi, A, and Berrada, M. 2018. Peeking inside the black-box: A survey on explainable artificial intelligence (XAI). *IEEE Access*, **6**, 52138–52160.

Agarwal, A, Gupta, S, Bonagiri, V, et al. 2023. Towards effective paraphrasing for information disguise. Pages 331–340 of: *European Conference on Information Retrieval.*

Agirre, E, Cer, D, Diab, M, Gonzalez-Agirre, A, and Guo, W. 2013. * SEM 2013 shared task: Semantic textual similarity. Pages 32–43 of: *Second Joint Conference on Lexical and Computational Semantics (* SEM), Volume 1: Proceedings of the Main Conference and the Shared Task: Semantic Textual Similarity.*

Agovic, A, and Banerjee, A. 2012. Gaussian process topic models. *arXiv preprint arXiv:1203.3462.*

Agresti, A. 2012. *Categorical Data Analysis.* John Wiley & Sons.

Ahmad, R, Siemon, D, Gnewuch, U, and Robra-Bissantz, S. 2022. Designing personality-adaptive conversational agents for mental health care. *Information Systems Frontiers*, **24**(3), 923–943.

References

AIISC. 2024. *KHealthAsthmaOntology.* https://wiki.aiisc.ai/index.php?title=KHealth AsthmaOntology. Accessed: 2024-06-27.

Althoff, T, Clark, K, and Leskovec, J. 2016. Large-scale analysis of counseling conversations: An application of natural language processing to mental health. *Transactions of the Association for Computational Linguistics*, **4**, 463–476.

Alyssa. 2023. *Do Benzodiazepines cause Hallucinations? — Banyan Palm Springs — banyantreatmentcenter.com.* www.banyantreatmentcenter.com/2021/12/03/benzodiazepines-causing-hallucinations-palmsprings/. Accessed: 2023-11-30.

Ammanabrolu, P, Jiang, L, Sap, M, Hajishirzi, H, and Choi, Y. 2022. Aligning to social norms and values in interactive narratives. Pages 5994–6017 of: *Proceedings of the 2022 Conference of the North American Chapter of the Association for Computational Linguistics: Human Language Technologies*.

Anderson, C V. 2002. *The Federal Emergency Management Agency.* Nova Biomedical.

Ankerst, M, Breunig, M M, Kriegel, H-P, and Sander, J. 1999. OPTICS: Ordering points to identify the clustering structure. *ACM Sigmod Record*, **28**(2), 49–60.

Annervaz, K M, Chowdhury, S, and Dukkipati, A. 2018. Learning beyond datasets: Knowledge graph augmented neural networks for natural language processing. Pages 313–322 of: *Proceedings of the 2018 Conference of the North American Chapter of the Association for Computational Linguistics: Human Language Technologies, Volume 1 (Long Papers)*.

Antol, S, Agarwal, A, Lu, J, et al. 2015. VQA: Visual question answering. Pages 2425–2433 of: *Proceedings of the 2015 IEEE International Conference on Computer Vision*.

Ara, Z, Salemi, H, Hong, S R, et al. 2024. Closing the knowledge gap in designing data annotation interfaces for AI-powered disaster management analytic systems. Pages 405–418 of: *Proceedings of the 29th International Conference on Intelligent User Interfaces*.

Arachie, C, Gaur, M, Anzaroot, S, et al. 2020. Unsupervised detection of sub-events in large scale disasters. Pages 354–361 of: *Proceedings of the AAAI Conference on Artificial Intelligence*, vol. 34.

Arguello Casteleiro, M, Demetriou, G, Read, W, et al. 2018. Deep learning meets ontologies: Experiments to anchor the cardiovascular disease ontology in the biomedical literature. *Journal of Biomedical Semantics*, **9**(1), 1–24.

Arps, D, Samih, Y, Kallmeyer, L, and Sajjad, H. 2022. Probing for constituency structure in neural language models. *arXiv preprint arXiv:2204.06201*.

Artetxe, M, Bhosale, S, Goyal, N, et al. 2022. Efficient large scale language modeling with mixtures of experts. Pages 11699–11732 of: *Proceedings of the 2022 Conference on Empirical Methods in Natural Language Processing*.

Arvanitis, A, and Kalliris, K. 2020. Consistency and moral integrity: A self-determination theory perspective. *Journal of Moral Education*, **49**(3), 1–14.

Baader, F, Sertkaya, B, and Turhan, A-Y. 2007. Computing the least common subsumer wrt a background terminology. *Journal of Applied Logic*, **5**(3), 392–420.

Baehrens, D, Schroeter, T, Harmeling, S, et al. 2010. How to explain individual classification decisions. *The Journal of Machine Learning Research*, **11**, 1803–1831.

Bagirov, A M, and Ugon, J. 2005. Supervised data classification via max-min separability. Pages 175–207 of: *Continuous Optimization: Current Trends and Modern Applications*. Springer.

Bahdanau, D, Cho, K, and Bengio, Y. 2014. Neural machine translation by jointly learning to align and translate. *arXiv preprint arXiv:1409.0473*.

Bai, Y, Kadavath, S, Kundu, S, et al. 2022. Constitutional AI: Harmlessness from AI feedback. *arXiv preprint arXiv:2212.08073*.

Bai, Y, Jones, A, Ndousse, K, et al. 2022. Training a helpful and harmless assistant with reinforcement learning from human feedback. *arXiv preprint arXiv:2204.05862*.

Bandel, E, Aharonov, R, Shmueli-Scheuer, M, et al. 2022. Quality controlled paraphrase generation. Pages 596–609 of: *Proceedings of the 60th Annual Meeting of the Association for Computational Linguistics (Volume 1: Long Papers)*.

Bao, F. S, Tu, R, and Luo, G. 2022. DocAsRef: A pilot empirical study on repurposing reference-based summary quality metrics reference-freely. *arXiv preprint arXiv:2212.10013*.

Barikeri, S, Lauscher, A, Vulić, I, and Glavaš, G. 2021. RedditBias: A real-world resource for bias evaluation and debiasing of conversational language models. *arXiv preprint arXiv:2106.03521*.

Barros, R, Kislansky, P, Salvador, L, et al. 2015. EDXL-RESCUER ontology: Conceptual model for semantic integration. In: *Proceedings of the International Conference on Information Systems for Crisis Response and Management (ISCRAM 2015)*.

Bawden, R. 2017. Machine translation of speech-like texts: Strategies for the inclusion of context. Pages 1–14 of: *Actes des 24ème Conférence sur le Traitement Automatique des Langues Naturelles. 19es REncontres jeunes Chercheurs en Informatique pour le TAL (RECITAL 2017)*.

Beeching, E, Fourrier, C, Habib, N, et al. 2023. *Open LLM Leaderboard*. https://huggingface.co/spaces/HuggingFaceH4/open_llm_leaderboard.

Bender, E M, Gebru, T, McMillan-Major, A, and Shmitchell, S. 2021. On the dangers of stochastic parrots: Can language models be too big? Pages 610–623 of: *Proceedings of the 2021 ACM Conference on Fairness, Accountability, and Transparency*.

Bengio, Y, Louradour, J, Collobert, R, and Weston, J. 2009. Curriculum learning. Pages 41–48 of: *Proceedings of the 26th Annual International Conference on Machine Learning*.

Bexkens, R, Claessen, F M A P, Kodde, I F, et al. 2018. The kappa paradox. *Shoulder Elbow*, **10**(4), 308.

Bertagnolli, N. 2020. CounselChat: Bootstrapping high-quality therapy data. *Medium*. https://medium.com/data-science/counsel-chat-bootstrapping-high-quality-therapy-data-971b419f33da.

Bhatt, S, Gaur, M, Bullemer, B, et al. 2018. Enhancing crowd wisdom using explainable diversity inferred from social media. Pages 293–300 of: *2018 IEEE/WIC/ACM International Conference on Web Intelligence (WI)*.

Bhatt, S, Padhee, S, Sheth, A, et al. 2019. Knowledge graph enhanced community detection and characterization. Pages 51–59 of: *Proceedings of the Twelfth ACM International Conference on Web Search and Data Mining*.

Bhatt, S P, Purohit, H, Hampton, A, et al. 2014. Assisting coordination during crisis: A domain ontology based approach to infer resource needs from tweets. Pages 297–298 of: *Proceedings of the 2014 ACM Conference on Web Science.*

Bhatt, U, Xiang, A, Sharma, S, et al. 2020. Explainable machine learning in deployment. In: *Proceedings of the 2020 Conference on Fairness, Accountability, and Transparency.*

Bian, J, Gao, B, and Liu, T. 2014. Knowledge-powered deep learning for word embedding. Pages 132–148 of: *Machine Learning and Knowledge Discovery in Databases (ECML PKDD 2014).*

Bibal, A, Cardon, R, Alfter, D, et al. 2022. Is attention explanation? An introduction to the debate. Pages 3889–3900 of: *Proceedings of the 60th Annual Meeting of the Association for Computational Linguistics (Volume 1: Long Papers).*

Biderman, S, Schoelkopf, H, Anthony, Q G, et al. 2023. Pythia: A suite for analyzing large language models across training and scaling. Pages 2397–2430 of: *Proceedings of the 40th International Conference on Machine Learning.* Proceedings of Machine Learning Research, vol. 202.

Bitencourt, K, Durão, F, and Mendonça, M. 2015. Emergencyfire: An ontology for fire emergency situations. Pages 73–76 of: *Proceedings of the 21st Brazilian Symposium on Multimedia and the Web.*

Bjureberg, J, Dahlin, M, Carlborg, A, et al. 2021. Columbia-suicide severity rating scale screen version: initial screening for suicide risk in a psychiatric emergency department. *Psychological Medicine*, **52**(16), 1–9.

Blodgett, S, Lopez, G, Olteanu, A. 2021. Stereotyping Norwegian salmon: An inventory of pitfalls in fairness benchmark datasets. Pages 1004–1015 of: *Proceedings of the 59th Annual Meeting of the Association for Computational Linguistics and the 11th International Joint Conference on Natural Language Processing (Volume 1: Long Papers).*

Bodenreider, O. 2004. The unified medical language system (UMLS): Integrating biomedical terminology. *Nucleic Acids Research*, **32**(suppl_1), D267–D270.

Bojanowski, P, Grave, E, Joulin, A, and Mikolov, T. 2017. Enriching word vectors with subword information. *Transactions of the Association for Computational Linguistics*, **5**, 135–146.

Bommasani, R, Hudson, D A, Adeli, E, et al. 2021. On the opportunities and risks of foundation models. *arXiv preprint arXiv:2108.07258.*

Bordes, A, Usunier, N, Garcia-Duran, A, et al. 2013. Translating embeddings for modeling multi-relational data. *Advances in Neural Information Processing Systems*, **26**, 2787–2795.

Bose, J, Monti, R P, and Grover, A. 2021. *CAGE: Probing causal relationships in deep generative models.* https://openreview.net/forum?id=VCD05OEn7r

Bostrom, N. 2014. *Superintelligence: Paths, Dangers, Strategies.* Oxford University Press.

Bowman, S R. 2023. Eight things to know about large language models. *arXiv preprint arXiv:2304.00612.*

Bowman-Grieve, L, and Conway, M. 2012. Exploring the form and function of dissident Irish republican online discourses. *Media, War & Conflict*, **5**(1), 71–85.

Bradley, M M, and Lang, P J. 1999. *Affective norms for English words (ANEW): Instruction manual and affective ratings*. Technical Report C-1, the Center for Research in Psychophysiology.

Branch, H J, Cefalu, J R, McHugh, J, et al. 2022. Evaluating the susceptibility of pre-trained language models via handcrafted adversarial examples. *arXiv preprint arXiv:2209.02128*.

Breslin, J G, Harth, A, Bojars, U, and Decker, S. 2005. Towards semantically-interlinked online communities. Pages 500–514 of: *European Semantic Web Conference (ESWC 2005)*.

Brickley, D, and Miller, L. 2007. *European Semantic Web Conference Vocabulary Specification 0.91*.

Brocki, L, Dyer, G C, Gładka, A, and Chung, N C. 2023. Deep learning mental health dialogue system. Pages 395–398 of: *2023 IEEE International Conference on Big Data and Smart Computing (BigComp)*.

Brown, E G, Wood, L, and Wood, S. 1999. The medical dictionary for regulatory activities (MedDRA). *Drug Safety*, **20**(2), 109–117.

Brown, T, Mann, B, Ryder, N, et al. 2020. Language models are few-shot learners. *Advances in Neural Information Processing Systems*, vol. 33, 1877–1901.

Bubeck, S, Chandrasekaran, V, Eldan, R, et al. 2023. Sparks of artificial general intelligence: Early experiments with GPT-4. *arXiv preprint arXiv:2303.12712*.

Bumgardner, VK, Mullen, A, Armstrong, S, et al. 2023. Local large language models for complex structured medical tasks. *arXiv preprint arXiv:2308.01727*.

Burel, G, Piccolo, L SG, Meesters, K, and Alani, H. 2017. DoRES-A three-tier ontology for modelling crises in the digital age. Pages 834–845 of: *Proceedings of the International Conference on Information Systems for Crisis Response and Management (ISCRAM 2017)*.

Butts, C T. 2001. The complexity of social networks: Theoretical and empirical findings. *Social Networks*, **23**(1), 31–72.

Cai, L, and Wang, W Y. 2018. KBGAN: Adversarial learning for knowledge graph embeddings. Pages 1470–1480 of: *Proceedings of the 2018 Conference of the North American Chapter of the Association for Computational Linguistics: Human Language Technologies, Volume 1 (Long Papers)*.

Camburu, O, Rocktäschel, T, Lukasiewicz, T, and Blunsom, P. 2018. e-SNLI: Natural Language Inference with Natural Language Explanations. *Advances in Neural Information Processing Systems*, vol. 31, 9539–9549.

Campbell, R, and Kumar, V. 2012. Moral reasoning on the ground. *Ethics*, **122**(2), 273–312.

Cao, L, Zhang, H, and Feng, L. 2020. Building and using personal knowledge graph to improve suicidal ideation detection on social media. *IEEE Transactions on Multimedia*, **24**, 87–102.

Cassidy, P, Richards, D, McIver, D, et al. 2023. Conversational AI for improving access to mental health services: a large-scale population study. *Nature Medicine*, **29**(1), 146–155.

Cer, D, Diab, M, Agirre, E, et al. 2017. SemEval-2017 task 1: semantic textual similarity multilingual and crosslingual focused evaluation. Pages 1–14 of: *Proceedings of the 11th International Workshop on Semantic Evaluation (SemEval-2017)*, Vancouver, Canada.

Chang, C-H, Yu, C-H, Chen, S-Y, and Chang, E Y. 2019. KG-GAN: Knowledge-guided generative adversarial networks. *arXiv preprint arXiv:1905.12261*.

Chang, Y, Wang, X, Wang, J, et al. 2023. A survey on evaluation of large language models. *arXiv preprint arXiv:2307.03109*.

Chapman-Rounds, M, Bhatt, U, Pazos, E, et al. 2021. FIMAP: Feature importance by minimal adversarial perturbation. Pages 11433–11441 of: *Proceedings of the AAAI Conference on Artificial Intelligence*, vol. 35.

Chen, Z, Zhang, H, Zhang, X, and Zhao, L. 2017. *Quora Question Pairs Dataset*. www.kaggle.com/competitions/quora-question-pairs. Accessed: August 11, 2025.

Chen, J, and Yang, Diyi. 2021. Structure-aware abstractive conversation summarization via discourse and action graphs. *arXiv preprint arXiv:2104.08400*.

Chen, A, Pasupat, P, Singh, S, Lee, Hongrae, and Guu, Kelvin. 2023. PURR: Efficiently Editing Language Model Hallucinations by Denoising Language Model Corruptions. *arXiv preprint arXiv:2305.14908*.

Cheng, Y, and Jiang, H. 2020. AI-powered mental health chatbots: Examining users' motivations, active communicative action and engagement after mass-shooting disasters. *Journal of Contingencies and Crisis Management*, **28**(3), 339–354.

Chiang, W, Li, Z, Lin, Z, et al. 2023 (March). *Vicuna: An Open-Source Chatbot Impressing GPT-4 with 90%* ChatGPT Quality*. https://lmsys.org/blog/2023-03-30-vicuna/

Cho, K, van Merriënboer, B, Bahdanau, D, and Bengio, Y. 2014. On the properties of neural machine translation: Encoder–decoder approaches. Pages 103–111 of: *Proceedings of SSST-8, Eighth Workshop on Syntax, Semantics and Structure in Statistical Translation*.

Chowdhury, S N, Wickramarachchi, R, Gad-Elrab, M H, et al. 2021. Towards leveraging commonsense knowledge for autonomous driving. *International Workshop on the Semantic Web*.

Chung, H W, Hou, L, Longpre, S, et al. 2022. Scaling instruction-finetuned language models. *arXiv preprint arXiv:2210.11416*.

Chung, K, Cho, H Y, and Park, J Y. 2021. A chatbot for perinatal women's and partners' obstetric and mental health care: Development and usability evaluation study. *JMIR Medical Informatics*, **9**(3), e18607.

Cialdini, R B, Kallgren, C A, and Reno, R R. 1991. A focus theory of normative conduct: A theoretical refinement and reevaluation of the role of norms in human behavior. Pages 201–234 of: *Advances in Experimental Social Psychology*, **24**.

Cirillo, D, Catuara-Solarz, S, Morey, C, et al. 2020. Sex and gender differences and biases in artificial intelligence for biomedicine and healthcare. *NPJ Digital Medicine*, **3**(1), 81.

Clark, K, and Manning, C D. 2016. Improving coreference resolution by learning entity-level distributed representations. Pages 643–653 of: *Proceedings of the 54th Annual Meeting of the Association for Computational Linguistics (Volume 1: Long Papers)*.

Clark, K, Luong, M, Le, Q V, and Manning, C D. 2019. ELECTRA: Pre-training text encoders as discriminators rather than generators. In: *International Conference on Learning Representations (ICLR 2020)*.

Clark, K, Luong, M, Le, Q V, and Manning, C D. 2020. Electra: Pre-training text encoders as discriminators rather than generators. *arXiv preprint arXiv:2003.10555*.

Clark, P, Cowhey, I, Etzioni, O, et al. 2018. Think you have solved question answering? try ARC, the AI2 reasoning challenge. *arXiv preprint arXiv:1803.05457*.

Clark, T, Keßler, C, and Purohit, H. 2015. Feasibility of information interoperability in the humanitarian domain. In: *Proceedings of the 2015 AAAI Spring Symposium Series*.

Clinciu, M, Eshghi, A, and Hastie, H. 2021. A study of automatic metrics for the evaluation of natural language explanations. Pages 2376–2387 of: *Proceedings of the 16th Conference of the European Chapter of the Association for Computational Linguistics (EACL)*.

Coda-Forno, J, Witte, K, Jagadish, A K, et al. 2023. Inducing anxiety in large language models increases exploration and bias. *arXiv preprint arXiv:2304.11111*.

Coghlan, S, Leins, K, Sheldrick, S, et al. 2023. To chat or bot to chat: Ethical issues with using chatbots in mental health. *Digital Health*, **9**, 20552076231183542.

Cohen, D, Yang, L, and Croft, W B. 2018. WikiPassageQA: A benchmark collection for research on non-factoid answer passage retrieval. Pages 1165–1168 of: *The 41st International ACM SIGIR Conference on Research & Development in Information Retrieval*.

CompanionMX, Inc. 2025. *Companion: Emotion and Conversation AI platform, clinically validated at Harvard Medical School and Veterans Affairs clinics*. www.companionmx.com/. Accessed: 2025-08-11.

Conneau, A, and Kiela, D. 2018. SentEval: An evaluation toolkit for universal sentence representations. Pages 1913–1923 of: *Proceedings of the Eleventh International Conference on Language Resources and Evaluation (LREC 2018)*. Miyazaki, Japan.

Connor L, and Gabriel A. 2023. *Cognitive Emulation: A Naive AI Safety Proposal*. www.alignmentforum.org/posts/ngEvKav9w57XrGQnb/cognitive-emulation-a-naive-ai-safety-proposal. Accessed 01-12-2023.

Cordì, V, and Mascardi, V. 2004. Checking the completeness of ontologies: A case study from the semantic web. In: *Proceedings of the Italian Conference on Computational Logic (CILC) Workshop*. www.cs.unipr.it/CILC04/DownloadArea/CordiM-CILC04.pdf

Cornelio, C, Dash, S, Austel, V, et al. 2021. AI Descartes: Combining data and theory for derivable scientific discovery. *arXiv preprint arXiv:2109.01634*.

Czeisler, M É, Lane, R I, Petrosky, E, et al. 2020. Mental health, substance use, and suicidal ideation during the COVID-19 pandemic. *Morbidity and Mortality Weekly Report*, **69**(32), 1049.

Dagan, I, Glickman, O, and Magnini, B. 2005. The PASCAL recognising textual entailment challenge. Pages 177–190 of: *Machine Learning Challenges Workshop*. Springer.

Dagan, I, Dolan, B, Magnini, B, and Roth, D. 2010. Recognizing textual entailment: Rational, evaluation and approaches–erratum. *Natural Language Engineering*, **16**(1), 105–105.

Dai, D, Dong, L, Hao, Y, et al. 2022. Knowledge neurons in pretrained transformers. Pages 8493–8502 of: *Proceedings of the 60th Annual Meeting of the Association for Computational Linguistics (Volume 1: Long Papers)*.

Dai, Z, Yang, Z, Yang, Y, et al. 2019. Transformer-XL: attentive language models beyond a fixed-length context. Pages 2978–2988 of: *Proceedings of the 57th Annual Meeting of the Association for Computational Linguistics*.

Dalal, S, Tilwani, D, Gaur, M, et al. 2023. A cross attention approach to diagnostic explainability using clinical practice guidelines for depression. IEEE *Journal of Biomedical and Health Informatics*, **29**(2), 1333–1342.

Dalton, J, Xiong, C, Kumar, V, and Callan, J. 2020. Cast-19: A dataset for conversational information seeking. Pages 1985–1988 of: *Proceedings of the 43rd International ACM SIGIR Conference on Research and Development in Information Retrieval*.

Dash, T, Chitlangia, S, Ahuja, A, and Srinivasan, A. 2022. A review of some techniques for inclusion of domain-knowledge into deep neural networks. *Scientific Reports*, **12**(1), 1040.

Davis, C R, Murphy, K J, Curtis, R G, and Maher, C A. 2020. A process evaluation examining the performance, adherence, and acceptability of a physical activity and diet artificial intelligence virtual health assistant. *International Journal of Environmental Research and Public Health*, **17**(23), 9137.

Daws, R. 2020. *Babylon Health lashes out at doctor who raised AI chatbot safety concerns*. www.artificialintelligence-news.com/2020/02/26/babylon-health-doctor-ai-chatbot-safety-concerns/.

Daws, R. 2023. *Medical chatbot using OpenAI's GPT-3 told a fake patient to kill themselves*. www.artificialintelligence-news.com/2020/10/28/medical-chatbot-openai-gpt3-patient-kill-themselves/. Accessed: 2023-11-30.

Defense Advanced Research Projects Agency (DARPA). 2019. *A DARPA perspective on artificial intelligence*. https://sites.nationalacademies.org/cs/groups/pgasite/documents/webpage/pga_177035.pdf. Accessed: 2024-06-22.

Dehghani, M, Tay, Y, Gritsenko, A A, et al. 2021. The benchmark lottery. *arXiv preprint arXiv:2107.07002*.

Dehmer, M, and Mowshowitz, A. 2011. A history of graph entropy measures. *Information Sciences*, **181**(1), 57–78.

Delforge, D, Wathelet, V, Below, R, et al. 2025. EM-DAT: The Emergency Events Database. *International Journal of Disaster Risk Reduction*, **124**, 105509. doi: 10.1016/j.ijdrr.2025.105509.

Demasi, O, Hearst, M A., and Recht, B. 2019. Towards augmenting crisis counselor training by improving message retrieval. Pages 1–11 of: *Proceedings of the Sixth Workshop on Computational Linguistics and Clinical Psychology*.

Demszky, D, Movshovitz-Attias, D, Ko, J, et al. 2020. GoEmotions: A dataset of fine-grained emotions. *arXiv preprint arXiv:2005.00547*.

Denecke, K, Vaaheesan, S, and Arulnathan, A. 2020. A mental health chatbot for regulating emotions (SERMO)-concept and usability test. *IEEE Transactions on Emerging Topics in Computing*, **9**(3), 1170–1182.

Deng, J, Sun, H, Zhang, Z, et al. 2023. Recent advances towards safe, responsible, and moral dialogue systems: A survey. *arXiv preprint arXiv:2302.09270*.

Derczynski, L, Ritter, A, Clark, S, and Bontcheva, K. 2013. Twitter part-of-speech tagging for all: Overcoming sparse and noisy data. Pages 198–206 of: *Proceedings of the International Conference Recent Advances in Natural Language Processing RANLP 2013*.

Deshpande, A, Murahari, V, Rajpurohit, T, et al. 2023. Toxicity in ChatGPT: Analyzing persona-assigned language models. *arXiv preprint arXiv:2304.05335*.

Dettmers, T, Minervini, P, Stenetorp, P, and Riedel, S. 2018. Convolutional 2D knowledge graph embeddings. *Proceedings of the AAAI Conference on Artificial Intelligence*, **32**(1).

Dettmers, T, Pagnoni, A, Holtzman, A, and Zettlemoyer, L. 2024. QLORA: Efficient finetuning of quantized LLMs. *Advances in Neural Information Processing Systems*, **36**, 10088–10115.

Devlin, J, Chang, M-W, Lee, K, and Toutanova, K. 2019. BERT: Pre-training of deep bidirectional transformers for language understanding. Pages 4171–4186 of: *Proceedings of the 2019 Conference of the North American Chapter of the Association for Computational Linguistics: Human Language Technologies, Volume 1 (Long and Short Papers)*.

Dhamala, J, Sun, T, Kumar, V, et al. 2021. BOLD: Dataset and metrics for measuring biases in open-ended language generation. Pages 862–872 of: *Proceedings of the 2021 ACM Conference on Fairness, Accountability, and Transparency*.

Dhavala, S, Faldu, K, and Avasthi, A. 2024. *System and method for generating diagnostic assessment question papers and evaluating their quality*. US Patent 12,125,412.

Dinan, E, Roller, S, Shuster, K, et al. 2018. Wizard of Wikipedia: Knowledge-powered conversational agents. *arXiv preprint arXiv:1811.01241*.

Dinan, E, Abercrombie, G, Bergman, A et al. 2021. Anticipating safety issues in E2E conversational AI: Framework and tooling. *arXiv preprint arXiv:2107.03451*.

Dinan, E, Abercrombie, G, Bergman, S A, et al. 2022. SafetyKit: First aid for measuring safety in open-domain conversational systems. In: *Proceedings of the 60th Annual Meeting of the Association for Computational Linguistics (Volume 1: Long Papers)*.

Dinkar, T, Attanasio, G, Curry, A C, et al. (eds). 2024. *Proceedings of Safety4ConvAI: The Third Workshop on Safety for Conversational AI @ LREC-COLING 2024*. Torino, Italia. ELRA and ICCL. https://aclanthology.org/2024.safety4convai-1.0.

Dolan, B, and Brockett, C. 2005. Automatically constructing a corpus of sentential paraphrases. In: *Third International Workshop on Paraphrasing (IWP2005)*.

Domingos, P. 2012. A few useful things to know about machine learning. *Communications of the ACM*, **55**(10), 78–87.

Donnelly, K, et al. 2006. SNOMED-CT: The advanced terminology and coding system for eHealth. *Studies in Health Technology and Informatics*, **121**, 279–290.

Du, K, Xing, F, and Cambria, E. 2023. Incorporating multiple knowledge sources for targeted aspect-based financial sentiment analysis. *ACM Transactions on Management Information Systems*, **14**(3), 1–24.

Dubois, Y, Li, X, Taori, R, et al. 2023. AlpacaFarm: A simulation framework for methods that learn from human feedback. *arXiv preprint arXiv:2305.14387*.

Dugas, C, Bengio, Y, Bélisle, F, et al. 2009. Incorporating functional knowledge in neural networks. *Journal of Machine Learning Research*, **10**, 1239–1262.

Dutt, R, Hiware, K, Ghosh, A, and Bhaskaran, R. 2018. SAVITR: A system for real-time location extraction from microblogs during emergencies. Pages 1643–1649 of: *WWW '18: Companion Proceedings of the The Web Conference 2018*.

Elazar, Y, Kassner, N, Ravfogel, S, et al. 2021. Measuring and improving consistency in pretrained language models. *Transactions of the Association for Computational Linguistics*, **9**, 1012–1031.

Fadhil, A. 2018. A conversational interface to improve medication adherence: towards AI support in patient's treatment. *arXiv preprint arXiv:1803.09844*.

Faldu, K, Sheth, A, Kikani, P, and Akbari, H. 2021a. KI-BERT: Infusing knowledge context for better language and domain understanding. *arXiv preprint arXiv:2104.08145*.

Faldu, K, Sheth, A, Kikani, P, et al. 2021b. Towards tractable mathematical reasoning: Challenges, strategies, and opportunities for solving math word problems. *arXiv preprint arXiv:2111.05364*.

Faruqui, M, Dodge, J, Jauhar, S K, et al. 2015. Retrofitting word vectors to semantic lexicons. Pages 1606–1615 of: *Proceedings of the 2015 Conference of the North American Chapter of the Association for Computational Linguistics: Human Language Technologies*.

Fawzi, A, Balog, M, Huang, A, et al. 2022. Discovering faster matrix multiplication algorithms with reinforcement learning. *Nature*, **610**(7930), 47–53.

Federal Emergency Management Agency. 2017. *ICS glossary*. https://training.fema.gov/emiweb/is/icsresource/assets/icsglossary.pdf. Accessed: 2024-05-29.

Feng, S, Park, C Y, Liu, Y, and Tsvetkov, Y. 2023. From pretraining data to language models to downstream tasks: Tracking the trails of political biases leading to unfair NLP models. *arXiv:2305.08283* [cs].

Fernández-López, M, Gómez-Pérez, A, and Juristo Juzgado, N. 1997. *Methontology: From Ontological Art towards Ontological Engineering*. American Association for Artificial Intelligence.

First, M B. 2014. Structured clinical interview for the DSM (SCID). *The Encyclopedia of Clinical Psychology*, 1–6.

Fitzpatrick, K K, Darcy, A, and Vierhile, M. 2017. Delivering cognitive behavior therapy to young adults with symptoms of depression and anxiety using a fully automated conversational agent (Woebot): a randomized controlled trial. *JMIR Mental Health*, **4**(2), e7785.

Fleiss, J L, Levin, B, Paik, Myunghee C, et al. 1981. The measurement of interrater agreement. *Statistical Methods for Rates and Proportions*, **2**(212–236), 22–23.

Floridi, L, and Chiriatti, M. 2020. GPT-3: Its nature, scope, limits, and consequences. *Minds and Machines*, **30**, 681–694.

Fluri, L, Paleka, D, and Tramèr, F. 2023. Evaluating superhuman models with consistency checks. *arXiv preprint arXiv:2306.09983*.

Foran, S, Swaine, A, and Burns, K. 2012. Improving the effectiveness of humanitarian action: progress in implementing the Inter-Agency Standing Committee (IASC) Gender Marker. *Gender & Development*, **20**(2), 233–247.

Forbes, M, Hwang, J D., Shwartz, V, et al. 2020. Social chemistry 101: learning to reason about social and moral norms. Pages 653–670 of: *Proceedings of the 2020 Conference on Empirical Methods in Natural Language Processing (EMNLP)*.

Fraunhofer IESE. 2023. *Fraunhofer Institute for Experimental Software Engineering IESE*. www.iese.fraunhofer.de. Accessed: 2023-05-29.

Fulmer, R, Joerin, A, Gentile, B, et al. 2018. Using psychological artificial intelligence (Tess) to relieve symptoms of depression and anxiety: randomized controlled trial. *JMIR Mental Health*, **5**(4), e9782.

Gabriel, I. 2020. Artificial intelligence, values, and alignment. *Minds and Machines*, **30**(3), 411–437.

Gao, L, and Huang, R. 2017. Detecting online hate speech using context aware models. *arXiv preprint arXiv:1710.07395*.

Gao, L, Dai, Z, Pasupat, P, et al. 2023. RARR: Researching and revising what language models say, using language models. Pages 16477–16508 of: *Proceedings of the 61st Annual Meeting of the Association for Computational Linguistics (Volume 1: Long Papers)*.

Gao, Y, Wu, C, Li, J, et al. 2020. Discern: Discourse-aware entailment reasoning network for conversational machine reading. Pages 2439–2449 of: *Proceedings of the 2020 Conference on Empirical Methods in Natural Language Processing (EMNLP)*.

Garcez, A and Lamb, L C. 2023. Neurosymbolic AI: The 3rd Wave. *Artificial Intelligence Review*, **56**(11), 12387–12406.

Garrido-Muñoz, I, Montejo-Ráez, A, Martínez-Santiago, F, and Ureña-López, L A. 2021. A survey on bias in deep NLP. *Applied Sciences*, **11**(7), 3184.

Gartner, Inc. 2023. *Exciting New Trends in the Gartner Emerging Technologies Hype Cycle*. www.gartner.com/en/documents/xyz. Accessed: 2023-08-11.

Gaur, M, and Sheth, A. 2017. *Knoesis alchemy of healthcare*. http://wiki.aiisc.ai/index.php/Knoesis_Alchemy_of_Healthcare. Accessed: 2024-06-25.

Gaur, M, Kursuncu, U, Alambo, A, et al. 2018. "Let me tell you about your mental health!" Contextualized classification of reddit posts to DSM-5 for web-based intervention. Pages 753–762 of: *Proceedings of the 27th ACM International Conference on Information and Knowledge Management*.

Gaur, M, Shekarpour, S, Gyrard, A, et al. 2019a. Empathi: An ontology for emergency managing and planning about hazard crisis. Pages 396–403 of: *2019 IEEE 13th International Conference on Semantic Computing (ICSC)*.

Gaur, M, Alambo, A, Sain, J P, et al. 2019b. Knowledge-aware assessment of severity of suicide risk for early intervention. Pages 514–525 of: *WWW '19:The World Wide Web Conference*.

Gaur, M, Desai, A, Faldu, K, and Sheth, A. 2020. Explainable AI using knowledge graphs. In: *ACM CoDS-COMAD Conference*.

Gaur, M, Aribandi, V, Alambo, A, et al. 2021a. Characterization of time-variant and time-invariant assessment of suicidality on Reddit using C-SSRS. *PloS one*, **16**(5), e0250448.

Gaur, M, Gunaratna, K, Srinivasan, V, and Jin, H. 2021b. ISEEQ: Information seeking question generation using dynamic meta-information retrieval and knowledge graphs. *arXiv preprint arXiv:2112.07622*.

Gaur, M, Aribandi, V, Kursuncu, U, 2021c. Knowledge-infused abstractive summarization of clinical diagnostic interviews: Framework development study. *JMIR Mental Health*, **8**(05), e20865.

Gaur, M, Faldu, K, and Sheth, A. 2021d. Semantics of the black-box: Can knowledge graphs help make deep learning systems more interpretable and explainable? *IEEE Internet Computing*, **25**(1), 51–59.

Gaur, M, Roy, K, Sharma, A, et al. 2021e. "Who can help me?": Knowledge infused matching of support seekers and support providers during COVID-19 on Reddit. Pages 265–269 of: *2021 IEEE 9th International Conference on Healthcare Informatics (ICHI)*.

Gaur, M, Gunaratna, K, Srinivasan, V, and Jin, H. 2022a. ISEEQ: Information seeking question generation using dynamic meta-information retrieval and knowledge graphs. Pages 10672–10680 of: *Proceedings of the AAAI Conference on Artificial Intelligence*, vol. 36.

Gaur, M, Gunaratna, K, Bhatt, S, and Sheth, A. 2022b. Knowledge-infused learning: a sweet spot in neuro-symbolic AI. *IEEE Internet Computing*, **26**(4), 5–11.

Gaur, M, Gunaratna, D A K S S, Srinivasan, V, and Jin, H. 2023. *Dynamic question generation for information-gathering*. US Patent App. 17/817,778.

Gautam, S, Jain, A, Gautam, M, et al. 2017. Clinical practice guidelines for the management of depression. *Indian Journal of Psychiatry*, **59**(Suppl 1), S34.

Gauthier, D. 1987. *Morals by Agreement*. Oxford University Press.

Gehrmann, S, Clark, E, and Sellam, T. 2023. Repairing the cracked foundation: A survey of obstacles in evaluation practices for generated text. *Journal of Artificial Intelligence Research*, **77**, 103–166.

Gentner, D. 1983. Structure-mapping: A theoretical framework for analogy. *Cognitive Science*, **7**(2), 155–170.

Geonames. 2006. *Geonames Ontology Documentation*. www.geonames.org/ontology/documentation.html. Accessed: 2024-05-29.

GeoNames Team. 2019. *The GeoNames Ontology*. www.geonames.org/ontology. Version 3.2, November 2019. Maintained by GeoNames.org. Licensed under Creative Commons Attribution 3.0 License.

Ghandeharioun, A, McDuff, D, Czerwinski, M, and Rowan, K. 2019. Emma: An emotion-aware wellbeing chatbot. Pages 1–7 of: *2019 8th International Conference on Affective Computing and Intelligent Interaction (ACII)*.

Ghoneim, Ahmed Elgohary, and Peskov, Denis. 2019. CANARD: A dataset for question-in-context rewriting. http://hdl.handle.net/1903/27595.

Ghosh, S, Ekbal, A, and Bhattacharyya, P. 2022. Am I no good? towards detecting perceived burdensomeness and thwarted belongingness from suicide notes. *arXiv preprint arXiv:2206.06141*.

Ginger. 2011. *In-the-Moment Care for Every Emotion*. www.ginger.com/.

Glass, M, Rossiello, G, Chowdhury, M F M, et al 2022. Re2G: Retrieve, Rerank, Generate. Pages 2701–2715 of: *Proceedings of the 2022 Conference of the North American Chapter of the Association for Computational Linguistics: Human Language Technologies*.

Goebel, R, Chander, A, Holzinger, K, et al. 2018. Explainable AI: the new 42? Pages 295–303 of: *International Cross-Domain Conference for Machine Learning and Knowledge Extraction*.

Goel, A, Sharma, C, and Kumaraguru, P. 2022. An unsupervised, geometric and syntax-aware quantification of polysemy. Pages 10565–10574 of: *Proceedings of the 2022 Conference on Empirical Methods in Natural Language Processing*.

Goferman, S, Zelnik-Manor, L, and Tal, A. 2011. Context-aware saliency detection. *IEEE Transactions on Pattern Analysis and Machine Intelligence*, **34**(10), 1915–1926.

Goldstein, A, Zada, Z, Buchnik, E, Schain, et al. 2022. Shared computational principles for language processing in humans and deep language models. *Nature Neuroscience*, **25**(3), 369–380.

Goodman, M W. 2023. *WN: A Python library for working with wordnets*. https://github.com/goodmami/wn. Accessed: 2023-05-29.

Govil, P, Bonagiri, V K, Gaur, M, et al. 2024. COBIAS: Contextual reliability in bias assessment. *arXiv preprint arXiv:2402.14889*.

Grigoruta, C. 2018. *Why we need mental health chatbots*. https://woebothealth.com/why-we-need-mental-health-chatbots/.

Gritta, M, Hu, R, and Iacobacci, I. 2022. CrossAligner & Co: Zero-shot transfer methods for task-oriented cross-lingual natural language understanding. Pages 4048–4061 of: *Findings of the Association for Computational Linguistics: ACL 2022*.

Group, Stanford Ermon. 2023. *Variational inference - CS228 class notes*. https://ermongroup.github.io/cs228-notes/inference/variational/. Accessed: 2023-05-29.

Gunaratna, K, Yazdavar, A H, Thirunarayan, K, et al. 2017. Relatedness-based multi-entity summarization. Page 1060 of: *IJCAI: Proceedings of the Conference*, vol. 2017.

Gunaratna, K, Wang, Y, and Jin, H. 2021. Entity context graph: Learning entity representations from semi-structured textual sources on the web. *arXiv preprint arXiv:2103.15950*.

Guo, Q, Zhuang, F, Qin, C, et al. 2020. A survey on knowledge graph-based recommender systems. *IEEE Transactions on Knowledge and Data Engineering*, **34**(8), 3549–3568.

Guo, Y, Yang, Y, and Abbasi, A. 2022. Auto-Debias: Debiasing masked language models with automated biased prompts. Pages 1012–1023 of: Muresan, S, Nakov, P, and Villavicencio, A (eds), *Proceedings of the 60th Annual Meeting of the Association for Computational Linguistics (Volume 1: Long Papers)*.

Gupta, S, Agarwal, A, Gaur, M, et al. 2022. Learning to automate follow-up question generation using process knowledge for depression triage on reddit posts. Pages 137–147 of: *Proceedings of the Eighth Workshop on Computational Linguistics and Clinical Psychology*.

Gururangan, S, Swayamdipta, S, Levy, O, et al. 2018. Annotation artifacts in natural language inference data. Pages 107–112 of: *Proceedings of NAACL-HLT*.

Guu, K, Lee, K, Tung, Z, et al. 2020. REALM: Retrieval Augmented Language Model Pre-Training. Pages 3929–3938 of: *Proceedings of the 37th International Conference on Machine Learning (ICML)*.

Gyrard, A. 2015. *Designing cross-domain semantic web of things applications*. Ph.D. thesis, Télécom ParisTech.

Gyrard, A, and Boudaoud, K. 2022. Interdisciplinary IoT and emotion knowledge graph-based recommendation system to boost mental health. *Applied Sciences*, **12**(19), 9712.

Gyrard, A, Gaur, M, Shekarpour, S, et al. 2018. Personalized health knowledge graph. In: *CEUR Workshop Proceedings*, Vol. 2317. NIH Public Access.

Gyrard, A, Mohammadi, S, Gaur, M, and Kung, A. 2024. IoT-based preventive mental health using knowledge graphs and standards for better well-being. *arXiv preprint arXiv:2406.13791*.

Habicht, J, Viswanathan, S, Carrington, B, et al. 2024. Closing the accessibility gap to mental health treatment with a personalized self-referral chatbot. *Nature Medicine*, **30**, 595–602.

Hadfield-Menell, D, Andrus, M, and Hadfield, G. 2019. Legible normativity for AI alignment: The value of silly rules. Pages 115–121 of: *Proceedings of the 2019 AAAI/ACM Conference on AI, Ethics, and Society*.

Hagendorff, T, Dasgupta, I, Binz, M, et al. 2023. Machine psychology. *arXiv preprint arXiv:2303.13988*.

Hamaguchi, T, Oiwa, Hidekazu, S, Masashi, and Matsumoto, Y. 2017. Knowledge transfer for out-of-knowledge-base entities: a graph neural network approach. *arXiv preprint arXiv:1706.05674*.

Hamilton, William L. 2022. *Graph representation learning*. Synthesis Lectures on Artificial Intelligence and Machine Learning, vol. 14, no. 3. Morgan & Claypool Publishers.

Harrison, Chase. 2023. *GitHub - langchain-ai/langchain: Building applications with LLMs through composability — github.com*. https://github.com/hwchase17/langchain. Accessed: 2023-07-30.

Hartmann, R, Sander, C, Lorenz, N, et al. 2019. Utilization of patient-generated data collected through mobile devices: insights from a survey on attitudes toward mobile self-monitoring and self-management apps for depression. *JMIR Mental Health*, **6**(4), e11671.

Hasan, K S, and Ng, V. 2014. Automatic keyphrase extraction: A survey of the state of the art. Pages 1262–1273 of: *Proceedings of the 52nd Annual Meeting of the Association for Computational Linguistics (Volume 1: Long Papers)*.

He, L, Lee, K, Lewis, M, and Zettlemoyer, L. 2017. Deep semantic role labeling: What works and what's next. Pages 473–483 of: *Proceedings of the 55th Annual Meeting of the Association for Computational Linguistics (Volume 1: Long Papers)*.

He, P, Liu, X, Gao, J, and Chen, W. 2021. DeBERTa: Decoding-enhanced BERT with disentangled attention. In: *Proceedings of the 9th International Conference on Learning Representations (ICLR)*. https://openreview.net/forum?id=XPZIaotutsD.

Heikkilä, M, et al. 2022. DeepMind's new chatbot uses google searches plus humans to give better answer. *MIT Technology Review*.

Henderson, P, Sinha, K, Angelard-Gontier, N, et al. 2018. Ethical challenges in data-driven dialogue systems. Pages 123–129 of: *Proceedings of the 2018 AAAI/ACM Conference on AI, Ethics, and Society*.

Hendrycks, D, Mazeika, M, and Woodside, T. 2023. An overview of catastrophic AI risks. *arXiv preprint arXiv:2306.12001*.

Hennemann, S, Kuhn, S, Witthöft, M, and Jungmann, S M. 2022. Diagnostic performance of an app-based symptom checker in mental disorders: Comparative study in psychotherapy outpatients. *JMIR Ment Health*, **9**(1), e32832.

Hensher, D A, and Stopher, P R. 2021. *Behavioural travel modelling*. Vol. 12. Routledge.

Hinton, G, Vinyals, O, and Dean, J. 2015. Distilling the knowledge in a neural network. *arXiv preprint arXiv:1503.02531*.

Hitzler, P, Eberhart, A, Ebrahimi, M, et al. 2022. Neuro-symbolic approaches in artificial intelligence. *National Science Review*, **9**(6), nwac035.

Hlomani, H, and Stacey, D. 2014. Approaches, methods, metrics, measures, and subjectivity in ontology evaluation: A survey. *Semantic Web Journal*.

Hochreiter, S, and Schmidhuber, J. 1997. Long short-term memory. *Neural Computation*, **9**(8), 1735–1780.

Hoffman, R R, Mueller, S T, Klein, G, and Litman, J. 2018. Metrics for explainable AI: Challenges and prospects. *arXiv preprint arXiv:1812.04608*.

Hofstadter, D R. 1979. Gödel. *Escher, Bach: An Eternal Golden Braid*. Basic Books.

Holohan, M. 2023. A boy saw 17 doctors over 3 years for chronic pain. ChatGPT found the diagnosis. *TODAY. com*.

Holtzman, A, Buys, J, Du, L, et al. 2019. The curious case of neural text degeneration. In: *International Conference on Learning Representations*.

Honnibal, M, Montani, I, Van Landeghem, S, and Boyd, A. 2020. *spaCy: Industrial-Strength Natural Language Processing in Python*. https://doi.org/10.5281/zenodo.1212303.

Honovich, O, Aharoni, R, Herzig, J, et al. 2022. TRUE: Re-evaluating factual consistency evaluation. Pages 3905–3920 of: *Proceedings of the 2022 Conference of the North American Chapter of the Association for Computational Linguistics: Human Language Technologies*.

Howard, J, and Ruder, S. 2018. Universal Language Model Fine-tuning for Text Classification. In: *Proceedings of the 56th Annual Meeting of the Association for Computational Linguistics (Volume 1: Long Papers)*.

Hu, P, Lu, Y, and Gong, Y. 2021. Dual humanness and trust in conversational AI: A person-centered approach. *Computers in Human Behavior*, **119**, 106727.

Hu, Z, Yang, Z, Salakhutdinov, R R, et al. 2018. Deep generative models with learnable knowledge constraints. *Advances in Neural Information Processing Systems*, **31**.

Huang, L, Sun, C, Qiu, X, and Huang, X. 2019. GlossBERT: BERT for word sense disambiguation with gloss knowledge. Pages 3509–3514 of: *Proceedings of the 2019 Conference on Empirical Methods in Natural Language Processing and the 9th International Joint Conference on Natural Language Processing (EMNLP-IJCNLP)*.

Huang, Q, Zhang, Y, Ko, T, et al. 2023. Personalized dialogue generation with persona-adaptive attention. Pages 12916–12923 of: *Proceedings of the AAAI Conference on Artificial Intelligence*, vol. 37.

Huang, Z, Yang, J, van Harmelen, F, and Hu, Q. 2017. Constructing knowledge graphs of depression. Pages 149–161 of: *International Conference on Health Information Science*.

Hudson, Christopher D, and Drew A, Manning. 2019. GQA: A new dataset for real-world visual reasoning and compositional question answering. Pages 6700–6709 of: *Proceedings of the IEEE/CVF Conference on Computer Vision and Pattern Recognition*.

HXL Standard. 2015. *HXL standard*. https://hxlstandard.org/. Accessed: 2024-05-29.

IBM. 2021. *IBM's Global AI adoption index 2021*.

Imran, M, Castillo, C, Diaz, F, and Vieweg, S. 2015. Processing social media messages in mass emergency: A survey. *ACM Computing Surveys (CSUR)*, **47**(4), 1–38.

Inkster, B, Sarda, S, Subramanian, V, et al. 2018. An empathy-driven, conversational artificial intelligence agent (Wysa) for digital mental well-being: real-world data evaluation mixed-methods study. *JMIR mHealth and uHealth*, **6**(11), e12106.

Inter-Agency Standing Committee. 2023. *IASC Products*. https://interagencystandingcommittee.org/resources/iasc-products. Accessed: 2023-05-29.

Irie, K, Csordás, R, and Schmidhuber, J. 2022. The dual form of neural networks revisited: Connecting test time predictions to training patterns via spotlights of attention. *arXiv preprint arXiv:2202.05798*.

Iyer, S, Dandekar, N, and Csernai, K, et al. 2017. *First Quora dataset release: Question pairs*. https://quoradata.quora.com/First-Quora-Dataset-Release-Question-Pairs. Accessed: 2024-08-13.

Jamnik, M R, and Lane, D J. 2017. The use of Reddit as an inexpensive source for high-quality data. *Practical Assessment, Research, and Evaluation*, **22**(1), 5.

Jang, M, and Lukasiewicz, T. 2023. *Consistency analysis of ChatGPT*. arXiv:2303.06273 [cs].

Jang, M, Kwon, D S, and Lukasiewicz, T. 2022a. BECEL: Benchmark for consistency evaluation of language models. Pages 3680–3696 of: *Proceedings of the 29th International Conference on Computational Linguistics*.

Jang, Y, Lim, J, Hur, Y, et al. 2022b. Call for customized conversation: Customized conversation grounding persona and knowledge. Pages 10803–10812 of: *Proceedings of the AAAI Conference on Artificial Intelligence*, vol. 36.

Janizek, J D, Sturmfels, P, and Lee, S. 2021. Explaining explanations: Axiomatic feature interactions for deep networks. *Journal of Machine Learning Research*, **22**, 1–54.

Ji, Z, Lee, N, Frieske, R, et al. 2022. Survey of Hallucination in Natural Language Generation. *ACM Computing Surveys*, **55**, 1–38.

Jiang, D, Ren, X, and Lin, B Y. 2023. LLM-Blender: Ensembling large language models with pairwise ranking and generative fusion. *arXiv preprint arXiv:2306.02561*.

Jiang, L, Hwang, J D, Bhagavatula, C, et al. 2021. Can machines learn morality? The delphi experiment. *arXiv preprint arXiv:2110.07574v1*.

Jiang, L, Hwang, J D., Bhagavatula, C, et al. 2022 (July). Can machines learn morality? The Delphi experiment. *arXiv:2110.07574v2* [cs].

Jiang, S, Groves, W, Anzaroot, S, and Jaimes, A. 2019 (June). Crisis Sub-Events on Social Media: A Case Study of Wildfires. In: *Proceedings of the ICML 2019 Workshop on AI for Social Good, Long Beach, CA, USA*. https://shanjiang.me/publications/aisg19_paper.pdf

Jie, R, Meng, X, Shang, L, 2023. Prompt-based length controlled generation with reinforcement learning. *arXiv preprint arXiv:2308.12030*.

Jin, Z, Levine, S, Gonzalez A, et al. 2022. When to make exceptions: Exploring language models as accounts of human moral judgment. *Advances in Neural Information Processing Systems*, **35**, 28458–28473.

Johnson, J, Douze, M, and Jégou, H. 2019. Billion-scale similarity search with GPUs. *IEEE Transactions on Big Data*, **7**(3), 535–547.

Johnson, J, Krishna, R, Stark, M, et al. 2015. Image retrieval using scene graphs. Pages 3668–3678 of: *Proceedings of the IEEE Conference on Computer Vision and Pattern Recognition.*

Jonkman, S N, Vrijling, J K, and Vrouwenvelder, H J. 2005. Global perspectives on loss of human life caused by floods. *Natural Hazards*, **34**(2), 151–175.

Joshi, C K., Mi, F, and Faltings, B. 2017. Personalization in Goal-oriented Dialog. Pages 1838–1848 of: *Proceedings of the 2017 Conference on Empirical Methods in Natural Language Processing.* https://aclanthology.org/D17-1197.

Joulin, A, Grave, E, Bojanowski, P, et al. 2016. Fasttext.zip: Compressing text classification models. *arXiv preprint arXiv:1612.03651.*

Joyce, D W, Kormilitzin, A, Smith, K A, and Cipriani, A. 2023. Explainable artificial intelligence for mental health through transparency and interpretability for understandability. *npj Digital Medicine*, **6**(1), 6.

Jumper, J, Evans, R, Pritzel, A, et al. 2021. Highly accurate protein structure prediction with AlphaFold. *Nature*, **596**(7873), 583–589.

Kahneman, D. 2011. *Thinking, Fast and Slow*. Farrar, Straus and Giroux.

Kané, H, Kocyigit, Y, Ajanoh, P, et al. 2019. Towards neural similarity evaluator. In: *Workshop on Document Intelligence at NeurIPS 2019.*

Kane, H, Kocyigit, M Y, Abdalla, A, et al. 2020. NUBIA: NeUral Based Interchangeability Assessor for Text Generation. Pages 28–37 of: *Proceedings of the 1st Workshop on Evaluating NLG Evaluation.*

Kaneko, M, and Okazaki, N. 2023. Reducing sequence length by predicting edit operations with large language models. *arXiv preprint arXiv:2305.11862.*

Karpukhin, V, Oguz, B, Min, S, et al. 2020. Dense Passage Retrieval for Open-Domain Question Answering. Pages 6769–6781 of: *Proceedings of the 2020 Conference on Empirical Methods in Natural Language Processing (EMNLP).*

Kautz, Henry A. 2020. The third AI summer: AAAI Robert S. Engelmore memorial lecture. *AI Magazine*, **41**(3), 93–104.

Kazi, H, Chowdhry, B S, and Memon, Z. 2012. MedChatBot: An UMLS based chatbot for medical students. *International Journal of Computer Applications*, **55**, 1–5.

Keßler, C, and Hendrix, C. 2015. The humanitarian eXchange language: Coordinating disaster response with semantic web technologies. *Semantic Web*, **6**(1), 5–21.

Khalatbari, L, Bang, Y, Su, D, et al. 2023. Learn what NOT to learn: Towards generative safety in chatbots. *arXiv preprint arXiv:2304.11220.*

Khare, P, Burel, G, and Alani, H. 2018. Classifying crises-information relevancy with semantics. Pages 367–383 of: *ESWC 2018: Proceedings of the 15th International Conference.*

Khattab, O, and Zaharia, M. 2020. ColBERT: Efficient and effective passage search via contextualized late interaction over BERT. Pages 39–48 of: *Proceedings of the 43rd International ACM SIGIR Conference on Research and Development in Information Retrieval.*

Kim, A-G, Dasom, H, Hong, K, Park, P, and Soyeon, T. 2021. Bridging knowledge graphs to generate scene graphs. Pages 606–623 of: *European Conference on Computer Vision.*

Kim, H, Yu, Y, Jiang, L, et al. 2022a. ProsocialDialog: A prosocial backbone for conversational agents. Pages 4005–4029 of: *Proceedings of the 2022 Conference on Empirical Methods in Natural Language Processing.*

Kim, H, Yu, Y, Jiang, L, et al. 2022b (Oct.). ProsocialDialog: A prosocial backbone for conversational agents. *arXiv:2205.12688* [cs].

Kim, J E, Henson, C, Huang, K, et al. 2021. Accelerating road sign ground truth construction with knowledge graph and machine learning. Pages 325–340 of: *Intelligent Computing: Proceedings of the 2021 Computing Conference, Volume 2*.

Kitaev, N, and Klein, D. 2018. Constituency parsing with a self-attentive encoder. Pages 2676–2686 of: *Proceedings of the 56th Annual Meeting of the Association for Computational Linguistics (Volume 1: Long Papers)*.

Kocaman, V, and Talby, D. 2022. Accurate clinical and biomedical named entity recognition at scale. *Software Impacts*, **13**, 100373.

Kodirov, E, Xiang, T, and Gong, S. 2017. Semantic autoencoder for zero-shot learning. *arXiv preprint arXiv:1704.08345*.

Koh, P W, and Liang, P. 2017. Understanding black-box predictions via influence functions. Pages 1885–1894 of: *International Conference on Machine Learning*.

Koulouri, T, Macredie, R D., and Olakitan, D. 2022. Chatbots to support young adults' mental health: An exploratory study of acceptability. *ACM Transactions on Interactive Intelligent Systems(TiiS)*, **12**(2), 1–39.

Koutsouleris, N, Hauser, T U, Skvortsova, V, and De Choudhury, M. 2022. From promise to practice: towards the realisation of AI-informed mental health care. *The Lancet Digital Health*, **4**(11), e829–e840.

Krishnaswamy, N, and Pustejovsky, J. 2020. Neurosymbolic AI for situated language understanding. *arXiv preprint arXiv:2012.02947*.

Krishna, R, Zhu, Y, Groth, O, et al. 2017. Visual genome: Connecting language and vision using crowdsourced dense image annotations. *International Journal of Computer Vision*, **123**(1), 32–73.

Kroenke, K, Spitzer, R L, and Williams, J B W. 2001. The PHQ-9: validity of a brief depression severity measure. *Journal of General Internal Medicine*, **16**(9), 606–613.

Kryściński, W, and McCann, B. 2021 (Apr. 29). *Evaluating the Factual Consistency of Abstractive Text Summarization*. US Patent App. 16/750, 598.

Krügel, S, Ostermaier, A, and Uhl, M. 2023. ChatGPT's inconsistent moral advice influences users' judgment. *Sci Rep*, **13**(1), 4569.

Kulkarni, M, Mahata, D, Arora, R, and Bhowmik, R. 2022. Learning rich representation of keyphrases from text. Pages 891–906 of: *Findings of the Association for Computational Linguistics: NAACL 2022*.

Kumar, R, Yadav, S, Daniulaityte, R, et al. 2020. eDarkFind: Unsupervised multi-view learning for sybil account detection. Pages 1955–1965 of: *Proceedings of The Web Conference 2020*.

Kursuncu, U, Gaur, M, Lokala, U, et al. 2018. "What's ur type?" Contextualized classification of user types in marijuana-related communications using compositional multiview embedding. In: *IEEE/WIC/ACM International Conference on Web Intelligence(WI'18)*.

Kursuncu, U, Gaur, M, Castillo, C, et al. 2019. Modeling islamist extremist communications on social media using contextual dimensions: Religion, ideology, and hate. *Proceedings of the ACM on Human-Computer Interaction*, **3**(CSCW), 1–22.

Kusner, M, Sun, Y, Kolkin, N, and Weinberger, K. 2015. From word embeddings to document distances. Pages 957–966 of: *ICML'15: Proceedings of the 32nd International Conference on Machine Learning*. PMLR.

Kwon, M, Xie, S M, Bullard, K, and Sadigh, D. 2023. Reward design with language models. In: *The Eleventh International Conference on Learning Representations*.

Lai, P, Phan, N, Hu, H, et al. 2020a. Ontology-based interpretable machine learning for textual data. *2020 International Joint Conference on Neural Networks (IJCNN)*, 1–10.

Lai, Y, Lalwani, G, and Zhang, Y. 2020b. Context analysis for pre-trained masked language models. In: *EMNLP 2020*.

Lakkaraju, H, Slack, D, Chen, Y, et al. 2022. Rethinking explainability as a dialogue: A practitioner's perspective. In: *NeurIPS Workshop on Human Centered AI*.

Lamb, A M, Alias P G, Anirudh G, et al. 2016. Professor forcing: A new algorithm for training recurrent networks. *NIPS'16: Proceedings of the 30th International Conference on Neural Information Processing Systems*.

Lan, Z, Chen, M, Goodman, S, et al. 2019. ALBERT: A Lite BERT for self-supervised learning of language representations. In: *International Conference on Learning Representations*.

Lauscher, A, Glavaš, G, Ponzetto, S P, and Vulić, I. 2020. A general framework for implicit and explicit debiasing of distributional word vector spaces. Pages 8131–8138 of: *Proceedings of the AAAI Conference on Artificial Intelligence*, vol. 34.

Lawrie, D, Yang, E, Oard, D W, and Mayfield, J. 2022. Multilingual ColBERT-X. *arXiv preprint arXiv:2209.01335*.

LeCun, Y, Bengio, Y, and Hinton, G. 2015. Deep learning. *Nature*, **521**(7553), 436–444.

Lee, G, Jin, W, Alvarez-Melis, D, and Jaakkola, T. 2019. Functional transparency for structured data: A game-theoretic approach. Pages 3723–3733 of: *International Conference on Machine Learning*. PMLR.

Lee, J S Y, Liang, B, and Fong, H HM. 2021. Restatement and question generation for counsellor chatbot. Pages 1–7 of: *1st Workshop on Natural Language Processing for Programming (NLP4Prog)*.

Lee, J, Shim, M, Son, S, et al. 2022. There is no rose without a thorn: Finding weaknesses on BlenderBot 2.0 in terms of model, data and user-centric approach. https://api.semanticscholar.org/CorpusID:250407996

Lee, R S.T. 2020. *Artificial Intelligence in Daily Life*. Springer.

Lee, W, Bailer, W, Bürger, T, et al. 2012. Ontology for media resources 1.0. *W3C recommendation*.

Leiter, C, Zhang, R, Chen, Y, et al. 2024. ChatGPT: A meta-analysis after 2.5 months. *Machine Learning with Applications*, **16**, 100541.

Levesque, Hector J, Davis, Ernest, and Morgenstern, Leora. 2012. The Winograd schema challenge. *Proceedings of the Thirteenth International Conference on Principles of Knowledge Representation and Reasoning*.

Levine, Y, Lenz, B, Dagan, O, et al. 2020. SenseBERT: Driving some sense into BERT. Pages 4656–4667 of: *Proceedings of the 58th Annual Meeting of the Association for Computational Linguistics*.

Levy, S, Allaway, E, Subbiah, M, et al. 2022. SafeText: A benchmark for exploring physical safety in language models. Pages 2407–2421 of: *Proceedings of the 2022 Conference on Empirical Methods in Natural Language Processing*.

References

Lewis, P, Perez, E, Piktus, A, et al. 2020. Retrieval-augmented generation for knowledge-intensive NLP tasks. *Advances in Neural Information Processing Systems*, **33**, 9459–9474.

Li, J, Monroe, W, Ritter, A, et al. 2016. Deep reinforcement learning for dialogue generation. Pages 1192–1202 of: *Proceedings of the 2016 Conference on Empirical Methods in Natural Language Processing*.

Li, Z, Guo, R, and Kumar, S. 2022. Decoupled context processing for context augmented language modeling. *ArXiv*, abs/2210.05758.

Liang, K, Lange, P, Oh, Y J, et al. 2021. Evaluation of in-person counseling strategies to develop physical activity chatbot for women. *arXiv preprint arXiv:2107.10410*.

Liang, P, Bommasani, R, Lee, T, et al. 2022. Holistic evaluation of language models. *arXiv preprint arXiv:2211.09110*.

Libben, G. 2021. From lexicon to flexicon: The principles of morphological transcendence and lexical superstates in the characterization of words in the mind. *Frontiers in Artificial Intelligence*, **4**.

Lim, J, Kang, M, Hur, Y, et al. 2022. You truly understand what I need: Intellectual and friendly dialog agents grounding persona and knowledge. In: Goldberg, Y, Kozareva, Z, and Zhang, Y (eds), *Findings of the Association for Computational Linguistics: EMNLP 2022*. Association for Computational Linguistics.

Limbic. 2017. *Enabling the best psychological therapy*. https://limbic.ai/.

Limsopatham, N, and Collier, N. 2016. Normalising medical concepts in social media texts by learning semantic representation. Pages 1014–1023 of: *Proceedings of the 54th Annual Meeting of the Association for Computational Linguistics (Volume 1: Long Papers)*.

Lin, C. 2004. ROUGE: A package for automatic evaluation of summaries. Pages 74–81 of: *Text Summarization Branches Out*. Association of Computational Linguistics.

Lin, C, and Och, F J. 2004. Automatic evaluation of machine translation quality using longest common subsequence and skip-bigram statistics. Pages 605–612 of: *Proceedings of the 42nd Annual Meeting of the Association for Computational Linguistics (ACL-04)*.

Lin, S, Hilton, J, and Evans, O. 2022a. Teaching models to express their uncertainty in words. *Transactions on Machine Learning Research*.

Lin, S, Hilton, J, and Evans, O. 2022b. TruthfulQA: Measuring how models mimic human falsehoods. Pages 3214–3252 of: *Proceedings of the 60th Annual Meeting of the Association for Computational Linguistics (Volume 1: Long Papers)*.

Linkedevents.org. 2021. *Linked Events Ontology*. http://linkedevents.org/ontology/. Accessed: 2024-05-29.

Lipton, Z, Li, X, Gao, J, Li, al. 2018. BBQ-networks: Efficient exploration in deep reinforcement learning for task-oriented dialogue systems. In: *Proceedings of the AAAI Conference on Artificial Intelligence*, vol. 32.

Liu, C S, and Lee, T. 2016. Service quality and price perception of service: Influence on word-of-mouth and revisit intention. *Journal of Air Transport Management*, **52**, 42–54.

Liu, H, and Singh, P. 2004. Commonsense reasoning in and over natural language. Pages 293–306 of: *International Conference on Knowledge-Based and Intelligent Information and Engineering Systems*.

Liu, M, Zhang, D, and Chen, S. 2014. Attribute relation learning for zero-shot classification. *Neurocomputing*, **139**, 34–46.

Liu, S, Brewster, C, and Shaw, D. 2013. Ontologies for crisis management: A review of state of the art in ontology design and usability. Pages 1–10 of: *Proceedings of the International Conference on Information Systems for Crisis Response and Management (ISCRAM 2013)*.

Liu, S, Cho, H J, Freedman, M, et al. 2023a. RECAP: Retrieval-enhanced context-aware prefix encoder for personalized dialogue response generation. *arXiv preprint arXiv:2306.07206*.

Liu, S, Ma, W, Moore, R, et al. 2005. RxNorm: prescription for electronic drug information exchange. *IT Professional*, **7**(5), 17–23.

Liu, S, Zhu, Z, Ye, N, et al. 2017. Improved image captioning via policy gradient optimization of spider. Pages 873–881 of: *Proceedings of the IEEE International Conference on Computer Vision*.

Liu, W, Zhou, P, Zhao, Z, et al. 2020. K-BERT: Enabling language representation with knowledge graph. Pages 2901–2908 of: *Proceedings of the AAAI Conference on Artificial Intelligence*, vol. 34.

Liu, Y, Iter, D, Xu, Y, et al. 2023b. G-Eval: NLG evaluation using GPT-4 with better human alignment. *arXiv preprint arXiv:2303.16634*.

Liu, Y, Yao, Y, Ton, J, et al. 2023c. Trustworthy LLMs: A survey and guideline for evaluating large language models' alignment. *arXiv:2308.05374* [cs].

Liu, Y, Ott, M, Goyal, N, et al. 2019a. RoBERTa: A robustly optimized BERT pretraining approach. *arXiv preprint arXiv:1907.11692*.

Liu, Z, Peng, Y, and Ni, S. 2022. Personalized dialogue generation model based on BERT and hierarchical copy mechanism. *Journal of Computer and Communications*, **10**(7), 35–52.

Liu, Z, Wang, Z, Liang, P P, et al. 2019b. Deep gamblers: Learning to abstain with portfolio theory. *Advances in Neural Information Processing Systems*, **32**.

Lokala, U, Daniulaityte, R, Lamy, F, et al. 2020. DAO: An ontology for substance use epidemiology on social media and dark web. *JMIR Public Health and Surveillance*, **8**(12), e24938.

Longo, L, Goebel, R, Lecue, F, et al. 2020a. Explainable artificial intelligence: Concepts, applications, research challenges and visions. Pages 1–16 of: *International Cross-Domain Conference for Machine Learning and Knowledge Extraction*.

Longpre, S, Hou, L, Vu, T, et al. 2023. The flan collection: Designing data and methods for effective instruction tuning. *arXiv preprint arXiv:2301.13688*.

Longworth, C. 2010. *Kernel methods for text-independent speaker verification*. Ph.D. thesis, University of Cambridge.

Loshchilov, I, and Hutter, F. 2019. Decoupled Weight Decay Regularization. In: *International Conference on Learning Representations*.

Lowry, S, and Macpherson, G. 1988. A blot on the profession. *British Medical Journal (Clinical Research Ed.)*, **296**(6523), 657.

Lu, J, Valois, F, Dohler, M, and Barthel, D. 2008. Quantifying organization by means of entropy. *IEEE Communications Letters*, **12**(3), 185–187.

Lundberg, Scott M, and Lee, S. 2017. A unified approach to interpreting model predictions. *Advances in Neural Information Processing Systems*, **30**.

Lyu, X, Grafberger, S, Biegel, S, et al. 2023. Improving retrieval-augmented large language models via data importance learning. *arXiv preprint arXiv:2307.03027*.

Ma, X, Mishra, S, Beirami, A, et al. 2023. Let's do a thought experiment: Using counterfactuals to improve moral reasoning. *arXiv preprint arXiv:2306.14308*.

MacDonald, B A. 1991. Instructable systems. *Knowledge Acquisition*, **3**(4), 381–420.

Madnani, N, Tetreault, J, and Chodorow, M. 2012. Re-examining machine translation metrics for paraphrase identification. Pages 182–190 of: *Proceedings of the 2012 Conference of the North American Chapter of the Association for Computational Linguistics: Human Language Technologies*.

Majumder, B P, Berg-Kirkpatrick, T, McAuley, J, and Jhamtani, H. 2021. Unsupervised enrichment of persona-grounded dialog with background stories. Pages 585–592 of: *Proceedings of the 59th Annual Meeting of the Association for Computational Linguistics and the 11th International Joint Conference on Natural Language Processing (Volume 2: Short Papers)*.

Makni, B, and Hendler, J. 2019. Deep learning for noise-tolerant RDFS reasoning. *Semantic Web*, **10**(5), 823–862.

Malmi, E, Krause, S, Rothe, S, et al. 2019. Encode, tag, realize: High-precision text editing. *arXiv preprint arXiv:1909.01187*.

Malmi, E, Dong, Y, Mallinson, J, et al. 2022. Text Generation with Text-Editing Models. *arXiv preprint arXiv:2206.07043*.

Manakul, P, Liusie, A, and Gales, M JF. 2023. SelfCheckGPT: Zero-resource black-box hallucination detection for generative large language models. *arXiv preprint arXiv:2303.08896*.

Manas, G, Aribandi, V, Kursuncu, U, et al. 2021. Knowledge-infused abstractive summarization of clinical diagnostic interviews: Framework development study. *JMIR Mental Health*, **8**(5), e20865.

Mao, J, Yang, X, Zhang, X, et al. 2022. CLEVRER-Humans: Describing physical and causal events the human way. *Advances in Neural Information Processing Systems*, **35**, 7755–7768.

Marcus, R B. 1980. Moral dilemmas and consistency. *The Journal of Philosophy*, **77**(3), 121–136.

Marcus, Gary. 2020. The next decade in AI: four steps towards robust artificial intelligence. *arXiv preprint arXiv:2002.06177*.

Marino, K, Salakhutdinov, R, and Gupta, A. 2017. The more you know: Using knowledge graphs for image classification. Pages 2673–2681 of: *Proceedings of the IEEE Conference on Computer Vision and Pattern Recognition*.

Masse, N Y, Grant, G D, and Freedman, D J. 2018. Alleviating catastrophic forgetting using context-dependent gating and synaptic stabilization. *Proceedings of the National Academy of Sciences*, **115**(44), E10467–E10475.

Massei, S, Palitta, D, and Robol, L. 2018. Solving rank-structured sylvester and lyapunov equations. *SIAM Journal on Matrix Analysis and Applications*, **39**(4), 1564–1590.

Mayer, R C., Davis, J H., and Schoorman, F. D. 1995. An integrative model of organizational trust. *The Academy of Management Review*, **20**(3), 709–734.

McCarthy, J, and Hayes, P J. 1981. Some philosophical problems from the standpoint of artificial intelligence. Pages 431–450 of: *Readings in Artificial Intelligence*. Elsevier.

McCullagh, P. 1996. Möbius transformation and Cauchy parameter estimation. *The Annals of Statistics*, **24**(2), 787–808.

McCullough, D. 2010. *Slides for MAA Presentation 2010*. www2.math.ou.edu/~dmccullough/teaching/slides/maa2010.pdf. Accessed: 2023-05-29.

McHugh, M L. 2012. Interrater reliability: the kappa statistic. *Biochemia Medica*, **22**(3), 276–282.

Meade, N, Gella, S, Hazarika, D, et al. 2023. Using In-Context Learning to Improve Dialogue Safety. *arXiv preprint arXiv:2302.00871*.

Menick, J, Trebacz, M, Mikulik, V, et al. 2022. Teaching language models to support answers with verified quotes. *arXiv preprint arXiv:2203.11147*.

Mertes, S, Huber, T, Weitz, K, et al. 2022. Ganterfactual-counterfactual explanations for medical non-experts using generative adversarial learning. *Frontiers in Artificial Intelligence*, **5**, 825565.

META. 2017. FAIR Principles. www.go-fair.org/fair-principles/.

Michael, J, Stanovsky, G, He, L, et al. 2017. Crowdsourcing question-answer meaning representations. *CoRR*, abs/1711.05885.

Microsoft Corporation. 2023. *Bing Web Search API*. www.microsoft.com/en-us/bing/apis/bing-web-search-api. Accessed: 2023-05-29.

Mikolov, T, Sutskever, I, Chen, K, et al. 2013. Distributed representations of words and phrases and their compositionality. *Advances in Neural Information Processing Systems*, **26**.

Miles, A, and Bechhofer, S. 2009 (Aug.). *SKOS Simple Knowledge Organization System Reference*. www.w3.org/TR/skos-reference/. W3C Recommendation, 18 August 2009.

Miles, A, Matthews, B, Wilson, M, et al. 2005. SKOS core: simple knowledge organisation for the web. In: *Proceedings of the International Conference on Dublin Core and Metadata Applications*.

Miller, G A. 1995. WordNet: a lexical database for English. *Communications of the ACM*, **38**(11), 39–41.

Miller, L, and Brickley, D. 2007. *FOAF Vocabulary Specification 0.99*. http://xmlns.com/foaf/0.1/.

Miner, A, Chow, A, Adler, S, et al. 2016. Conversational agents and mental health: Theory-informed assessment of language and affect. Pages 123–130 of: *Proceedings of the Fourth International Conference on Human Agent Interaction*.

Mirzadeh, S I, Chaudhry, A, Yin, D, et al. 2022. Architecture matters in continual learning. *arXiv preprint arXiv:2202.00275*.

Mitchell, E, Noh, J, Li, S, et al. 2022. Enhancing self-consistency and performance of pre-trained language models through natural language inference. Pages 1754–1768 of: *Proceedings of the 2022 Conference on Empirical Methods in Natural Language Processing*.

Mohammadi, S, Raff, E, Malekar, J, et al. 2024. WellDunn: On the robustness and explainability of language models and large language models in identifying wellness dimensions. Pages 364–388 of: *Proceedings of the 7th BlackboxNLP Workshop: Analyzing and Interpreting Neural Networks for NLP*.

Moi, M, Rodehutskors, N, and Koch, R. 2016. An Ontology for the Use of Quality Evaluated Social Media Data in Emergencies. *IADIS International Journal on WWW/Internet*, **14**(2).

Monka, S, Halilaj, L, and Rettinger, A. 2022. A survey on visual transfer learning using knowledge graphs. *Semantic Web*, **13**(3), 477–510.

Monka, A, Halilaj, L, and Rettinger, S. 2022. A survey on visual question answering using knowledge graphs. *Frontiers in Big Data*, **5**, 838888.

Montavon, G, Binder, A, Lapuschkin, S, et al. 2019. Layer-wise relevance propagation: an overview. Pages 193–209 of: *Explainable AI: Interpreting, Explaining and Visualizing Deep Learning*. Springer

Morowitz, H J. 1955. Some order-disorder considerations in living systems. *The Bulletin of Mathematical Biophysics*, **17**(2), 81–86.

Morris, J, Lifland, E, Yoo, J, et al. 2020. TextAttack: A framework for adversarial attacks, data augmentation, and adversarial training in NLP. Pages 119–126 of: *Proceedings of the 2020 Conference on Empirical Methods in Natural Language Processing: System Demonstrations*.

Mosbach, M, Andriushchenko, M, and Klakow, D. 2020. On the stability of fine-tuning BERT: Misconceptions, explanations, and strong baselines. In: *International Conference on Learning Representations*.

Mrkšić, N, Séaghdha, D, Thomson, B, et al. 2016. Counter-fitting word vectors to linguistic constraints. Pages 142–148 of: *Proceedings of the 2016 Conference of the North American Chapter of the Association for Computational Linguistics: Human Language Technologies*.

Nabla. 2020. *Medical Chatbot Using OpenAI's GPT-3 Told a Fake Patient to Kill Themselves*. https://incidentdatabase.ai/cite/236. AI Incident Database Record #236.

Nadeem, M, Bethke, A, and Reddy, S. 2021. StereoSet: Measuring stereotypical bias in pretrained language models. In: Zong, C, Xia, F, Li, W, and Navigli, R (eds), Pages 5356–5371 of: *Proceedings of the 59th Annual Meeting of the Association for Computational Linguistics and the 11th International Joint Conference on Natural Language Processing (Volume 1: Long Papers)*.

Namvarpour, M, Pauwels, H, and Razi, A. 2025. AI-induced sexual harassment: investigating contextual characteristics and user reactions of sexual harassment by a companion chatbot. *Proceedings of the ACM on Human-Computer Interaction (CSCW)*, **9**(7), 1–28.

Nalchigar, S, and Fox, M S. 2010. An ontology for open 311 Data. *AAAI Workshop Papers 2014*.

Nangia, N, Vania, C, Bhalerao, R, et al. 2020. CrowS-Pairs: A challenge dataset for measuring social biases in masked language models. Pages 1953–1967 of: Webber, B, Cohn, T, He, Y, and Liu, Y (eds), *Proceedings of the 2020 Conference on Empirical Methods in Natural Language Processing (EMNLP)*.

Narasimhan, A G, Lazebnik, M, and Schwing, S. 2018. Out of the box: Reasoning with graph convolution nets for factual visual question answering. In: *Advances in Neural Information Processing Systems*, vol. 31.

National Library of Medicine. 2023. *Unified Medical Language System (UMLS)*. www.nlm.nih.gov/research/umls/index.html. Accessed: 2023-05-29.

Navigli, R, and Ponzetto, S P. 2010. BabelNet: Building a very large multilingual semantic network. Pages 216–225 of: *Proceedings of the 48th Annual Meeting of the Association for Computational Linguistics*.

Nelson, S J, Zeng, K, Kilbourne, J, et al. 2011. Normalized names for clinical drugs: RxNorm at 6 years. *Journal of the American Medical Informatics Association*, **18**(4), 441–448.

Nema, P, and Khapra, M M. 2018. Towards a better metric for evaluating question generation systems. Pages 3950–3959 of: *Proceedings of the 2018 Conference on Empirical Methods in Natural Language Processing*.

Névéol, A, Dupont, Y, Bezançon, J, et al. 2022. French CrowS-Pairs: Extending a challenge dataset for measuring social bias in masked language models to a language other than English. Pages 8521–8531 of: Muresan, S, Nakov, P, and Villavicencio, A (eds), *Proceedings of the 60th Annual Meeting of the Association for Computational Linguistics (Volume 1: Long Papers)*.

Ng, A Y, Jordan, M I, and Weiss, Y. 2002. On spectral clustering: Analysis and an algorithm. In: *NIPS'01: Proceedings of the 15th International Conference on Neural Information Processing Systems*.

Ngo, R, Chan, L, and Mindermann, S. 2022. The alignment problem from a deep learning perspective. *arXiv preprint arXiv:2209.00626*.

Nickel, M, Rosasco, L, Poggio, T A, et al. 2016. Holographic embeddings of knowledge graphs. Pages 1955–1961 of: *AAAI'16: Proceedings of the Thirtieth AAAI Conference on Artificial Intelligence*.

Noble, J M, Zamani, A, Gharaat, M A, et al. 2022. Developing, implementing, and evaluating an artificial intelligence–guided mental health resource navigation chatbot for health care workers and their families during and following the COVID-19 pandemic: protocol for a cross-sectional study. *JMIR Research Protocols*, **11**(7), e33717.

Norcliffe-Brown, W, Parisot, S, and Vafeias, S. 2018. Learning conditioned graph structures for interpretable visual question answering. In: *Advances in Neural Information Processing Systems*, vol. 31.

Onki Finnish Ontology Library. 2000. *Disaster - Onki Browser*. http://onki.fi/en/browser/overview/disaster. Accessed: 2024-05-29.

OpenAI. 2023. *GPT-4 Technical Report*. https://cdn.openai.com/papers/gpt-4.pdf.

Pan, A, Chan, J S, Zou, A, et al. 2023a. Do the rewards justify the means? Measuring trade-offs between rewards and ethical behavior in the MACHIAVELLI benchmark. Pages 26837–26867 of: *Proceedings of the 40th International Conference on Machine Learning*.

Pan, L, Albalak, A, Wang, X, et al. 2023b. Logic-LM: empowering large language models with symbolic solvers for faithful logical reasoning. Pages 3806–3824 of: *Findings of the Association for Computational Linguistics: EMNLP 2023*.

Papers With Code. 2023. *Natural language inference*. https://paperswithcode.com/task/natural-language-inference. Accessed: 2023-05-29.

Papineni, K, Roukos, S, Ward, T, et al. 2002. BLEU: a method for automatic evaluation of machine translation. Pages 311–318 of: *Proceedings of the 40th Annual Meeting of the Association for Computational Linguistics*.

Passant, A, Bojārs, U, Breslin, J G, et al. 2010. The SIOC project: semantically-interlinked online communities, from humans to machines. Pages 179–194 of:

Coordination, Organizations, Institutions and Norms in Agent Systems V (COIN 2009), Lecture Notes in Computer Science, vol. 6069.

Paton, H J. 1971. *The Categorical Imperative: A Study in Kant's Moral Philosophy*. University of Pennsylvania Press.

Penedo, G, Malartic, Q, Hesslow, D, et al. 2023. The RefinedWeb dataset for Falcon LLM: Outperforming curated corpora with web data, and web data only. *arXiv preprint arXiv:2306.01116*.

Peng, B, Galley, M, He, P, et al. 2022. GODEL: Large-scale pre-training for goal-directed dialog. *arXiv preprint arXiv:2206.11309*.

Pennebaker, J W, Francis, M E, Booth, R J, et al. 2001. Linguistic Inquiry and Word Count: LIWC. Lawrence Erlbaum Associates.

Pennington, J, Socher, R, and Manning, C. 2014. GloVe: Global vectors for word representation. In: *Proceedings of the 2014 Conference on Empirical Methods in Natural Language Processing (EMNLP)*.

Perez, E, Huang, S, Song, F, et al. 2022. Red teaming language models with language models. *arXiv preprint arXiv:2202.03286*.

Perry, T. 2021. LightTag: Text annotation platform. *arXiv:2109.02320* [cs].

Peters, M E., Neumann, M, Iyyer, M, et al. 2018. Deep contextualized word representations. Pages 2227–2237 of: *Proceedings of the 2018 Conference of the North American Chapter of the Association for Computational Linguistics: Human Language Technologies, Volume 1 (Long Papers)*.

Peterson, C. 2023. ChatGPT and medicine: Fears, fantasy, and the future of physicians. *The Southwest Respiratory and Critical Care Chronicles*, **11**(48), 18–30.

Petroni, F, Rocktäschel, T, Riedel, S, et al. 2019a. Language Models as Knowledge Bases? Pages 2463–2473 of: *Proceedings of the 2019 Conference on Empirical Methods in Natural Language Processing and the 9th International Joint Conference on Natural Language Processing (EMNLP-IJCNLP)*.

Petroni, F, Rocktäschel, T, Lewis, S, et al. 2019b. Language Models as Knowledge Bases? *arXiv:1909.01066* [cs].

Petroni, F, Piktus, A, Fan, A, et al. 2020. KILT: a benchmark for knowledge intensive language tasks. *arXiv preprint arXiv:2009.02252*.

Petroni, F, Piktus, A, Fan, A, et al. 2021. KILT: a benchmark for knowledge intensive language tasks. Pages 2523–2544 of: *Proceedings of the 2021 Conference of the North American Chapter of the Association for Computational Linguistics: Human Language Technologies*.

Pillutla, K, Swayamdipta, S, Zellers, R, et al. 2021. MAUVE: Measuring the gap between neural text and human text using divergence frontiers. *Advances in Neural Information Processing Systems*, vol. 34.

Posner, K, Brent, D, Lucas, C, et al. 2010. *Columbia-Suicide Severity Rating Scale (C-SSRS)*. The Research Foundation for Mental Hygiene, Inc.

Possati, L M. 2022. Psychoanalyzing artificial intelligence: the case of Replika. *AI & Society*, **38**, 1725–1738.

Pothirattanachaikul, S, Yamamoto, T, Yamamoto, Y, et al. 2020. Analyzing the effects of "people also ask" on search behaviors and beliefs. Pages 101–110 of: *Proceedings of the 31st ACM Conference on Hypertext and Social Media*.

Powell, J. 2019. Trust Me, I'm a chatbot: how artificial intelligence in health care fails the Turing test. *Journal of Medical Internet Research*, **21**(10), e16222.

Prabhakar, Arati. 2017. *A DARPA Perspective on Artificial Intelligence: The Three Waves of AI*. https://sites.nationalacademies.org/cs/groups/pgasite/documents/webpage/pga_177035.pdf. Accessed: August 11, 2025.

Prior, A, and Geffet, M. 2003. Mutual information and semantic similarity as predictors of word association strength: Modulation by association type and semantic relation. Pages 265–270 of: *Proceedings of EuroCogSci 03*.

Purohit, H, Hampton, A, Bhatt, S, et al. 2014. Identifying seekers and suppliers in social media communities to support crisis coordination. *Computer Supported Cooperative Work*, **23**, 513–545.

Purohit, H, Shalin, V L, and Sheth, A P. 2020. Knowledge graphs to empower humanity-inspired AI systems. *IEEE Internet Computing*, **24**(4), 48–54.

Pyatkin, V, Klein, A, Tsarfaty, R, et al. 2020. QADiscourse–discourse relations as QA pairs: representation, crowdsourcing and baselines. Pages 2804–2819 of: *Proceedings of the 2020 Conference on Empirical Methods in Natural Language Processing (EMNLP)*.

Qatar Computing Research Institute. 2023. *QCRI CrisisNLP*. https://crisisnlp.qcri.org/. Accessed: 2023-05-29.

Qi, W, Gong, Y, Yan, Y, et al. 2020. ProphetNet-Ads: A looking ahead strategy for generative retrieval models in sponsored search engine. Pages 305–317 of: *CCF International Conference on Natural Language Processing and Chinese Computing, 9th CCF International Conference, NLPCC 2020, Zhengzhou, China, October 14–18, 2020, Proceedings, Part II*.

Qi, X, Zeng, Y, Xie, T, Chen, P Y, Jia, R, Mittal, P, and Henderson, P. 2024. Fine-tuning aligned language models compromises safety, even when users do not intend to! In: *International Conference on Learning Representations (ICLR 2024)*.

Qian, H, Dou, Z, Zhu, Y, et al. 2021. Learning implicit user profile for personalized retrieval-based chatbot. Pages 1467–1477 of: *Proceedings of the 30th ACM International Conference on Information & Knowledge Management*.

Qian, Q, Huang, M, Zhao, H, et al. 2018. Assigning personality/profile to a chatting machine for coherent conversation generation. Pages 4279–4285 of: *Proceedings of the Twenty-Seventh International Joint Conference on Artificial Intelligence*.

Qian, X, and Oard, D W. 2021. Full-collection search with passage and document evidence: Maryland at the TREC 2021 conversational assistance track. *Proceedings of the Thirtieth Text REtrieval Conference*. https://trec.nist.gov/pubs/trec30/papers/UMD.pdf

Qiu, S, and Zhang, K. 2021. Learning personalized end-to-end task-oriented dialogue for fast and reliable adaptation. Pages 62–66 of: *2021 International Conference on Digital Society and Intelligent Systems (DSInS)*.

Quan, H, Sundararajan, V, Halfon, P, et al. 2005. Coding algorithms for defining comorbidities in ICD-9-CM and ICD-10 administrative data. *Medical Care*, **43**(11), 1130–1139.

Quartet Health. 2020 (Oct.). *How AI is helping to diagnose and treat mental health conditions*. www.quartethealth.com/coverage/how-ai-is-helping-to-diagnose-and-treat-mental-health-conditions. Accessed: 2025-08-02.

Quora. 2017. *First Quora Dataset Release: Question Pairs*. https://quoradata.quora.com/First-Quora-Dataset-Release-Question-Pairs. Accessed: 2024-08-13.

Radziwill, Nicole M. 2017. *Statistics (the Easier Way) with R*. 2nd edn. Lapis Lucera.

Rai, A. 2020. Explainable AI: From black box to glass box. *Journal of the Academy of Marketing Science*, **48**, 137–141.

Raj, H, Rosati, D, and Majumdar, S. 2022. Measuring reliability of large language models through semantic consistency. *arXiv preprint arXiv:2211.05853*.

Rajpurkar, P, Zhang, J, Lopyrev, K, et al. 2016. SQuAD: 100,000+ questions for machine comprehension of text. *arXiv preprint arXiv:1606.05250*.

Rajpurkar, P, Jia, R, and Liang, P. 2018. Know what you don't know: Unanswerable questions for SQuAD. Pages 784–789 of: *Proceedings of the 56th Annual Meeting of the Association for Computational Linguistics (Volume 2: Short Papers)*.

Rao, S, and Daumé III, H. 2018. Learning to ask good questions: Ranking clarification questions using neural expected value of perfect information. *arXiv preprint arXiv:1805.04655*.

Rashevsky, N. 1955. Life, information theory, and topology. *The Bulletin of Mathematical Biophysics*, **17**, 229–235.

Rashkin, H, Smith, E M, Li, M, et al. 2018. Towards empathetic open-domain conversation models: A new benchmark and dataset. *arXiv preprint arXiv:1811.00207*.

Rawte, V, Chakraborty, M, Roy, K, et al. TDLR: Top semantic-down syntactic language representation. In: *NeurIPS'22 Workshop on All Things Attention: Bridging Different Perspectives on Attention*.

Raza, S, Schwartz, B, and Rosella, L C. 2022. CoQUAD: A COVID-19 question answering dataset system, facilitating research, benchmarking, and practice. *BMC Bioinformatics*, **23**(1), 1–28.

Reagle, J, and Gaur, M. 2022. Spinning words as disguise: Shady services for ethical research? *First Monday*. https://firstmonday.org/ojs/index.php/fm/article/view/12350

Rebedea, T, Dinu, R, Sreedhar, M, et al. 2023. NeMo Guardrails: A toolkit for controllable and safe LLM applications with programmable rails. In: *Proceedings of the EMNLP 2023 Demo Track*. https://aclanthology.org/2023.emnlp-demo.40

Regier, D A, Kuhl, E A, and Kupfer, D J. 2013. The DSM-5: Classification and criteria changes. *World Psychiatry*, **12**(2), 92–98.

The Register. 2023. Google grilled over AI bot Med-PaLM 2 used in hospitals. *The Register*, August 8. Article covers Senator Mark Warner's questioning of Google regarding AI use in healthcare.

Řehůřek, Radim. 2023. *Phrases Model Documentation*. https://radimrehurek.com/gensim/models/phrases.html. Accessed: 2025-08-02.

Reimers, N, and Gurevych, I. 2019. Sentence-BERT: Sentence embeddings using Siamese BERT-networks. Pages 3982–3992 of: *Proceedings of the 2019 Conference on Empirical Methods in Natural Language Processing and the 9th International Joint Conference on Natural Language Processing (EMNLP-IJCNLP)*.

ReliefWeb. 1996. *ReliefWeb Taxonomy Descriptions - Disaster Types*. https://reliefweb.int/taxonomy-descriptions#disastertype. Accessed: 2024-05-29.

Ribeiro, M T, Singh, S, and Guestrin, C. 2016. "Why should I trust you?" Explaining the predictions of any classifier. Pages 1135–1144 of: *Proceedings of the 22nd ACM SIGKDD International Conference on Knowledge Discovery and Data Mining*.

Richardson, L. 2023. Our responsible approach to building guardrails for generative AI. *Google AI Blog*. https://blog.google/technology/ai/our-responsible-approach-to-building-guardrails-for-generative-ai.

Riveiro, M, and Thill, S. 2021. "That's (not) the output I expected!" On the role of end user expectations in creating explanations of AI systems. *Artificial Intelligence*, **298**, 103507.

Rodriguez, P, Crook, P A, Moon, S, et al. 2020. Information seeking in the spirit of learning: A dataset for conversational curiosity. Pages 8153–8172 of: *Proceedings of the 2020 Conference on Empirical Methods in Natural Language Processing (EMNLP)*.

Rollwage, M, Juchems, K, Habicht, J, et al. 2022. Conversational AI facilitates mental health assessments and is associated with improved recovery rates. *medRxiv*, 2022–11.

Rollwage, M, Habicht, J, Juechems, K, et al. 2023. Using conversational AI to facilitate mental health assessments and improve clinical efficiency within psychotherapy services: Real-world observational study. *JMIR AI*, 2023;2:e44358.

Romanov, A, and Shivade, C. 2018. Lessons from natural language inference in the clinical domain. Pages 1586–1596 of: *Proceedings of the 2018 Conference on Empirical Methods in Natural Language Processing*.

Rotmensch, M, Halpern, Y, Tlimat, A, et al. 2017. Learning a health knowledge graph from electronic medical records. *Scientific Reports*, **7**(1), 5994.

Roy, K, Zhang, Q, Gaur, M, et al. 2021. Knowledge infused policy gradients with upper confidence bound for relational bandits. Pages 35–50 of: *Joint European Conference on Machine Learning and Knowledge Discovery in Databases. (ECML PKDD 2021)*.

Roy, K, Gaur, M, Zhang, Q, et al. 2022a. Process knowledge-infused learning for suicidality assessment on social media. *arXiv, abs/2204.12560*.

Roy, K, Gaur, M, Rawte, V, et al. 2022b. ProKnow: process knowledge for safety constrained and explainable question generation for mental health diagnostic assistance. *UMBC Faculty Collection*.

Roy, K, Zi, Y, Gaur, M, et al. 2023a. Process knowledge-infused learning for clinician-friendly explanations. Pages 154–160 of: *Proceedings of the AAAI Second Symposium on Human Partnership with Medical Artificial Intelligence*. https://arxiv.org/abs/2306.09824.

Roy, K, Gaur, M, Soltani, M, et al. 2023b. ProKnow: Process knowledge for safety constrained and explainable question generation for mental health diagnostic assistance. *Frontiers in Big Data*, **5**, 1056728.

Rücklé, A., Eger, S, Peyrard, M, et al. 2018. Concatenated power mean word embeddings as universal cross-lingual sentence representations. *arXiv preprint arXiv:1803.01400*.

Rudin, C. 2019. Stop explaining black box machine learning models for high stakes decisions and use interpretable models instead. *Nature Machine Intelligence*, **1**(5), 206–215.

Rudinger, R, Naradowsky, J, Leonard, B, et al. 2018. Gender bias in coreference resolution. Pages 8–14 of: *Proceedings of the 2018 Conference of the North American Chapter of the Association for Computational Linguistics: Human Language Technologies, Volume 2 (Short Papers)*.

Rudra, K, Goyal, P, Ganguly, N, et al. 2018. Identifying sub-events and summarizing disaster-related information from microblogs. In: *41st AC SIGIR*.

Salazar, J, Liang, D, Nguyen, T Q., et al. 2020. Masked language model scoring. Pages 2699–2712 of: *Proceedings of the 58th Annual Meeting of the Association for Computational Linguistics*. arXiv:1910.14659 [cs, eess, stat].

Sallam, M. 2023. ChatGPT utility in healthcare education, research, and practice: systematic review on the promising perspectives and valid concerns. Page 887 of: *Healthcare*, **11**(6).

Samek, W, Montavon, G, Binder, A, et al. 2016. Interpreting the predictions of complex ML models by layer-wise relevance propagation. *arXiv preprint arXiv:1611.08191*.

Santy, S, Liang, J T, Bras, R L, et al. 2023. NLPositionality: Characterizing design biases of datasets and models. Pages 9080–9102 of: *Proceedings of the 61st Annual Meeting of the Association for Computational Linguistics (Volume 1: Long Papers)*.

Sap, M, Swayamdipta, S, Vianna, L, et al. 2022. Annotators with attitudes: How annotator beliefs and identities bias toxic language detection. Pages 5884–5906 of: *Proceedings of the 2022 Conference of the North American Chapter of the Association for Computational Linguistics: Human Language Technologies*.

Sarkar, S, Gaur, M, Chen, L K, et al. 2023. A review of the explainability and safety of conversational agents for mental health to identify avenues for improvement. *Frontiers in Artificial Intelligence*, **6**. www.frontiersin.org/journals/artificial-intelligence/articles/10.3389/frai.2023.1229805

Sarker, M K, Xie, N, Doran, D, et al. 2017. Explaining trained neural networks with semantic web technologies: First steps. In: *Proceedings of the Twelfth International Workshop on Neural-Symbolic Learning and Reasoning (NeSy 2017)*.

Sawhney, R, Neerkaje, A, and Gaur, M. 2022. A Risk-averse mechanism for suicidality assessment on social media. Pages 628–635 of: *Proceedings of the 60th Annual Meeting of the Association for Computational Linguistics (Volume 2: Short Papers)*.

Scarlini, B, Pasini, T, and Navigli, R. 2020. SensEmBERT: Context-enhanced sense embeddings for multilingual word sense disambiguation. Pages 8758–8765 of: *Proceedings of the AAAI Conference on Artificial Intelligence*, Vol. 34.

Scarselli, F, Gori, M, Tsoi, A C, et al. 2008. The graph neural network model. *IEEE Transactions on Neural Networks*, **20**(1), 61–80.

Scherrer, N, Shi, C, Feder, A, et al. 2023. Evaluating the moral beliefs encoded in LLMs. Pages 51778–51809 of: *Thirty-seventh Conference on Neural Information Processing Systems*.

Schick, T, Udupa, S, and Schütze, H. 2021. Self-diagnosis and self-debiasing: A proposal for reducing corpus-based bias in NLP. *Transactions of the Association for Computational Linguistics*, **9**(Dec.), 1408–1424.

Schlag, I, Irie, K, and Schmidhuber, J. 2021. Linear transformers are secretly fast weight programmers. Pages 9355–9366 of: *Proceedings of the 38th International Conference on Machine Learning*.

Schubert, E, Sander, J, Ester, M, et al. 2017. DBSCAN revisited, revisited: Why and how you should (still) use DBSCAN. *ACM Transactions on Database Systems (TODS)*, **42**(3), 1–21.

Sekulić, I, Aliannejadi, M, and Crestani, F. 2021. Towards facet-driven generation of clarifying questions for conversational search. Pages 167–175 of: *Proceedings* of the 2021 ACM SIGIR International Conference on Theory of Information Retrieval.

Sellam, T, Das, D, and Parikh, A. 2020. BLEURT: Learning robust metrics for text generation. Pages 7881–7892 of: *Proceedings of the 58th Annual Meeting of the Association for Computational Linguistics*.

Senarath, Y, Chan, J, Purohit, H, et al. 2021. Evaluating the relevance of UMLS knowledge base for public health informatics during disasters. In: *Proceedings of the International Conference on Information Systems for Crisis Response and Management (ISCRAM 2021)*.

SerpAPI. 2023. *SerpAPI: Search Engine Results API*. https://serpapi.com/. Accessed: 2023-05-29.

Shah, R S, Holt, F, Hayati, S A, et al. 2022a. Modeling motivational interviewing strategies on an online peer-to-peer counseling platform. *Proceedings of the ACM on Human-Computer Interaction*, **6**(CSCW2), 1–24.

Shah, R, Varma, V, Kumar, R, et al. 2022b. Goal misgeneralization: Why correct specifications aren't enough for correct goals. *arXiv preprint arXiv:2210.01790*.

Shah, A, Mishra, N, Partha Pratim, S, and Talukdar, Y. 2019. KVQA: Knowledge-aware visual question answering. Pages 8876–8884 of: *Proceedings of the AAAI Conference on Artificial Intelligence*, vol. 33.

Shaham, U, and Levy, O. 2022. What do you get when you cross beam search with nucleus sampling? Pages 38–45 of: *Proceedings of the Third Workshop on Insights from Negative Results in NLP*.

Shannon, C E. 1948. A mathematical theory of communication. *The Bell System Technical Journal*, **27**(3), 379–423.

Sharma, A, Lin, I W, Miner, A S, et al. 2021. Towards facilitating empathic conversations in online mental health support: A reinforcement learning approach. Pages 194–205 of: *Proceedings of the Web Conference 2021*.

Sharma, A, Lin, I W, Miner, A S, et al. 2023. Human–AI collaboration enables more empathic conversations in text-based peer-to-peer mental health support. *Nature Machine Intelligence*, **5**(1), 46–57.

Sharma, L, Graesser, L, Nangia, N, and Evci, U. 2019. Natural language understanding with the quora question pairs dataset. *arXiv preprint arXiv:1907.01041*.

Shaw, P, Uszkoreit, J, and Vaswani, A. 2018. Self-attention with relative position representations. Pages 464–468 of: *Proceedings of the 2018 Conference of the North American Chapter of the Association for Computational Linguistics: Human Language Technologies, Volume 2 (Short Papers)*.

Shelter Cluster. 2010. *Haiti Earthquake 2010 Response*. https://sheltercluster.org/response/haiti-earthquake-2010. Accessed: 2023-05-29.

Shen, L, Liu, L, Jiang, H, and Shi, S. 2022. On the evaluation metrics for paraphrase generation. Pages 3178–3190 of: *Proceedings of the 2022 Conference on Empirical Methods in Natural Language Processing*.

Shen, Y, Deng, Y, Yang, M, et al. 2018. Knowledge-aware attentive neural network for ranking question answer pairs. Pages 901–904 of: *The 41st International ACM SIGIR Conference on Research & Development in Information Retrieval*.

Sheth, A, and Kapanipathi, P. 2016. Semantic filtering for social data. *IEEE Internet Computing*, **20**(4), 74–78.

Sheth, A, and Thirunarayan, K. 2021. The duality of data and knowledge across the three waves of AI. *IT Professional*, **23**(3), 35–45.

Sheth, A, Avant, D, and Bertram, C. 2001. *System and method for creating a semantic web and its applications in browsing, searching, profiling, personalization and advertising*. US Patent US6311194B1.

Sheth, A, Bertram, C, Avant, D, et al. 2002. Managing semantic content for the web. *IEEE Internet Computing*, **6**(4), 80–87.

Sheth, A, Arpinar, I B, and Kashyap, V. 2004. Relationships at the heart of semantic web: Modeling, discovering, and exploiting complex semantic relationships. Pages 63–94 of: *Enhancing the Power of the Internet*. Springer.

Sheth, A, Anantharam, P, and H, Cory. 2013. Physical-cyber-social computing: An early 21st century approach. *IEEE Intelligent Systems*, **28**(1), 78–82.

Sheth, A, Anantharam, P, and Thirunarayan, K. 2014. kHealth: Proactive personalized actionable information for better healthcare. In: *Proceedings of the VLDB (Very Large Databases) Workshop on Personal Data Analytics in the Internet of Things*.

Sheth, A, Anantharam, P, and Henson, C. 2016. Semantic, cognitive, and perceptual computing: Paradigms that shape human experience. *Computer*, **49**(3), 64–72.

Sheth, A, Perera, S, Wijeratne, S, et al. 2017. Knowledge will propel machine understanding of content: extrapolating from current examples. *arXiv preprint arXiv:1707.05308*.

Sheth, A, Yip, H Y, and Shekarpour, S. 2019a. Extending patient-chatbot experience with internet-of-things and background knowledge: case studies with healthcare applications. *IEEE Intelligent Systems*, **34**(4), 24–30.

Sheth, A, Padhee, S, and Gyrard, A. 2019b. Knowledge graphs and knowledge networks: the story in brief. *IEEE Internet Computing*, **23**(4), 67–75.

Sheth, A, Gaur, M, Kursuncu, U, and Wickramarachchi, Ruwan. 2019c. Shades of knowledge-infused learning for enhancing deep learning. *IEEE Internet Computing*, **23**(6), 54–63.

Sheth, A, Gaur, M, Roy, K, et al. 2021. Knowledge-intensive language understanding for explainable AI. *IEEE Internet Computing*, **25**(5), 19–24.

Sheth, A, Gaur, M, Roy, K, et al. 2022. Process knowledge-infused AI: Toward user-level explainability, interpretability, and safety. *IEEE Internet Computing*, **26**(5), 76–84.

Sheth, A, Roy, K, and Gaur, M. 2023. Neurosymbolic artificial intelligence (why, what, and how). *IEEE Intelligent Systems*, **38**(3), 56–62.

Sheth, A P. 2003. Semantic web in action: Ontology-driven information search, integration and analysis. https://corescholar.libraries.wright.edu/knoesis/32.

Shi, L, Li, S, Yang, X, et al. 2017. Semantic health knowledge graph: semantic integration of heterogeneous medical knowledge and services. *BioMed Research International*, **2017**(1), 2858423.

Shin, R. 2023. *Google Wants its A.I. to Transform Health Care Next, as it Partners with the Mayo Clinic, Report Says*. https://fortune.com/2023/07/10/google-ai-mayo-clinic-healthcare-med-palm-2-large-language-model/#. Accessed: 2023-11-30.

Shivakumar, P G, Li, H, Knight, K, et al. 2018. Learning from past mistakes: Improving automatic speech recognition output via noisy-clean phrase context modeling. *arXiv preprint arXiv:1802.02607*.

Shuster, K, Poff, S, Chen, M, et al. 2021. Retrieval augmentation reduces hallucination in conversation. Pages 3784–3803 of: *Findings of the Association for Computational Linguistics: EMNLP 2021*.

Shwartz-Altshuler, T. 2023. *Yom Kippur War: ChatGPT Can Be Used or Military Intel, War Simulation*. www.jpost.com/business-and-innovation/opinion/article-760273. Accessed: 2023-11-30.

Siervo, M, Lara, J, Chowdhury, S, et al. 2015. Effects of the dietary approach to stop hypertension (DASH) diet on cardiovascular risk factors: a systematic review and meta-analysis. *British Journal of Nutrition*, **113**(1), 1–15.

Silver, D, Huang, A, Maddison, C J, et al. 2016. Mastering the game of Go with deep neural networks and tree search. *Nature*, **529**(7587), 484–489.

Škrlj, B, Eržen, N, Sheehan, S, et al. 2020. AttViz: Online exploration of self-attention for transparent neural language modeling. *arXiv preprint arXiv:2005.05716*.

Slack, D, Krishna, S, Lakkaraju, H, et al. 2023. Explaining machine learning models with interactive natural language conversations using TalkToModel. *Nature Machine Intelligence*, **5**(8), 873–883.

So, D R, Mańke, W, Liu, H, et al. 2021. Primer: Searching for efficient transformers for language modeling. *arXiv preprint arXiv:2109.08668*.

Soberón, G, Aroyo, L, Welty, C, et al. 2013. Measuring crowd truth: Disagreement metrics combined with worker behavior filters. In: *CrowdSem 2013 Workshop*, vol. 2.

Socher, R, Perelygin, A, Wu, J, et al. 2013. Recursive deep models for semantic compositionality over a sentiment treebank. Pages 1631–1642 of: *Proceedings of the 2013 Conference on Empirical Methods in Natural Language Processing*.

Sohail, S H. 2023. *AI Mental Health Chatbot Diagnoses Disorders with 93% Accuracy —*. https://hitconsultant.net/2023/01/23/ai-mental-health-chatbot-diagnoses-disorders-with-93-accuracy/. Accessed: 2023-07-29.

Solaiman, I, Talat, Z, Agnew, W, et al. 2023. Evaluating the social impact of generative AI systems in systems and society. *arXiv preprint arXiv:2306.05949*.

Song, K, Tan, X, Qin, T, et al. 2020. MPNet: Masked and permuted pre-training for language understanding. *Advances in Neural Information Processing Systems*, **33**, 16857–16867.

Sparrow. 2023. *Building Safer Dialogue Agents*. www.deepmind.com/blog/building-safer-dialogue-agents. Accessed: 2023-11-30.

Speer, R, Chin, J, and Havasi, C. 2017. ConceptNet 5.5: An open multilingual graph of general knowledge. Pages 4444–4451 of: *Proceedings of the Thirty-First AAAI Conference on Artificial Intelligence (AAAI-17)*.

Srivastava, B. 2021. Did chatbots miss their "Apollo Moment"? Potential, gaps, and lessons from using collaboration assistants during COVID-19. *Patterns*, **2**(8), 100308.

Srivastava, M, and Goodman, N D. 2021. Question generation for adaptive education. Pages 692–701 of: *Proceedings of the 59th Annual Meeting of the Association for Computational Linguistics and the 11th International Joint Conference on Natural Language Processing (Volume 2: Short Papers)*.

Stasaski, K, and Hearst, M A. 2017. Multiple choice question generation utilizing an ontology. Pages 303–312 of: *Proceedings of the 12th Workshop on Innovative Use of NLP for Building Educational Applications*.

Stasaski, K, and Hearst, M A. 2022. Semantic diversity in dialogue with natural language inference. Pages 85–98 of: *Proceedings of the 2022 Conference of the North American Chapter of the Association for Computational Linguistics: Human Language Technologies*.

Stefanidis, K, Pitoura, E, and Vassiliadis, P. 2006. Adding context to preferences. Pages 846–855 of: *2007 IEEE 23rd International Conference on Data Engineering*.

Stoltz, D S, and Taylor, M A. 2019. Concept mover's distance: measuring concept engagement via word embeddings in texts. *Journal of Computational Social Science*, **2**(2), 293–313.

Su, H, Shen, X, Zhao, S, et al. 2020. Diversifying dialogue generation with non-conversational text. Pages 7087–7097 of: *58th Annual Meeting of the Association for Computational Linguistics*.

Su, J, Ahmed, M, Lu, Y, et al. 2024. RoFormer: Enhanced transformer with rotary position embedding. *Neurocomputing*, **568**, 127063.

Suarez-Figueroa, M C, Gomez-Perez, A, and Fernandez-Lopez, M. 2012. The NeOn methodology for ontology engineering. Pages 9–34 of: *Ontology Engineering in a Networked World*. Springer.

Sun, C, Shrivastava, A, Singh, S, et al. 2017. Revisiting unreasonable effectiveness of data in deep learning era. Pages 843–852 of: *Proceedings of the 2017 IEEE International Conference on Computer Vision*.

Sun, Siqi, Cheng, Yu, Gan, Zhe, and Liu, Jingjing. 2019. Patient Knowledge Distillation for BERT Model Compression. Pages 4323–4332 of: *Proceedings of the 2019 Conference on Empirical Methods in Natural Language Processing and the 9th International Joint Conference on Natural Language Processing (EMNLP-IJCNLP)*.

Sun, J, Xu, C, Tang, L, et al. 2023. Think-on-Graph: Deep and responsible reasoning of large language model on knowledge graph. In: *International Conference on Representation Learning 2024 (ICLR 2024)*.

Sun, L, Huang, Y, W, H, et al. 2024. TrustLLM: Trustworthiness in large language models. *arXiv preprint arXiv:2401.05561*.

Sun, Y, Wang, S, Li, Y, et al. 2020. Ernie 2.0: A continual pre-training framework for language understanding. Pages 8968–8975 of: *Proceedings of the AAAI Conference on Artificial Intelligence*, vol. 34.

Sun, Y, Wang, S, Feng, S, et al. 2021. Ernie 3.0: Large-scale knowledge enhanced pre-training for language understanding and generation. *arXiv preprint arXiv:2107.02137*.

Sundararajan, M, Taly, A, and Yan, Q. 2017. Axiomatic attribution for deep networks. Pages 3319–3328 of: *Proceedings of the 34th International Conference on Machine Learning*.

Sutskever, I, Martens, J, Dahl, G, et al. 2013. On the importance of initialization and momentum in deep learning. Pages 1139–1147 of: *Proceedings of the 30th International Conference on International Conference on Machine Learning*.

Sweeney, C, Potts, C, Ennis, E, et al. 2021. Can Chatbots help support a person's mental health? Perceptions and views from mental healthcare professionals and experts. *ACM Transactions on Computing for Healthcare*, **2**(3), 1–15.

Tai, K S, Socher, R, and Manning, C D. 2015. Improved semantic representations From tree-structured long short-term memory networks. Pages 1556–1566 of:

Proceedings of the 53rd Annual Meeting of the Association for Computational Linguistics and the 7th International Joint Conference on Natural Language Processing (Volume 1: Long Papers).

Talat, Z, Blix, H, Valvoda, J, et al. 2021. A Word on Machine Ethics: A Response to Jiang et al. (2021). *arXiv preprint arXiv:2111.04158.*

Tang, T, Lu, H, Jiang, Y E, et al. 2023. Not All Metrics Are Guilty: Improving NLG Evaluation with LLM Paraphrasing. *arXiv preprint arXiv:2305.15067.*

Tarunesh, I, Aditya, S, and Choudhury, M. 2021. Trusting ROBERTA over BERT: Insights from checklisting the natural language inference task. *arXiv preprint arXiv:2107.07229.*

Tatman, R. 2023. *EmojiNet.* www.kaggle.com/datasets/rtatman/emojinet. Accessed: 2023-05-29.

Tavakol, M, and Dennick, R. 2011. Making sense of Cronbach's alpha. *International Journal of Medical Education*, **2**, 53.

Teney, D, Liu, L, and Van Den Hengel, A. 2017. Graph-structured representations for visual question answering. Pages 1–9 of: *Proceedings of the 2017 IEEE Conference on Computer Vision and Pattern Recognition.*

Tenney, I, Xia, P, Chen, B, et al. 2018. What do you learn from context? Probing for sentence structure in contextualized word representations. In: *7th International Conference on Learning Representations, ICLR 2019.*

Thiruvalluru, R K, Gaur, M, Thirunarayan, K, et al. 2021. Comparing suicide risk insights derived from clinical and social media data. *AMIA Summits on Translational Science Proceedings*, **2021**, 364.

Thoppilan, R, De Freitas, D, Hall, J, et al. 2022a. LaMDA: Language Models for Dialog Applications. *arXiv preprint arXiv:2201.08239.*

Thoppilan, R, De Freitas, D, Hall, J, et al. 2022b. LaMDA: Language Models for Dialog Applications. *CoRR*, abs/2201.08239.

Tilwani, D, Bradshaw, J, Sheth, A, et al. 2023. ECG recordings as predictors of very early autism likelihood: a machine learning approach. *Bioengineering*, **10**(7), 827.

Tlili, A, Shehata, B, Adarkwah, M A, et al. 2023. What if the devil is my guardian angel: ChatGPT as a case study of using chatbots in education. *Smart Learning Environments*, **10**(1), 15.

Tonon, A, Khare, P, Burel, G, et al. 2018 (June). Classifying crises-information relevancy with semantics. In: *Proceedings of the Extended Semantic Web Conference (ESWC 2018).*

Topp, C W, Østergaard, S D, Søndergaard, S, et al. 2015. The WHO-5 Well-Being Index: a systematic review of the literature. *Psychotherapy and Psychosomatics*, **84**(3), 167–176.

Touvron, H, Martin, L, Stone, K, et al. 2023. Llama 2: Open foundation and fine-tuned chat models. *arXiv preprint arXiv:2307.09288.*

Trella, A L, Zhang, K W, Nahum-Shani, I, et al. 2022. Designing reinforcement learning algorithms for digital interventions: pre-implementation guidelines. *Algorithms*, **15**(8), 255.

Tyagi, N, Sarkar, S, and Gaur, M. 2023a. Leveraging knowledge and reinforcement learning for enhanced reliability of language models. Pages 4320–4324 of: *Proceedings of the 32nd ACM International Conference on Information and Knowledge Management.*

Tyagi, N, Shiri, A, Sarkar, S, et al. 2023b. Simple is better and large is not enough: Towards ensembling of foundational language models. *arXiv preprint arXiv:2308.12272.*

Uban, A, Chulvi, B, and Rosso, P. 2021. An emotion and cognitive based analysis of mental health disorders from social media data. *Future Generation Computer Systems*, **124**, 480–494.

United Nations Office for the Coordination of Humanitarian Affairs (OCHA), Centre for Humanitarian Data. 2023. *The State of Open Humanitarian Data 2023: Assessing Data Availability across Humanitarian Crises.* United Nations OCHA Centre for Humanitarian Data. https://data.humdata.org/dataset/2048a947-5714-4220-905b-e662cbcd14c8/resource/9d4121c6-b32b-4eb8-a707-209c79241970/download/state-of-open-humanitarian-data-2023.pdf.

United Nations Office for the Coordination of Humanitarian Affairs (UNOCHA). 2024. *UNOCHA Humanitarian Response Vocabulary.* https://vocabulary.unocha.org/. Accessed: 2024-05-29.

United Nations Office for the Coordination of Humanitarian Affairs (OCHA), Centre for Humanitarian Data. 2023 (February). *The State of Open Humanitarian Data 2023: Assessing Data Availability Across Humanitarian Crises.* Tech. rept. United Nations OCHA Centre for Humanitarian Data, The Hague. Fourth edition.

University of Toronto. 2010. *IContact - Institute for Aerospace Studies (UTIAS).* http://ontology.eil.utoronto.ca/icontact.html. Accessed: 2024-05-29.

U.S. Department of Health and Human Services. 2015. *2015 Dietary Guidelines.* https://health.gov/our-work/nutrition-physical-activity/dietary-guidelines/previous-dietary-guidelines/2015. Accessed: 2023-05-29.

U.S. Department of Health and Human Services and U.S. Department of Agriculture. 2023. *Dietary guidelines for Americans.* www.dietaryguidelines.gov. Accessed: 2023-05-29.

Ushahidi. 2023. *Crisis preparedness platform.* www.ushahidi.com/case-studies/crisis-preparedness-platform. Accessed: 2023-05-29.

Van der Maaten, L, and Hinton, G. 2008. Visualizing data using t-SNE. *Journal of Machine Learning Research*, **9**(11).

Varshney, K R. 2022. *Trustworthy Machine Learning.* Self-published / Available at trustworthymachinelearning.com. ISBN 979-8-41-190395-9, licensed under CC BY-ND 2.0.

Vaswani, A, Shazeer, N, Parmar, N, et al. 2017a. Attention is all you need. Pages 5998–6008 of: *Advances in Neural Information Processing Systems (NeurIPS) 2017.*

Vo, K, Pham, D, Nguyen, M, et al 2017. Combination of domain knowledge and deep learning for sentiment analysis. Pages 162–173 of: *International Workshop on Multi-disciplinary Trends in Artificial Intelligence (MIWAI 2017).*

Vrandečić, D, and Krötzsch, M. 2014. Wikidata: a free collaborative knowledgebase. *Communications of the ACM*, **57**(10), 78–85.

Walker, M A, Litman, D J, Kamm, C A, and Abella, A. 1997. PARADISE: A framework for evaluating spoken dialogue agents. *arXiv preprint cmp-lg/9704004.*

Wang, A, Singh, A, Michael, J, et al. 2018a. GLUE: A multi-task benchmark and analysis platform for natural language understanding. Pages 353–355 of: *Proceedings of the 2018 EMNLP Workshop BlackboxNLP: Analyzing and Interpreting Neural Networks for NLP.*

Wang, A, Singh, A, Michael, J, et al. 2018b. GLUE: A multi-task benchmark and analysis platform for natural language understanding. Pages 353–355 of: *Proceedings of the 2018 EMNLP Workshop BlackboxNLP: Analyzing and Interpreting Neural Networks for NLP.*

Wang, A, Pruksachatkun, Y, Nangia, N, et al. 2019a. Superglue: A stickier benchmark for general-purpose language understanding systems. *Advances in Neural Information Processing Systems*, vol. 32.

Wang, P, Li, L, Chen, L, et al. 2023a. Large language models are not fair evaluators. Pages 9440–9450 of: *Proceedings of the 62nd Annual Meeting of the Association for Computational Linguistics (Volume 1: Long Papers).*

Wang, Q, Mao, Z, Wang, B, and Guo, L. 2017. Knowledge graph embedding: A survey of approaches and applications. *IEEE Transactions on Knowledge and Data Engineering*, **29**(12), 2724–2743.

Wang, R, Tang, D, Duan, N, et al. 2020. K-adapter: Infusing knowledge into pre-trained models with adapters. *arXiv preprint arXiv:2002.01808.*

Wang, R, Tang, D, Duan, N, et al. 2021a. K-Adapter: Infusing Knowledge into Pre-Trained Models with Adapters. Pages 1405–1418 of: *Findings of the Association for Computational Linguistics: ACL-IJCNLP 2021.*

Wang, X, Wang, D, Xu, C, et al. 2019b. Explainable reasoning over knowledge graphs for recommendation. Pages 5329–5336 of: *Proceedings of the AAAI Conference on Artificial Intelligence*, vol. 33.

Wang, X, Kapanipathi, P, Musa, R, et al. 2019c. Improving natural language inference using external knowledge in the science questions domain. Pages 7208–7215 of: *Proceedings of the AAAI Conference on Artificial Intelligence*, vol. 33.

Wang, X, Gao, T, Zhu, Z, et al. 2021c. KEPLER: A unified model for knowledge embedding and pre-trained language representation. *Transactions of the Association for Computational Linguistics*, **9**, 176–194.

Wang, X, Wei, J, Schuurmans, D, et al. 2022. Self-consistency improves chain of thought reasoning in language models. In: *The Eleventh International Conference on Learning Representations.* https://openreview.net/forum?id=1PL1NIMMrw

Wang, Y, Yu, Z, Zeng, Z, et al. 2023b. PandaLM: An automatic evaluation benchmark for LLM instruction tuning optimization. *arXiv preprint arXiv:2306.05087.*

Wang, Z, Zhang, J, Feng, J, and Chen, Z. 2014. Knowledge graph embedding by translating on hyperplanes. Pages 1112–1119 of: *AAAI*, vol. 14.

Warstadt, A, Singh, A, and Bowman, S R. 2019. Neural network acceptability judgments. *Transactions of the Association for Computational Linguistics*, **7**, 625–641.

Wei, J, Tay, Y, Bommasani, R, et al. 2022. Emergent abilities of large language models. *arXiv preprint arXiv:2206.07682.*

Weick, Karl E. 1995. *Sensemaking in Organizations.* Vol. 3. Sage.

Weidinger, L, Mellor, J, Rauh, M, et al. 2021. Ethical and social risks of harm from language models. *arXiv preprint arXiv:2112.04359.*

Welbl, J, Glaese, A, Uesato, J, et al. 2021. Challenges in detoxifying language models. *arXiv preprint arXiv:2109.07445.*

Weld, H, Huang, G, Lee, J, et al. 2021. CONDA: a contextual dual-annotated dataset for in-game toxicity understanding and detection. *arXiv preprint arXiv:2106.06213.*

References

Welivita, A, and Pu, P. 2022a. Curating a large-scale motivational interviewing dataset using peer support forums. Pages 3315–3330 of: *Proceedings of the 29th International Conference on Computational Linguistics*.

Welivita, A, and Pu, P. 2022b. HEAL: A knowledge graph for distress management conversations. Pages 11459–11467 of: *Proceedings of the AAAI Conference on Artificial Intelligence*, vol. 36.

Westra, H A., Aviram, A, and Doell, F K. 2011. Extending Motivational Interviewing to the Treatment of Major Mental Health Problems: Current Directions and Evidence. Extending motivational interviewing to the treatment of major mental health problems: Current directions and evidence. *Canadian Journal of Psychiatry*, **56**(11), 643–650.

Wick, M, Vatant, B., and Christophe, B. 2015. Geonames ontology. www.geonames.org/ontology.

Wickramarachchi, R, Henson, C, and Sheth, A. 2021. Knowledge-infused learning for entity prediction in driving scenes. *Frontiers in Big Data*, **4**, 759110.

Wijeratne, S, Balasuriya, L, Sheth, A, and Doran, D. 2017. Emojinet: An open service and API for emoji sense discovery. *arXiv preprint arXiv:1707.04652*.

Wijesiriwardene, T, Inan, H, Kursuncu, U, et al. 2020. ALONE: A dataset for toxic behavior among adolescents on Twitter. Pages 427–439 of: *12th International Conference on Social Informatics*.

Williams, A, Nangia, N, and Bowman, S R. 2018a. A broad-coverage challenge corpus for sentence understanding through inference. Pages 1112–1122 of: *Proceedings of the 2018 Conference of the North American Chapter of the Association for Computational Linguistics: Human Language Technologies, Volume 1 (Long Papers)*.

Williams, A, Nangia, N, and Bowman, S R. 2018b. The multi-genre NLI corpus. https://cims.nyu.edu/~sbowman/multinli/.

Williams, R J, and Z, D. 1989. A learning algorithm for continually running fully recurrent neural networks. *Neural Computation*, **1**(2), 270–280.

Wiseman, S, and Rush, A M. 2016. Sequence-to-sequence learning as beam-search optimization. Pages 1296–1306 of: *Proceedings of the 2016 Conference on Empirical Methods in Natural Language Processing*.

Wolf, M J, Miller, K, and Grodzinsky, F S. 2017. Why we should have seen that coming: comments on Microsoft's Tay "experiment," and wider implications. *ACM SIGCAS Computers and Society*, **47**(3), 54–64.

Wolf, T, Sanh, V, Chaumond, J, and Delangue, C. 2019a. TransferTransfo: A Transfer Learning Approach for Neural Network Based Conversational Agents. *arXiv preprint arXiv:1901.08149*.

Wolf, T, Debut, L, Sanh, V, et al. 2019b. Hugging Face's transformers: State-of-the-art natural language processing. *arXiv preprint arXiv:1910.03771*.

Woo, T, Nam, W, Ju, Y, and Lee, S. 2023. Compensatory debiasing For gender imbalances in language models. Pages 1–5 of: *ICASSP 2023-2023 IEEE International Conference on Acoustics, Speech and Signal Processing (ICASSP)*.

Wu, B, Li, M, Wang, Z, Chen, et al. 2020a. Guiding variational response generator to exploit persona. Pages 53–65 of: *Proceedings of the 58th Annual Meeting of the Association for Computational Linguistics*.

Wu, Z, Helaoui, R, Kumar, V, et al. 2020b. Towards detecting need for empathetic response in motivational interviewing. Pages 497–502 of: *Companion Publication of the 2020 International Conference on Multimodal Interaction.*

Xenos, A, Pavlopoulos, J, and Androutsopoulos, I. 2021. Context sensitivity estimation in toxicity detection. Pages 140–145 of: *Proceedings of the 5th Workshop on Online Abuse and Harms (WOAH 2021).*

Xiao, D, Li, Y, Zhang, H, et al. 2021. ERNIE-Gram: Pre-training with explicitly NGram masked language modeling for natural language understanding. Pages 1702–1715 of: *Proceedings of the 2021 Conference of the North American Chapter of the Association for Computational Linguistics: Human Language Technologies.*

Xu, J, Ju, Da, Li, M, et al. 2020. Recipes for safety in open-domain chatbots. *arXiv preprint arXiv:2010.07079.*

Xu, Y, Zhu, C, Wang, S, et al. Human parity on commonsense QA: Augmenting self-attention with external attention. Pages 2767–2775 of: *Proceedings of the Thirty-First International Joint Conference on Artificial Intelligence (IJCAI-22).*

Xu, Z, and Ke, Y. 2016. Effective and efficient spectral clustering on text and link data. Pages 357–366 of: *Proceedings of the 25th ACM International on Conference on Information and Knowledge Management.*

Yadav, S, Ekbal, A, Saha, S, et al. 2018. Multi-Task Learning Framework for Mining Crowd Intelligence towards Clinical Treatment. Pages 271–277 of: *Proceedings of the 2018 Conference of the North American Chapter of the Association for Computational Linguistics: Human Language Technologies, Volume 2 (Short Papers).*

Yamada, I, Asai, A, Sakuma, J, et al. 2020. Wikipedia2Vec: An efficient toolkit for learning and visualizing the embeddings of words and entities from Wikipedia. Pages 23–30 of: *Proceedings of the 2020 Conference on Empirical Methods in Natural Language Processing: System Demonstrations.*

Yang, B, and Mitchell, T M. 2017. Leveraging knowledge bases in LSTMs for improving machine reading. Pages 1436–1446 of: *Proceedings of the 55th Annual Meeting of the Association for Computational Linguistics (Volume 1: Long Papers).*

Yang, C, Wang, X, Lu, Y, et al. 2024. Large language models as optimizers. In: *International Conference on Learning Representations (ICLR) 2024.*

Yang, J, Xiao, G, Shen, Y, et al. 2021. A survey of knowledge enhanced pre-trained models. *arXiv preprint arXiv:2110.00269.*

Yang, L, Chen, H, Li, Z, et al. 2025. ChatGPT is not enough: Enhancing large language models with knowledge graphs for fact-aware language modeling. *Proceedings of the 34th ACM International Conference on Information and Knowledge Management (CIKM).*

Yang, Y, Tresp, V, Wunderle, M, and Fasching, P A. 2018a. Explaining therapy predictions with layer-wise relevance propagation in neural networks. Pages 152–162 of: *2018 IEEE International Conference on Healthcare Informatics (ICHI).*

Yang, Y, Tau Y, Wen, and Meek, C. 2018b. HotpotQA: A Dataset for Diverse, Explainable Multi-hop Question Answering. Pages 2369–2380 of: *Proceedings* of the 2018 Conference on Empirical Methods in Natural Language Processing (EMNLP).

Yang, Z, Dai, Z, Yang, Y, et al. 2019. XLNet: Generalized autoregressive pretraining for language understanding. Pages 5753–5763 of: *Advances in Neural Information Processing Systems (NeurIPS) 2019*.

Yang, Z, Yang, D, Dyer, C, et al. 2016. Hierarchical attention networks for document classification. Pages 1480–1489 of: *Proceedings of the 2016 Conference of the North American Chapter of the Association for Computational Linguistics: Human Language Technologies (NAACL-HLT)*.

Yao, S, Zhao, J, Yu, D, et al. 2023. ReAct: Synergizing reasoning and acting in language models. In: *Proceedings of the International Conference on Learning Representations (ICLR) 2023*.

Yao, S, Yu, D, Zhao, J, et al. 2023a. Tree of thoughts: Deliberate problem solving with large language models. In: *Advances in Neural Information Processing Systems (NeurIPS) 2023*.

Yao, X, Mikhelson, M, Watkins, S C, et al. 2023b. Development and evaluation of three chatbots for postpartum mood and anxiety disorders. *arXiv preprint arXiv:2308.07407*.

Yazdavar, A Hossein, A, Hussein S., et al. 2017. Semi-supervised approach to monitoring clinical depressive symptoms in social media. Pages 1191–1198 of: *Proceedings of the IEEE/ACM International Conference on Advances in Social Networks Analysis and Mining (ASONAM)*.

Yin, W, Hay, J, and Roth, D. 2019. Benchmarking zero-shot text classification: Datasets, evaluation and entailment approach. Pages 3914–3923 of: *Proceedings of the 2019 Conference on Empirical Methods in Natural Language Processing and the 9th International Joint Conference on Natural Language Processing (EMNLP-IJCNLP)*.

Young, T, Xing, F, Pandelea, V, et al. 2022. Fusing task-oriented and open-domain dialogues in conversational agents. In: *Proceedings of the Thirty-Sixth AAAI Conference on Artificial Intelligence (AAAI) 2022*.

Zafar, M R, and Khan, N M. 2019. DLIME: A deterministic local interpretable model-agnostic explanations approach for computer-aided diagnosis systems. In: *Proceedings of the ACM SIGKDD Workshop on Explainable AI/ML (XAI) for Accountability, Fairness, and Transparency*. ACM.

Zamani, H, Dumais, S, Craswell, N, et al. 2020. Generating clarifying questions for information retrieval. Pages 418–428 of: *Proceedings of The Web Conference 2020*.

Zellers, R, Holtzman, A, Bisk, Y, et al. 2019. HellaSwag: Can a machine really finish your sentence? Pages 4791–4800 of: *Proceedings of the 57th Annual Meeting of the Association for Computational Linguistics*.

Zhang, H, Goodfellow, I, Metaxas, D, and Odena, A. 2019a. Self-attention generative adversarial networks. Pages 7354–7363 of: *Proceedings of the 36th International Conference on Machine Learning*.

Zhang, H, Liu, Z, Xiong, C, and Liu, Z. 2019b. Grounded conversation generation as guided traverses in commonsense knowledge graphs. Pages 2031–2043 of: *Proceedings of the 58th Annual Meeting of the Association for Computational Linguistics (ACL)*.

Zhang, S, Dinan, E, Urbanek, J, et al. 2018. Personalizing dialogue agents: I have a dog, do you have pets too? Pages 2204–2213 of: *Proceedings of the 56th Annual Meeting of the Association for Computational Linguistics (Volume 1: Long Papers)*.

Zhang, T, Kishore, V, Wu, F, et al. 2020. BERTScore: Evaluating Text Generation with BERT. In: *8th International Conference on Learning Representations, ICLR 2020*.

Zhang, Y, Li, Y, Cui, L, et al. 2023. Siren's song in the AI ocean: A survey on hallucination in large language models. *Transactions of the Association for Computational Linguistics*, **12**, 1234–1260.

Zhang, Z, Han, X, Liu, Z, et al. 2019d. ERNIE: Enhanced language representation with informative entities. *arXiv preprint arXiv:1905.07129*.

Zhang, Z, Han, X, Liu, Z, et al. 2019e. ERNIE: enhanced language representation with informative entities. Pages 1441–1451 of: *Proceedings of the 57th Annual Meeting of the Association for Computational Linguistics*.

Zhao, J, Wang, T, Yatskar, M, et al. 2018. Gender bias in coreference resolution: evaluation and debiasing methods. Pages 15–20 of: *Proceedings of the 2018 Conference of the North American Chapter of the Association for Computational Linguistics: Human Language Technologies, Volume 2 (Short Papers)*.

Zheng, L, Chiang, W, Sheng, Y, et al. 2023. Judging LLM-as-a-judge with MT-bench and chatbot arena. *arXiv preprint arXiv:2306.05685*.

Zhong, C, Jianwei, J, Li, S, Xu, Y, and Yin, Y. 2021. Learning to generate scene graph from natural language supervision. Pages 1803–1814 of: *Proceedings of the 2021 IEEE/CVF International Conference on Computer Vision*.

Zhou, J, and Bhat, S. 2021. Paraphrase generation: A survey of the state of the art. Pages 5075–5086 of: *Proceedings of the 2021 Conference on Empirical Methods in Natural Language Processing*.

Zhou, J, Jiawen, D, Mi, F, et al. 2022a. Towards identifying social bias in dialog systems: framework, dataset, and benchmark. Pages 3577–3587 of: *Findings of the Association for Computational Linguistics: EMNLP 2022*.

Zhou, K, Jurafsky, D, and Hashimoto, T. 2023. Navigating the grey area: How expressions of uncertainty and overconfidence affect language models. Pages 5506–5524 of: *Proceedings of the 2023 Conference on Empirical Methods in Natural Language Processing (EMNLP)*.

Zhou, Y, Booth, S, Ribeiro, M T, and Shah, J. 2022b. Do feature attribution methods correctly attribute features? Pages 9623–9633 of: *Proceedings of the AAAI Conference on Artificial Intelligence*, vol. 36.

Zielasek, J, Reinhardt, I, Schmidt, L, et al. 2022. Adapting and implementing apps for mental healthcare. *Current Psychiatry Reports*, **24**(9), 407–417.

Ziems, C, Yu, J, Wang, Y, et al. 2022. The moral integrity corpus: A benchmark for ethical dialogue systems. Pages 3755–3773 of: *Proceedings of the 60th Annual Meeting of the Association for Computational Linguistics (Volume 1: Long Papers)*.

Zirikly, A, and Dredze, M. 2022. Explaining models of mental health via clinically grounded auxiliary tasks. Pages 30–39 of: *Proceedings of the Eighth Workshop on Computational Linguistics and Clinical Psychology*.

Index

AAAI conference, ix
ablation study, 118
absolute learning, 219
abstention rule, 217
abstraction, 50, 221
accessible, ix
accessible technologies, ix
activation function, 96
active communication, 185
active learning, 8
AdamW optimizer, 116
additive consistency, 230
adherence
   VMHA, 198
adherence to standards, ix
ADOS, 59
adversarial attacks, 49, 231
adversarial perturbation, 210
adversarial prompting, 209
Aggregation Ensemble (AE), 113
AI, *see* artificial intelligence
AI alignment, 226
AI for social good, x
albert-xxlarge-v2, 253
Alchemy API, 38
ALLEVIATE, 194
AlpacaFarm, 225
AlphaFold, ix
AlphaGo, 100
Amazon Mechanical Turk, 34
ambiguous entities, 61
analogy, 50
ANEW, 56
annotation, 88
annotator agreement, 88

annotators, 237
ANOVA (Analysis of Variance), 170
answerability test, 217
anti-stereotype, 246
anti-stereotypical statements, 247
anxiety, 219
Anxiety Disorder (AD), 139
API limitations, 236
application-specific evaluation methods, x
artificial intelligence, ix
asthma, 36
attention mechanism, 40, 71, 213
attribution scores, 213
Attviz, 199
AUC (Area Under Curve), 87
AUROC (Area Under ROC), 136
autoencoders, 45, 100
automatic KG construction, x
autonomous vehicles, 6, 75
autoregressive models, 203
average number of unsafe matches, 138

BabelNet, 61
Babylon, 201
backpropagation, 98
BART sentiment score, 208
BARTScore, 225
batch normalization, 116
batch size, 116
Bayes' rule, 109
Bayesian framework, 109
beam search, 178
beam search optimization, 129
benchmarking, x, 236, 246
Bengio, Yoshua, ix

300

Index

BERT, 11, 58, 204
bert-large-uncased, 253
bert-viz, 152
BERTScore, 70, 156, 205
Bessel's correction, 253
Bi-LSTM, 74
bias awareness, 245
bias benchmarks, 246
bias detection, 244
bias determination, 257
bias mitigation, 243
bias-benchmark datasets, 244
Bilingual Evaluation Understudy (BLEU), 209
binary classification task, 249
binary cross entropy loss, 114
Bing Search API, 137
BioBert, 102
biological differences, 244
BioPortal, 190
black box effect, 187
black box models, 187, 203
blanks, 248
Blenderbot, 191
BLEU, 44
BLEU score, 177, 208
BLEURT, 44, 164, 226
blind evaluation, 170
bot baked in, 192
bot-adversarial dialogue, 192
branch and bound method, 141
brittleness, 223
broader analysis, 257

C-SSRS (Columbia Suicide Severity Rating Scale), 191
CAGE, 99
CalibratedMath, 210
calibration, 211, 250
CANARD dataset, 166
Cardiovascular Disease Ontology (CDO), 104
CAsT-19 (Conversational Assistance Track) dataset, 159
CBOW, 73
CC dataset, 196
CC-44 dataset, 196
chain-of-thought reasoning, 53, 220
chance-adjusted measures, 250
ChaosGPT, 199
chatbot, 9
ChatGPT, 181, 203
chi-square test, 245, 255

chit-chat conversations, 172
CI, *see* confidence interval
clarifying questions, 156
Claude, 207
CLEVERER-Humans, 206
clinical assessment methods, 205
clinical decision-making, 206
Clinical Diagnostic Interviewing (CDI), 201
clinical expertise, 204
clinical knowledge, 205
clinical named entity recognition, 192
clinical practice guidelines (CPGs), 131, 205
clinical specifications, 189
ClinicalT5-large, 215
closed world assumption, 130
CLS token, 152
co-occurrence probability, 111
COBIAS, *see* context-oriented bias indicator and assessment score
cognition, 47
Cognitive Behavioral Therapy (CBT), 195
cognitive theories, x
Cohen's kappa, 112, 211, 250
cohort, 248
cold start problem, 67
Columbia Suicide Severity Rating Scale (C-SSRS), 70
common-sense knowledge, 120, 210
CommonSense, 221
commonsense inference, 228
commonsense inference task, 175
Commonsense Norm Bank, 228
commonsense reasoning, 102, 228
CompanionMX, 194
compositional diversity, 157
computational social science, 128
computationally infeasible, 254
compute constraints, 242
computer vision, 68, 206
concept abstraction, 216
concept classes, 69
Concept Mover Distance, 157
concept phrases, 79
ConceptNet, 61
conceptual entities, 61
conceptual flow, 58, 131
conceptual reasoning, 206
condition evaluation function, 146
confidence interval, 255
consistency checks, 228

consistency lexicons, 225
constituency parser, 160
constituency parsing, 78
constitution (Anthropic), 199
constraints, 213
constraints-based loss function, 96
content moderation, 245
context, 243, 245
Context Awareness (CA), 220
context insertion, 246
context vector, 144
context-added versions, 251
context-addition, 248
context-addition points, 245
context-free grammar, 75
context-oriented bias indicator and assessment score, 245
context-sensitivity estimation, 246
context-variance, 253
contextual considerations, 244
contextual reliability, 245
Contextual Rewards (CR), 220
contextualization, 66, 172, 221
contrastive fine-tuning, 174
convergence pattern, 254
conversation templates, 202
conversational agents, x, 56, 134, 141, 230
conversational information seeking, 155
convex optimization, 147
convolutional neural network (CNN), 45, 76
CoPilots, x
coreference, 115
coreference resolution, 160, 246
cosine distance, 234
cosine similarity, 19, 70, 205
CounselChat dataset, 196
counter-fitting, 73
CREST framework, 203
 assessment, 224
crisis informatics, 93
crisis management, ix, 8, 13, 75
CrisisNLP, 25
Cronbach's alpha, 255
cross-correlation matrix, 94
cross-domain performance, 171
cross-encoder and bi-encoder, 174
cross-entropy loss, 141
crowd-sourced pairs, 247
crowd-sourced training data, 243
crowdsourcing, 112
CrowS-Pairs, 246, 257

CSSRS 2.0, 148
cumulative study, 82
curiosity-driven question generation, 155
curriculum learning, 98

DASH Diet Plan, 132
data augmentation, 231
data collection, 248
data creation agent, 157
data imbalance, 250
data mining, x
DBPedia, 55
DBSCAN, 27
debiasing, 246
debiasing LLMs, 243
deceptive alignment, 220
decision trees, 134
decoding step, 238
deep infusion, 55, 121
Deep Learning, 12
deep neural language models, 74
definitive judgments, 257
degree of freedom, 253
Delphi, 228
demographics, 243
Dense Passage Retriever (DPR), 162, 217
dependency parsing, 78
depression, 215
depression assessment, 152
Depression Ontology, 216
DepressionKG, 36
DEPSUB, 27
depth-first search, 161
descriptive evaluation, 230
desiderata, 254
deterministic, 238
deterministic dropout, 130
Diagnostic and Statistical Manual for Mental Health Disorders, 205
DialoGPT, 192
dialogue system, 214
differential knowledge, 125
differential knowledge engine, 127
differential sub-knowledge graph, 127
differing spans, 247
DIKW pyramid, 36
dimensionality reduction, 81
DiSafety dataset, 199, 218
disambiguation, 244
discriminative weight matrix, 104
distillation, 141

Index

distributional drift, 128
distributional semantics, 61
Diversity in Generation (DiG), 190
diversity of contexts, 257
domain constraints, 52
domain knowledge, 206
drastic shift, 256
DSM-5, 64, 189, *see also Diagnostic and Statistical Manual for Mental Health Disorders*
dual form of neural network, 129
dynamic knowledge retrieval, 172
dynamic knowledge-aware passage retrieval, 157

e-LLMs, *see* ensemble of LLMs
early stopping, 150
ELECTRA, 177
Electronic Medical Records (EMR), 37
ELMo, 74
Elo Rating, 225
embeddings, 26
EMMA (VMHA), 194
EmojiNet, 64
EmoKG, 190
emotion ontologies, 190
Empathetic Dialogues dataset, 196
enriched word embeddings, 73
ensemble learning, 112
ensemble of LLMs, 206
   deep ensemble, 213
   semi-deep ensembling, 212
   shallow ensembling, 211
entailment constraints, 157
entity normalization (EN), 69
entropy of distribution, 237
epidemiology, 75
ERNIE, 58
ethical assumptions, 240
ethics, 227
Euclidean distance, 83
evaluation dataset, 241
evaluation strategies, 239
evaluator, 213
event detection, 98
explainability, 1, 10, 40, 49, 203
   system-level, 40, 69
   user-level, 41, 69
explainability by design, 214
explainable AI (XAI), 43, 49

explainable data, 78
external knowledge integration, 212
external knowledge sources, 246
extrinsic methods, 238

F1 score, 28, 136, 220
fabrication
   in AI, 184
Facebook Curiosity (FBC) dataset, 159
FactCC, 225
factual knowledge-based scoring, 213
factuality, 211
FAIR principles, 196
FAISS (Facebook AI Semantic Search), 174
Falcon, 208
false alarms, 102
false beliefs, 238
false negatives, 82
false positive rate (FPR), 85
false positives, 85
FastText, 26, 74
feature attribution, 49
federated pipelines, 53
feedforward neural networks, 204
FEMA, 11
few-shot approach, 232
few-shot learning, 173
fill-in-blanks, 245
fine-grained features (FGF), 105
fine-tuning, 11, 99, 204
first-order logic, 51
Fitbit, 37
Flan T5, 205
Fleiss' kappa, 211, 250
FOAF, 15
FoCus dataset, 178
follow-up questions, 156
formal logic, 51
forward-backward pass, 110
fragments, 256
frequency of occurrence, 252
Frobenius norm, 105, 128
fused embeddings, 114
future directions, x
future research, 257

GAD-7 (Generalized Anxiety Disorder-7), 65, 132, 219
Gambler Loss, 82
game-theoretic transparency, 200

GANs (Generative Adversarial Networks), 99
Gaussian kernel, 147
gender bias, 244
generation randomness, 238
generative AI, 48, 205
generative evaluator tuning, 224
generative language models, 134
generative models, 4
generative-adversarial reinforcement learning, 160
Gensim, 26
GeoNames, 15
Ginger (VMHA), 194
GLoVe, 26, 74
GLUE, 63
GODEL, 179
GoEmotions, 56
goodness-of-fit metrics, 255
Google SERP API, 137
GopherCite, 217
GPT 3.5 Turbo, 208
GPT 4.0, 208
GPT-2, 74
GPT-3, 74, 204
GPT-4, 1, 48, *see also* GPT 4.0
graph embeddings, 71
graph entropy, 233
Graph Neural Network (GNN), 45, 50, 102
graph-based knowledge, 203
graphical data, x
grid search, 147
ground truth data, 227
grounded language learning, 206
groundedness, 218
Gumble Max function, 224

Hadamard pointwise multiplication, 126
hallucination, 58, 134, 211
   in AI, 184
harmlessness
   in VMHAs, 199
hate speech detection, 246
HCI, *see* Human-Computer Interaction
HEAL KG, 190
health and well-being, 203
Health Knowledge Graph, 36
healthcare, 1, 204
healthcare informatics, ix
heat map, 96
HellaSwag, 239
heterogeneous knowledge infusion, 120

hierarchical attention mechanisms, 173
high-level abstraction, 185
high-stakes decision-making, ix
highway connections, 98
Hinton, Geoffrey, ix
Hit Rate (HR), 162
HOLE, 124
honesty, 211
Horizontal Linguistic Features (HLF), 105
Huggingface, 45
human annotations, 237
human biases, 243
human feedback, 203
human judgments, 237
human values, 226
human-centered applications, ix
human-computer interaction, 250
human-in-the-loop evaluation, 197
human-understandable knowledge, ix
Hurricane Harvey, 24
Hurricane Sandy, 18
hybrid neural-symbolic learning, 130
hyperparameters, 235, 252

ICD-10, 37, 189
ICD-9, 36
IEEE W. Wallace McDowell Award, ix
implicit assumptions, 210
implicit biases, 245
imposter effect
   in VMHAs, 189
indicator function, 146
inductive biases, 52
inductive logic programming, 96
industry researchers and practitioners, x
inference tasks, 118
information fidelity, 9
information functional, 234
information gain, 126
information loss, 121
information retrieval, x
information systems, x
information-seeking questions (ISQs), 155
information-theoretic metric, 228
inherent biases, 257
inherent safety, 207
inherited limitations, 257
instigator (Tay) effect, 189
instruct-tuned LLMs, 231
InstructGPT, 207
instruction following tuning, 224

instruction-guided tuning, 203
insufficient context, 246
integer linear programming, 96
integrated gradients, 100, 187
integrated Hessians, 100
inter-annotator agreement, 112
inter-rater reliability, 89, 211
interdisciplinary centers, x
Interpolation Ensemble (IE), 113
interpretability, ix, 6, 44, 49, 211
   autoencoder, 45
   fine-tuning, 45
   multi-task learning, 45
   probing, 44
interpretable learning, x
interpretable machine learning, 134
intersentence, 247
intrasentence, 247
intrinsic property, 235
IoT
   healthcare, 36
ISEEQ, 100, 215
ISEEQ (Information SEEking Question generation), 155
ISEEQ-ERL, 157
ISEEQ-RL, 157
iterative quantization, 162

K-Adapter, 99
K-BERT, 45, 99
K-Means, 27
K-PERM (Knowledge-guided Personalization with Reward Modulation), 172
Kahneman, Daniel, ix
KakaoTalk, 191
Kappa paradox, 250
KB-LSTM, 99
KB-RANN, 103
KG embedding, 224
KG-GAN, 99
KG-Guided Attention, 99
KG-LSTM, 99
KGs, *see* knowledge graph
kHealth, 37
   reasoner, 38
KI-BERT, 99
KiL, *see* knowledge-infused learning
KILT, 63
knowledge attention matrix, 122
knowledge base, 211

knowledge concept to word attention map, 225
knowledge distillation, 103
knowledge embedding, 123
Knowledge Ensemble (KE), 113
knowledge graph (KGs), 4, 8, 11, 50, 212
   definition, 11
   education, 12
   embedding, 50
   explainability, 40
   interpretability, 44
   masking, 50
   masks, 109
knowledge graph embedding, 51
knowledge infusion layer (Ki-layer), 124
knowledge infusion techniques, x
knowledge injection, 121
Knowledge Intensive Language Understanding (KILU), 63
Knowledge Modulation Function (K-MF), 123
knowledge neuron, 121
knowledge proximation function, 127
knowledge retrieval, 9
knowledge retriever, 214
knowledge-augmented query, 161
Knowledge-aware Loss Function (K-LF), 123
Knowledge-aware Passage Retriever (KPR), 160
knowledge-based systems, 240
knowledge-infused ensembling, 223
Knowledge-infused Learning (KiL), ix, x, 11, 55, 206
Knowledge-Intensive Language Understanding Tasks, 206
KnowLLM, 222
Krippendorff's alpha, 88, 237
Kronecker delta function, 238
Kullback Leibler (KL) divergence, 101, 126

labeled property graph, 11
LAMA, 217
LangChain, 53, 148
language translation, 1
large language models (LLMs), 1, 9, 53, 151, 203
Latent Dirichlet Allocation (LDA), 74
latent representations, 220
layer-wise knowledge augmentation, 122
layer-wise relevance propagation, 40
learning momentum, 126
learning rate, 116

least common subsumer, 124
LeCun, Yann, ix
lexical and linguistic knowledge, 189
lexical divergence, 232
lexical diversity, 232
lexical similarity, 236
lifting, 50
LightTag, 249
likelihood probability, 110
Likert score, 170
Limbic (VMHA), 194
LIME (Local Interpretable Model-agnostic Explanations), 144, 213
linear algebra, x
linear relation, 252
linear scale, 257
linguist, 248
linguistic expert, 248
linguistic intuition, 252
linguistics, x
Linked Open Data (LOD), 39
Lipschitz functions, 103
LIWC, 56
LLama2, 208
LLMs, *see* large language models (LLMs)
LLMs over KGs, 223
locality sensitive hashing (LSH), 162
LODE, 15
log-likelihood, 253
logarithmic transformation, 254
logical agreement score, 139
logical coherence, 156, 212
logical consistency, 212
logit, 238
long tail entities, 61
longest common subsequence (LCS), 163
Longformer, 74, 149
longitudinal study, 82
loss function, 94
low-level abstraction, 185
low-resource problems, 11
lowering, 51
LSD (Least Significant Difference) post-hoc analysis, 170
LSTM, 45, 81
Lyapunov stability theorem, 127

MACHIAVELLI benchmark, 230
machine cognition, 47
machine learning, 12
machine perception, 47
machine translation, 246
Major Depressive Disorder (MDD), 139
majority vote, 250
many-to-one NLM, 124
marginalization, 223
marginalized loss, 129
masked language modeling setting, 252
mathematics, x
MAUVE, 44
MCC, *see* Moral Consistency Corpus
McFadden's R^2, 255
Mean Average Precision (MAP), 162
meaningless stereotypes, 244
Med-PaLM2, 204
MedChatbot, 185
MedDRA, 190
medication adherence, 198
MedNLI dataset, 200
MedNorm, 92
MedPaLM, 203
mental health, ix, 8, 11, 54, 206
mental health services, ix
mental health triage, 200
metadata, 246
methontology, 15
MIC, *see* Moral Integrity Corpus
Microsoft's Tay, 243
min-max separability, 105
MIPS (Maximum Inner Product Search), 162
MIRA, 191
misaligned stereotypes, 244
misalignment, 220
misconceptions, 238
missing data, 250
Mistral, 232
MITI dataset, 196
Mixture of Experts, 213
Möbius transformation, 254
MoCA, 59
model ensembles, 8
model fit, 255
model interpretability, 92
model parameters, 236
model-agnostic, 228
monetary compensation, 257
Monte-Carlo tree search, 100
moral consistency, 227
Moral Consistency Corpus, 228
moral decision-making, 228
Moral Integrity Corpus, 228
moral integrity dataset, 208

moral scenarios, 218, 227
MoralExceptQA, 230
morality, 226
morally aligned agents, 242
Motivational Interviewing (MI), 201, 213
MPNet model, 174
MS-MARCO, 65
multi-agent systems, 128
multi-hop question answering, 61
multi-hop traversal, 96
multi-hop triple extraction, 161
multi-label classification, 102
multi-label classifier, 175
multi-relational reinforcement learning, 100
multinomial regression analysis, 255
multiple-choice question-answering, 173
mutual information, 234

n-grams, 78
named entities, 221
NASARI, 103
National Institute on Drug Abuse, 218
natural language generation (NLG), 134
natural language generation evaluation, 231
natural language inference, 115, 234
natural language processing, 203
negation capturing, 153
negation detection, 75
negational consistency, 230
NELL, 103
NeMo Guardrails, 217
NeOn methodology, 15
Nepal Earthquake, 24
NeSy-AI, *see* NeuroSymbolic AI
Neural Attention Models (NAMs), 101
neural keyphrase extraction, 192
neural language models, 102
neural networks, 4, 47, 206
NeuralCoref, 160
neurosymbolic, 8
NeuroSymbolic AI, 47, 203
neutral statements, 256
Newton's method, 147
next generation, x
next word prediction strategy, 199
NIDA, *see* National Institute on Drug Abuse
NIDA ADHD Test, 217
NLI, *see* natural language inference
NLP, *see* natural language processing
Nobel Prize winner, ix
normalized entity score (NES), 162

normalized PLL scoring, 247
normative evaluation, 230
noun phrase extraction, 161
noun phrases, 79
noun-verb pairs, 24
NUBIA score, 178
nucleus sampling, 164

obesity, 37
one-shot prompt, 231
ontologies, 4, 59
ontology
  definition, 11
  disaster ontology, 14
  DoRES, 14
  EDXL-RESCUER, 14
  emergency fire, 14
  Empathi, 11
    age group, 16
    construction, 13
    core concepts, 16
    evaluation, 21
    event, 16
    facility, 17
    Hazard Phase, 17
    Hazard Type, 17
    impact, 17
    involved actors, 17
    modality of data, 17
    place, 17
    population, 18
    report, 17
    service, 17
    status, 17
    surveillance information, 18
    vocabulary integration, 14
  evaluation
    lexical, 21
    semantic relational, 21
    structural, 21
  HXL, 13
  iContact, 15
  kAO, 37
  MA-Ont, 15
  MOAC, 13
  SMEM, 14
opacity, ix
OPT, 232
OPTICS, 27
optimization algorithms, 220
optimization function, 94

ordered knowledge, 56
ordinal labels, 88

p-value, 245
pairwise semantic dissimilarity, 254
PandaLM, 225
parametric knowledge, 121
paraphrase generation, 231
paraphrasing, 207
paraphrasing model, 141
ParaScore, 210
Parkinson's disease, 38
parse tree, 78
passage retriever, 134
Patient Health Questionnaire-9, 134, 205
Pearson correlations, 107, 237
People Also Ask (PAA), 139
Perceived Risk Measure (PRM), 85, 91
perceived toxicity, 246
percentage variance, 253
perception, 47
perceptual, 4
perfect agreement, 249
performance maximization function, 213
persona, 172
persona selection, 173
PersonaChat dataset, 173
personalization, 66
    conversational AI, 172
Personalized Health Knowledge Graph (PHKG), 36
personalized response generation, 173
perverse instantiations, 220
PhD dissertation, ix
PHKG, *see* Personalized Health Knowledge Graph
    design, 36
PHQ-9, *see* Patient Health Questionnaire-9
PHQ9-DO, 216
PKiL (Process Knowledge-infused Learning), 100, 145
PLL, *see* pseudo-log-likelihood
PMF, *see* probability mass function
policy gradient-based learning, 192
policy gradients, 8
policymakers, 1
polysemic words, 61
population mean, 253
positional encoding, 44
post-hoc explainability, 9, 70, 213

posterior potential function, 111
posterior probability, 110
posterior regularizer, 101
potentially harmful, 257
practitioners, 1
pre-existing biases, 242
pre-trained models, 41
precision, 28
predictive power, 255
predictor variable, 255
PRIMATE dataset, 148, 196, 226
primer, x
Principal Component Analysis (PCA), 116
prior probability, 110
privacy, 1
probabilistic models, 203
probability, x
probability distribution, 237, 238
probability mass function, 238
probability vector, 233
procedural knowledge, 57, 190
process knowledge, 57, 131, 217
process knowledge-guided generation, 217
process knowledge-infused learning, 10, 224
professor forcing, 99
programmable guardrail systems, 243
projected Newton's method, 147
ProKnow dataset, 139
prompt engineering, 257
prompt injection, 209
prompt template, 150, 232
prompting methods, 207
ProphetNet, 74, 166
propositional logic, 51
ProsocialDialog dataset, 200
protein folding, 48
pruning methods, 217
pseudo-log-likelihood, 247
psychology, x
public health, 75
publicly available corpora, 243
PURR, 215

QADiscourse (QAD) dataset, 158
QAMR (Question Answer Meaning Representations) dataset, 158
QG-LSTM, 142
QG-Transformer (QG-T), 142
Quartet (VMHA), 194
query-rewriting model, 178
question generation, 9, 136

Index

question rewriting, 221
Quora Question Pairs (QQP), 61

r/SuicideWatch, 86
RAG, *see* retrieval augmented generation
Random Forest, 107
rapidly evolving AI landscape, x
RARR, 215
rate limits, 255
Rawlsian social welfare functions, 212
RDF, 11
RDFS (Resource Description Framework Schema), 104
ReACT, 217
real-world datasets, x
REALM, 217
reasoning, x
recall, 28, 82
recommender systems, 67
red-teaming, 218
Reddit, 75, 245
RedditBias, 256
reduced embeddings, 116
reference-based metrics, 197
regression model, 255
regularization, 106
reinforcement learning, 8, 74, 224
Relational Frame Theory (RFT), 191
relationship extraction, 98
relative comparison, 246
relative entropy, 126
reliability, 2, 10, 203
  of language models, 112
Replika, 187
response generation, 9
restricted Boltzmann machines, 44
retrieval augmented generation, 173, 217
retrieval-augmented LMs, 63
retrofitting, 74
Reverse Cross Entropy (RCE), 164
reward function, 114
  ISEEQ, 163
reward functions, 212
reward-based learning, 223
rewards, 206
RNN, 81
RoBERTa, 71
roberta-large, 253
robust learning, x
robustness, 2, 211

ROC curve, 28, 85
Roleplay dataset, 196
RoT, *see* Rule of Thumb
RoT prompting, 242
ROUGE, 236
ROUGE-L, 44, 164
Rouge–1/2/L/L-Sum, 178
Rule of Thumb (RoTs), 199, 208
rules, 4
  tag and rank, 136
RXNorm, 70, 213
RxNORM, 190

SafeTexT, 218
safety, 9, 49, 203
  alignment, 218
  grounding, 218
  instructability, 218
safety guardrails, 203
safety lexicon, 141
safety-critical applications, 49
SaGE, *see* semantic graph entropy
saliency maps, 40, 49, 200
sampling methods, 228
sarcasm detection, 154
SBERT (Sentence BERT), 113
SBERT DeBERTa, 234
scatter plot, 241
scene graph, 68
SciBERT, 102
SCID (Structured Clinical Interviews for DSM-5), 139
scientific discovery, 1
scoring function, 254
search algorithm, 141
SEDO (Semantic Encoding and Decoding Optimization), 104
Seeded SubKG, 123
selector module, 173
self-attention, 52
  interpretability, 153
  matrices, 94
self-correlation, 106
self-supervised learning, 47
SelfCheckGPT, 210
semantic, 4
semantic annotation, 18
semantic consistency, 230
semantic data transformation, 69
semantic dissimilarity, 251
semantic embedding loss, 83

semantic embeddings, 233
semantic graph, 234
semantic graph entropy, 228
semantic lexicons, 4, 56
Semantic Query Expander (SQE), 160
semantic relatedness, 212
semantic relations, 156
semantic relations and logical agreement measures, 138
semantic role labeling, 74
semantic similarity, 69, 232
semantic similarity metrics, 236
semantic textual similarity, 252
semantically equivalent contexts, 227
semi-deep infusion, 55, 94, 121
seminar course, x
SenseBERT, 99
Sentence BERT, 78
  SentenceBERT all-miniLM-L6-v2, 255
sentence embeddings, 234
sentence transformer, 113
sentiment analysis, 1
sequence-to-sequence model, 143
SERMO (VMHA), 194
shallow infusion, 55, 69, 121
Shannon's entropy, 233
SHAP (SHapley Additive exPlanations), 144
Sheth, Amit P., ix
SIDER, 38
similarity function, 146
similarity tasks, 118
similarity threshold, 146
simulated conversations, 201
single-sentence tasks, 118
Singular Value Decomposition (SVD), 81
SIOC, 15
SITQ (Simple-LSH and Iterative Quantization), 162
situation-dependent context, 244
situational awareness, 27
skip connections, 98
skip-gram, 73
SKOS, 16
SNAP Counseling dataset, 196
SNLI (Stanford Natural Language Inference), 144
SNOMED-CT, 8, 37, 57, 189, 213
social media, 75
  emergency management, 14
social norms, 226
social risks, 230

social science, x
social stereotypes, 243
socially impactful applications, ix
society at large, x
SOSA ontology, 37
spaCy, 26
Sparrow, 189, 207
specific pattern, 257
spectral clustering, 27
spurious generation, 217
SQUAD dataset, 166
Stanford CoreNLP, 148
statement score, 252
statistically representative, 257
statistics, x
StereoSet, 246, 257
stereotype, 246
stereotypical statements, 245, 247
stratified knowledge infusion, 120
stratified sample, 250
structural information content, 233
Structured Clinical Interviews for DSM-5, 205
STS, *see* semantic textual similarity
sub-event detection, 24, 93
  clustering, 24
  evaluation
    qualitative, 32
    quantitative, 28
  extraction, 25
  human evaluation, 34
  ranking, 26
sub-word information, 74
subgraph construction, 197
subjective, 245
subjective nature of bias, 248
subreddit, 90
suicidality assessment, 151
suicide KG, 190
suicide risk, 70
  severity lexicon, 78
SuperGLUE, 63
superintelligence, 220
supervised learning, 218
Support Vector Machine (SVM), 77
supportive users, 83
surrogate model, 144, 213
survey respondents, 230
Sylvester equation, 104
Sylvester optimization, 127
symbolic AI, 47, 203
symbolic knowledge, 206

Index

symbolic knowledge structures, 47
symbolic reasoning, 50
symmetric consistency, 230
System 1, 2, 48
System 2, 48
system-level explainability, 187, 213
systematic differences, 250

T-SNE, 73, 200
T5, 74
T5-XL, 205
target terms, 248
task accuracy, 239
Tay, *see* Microsoft's Tay
TDLR (Top-Down Language Representation), 108
teacher forcing, 99
temperature, 238
temperature-based sampling, 238
template-cum-human annotation strategy, 256
templates, 247
Tess (VMHA), 194
text editing task, 246
Text-Davinci-003, 148
textual entailment, 115
Textual Entailment Constraints (TEC), 136
TF-IDF, 74
therapeutic alliance, 197
three-rater system, 237
throwaway account, 89
TIFU, *see* Transparency and Interpretability Framework for Understandability
time-invariant assessment, 89
time-invariant model (TinvM), 83
time-variant assessment, 89
time-variant model (TvarM), 83
toxicity detection, 246
toxicity-focused studies, 245
trade-off, 252
TRANS-E, 124
TRANS-H, 124
transferability, 92
transferability test, 170
transformative potential, ix
transformer language models fine-tuned (TLMs-FT), 166
transformer models, 44, 52
transformer-based masked language modeling, 252

Transformer-XL, 71
transformers, 204
transitive consistency, 230
transparency
  in VMHAs, 199
Transparency and Interpretability Framework for Understandability, 214
transparent, x
Tree LSTM, 103
tree of thoughts, 220
true positive rate (TPR), 85
trust, 203
trusted AI, x
trustworthiness, 209
  in AI, 183
trustworthy, x
truthful question-answering, 228
truthfulness, 211
TruthfulQA, 238
Turing laureates, ix

UExMs, 214
  abstention, 217
  generating evaluator pairing, 214
  retriever augmentation, 217
ULMFiT, 74
UMLS, *see* Unified Medical Language System
unbiased model, 246
uncertainty
  modeling, 93
underlying context, 243
underlying distribution, 255
understandability, 1
Unified Medical Language System, 36, 55, 213
unordered knowledge, 55
unsafe responses, 203
usability, 1
use cases, x
user understandability, 153
user-level explainability (UsEx), 187, 206
User-level Explainable LLMs, *see* UExMs
utilitarian functions, 212

variational autoencoders, 127
variational inference, 128
variety of contexts, 257
verb phrases, 79
verbosity, 256
vertex probability, 234
Vertical Linguistic Features (VLF), 105

Vicuna, 208
Virtual Mental Health Assistants (VMHAs), 181
visual question answering, 68
visualization methods, 213

weight decay, 116
weighted average, 114
weighted averaging, 212
WHO Wellness Indices, 217
Wikidata, 8, 189
WikipassageQA, 166
Wikipedia, 113
WinoBias, 246
WinoGender, 256
Wireheading, 220
WNLI, 115

WoeBot, 186
Woebot (VMHA), 194
word embeddings, 19, 71
Word Mover Distance (WMD), 70, 156
Word2Vec, 11, 57
WordNet, 8, 61, 221
World Model, 4
Wysa (VMHA), 186, 194

Xiaoice, 192
XLNET, 177
XLNet, 71

YEA-SAYER (ELIZA) effect, 189

zero-shot learning, 8, 96, 127
zero-shot prompting, 181, 227

For EU product safety concerns, contact us at Calle de José Abascal, 56–1°,
28003 Madrid, Spain or eugpsr@cambridge.org.

www.ingramcontent.com/pod-product-compliance
Lightning Source LLC
LaVergne TN
LVHW022003060526
838200LV00003B/77